NEILL'S "BLUE CAPS"

NEILL'S "BLUE CAPS"

Vol. 3
1914–1922

by
COLONEL H. C. WYLLY, C.B.

The Naval & Military Press Ltd
in association with
The Imperial War Museum
Department of Printed Books

Published jointly by
The Naval & Military Press Ltd
Unit 10 Ridgewood Industrial Park,
Uckfield, East Sussex,
TN22 5QE England
Tel: +44 (0) 1825 749494
Fax: +44 (0) 1825 765701
www.naval-military-press.com

and

The Imperial War Museum, London
Department of Printed Books
www.iwm.org.uk

In reprinting in facsimile from the original, any imperfections are inevitably reproduced and the quality may fall short of modern type and cartographic standards.

[Photo. Gale & Polden, Ltd.

Dedicated

TO

FIELD-MARSHAL

HIS ROYAL HIGHNESS ARTHUR W. P. A.

THE DUKE OF CONNAUGHT AND STRATHEARN,

K.G., K.T., K.P., G.C.B., G.C.S.I., G.C.M.G., G.C.I.E., G.C.V.O., G.B.E.,

COLONEL-IN-CHIEF

THE ROYAL DUBLIN FUSILIERS,

IN GRATEFUL RECOGNITION

OF HIS NEVER-FAILING SYMPATHY AND INTEREST

IN ALL MATTERS RELATING TO

NEILL'S "BLUE CAPS"

1903—1922

FOREWORD

Now that Volume III of the History of "Neill's 'Blue Caps'" is ready for issue, I feel it would not be amiss to express to the Author, Colonel H. C. Wylly, C.B., the best thanks of the "Blue Caps" for the admirable manner in which he has narrated their achievements during the Great War.

His task was made harder owing to the difficulty of obtaining the personal diaries of individuals now scattered over every part of the Empire. The appalling casualties accounted, alas, for many a gallant "Blue Cap" whose personal quota to this history, had he lived, would have been invaluable. I feel sure, however, that past and present "Blue Caps" will endorse my appreciation of the Author's efforts.

Our best thanks are also due to Mr. C. S. Seager, Director of Messrs. Gale & Polden, Ltd. (the publishers), an old friend of both Battalions. He has spared himself no trouble in carrying out, with great success, the wishes of the officers of the "Blue Caps."

No words of mine can express the feelings of the Battalion when definite orders were received for its disbandment, and the horrible weeks spent in carrying this order into effect. Our feelings were greatly alleviated by the sympathy of our well-beloved Colonel-in-Chief, and the Colonel of the Regiment, as expressed in their farewell orders.

The final solemn ceremony of handing over the Colours revealed to all the depth of sympathy of their Majesties, and their sorrow at the disbandment of their loyal Irish Regiments.

All those privileged to be present on that occasion will never forget it; nothing could have been more human, sympathetic, and in every way perfect.

FOREWORD

In conclusion, we may feel thankful that no one can remove our traditions of 279 years, and if, at the time, long and faithful service, glorious traditions, and intense *esprit de corps*, coupled with military efficiency, were factors not considered sufficiently worthy to retain the services of the old "Blue Caps," nevertheless the decision of this country on November 15th, 1922, showed that right-minded people were not in sympathy with the astounding decisions of the Government then in force.

Lieut.-Colonel,
late Comdg. 1st Bn. The Royal Dublin Fusiliers
(Neill's " Blue Caps ").

DONNINGTON ELMS,
   NEWBURY, BERKS.
  February 1st, 1923.

[Photo, H. Seymour Cousens

MAJOR-GENERAL C. D. COOPER, C.B.,
COLONEL THE ROYAL DUBLIN FUSILIERS.

CONTENTS

CHAPTER		PAGE
I.	The Opening of the Great War	1
II.	The Gallipoli Landing	18
III.	Gallipoli: The Long Struggle—The Evacuation	44
IV.	France: Battles of the Somme, 1916—Battles of Arras, 1917—Battles of Ypres, 1917	64
V.	The Last Year of the Great War—First Battles of the Somme, 1918—The Battle of the Lys...	93
VI.	The End of the War and the Occupation of Germany	119
VII.	The Stormy Days of Peace: Disbandment—"Ave Atque Vale"	134

APPENDIX

1.	List of Commanding Officers of the "Blue Caps"	154
2.	List of Stations	156
3.	First Battalion Headquarters Strength Previous to Proceeding to Gallipoli	158
4.	Roll of Honour: Officers, Warrant Officers, Non-Commissioned Officers and Men	161
5.	List of Honours and Rewards Issued to the Royal Dublin Fusiliers for Services in the Great War, 1914-18	167
6.	Honours Selected for Regimental Colours and Army List	199
7.	Description of Memorials Erected: Great War, 1914-18	202
8.	What our Women did for the Regiment	205
9.	Special Orders on Disbandment	207
10.	Officers on the Strength of the "Blue Caps" at Date of Disbandment, July 31st, 1922	211
11.	List of Officers of the 1st and 2nd Battalions Serving on Disbandment, Showing Units to Which They Were Transferred, Etc.	212
12.	Copy of Army List for July, 1922	215

CONTENTS

APPENDIX

	PAGE
13. Distribution of Officers' and Sergeants' Mess Property	216
14. Disposal of the Silver and Mess Property	218
15. Ceremonial of the Reception of the Colours of the Disbanded Southern Irish Regiments by the King	222
16. Army Rifle Association Meeting: 1921 Meeting—Successes of the "Blue Caps"	226
17. Sporting Successes of the "Blue Caps" from August, 1919, to Disbandment, July, 1922	228
18. Battalion Magazine	231
19. Particulars of Bequests Made to the "Blue Caps"	232
20. The Royal Dublin Fusiliers' Association	234
21. Regimental Army Agents	236
22. Regimental Song	237
Index	241

LIST OF ILLUSTRATIONS

	FACING PAGE
Field-Marshal H.R.H. The Duke of Connaught, K.G., Etc., Colonel-in-Chief The Royal Dublin Fusiliers	*Frontispiece*
Major-General C. D. Cooper, C.B., Colonel The Royal Dublin Fusiliers	viii
Officer's Field Service Cap and Hackle	1
Handing over the Colours to Safe Custody of the Mayor of Torquay, January 7th, 1915	11
Memorial to the 29th Division at Dymchurch	14
Officers of the "Blue Caps" Taken Immediately Prior to Embarkation for Gallipoli, March, 1915	15
Divisional Sign	16
Gallipoli: "V" Beach and Fort Sedd-el-Bahr	19
Lieut.-Colonel R. A. Rooth	23
s.s. "River Clyde" Below the Walls of Sedd-el-Bahr Fort—Tenedos	25
s.s. "River Clyde"	26
Major C. T. W. Grimshaw, D.S.O.	36
Captain H. D. O'Hara, D.S.O.	38
Fort Sedd-el-Bahr	40
Gallipoli Trophies	50
Gallipoli Views (3)	62
Beaumont Hamel: Mine Crater and Shell Holes	67
Vlamertinghe—A Convent in Ypres	74
Delville Wood—Corbie from the Church Steeple	76
H.M. the King Visits Quesnoy—Sailly-Saillisel	77
Ammunition under Church, Le Neuville—Tanks Going through Meaulte	79
Hotel de Ville, Arras—Scene on the Battlefield, St. Jean, July, 1917	83
Sergeant J. Ockenden, V.C.	89
Regimental Dog "Jack"	114
The Hindenburg Line near Bellicourt	120
Certificate of Service, Great War, 1914-19	132
Original Expeditionary Force, Serving on March 17th, 1920	134
Gallipoli Landing Party, Serving on March 17th, 1920	135

LIST OF ILLUSTRATIONS

	FACING PAGE
THE COLONEL-IN-CHIEF LEADING THE "BLUE CAPS" PAST THE KING, ALDERSHOT, MAY, 1920	136
THE OFFICERS, SEPTEMBER, 1920	137
RESERVISTS, APRIL, 1921	138
PAST AND PRESENT OFFICERS "BLUE CAPS" AND "OLD TOUGHS," LUCKNOW DAY, SEPTEMBER 25TH, 1921	141
MEMBERS OF THE SERGEANTS' MESS, BORDON, 1922	143
REGIMENTAL COLOURS AND COLOUR BELTS, MAY, 1922	144
COLOUR PARTIES "BLUE CAPS" AND "OLD TOUGHS" WHO PROCEEDED WITH THE COLOURS TO WINDSOR CASTLE	148
COLOUR PARTIES ENTERING WINDSOR CASTLE	149
HANDING OVER COLOURS TO H.M. THE KING, JUNE 12TH, 1922	150
WOMEN'S CERTIFICATE	205
CERTIFICATE OF SERVICE ON DISBANDMENT	210
OFFICERS' MESS SILVER	218
SERGEANTS' MESS SILVER	219
SILVER CUP AND TRAY	220
COPY OF LETTER FROM H.M. THE KING ON DISBANDMENT	222
WINNERS OF THE HENRY WHITEHEAD CUP	226
THE KING GEORGE CUP—THE HENRY WHITEHEAD CUP	227
BATTALION FOOTBALL TEAM—HOCKEY TEAM	228
TUG-OF-WAR TEAM—BOXING TEAM	229
CROSS-COUNTRY RUNNING TEAM	230
REGIMENTAL SPOON AND MEDAL	231
BADGES AND BUTTONS	233

LIST OF MAPS

GALLIPOLI PENINSULA	20
CAPE HELLES AND THE SOUTHERN AREA, GALLIPOLI	26
POSITION AT SUVLA (END OF AUGUST, 1915)	52
THE YPRES SALIENT	72
ARRAS—BAPAUME	84
AMIENS AND ALBERT	102
COURTRAI AREA	120
29TH DIVISION MARCH THROUGH BELGIUM AND GERMANY, TO BRIDGEHEAD	124

THE COLOURED PLATES AND MAPS IN THIS NAVAL AND MILITARY PRESS REPRINT ARE PLACED AFTER THIS PAGE

OFFICER'S BLUE FIELD SERVICE CAP OF BLUE CLOTH.

Specially authorized by the War Office in commemoration of the Regimental Nickname, "Neill's Blue Caps," granted for distinguished services in the Indian Mutiny

HACKLE WORN IN OFFICER'S BUSBY OF THE ROYAL DUBLIN FUSILIERS.

Granted by H.M. Queen Victoria for the distinguished services of the Regiment in the South African Campaign.

REGIMENTAL BADGE

Worn by "THE BLUE CAPS" on the back of the S.D. Jacket below collar, throughout the Great War. This badge was also painted on the sides of the steel helmets.

The badge was the suggestion of the late Major E. Fetherstonhaugh, 1st Royal Dublin Fusiliers, who was killed in action at Gallipoli on the 25th April, 1915.

DIVISIONAL BADGES

Of the 29th DIVISION
Worn on the sleeve of the S.D. Jacket.

Of the 16th DIVISION
Worn on the sleeve of the S.D. Jacket.

Commanders of 29th and 16th Divisions under whom "The Blue Caps" served during the Great War.

29th Division. March, 1915, to October, 1917.
    Lieutenant-General Sir A. G. Hunter-Weston, K.C.B., D.S.O.
    Lieutenant-General Sir H. de B. De Lisle, K.C.B., K.C.M.G., D.S.O.

16th Division. October, 1917, to April, 1918.
    Major-General Sir W. B. Hickie, K.C.B.
    Major-General Sir C. P. A. Hull, K.C.B.

29th Division. April, 1918, to July, 1919.
    Major-General Sir W. de S. Cayley, K.C.M.G., C.B.

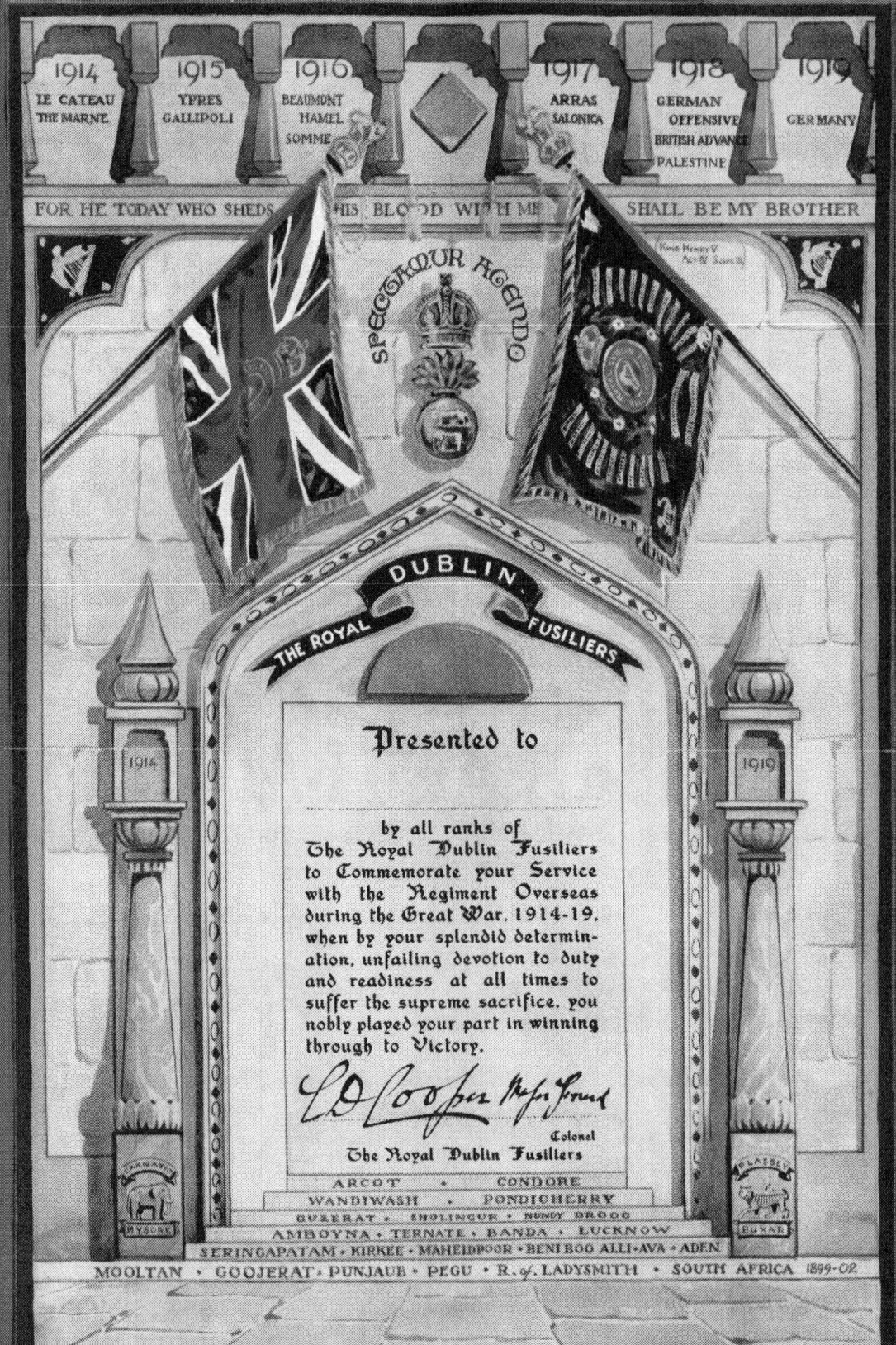

"PLASSEY" "BUXAR"

102ND "BLUE CAPS"

"CARNATIC" "MYSORE"

103RD "OLD TOUGHS"

THE ROYAL DUBLIN FUSILIERS

Raised 1644   *Disbanded 1922*

FIELD MARSHAL H.R.H. THE DUKE OF CONNAUGHT & STRATHEARN K.G. ETC
COLONEL-IN-CHIEF

Presented to :—

In recognition of his faithful service and as a memento of the old regiment on its disbandment.

Lt. Col.
Commanding 1st Bn. The Royal Dublin Fusiliers "Blue Caps"

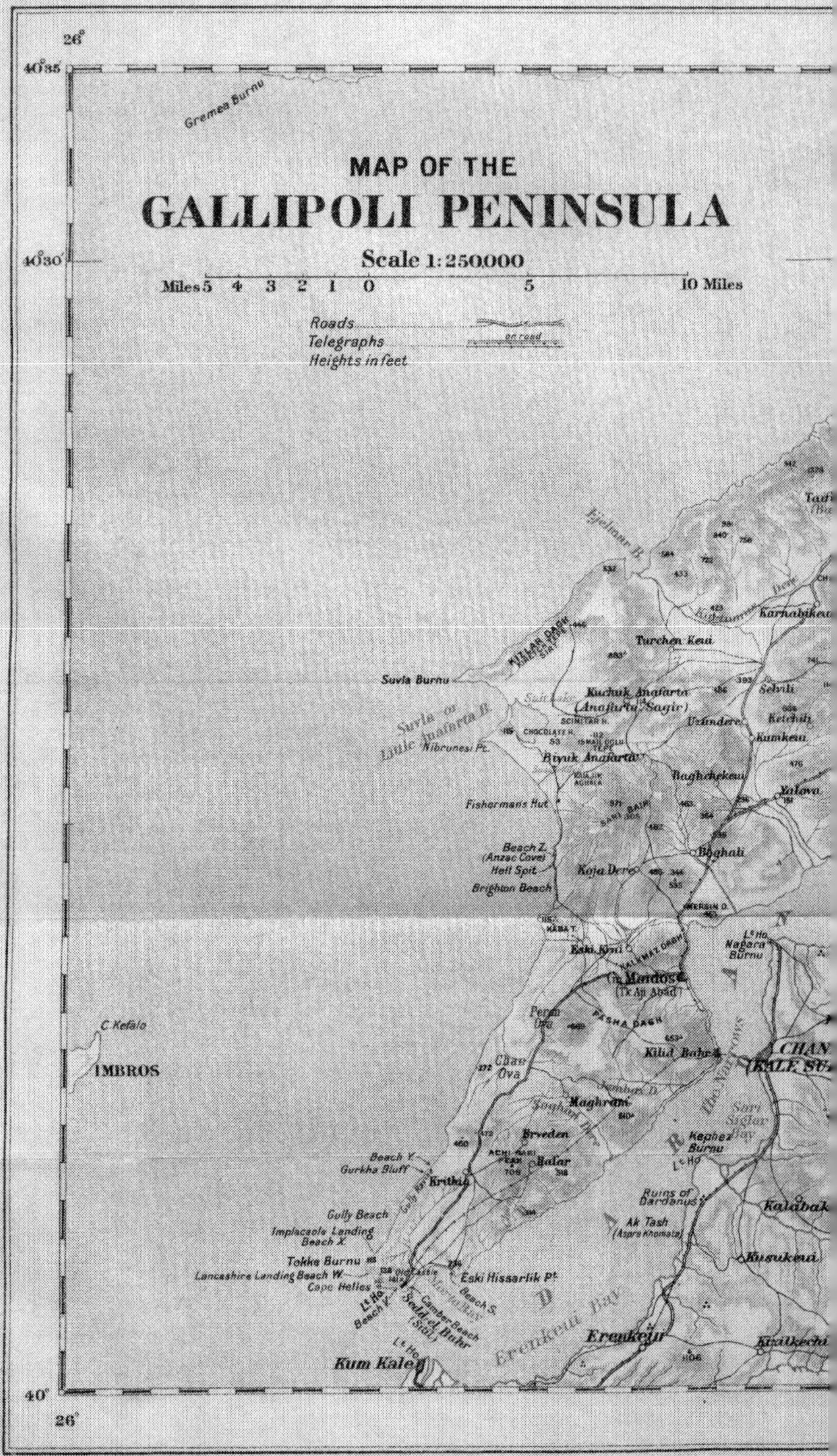

MAP OF THE
GALLIPOLI PENINSULA
Scale 1:250,000
Miles 5 4 3 2 1 0 5 10 Miles
Roads
Telegraphs
on road
Heights in feet
26°
40°35'
40°30'
40°
Gremea Burnu
Suvla Burnu
Suvla or Little Anafarta B.
Nibrunesi Pt.
Kuchuk Anafarta (Anafarta Sagir)
Biyuk Anafarta
Turchen Keui
Selvili
Uzundere
Ketchili
Kumkeui
Baghchekeui
Yalova
Karnabikeui
Fishermans Hut
Beach Z (Anzac Cove)
Hell Spit
Brighton Beach
Koja Dere
Boghali
Kabatepe
Eski Keui
Maidos
(Tk Ali Abad)
Pasha Dagh
Kilid Bahr
Nagara Burnu
Chanak Kale Su
Chai Ova
Maghram
Sari Siglar Bay
Kephez Burnu
Erveden
Beach Y
Gurkha Bluff
Krithia
Achi Baba Peak
Gully Beach
Implacable Landing Beach X
Tekke Burnu
Lancashire Landing Beach W
Cape Helles
Beach V
Eski Hissarlik Pt.
Morto Bay
Beach S
Camber Beach
Sedd el Bahr
Ruins of Dardanus
Ak Tash
Kalabak
Kusukeui
Erenkeui
Erenkeui Bay
Kum Kale
Kumkeui
C. Kefalo
IMBROS
26°

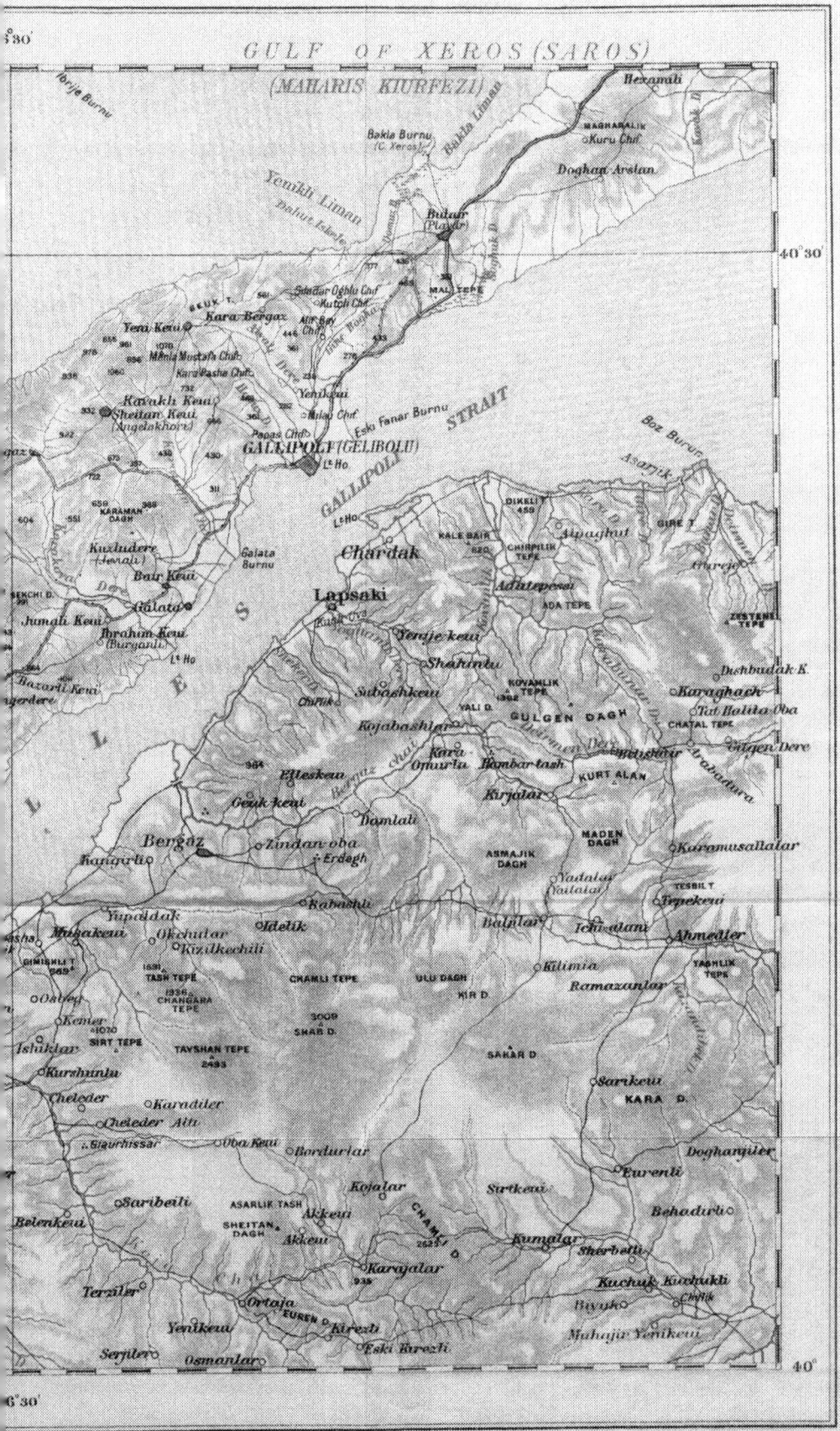

Reproduced by permission of the War Office, March, 1923.

THE YPRES

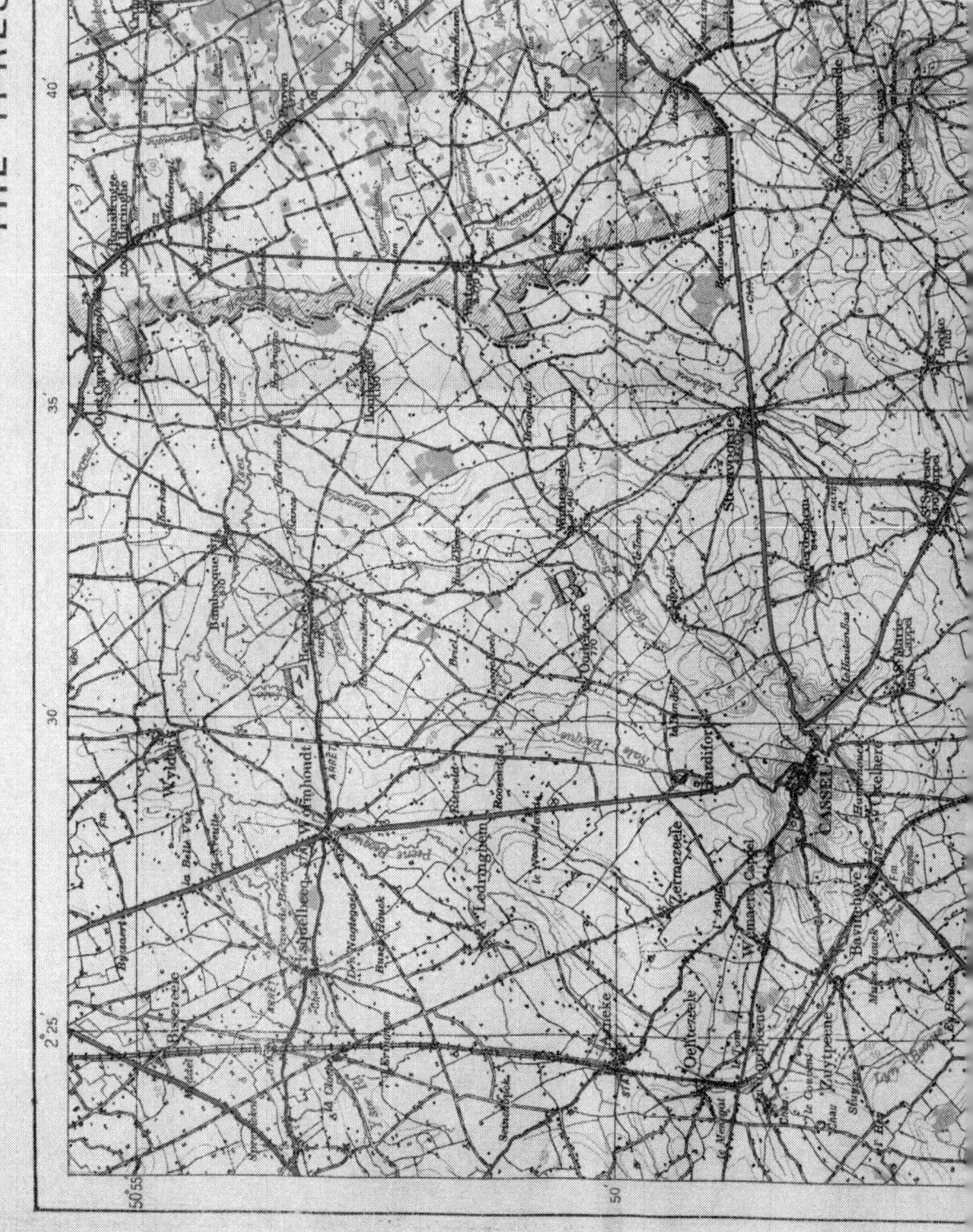

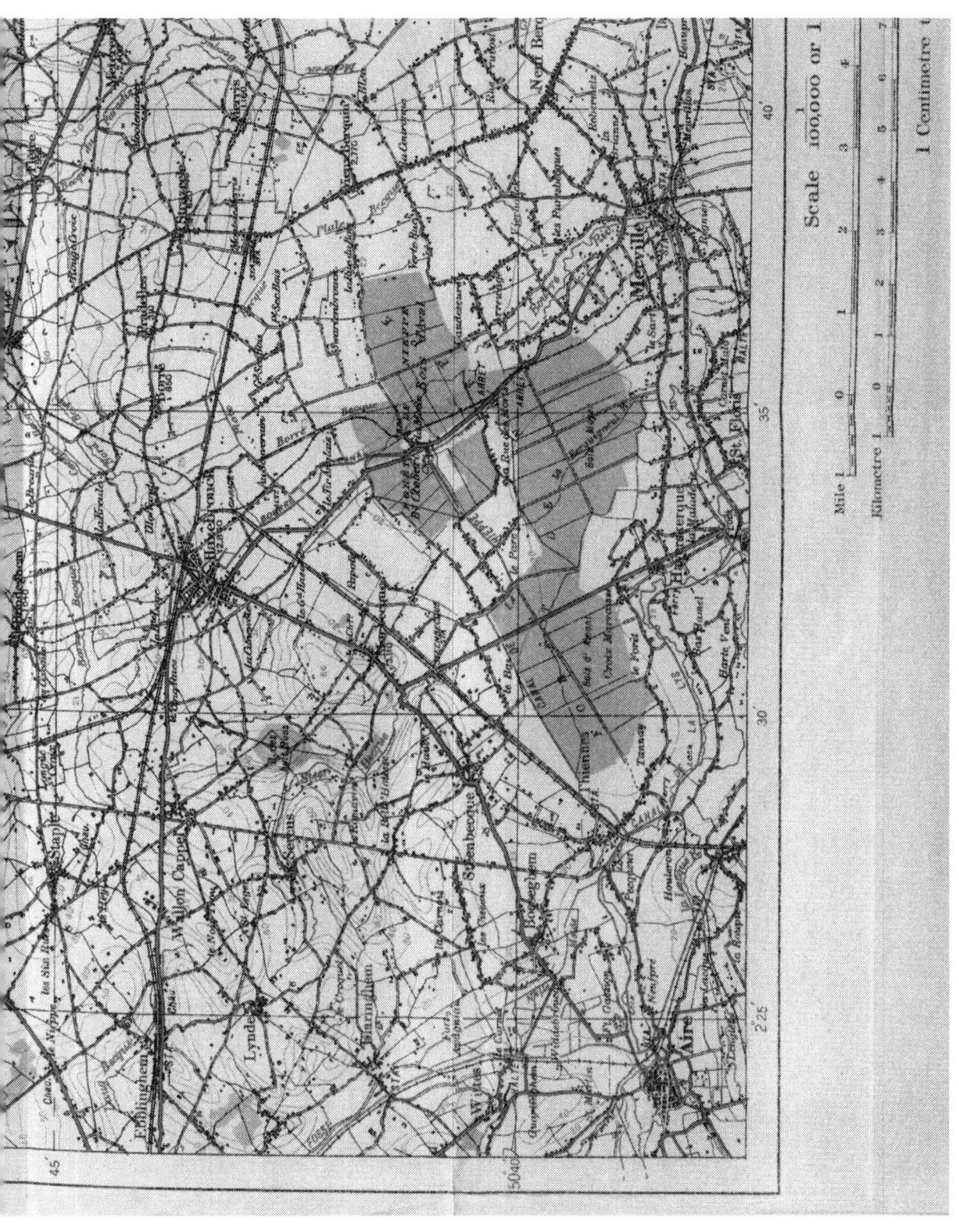

SALIENT

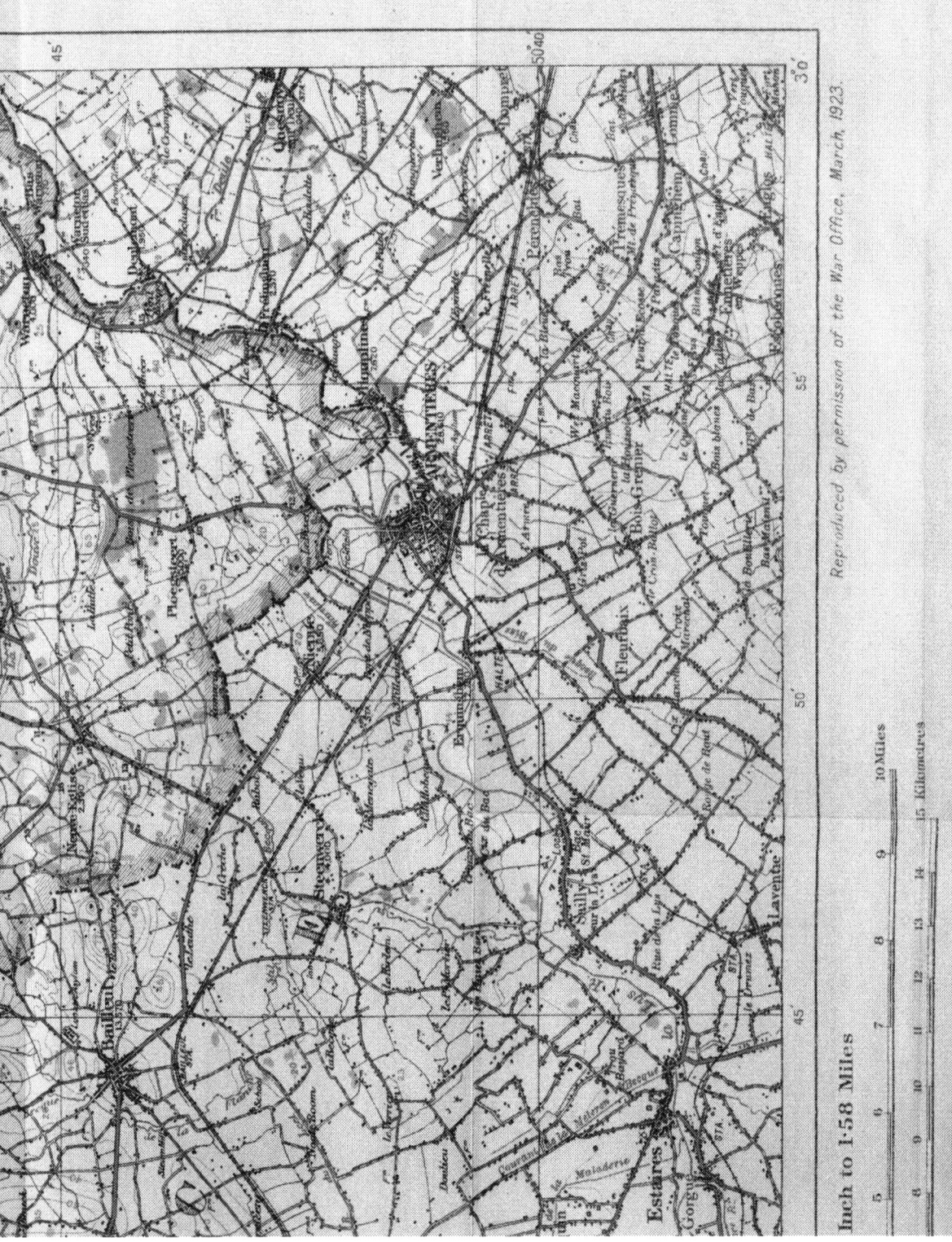

ARRAS

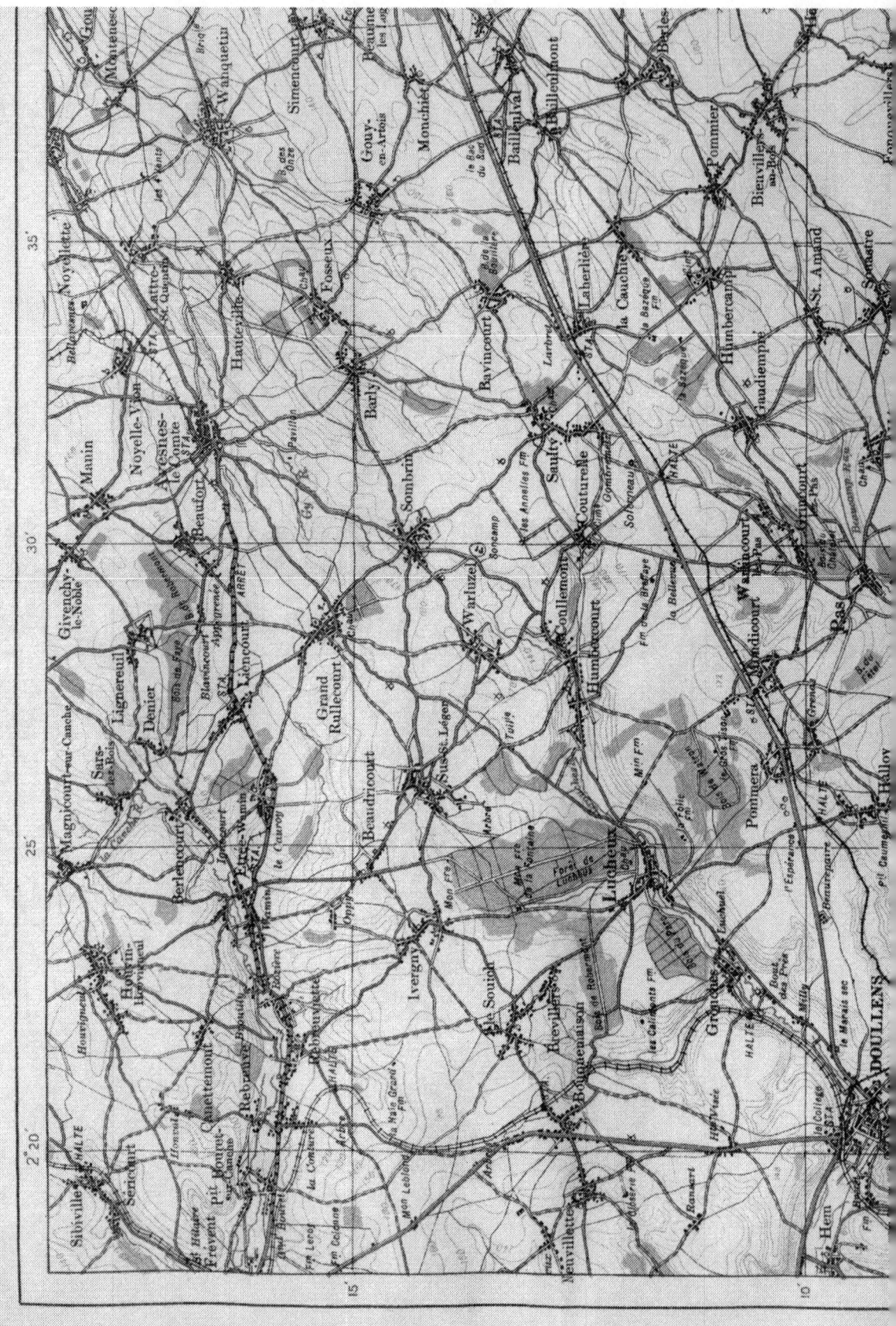

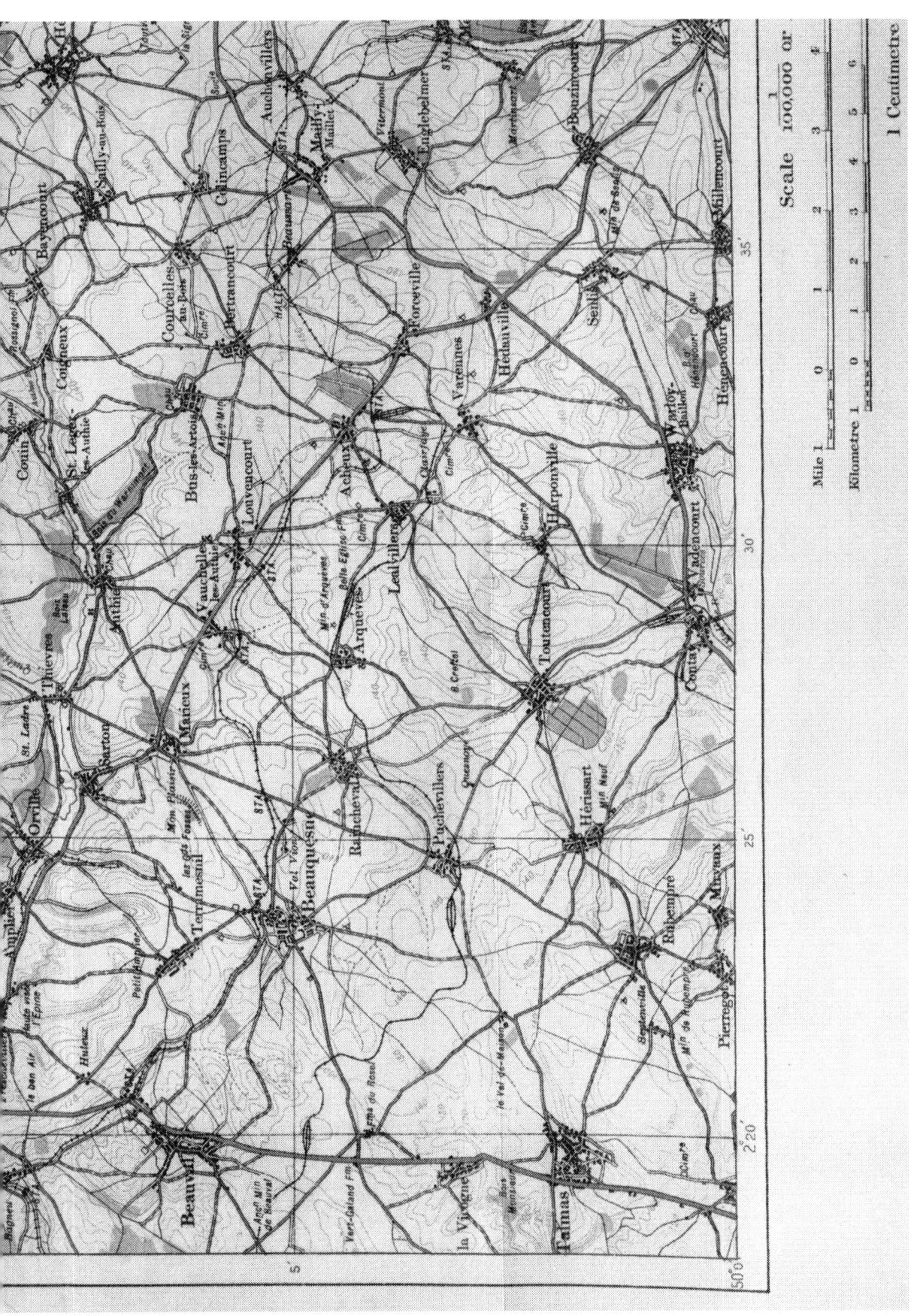

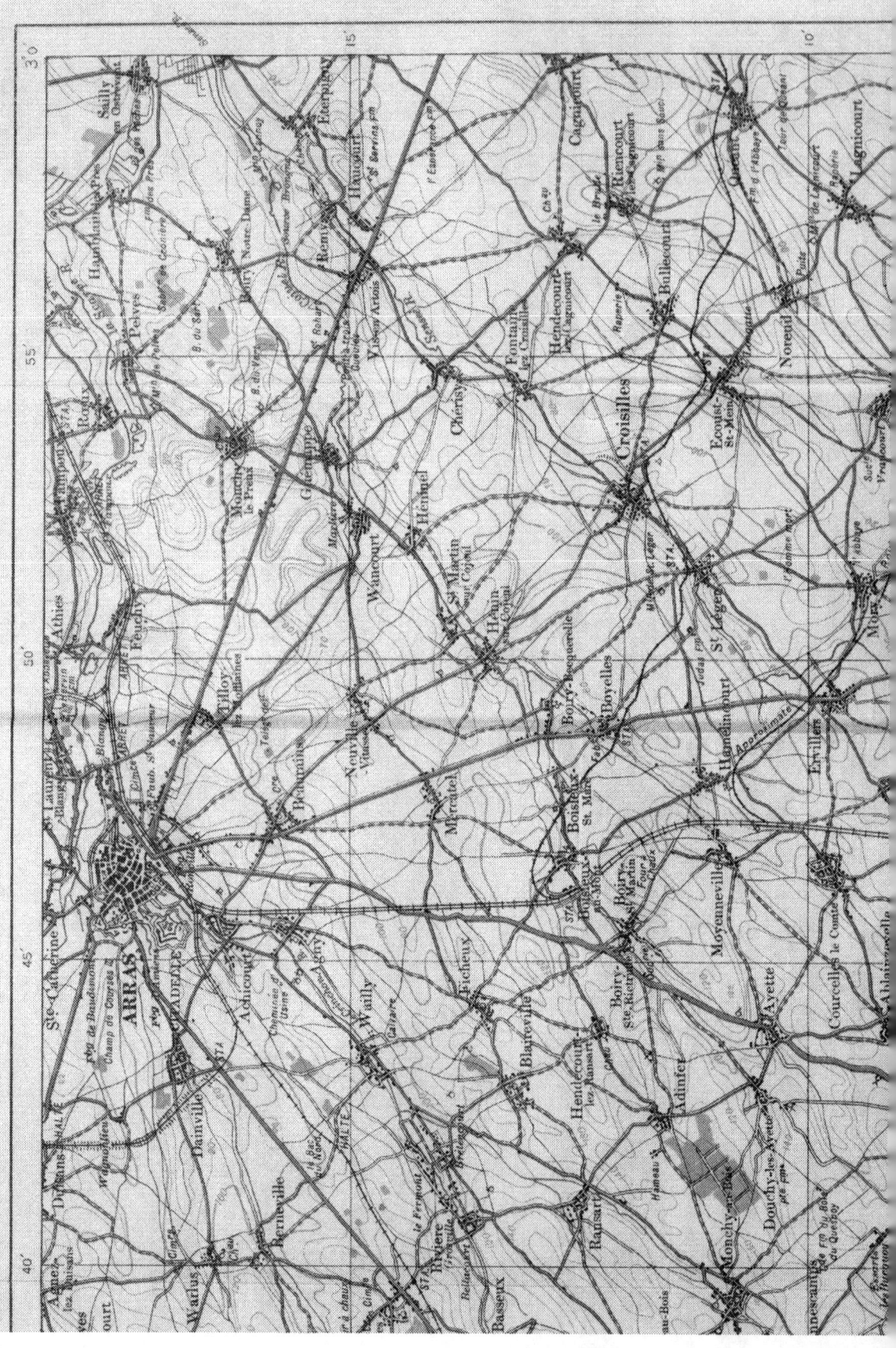

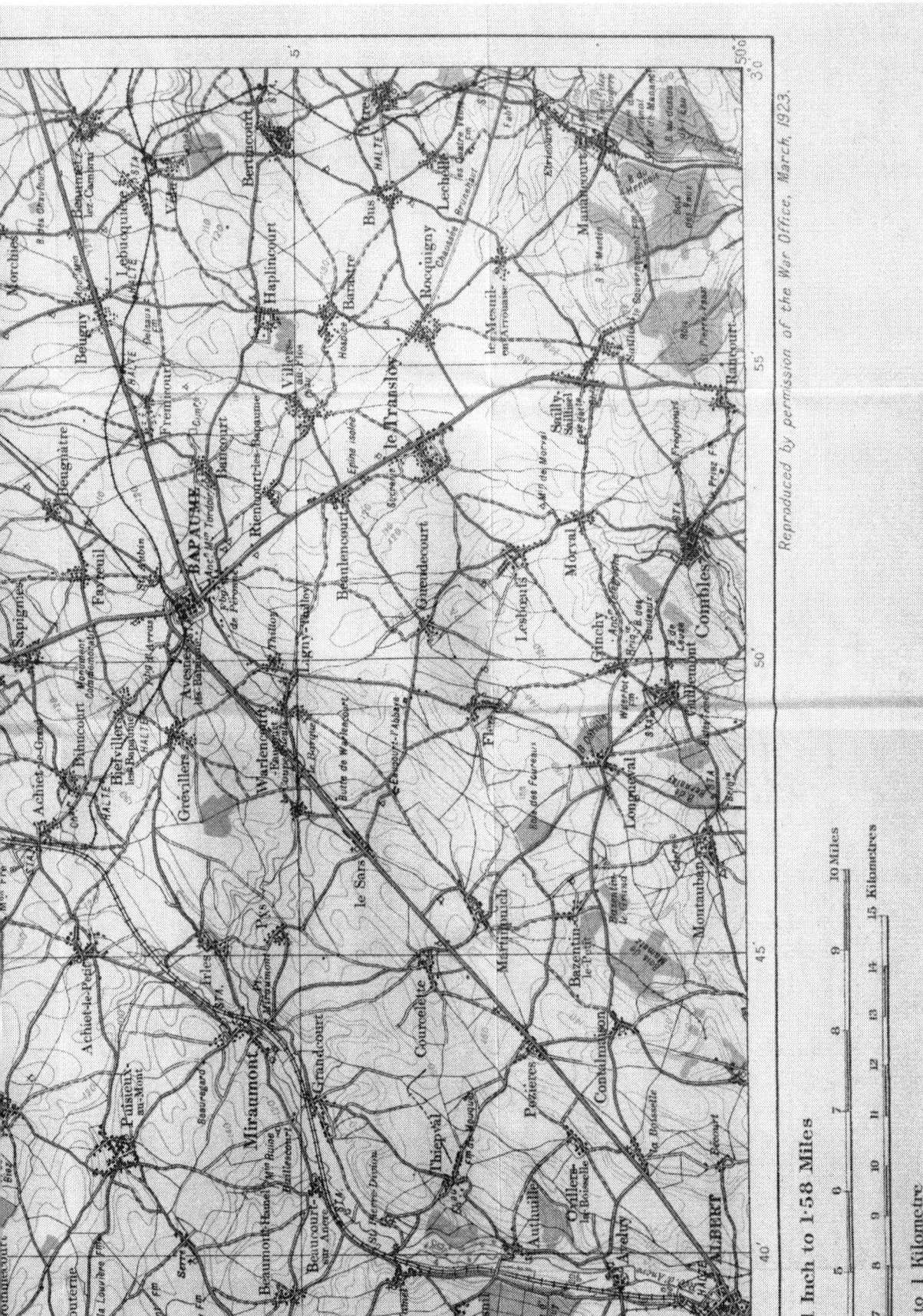

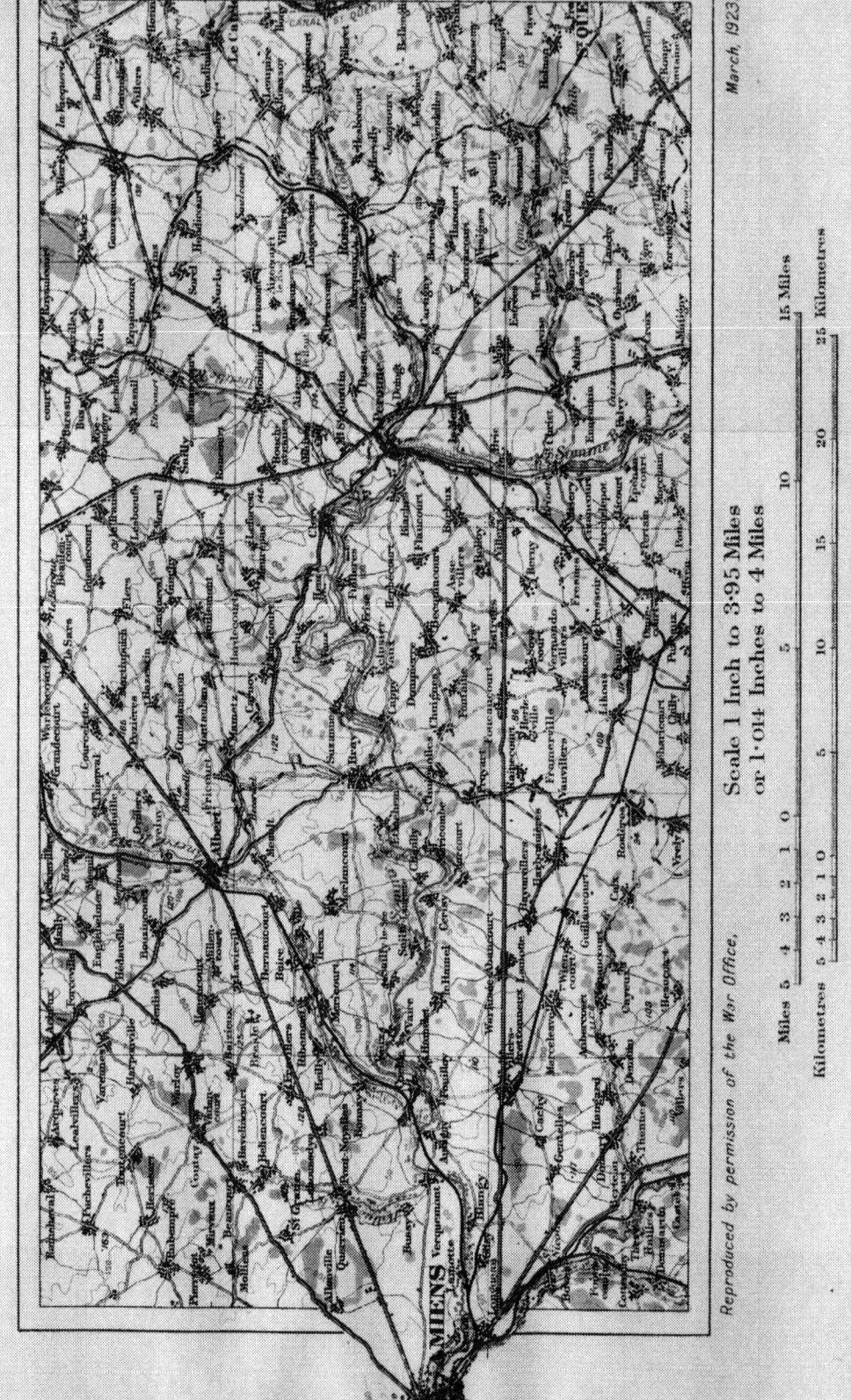

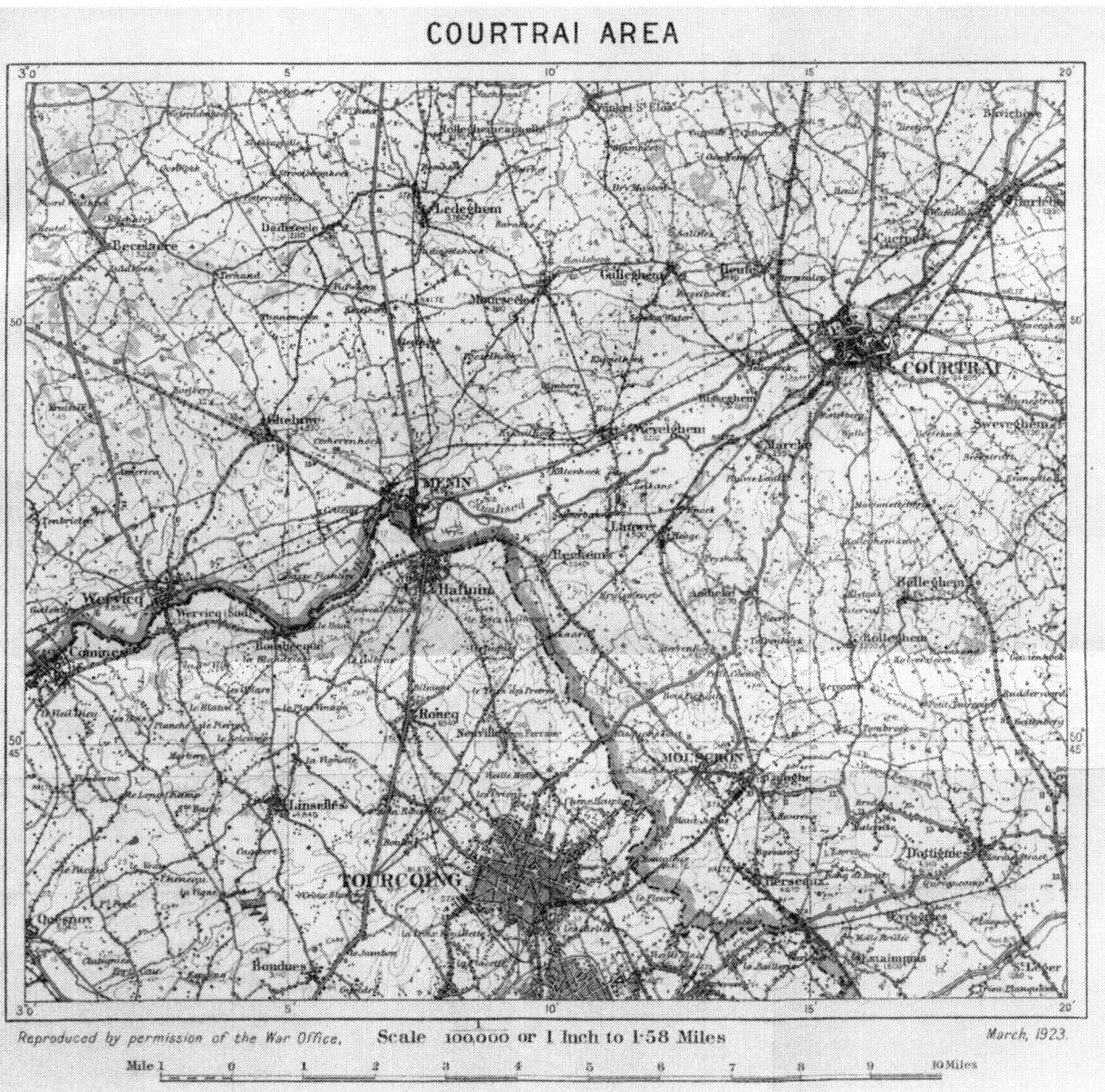

COURTRAI AREA

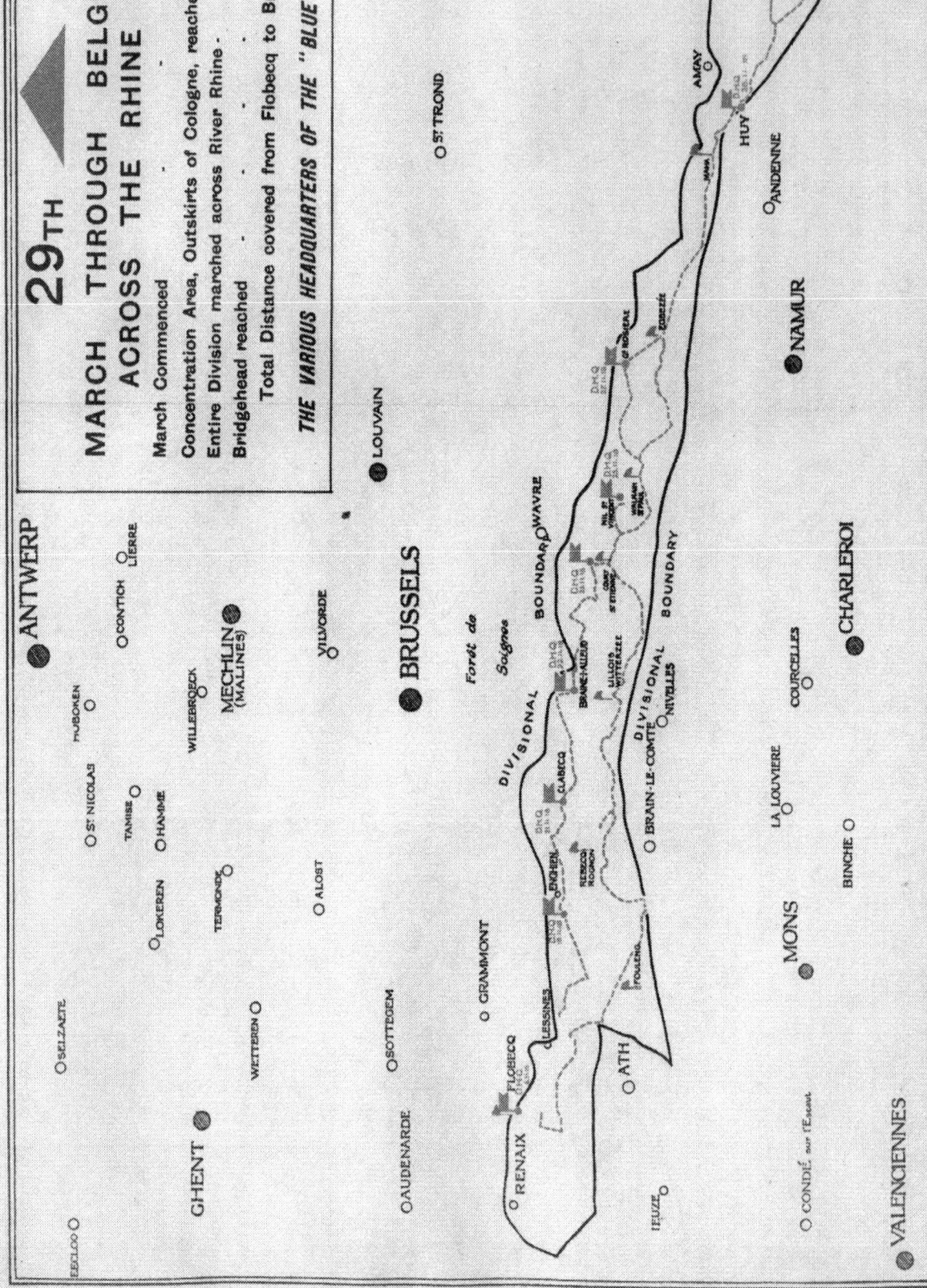

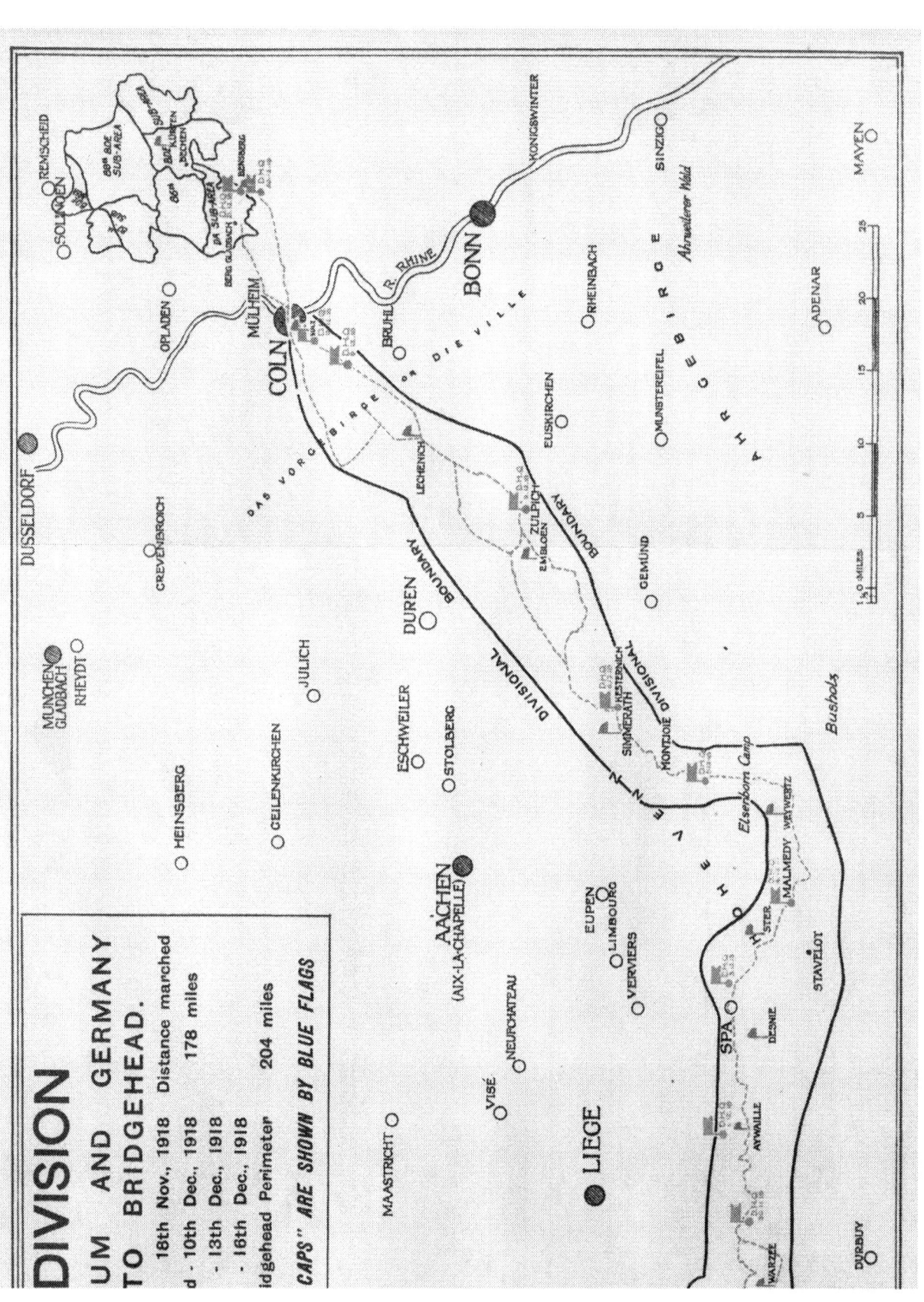

NEILL'S "BLUE CAPS"

CHAPTER I

THE OPENING OF THE GREAT WAR

1914 In the late summer of 1914, when the 1st Battalion Royal Dublin Fusiliers had been some eighteen months in Madras and rather more than four and a half years in India, those events rapidly came to pass which led to the outbreak of the greatest of all wars—a war in which India and her army were to play a very notable part, and to which she was to send some of her bravest and best, British and Indian.

The outstanding feature in the great crisis which had arisen was the speed at which events moved; the Austrian Archduke was murdered on June 28th, but while the ultimatum was not presented to Serbia until July 23rd, within a fortnight of this latter date Europe was at war. Great Britain had done her best to avert hostilities, and all had hoped that even at the eleventh hour the peaceful counsels might prevail which English statesmen had offered; but so soon as war was declared upon Germany there came, from all quarters of the world, " evidences of United Empire. The Sovereign of the Empire had not to summon; he had only to respond "; while, so far as India was concerned, " in the words of the prophetess Deborah, ' the people willingly offered themselves, and the Princes offered themselves willingly among the people.' "*

On September 10th the following Royal Message was addressed to " *the Princes and Peoples of My Indian Empire* " :—

" *During the past few weeks the peoples of My whole Empire at Home and Overseas have moved with one mind and purpose to*

---

* *The Empire at War.* Vol. I, pp. 276, 298, 302.

confront and overthrow an unparalleled assault upon the continuity of civilization and the peace of mankind.

"*The calamitous conflict is not of My seeking. My voice has been cast throughout on the side of peace. My Ministers earnestly strove to allay the causes of strife and to appease differences with which My Empire was not concerned. Had I stood aside when, in defiance of pledges to which My Empire was a party, the soil of Belgium was violated and her cities laid desolate, when the very life of the French nation was threatened with extinction, I should have sacrificed My honour and given to destruction the liberties of My Empire and of mankind. I rejoice that every part of the Empire is with Me in this decision.*

"*Paramount regard for treaty faith and the pledged word of rulers and peoples is the common heritage of England and of India.*

"*Among the many incidents which have marked the unanimous uprising of the populations of My Empire in defence of its unity and integrity, nothing has moved Me more than the passionate devotion to My Throne expressed both by My Indian subjects, and by the Feudatory Princes and the Ruling Chiefs of India, and their prodigal offers of their lives and their resources in the cause of the Realm. Their one-voiced demand to be foremost in the conflict has touched My heart and has inspired to the highest issues the love and devotion which, as I well know, have ever linked My Indian subjects and Myself. I recall to mind India's gracious message to the British nation of goodwill and fellowship, which greeted My return in February, 1912, after the solemn ceremony of My Coronation Durbar at Delhi; and I find in this hour of trial a full harvest and a noble fulfilment of the assurance given by you that the destinies of Great Britain and India are indissolubly linked.*"

In a leading article *The Times* of September 15th voiced the feeling experienced by all men of British birth on learning of the whole-hearted way in which India had accepted her share of the burdens of Empire, and was preparing to play her part in the mighty struggle upon which the British Government had entered.

"*In all its long annals,*" we read, "*the House of Commons has never been more moved than it was yesterday upon the reading of the wonderful message from the Viceroy of India. The Indian Empire has overwhelmed the British nation by the completeness and the immensity of its enthusiastic aid. India is sending 70,000 men—horse, foot, and artillery—British and Indian, Rajput and Gurkha, Sikh and Pathan, a formidable fighting force trained and maintained in constant readiness for warfare, to fall into line beside their brethren and the French. The proudest princes of India have buckled on their swords and are hastening to battle in the fair land of France. At their head comes the gallant Sir Pertab Singh, the Nestor of Rajput chivalry, who vowed long ago that he would not die in his bed, and at seventy years of age claims to face the foe once more upon the battlefield. With him is the knightly figure of the Maharaja of Bikanir; the young Maharaja of Patiala, the head of the Sikhs; the heir-apparent of Bhopal, the hope of a powerful Musulman ruling family; the Maharaja of Jodhpur, another famous Rajput ruler; and many more representatives of the most ancient and honoured princely families of India. Seven hundred Princes and Chiefs of India have placed the whole of their resources at the disposal of the King-Emperor. They have offered their swords, their treasuries, their troops, their lives. The peoples of British India—the innumerable millions under the sole control of the Government—have been equally lavish in their outpourings and their demonstrations of loyalty. From the grim Khyber, from far Baluchistan, from the mountain heights of Chitral, promises of assistance and appeals for enrolment are being pressed upon the Government of India. Nor is this all. The Prime Minister of Nepal, the great Gurkha state, has offered the formidable troops he controls, an offer of inestimable value. Such is India's glorious answer to the Kaiser and his misguided dream of revolt in the East. Asia has joined in the battle against brutal lust for power, and her weapons are turned against him. . . . The Kaiser has lighted a torch indeed, for he has set the West and East alike afire against him."*

But splendid and full of promise for the conduct and future issue of the war as were the offers of men and treasure daily coming in from India as from all parts of the Empire, it was to the Regular

Army, to the Army already in being, that the authorities looked to check the first onslaught of the enemy, and to form a human barrier behind which the Empire might fashion fresh armies and perfect new weapons; and the first great need of the moment was to transfer to the European theatre of war with the utmost possible dispatch all the admirably trained and seasoned units of the Regular Army which at this time formed the garrison of British India, replacing them by such troops of the Second Line as could be induced to volunteer for garrison duty in the East.

In the late summer of 1914 there were no fewer than 52 British infantry battalions serving in India—17 battalions in Bengal, 14 in the Punjab, 12 in Bombay, 6 in Madras, and 3 in Burma. Before the end of September ten of these battalions had already left India for Europe, some of them proceeding to France with the two divisions composing the Indian Army Corps, others voyaging to England to join the 8th Division then getting ready for service on the Western front; before the year 1914 came to an end fifteen more battalions had sailed for the seat of war in Europe or elsewhere; and when 1915 opened something less than a dozen battalions of regular British infantry remained in the country, while the place of every one of those which had left had been filled, almost automatically as it seemed, by fine strong battalions of the Territorial Army. The reliefs had thus expeditiously been effected without anything even remotely resembling serious interference by the naval forces of the Central Powers.

When war broke out early in August, 1914, the 1st Battalion Royal Dublin Fusiliers was in occupation of two stations in the Madras presidency, "A," "B," "F," "G," and "H" Companies being with headquarters at Fort St. George, Madras; while "C," "D," and "E" Companies were at Bellary under the command of Captain E. A. Molesworth, who had then only just returned to India from eight months' leave in England. At this time or a little later the following officers were with the detachment at Bellary—viz., Captains A. M. Johnson (who was also station staff officer) and H. C. Crozier, Lieutenants H. M. Floyd, J. O. W. Shine, and F. S. Lanigan-

THE OPENING OF THE WAR

O'Keeffe. The following officers were at headquarters:—Lieut.-Colonel R. A. Rooth, Major E. Fetherstonhaugh, Captains C. T. W. Grimshaw, D.S.O. (Adjutant), A. Brodhurst-Hill, W. F. Higginson, D. French, A. W. Molony, and J. M. Mood; Lieutenants T. L. M. L. Mansfield, J. F. K. Dobbs, G. M. Dunlop, D. D. Philby, R. Bernard, and A. B. Bagley; Second-Lieutenants C. G. Carruthers, L. C. Boustead, R. de Lusignan, and R. V. C. Corbet.

Captains S. G. Smithwick and C. B. R. Hoey and Lieutenant R. J. H. Carew were serving at the regimental depot, Lieutenant J. R. W. Grove was officiating as extra A.D.C. to the Governor of Madras, while Lieutenant D. V. F. Anderson was at Wellington and Lieutenant H. D. O'Hara at Poonamallee; Hon. Lieutenant M. J. Kennedy was Quartermaster of the Battalion.

It will have been noticed above that the companies have been described as lettered from "A" to "H," for actually the four-company battalion organization introduced in the Army quartered in the United Kingdom by special Army Order of September 26th, 1913, was not introduced into the British corps serving in India until rather less than a year later; and it is only on August 1st, 1914, that a notice appears in Battalion Orders directing that in future companies are to be trained as double companies. The following officers were appointed double-company commanders:—

"A" Double Company—Captain A. Brodhurst-Hill.
"B" Double Company—Captain E. A. Molesworth.
"C" Double Company—Captain A. M. Johnson.
"D" Double Company—Captain W. F. Higginson.

There being a considerable number of Germans and Austrians resident in the city of Madras, the duties became at once more than usually heavy owing to the necessity which arose for safeguarding the water-supply, the oil tanks, and all the public buildings and telephones, and accordingly "E" Company, under Captain Johnson, was called in to Headquarters from Bellary, and arrived on August 9th at a strength of 80 all ranks.

For some little time, however, there is no indication in Battalion Orders that war had broken out; there are certain announcements which show that an unusual situation had arisen: thus, on August 11th that the holding of "Lucknow Week" must be postponed *sine die;* on the 21st that Captain Higginson is appointed Assistant Press Censor; while on the 25th an order was published notifying that "certain German and Austrian subjects will shortly be interned in the new Supper Room, Fort St. George, pending their dispatch to Ahmednagar," and that they are to be treated with " as much consideration as orders on the subject allow, and soldiers should avoid doing anything to aggravate their unfortunate position." But of the first real act of war there is no mention whatever in the Battalion Orders of the Royal Dublin Fusiliers.

When at the end of July, 1914, the "War Imminent" message was sent out by the German Admiralty to all ships on foreign stations, the *Emden* (Captain von Müller), a German light cruiser of 3,592 tons, having a speed of 24.1 knots, and mounting ten 4.1 guns, had just left Tsingtau on a cruise to the entrance of the Japan Sea; on August 2nd news of the declaration of war against France and Russia was received; and early on the following morning the *Emden* captured a vessel of the Russian Volunteer Fleet and took her in to Tsingtau as prize. At this port the cruiser received orders from Admiral von Spee to join him at Pagan Island, which was reached on August 12th. From here the *Emden*, accompanied by the tender *Markomania,* was ordered on an independent visit to the south, and at the end of the first week in September she had entered the Bay of Bengal, and for some days she cruised between Calcutta and Colombo; about 9.30 p.m. on the 22nd the *Emden* appeared off Madras.

"Only on the preceding day had the gladsome news been officially announced in Madras that the *Emden* was disposed of. To celebrate the event, a festive gathering had assembled at the Club. Unfortunately, since we did not know of this at the time, we were unable to prevent our shells falling into the soup; otherwise we should naturally have postponed our bombardment until the following day. One should not unnecessarily irritate one's opponent.

As far as possible all sacred institutions should be spared, and Englishmen are specially sensitive as regards their dinner."*

The following are extracts from an account of the bombardment which appeared in the *Madras Mail* of September 23rd :—

" The German cruiser, *Emden*, which has been creating such havoc among the merchant shipping at the mouth of the Hooghly and on the Burma coast, is still at large in the Bay of Bengal, as the citizens of Madras now know to their cost, for she visited Madras between 9 and 10 o'clock last night, accompanied by the *Markomania*, stood in the offing to the south-east of the harbour within range of the beach, and proceeded to bombard the port. . . . Subsequent shots set the petroleum tanks on fire. The oil in the tanks immediately blazed up, rendering the sea face of the town as brilliant as day, aiding probably in the short, sharp cannonade that took place ; but this was hardly necessary, as the *Emden* was using a particularly brilliant searchlight, under which every detail of the sea face was distinctly visible. That the visit was altogether unexpected may be judged from the fact that the lighthouse was working as usual, and undoubtedly helped the cruiser to take up its bearings and fire with the accuracy with which it did. . . . The call was paid early enough to find the shore lights all ablaze, the trams working, and all the business of the town at that time of night going on as usual.

" As far as we can make out from personal observation, and from information received, she fired the guns of both broadsides before she extinguished her searchlight, in response, we believe, to a return fire from the shore, and vanished silently in the darkness with all her lights extinguished."

On the alarm being given, the Battalion paraded and occupied different prearranged defensive positions, but after a couple of hours the men were dismissed. Beyond the material damage done, the loss of life was not great, five people in all being killed, while something like a dozen received wounds.

* " *Emden*, paraphrased from von Mücke's account," R.U.S.I. Journal, Nov., 1917.

Things now quieted down again, and it was not until a month later that the 1st Battalion Royal Dublin Fusiliers received intimation that it was to play its part before long in a European theatre of war. On Wednesday, October 21st, the following was published in Battalion Orders :—

> "Orders have been received for the Battalion to hold itself in readiness to proceed to England at short notice.
> "It will proceed on relief scale.
> "Families will not accompany the Battalion.
> "Companies will get packed up ready to move.
> "All British kit-bags and *suleetahs* will be handed into Quartermaster's Stores, commencing with 'A' Company, at 11.30 a.m. on Friday next, 23rd inst.
> "All surplus S. and T. Stores will be handed in at the same time.
> "All Reflectors, Mirrors, Axes, felling, Binoculars, Compasses, Handcuffs, Pouch weights, Dummy drill cartridges will be handed in at the same time."

Battalion Orders of October 31st contained the names of some sixty-five non-commissioned officers and men of the Battalion who, by reason of ill-health or employment on important duties, were not to proceed with the corps to England; but some at least of the sick were found fit to accompany the Battalion when the time of departure actually arrived.

Finally, on Thursday, November 12th, the long-looked-for announcement appeared in Battalion Orders that embarkation was actually at hand; we read :—

> "Orders have been received for the Battalion to embark for passage to England.
> "The Battalion will parade at 4 p.m. to-morrow to march to the Railway Station. Dress—Marching Order.
> "Officers to carry the Colours (cased)—Lieutenant Boustead and Second-Lieutenant Corbet.
> "The Battalion will entrain in two trains :—

1st Train—Headquarters, Band, 'A,' 'B,' and 'E' Companies.

2nd Train—' F,' ' G,' and ' H ' Companies."

In accordance with the above, the 1st Battalion Royal Dublin Fusiliers marched for the last time out of Fort St. George on the afternoon of November 13th; many times previously in its history had the Regiment started out from the city of its birth to take part in the wars of old John Company and of the Empire, and now it marched away to the greatest of all wars, upon a Great Adventure from which few of those then serving with the Battalion would return, and after the close of which the very name of the Battalion was to disappear.

The duties of Fort St. George were handed over to the Madras Volunteer Guards, pending the arrival of the 4th Battalion Somerset Light Infantry, who were to relieve the Dublin Fusiliers, and, escorted by the Southern Provinces Mounted Rifles, the Battalion marched to the railway station, the route lined by the Madras Volunteer Artillery, the Madras Volunteer Guards, and the Southern Mahratta Railway Volunteers.

His Excellency the Governor, Lord Pentland, had come to bid the Battalion Godspeed, and in a short address said that he knew the good work " the Blue Caps" had done; that the people of Madras were proud of their Regiment, who had behaved in a most excellent way during their stay in the city; and that he and their many friends in Madras would follow their doings at the front with pride and sympathy.

In replying, Lieut.-Colonel Rooth spoke as follows :—

" Your Excellency,—

" We are very grateful to you for the honour you have done us in coming to bid us farewell. I think my Battalion has behaved well in Madras, and I hope that the inhabitants of this city are as sorry to lose us as we are to say good-bye to them."

Then, turning to the Battalion, Lieut.-Colonel Rooth added :—

" Men of the Old Madras Fusiliers! These walls have often resounded to the shouts of our forerunners. I want you now to reawaken the echoes with three cheers for His Excellency Lord Pentland, and the inhabitants of this ancient city of our birth."

The men of the Battalion gave three hearty cheers, the ceremony ended, and "the Blue Caps" then departed in two trains for Bombay. Halts were made for meals on the 14th and 15th at Guntakal, Raichur, Dhond, and Khalyan, the companies from Bellary joining at the first-named halting-place, and Bombay was finally reached on the 16th. Here the 1st Battalion Royal Dublin Fusiliers embarked on two hired transports; Headquarters and six companies under Lieut.-Colonel Rooth were accommodated on the British India steamship *Malda*, while Major Fetherstonhaugh embarked with " A " and " B " Companies in the P. and O. steamer *Assaye*. The following were the officers who left India with the Battalion :—Lieut.-Colonel R. A. Rooth ; Major E. Fetherstonhaugh ; Captains E. A. Molesworth, C. T. W. Grimshaw (Adjutant), A. Brodhurst-Hill, W. F. Higginson, A. M. Johnson, H. C. Crozier, D. French, A. W. Molony, J. M. Mood, and J. R. W. Grove ; Lieutenants G. M. Dunlop, H. M. Floyd, J. O. W. Shine, F. S. Lanigan-O'Keeffe, R. Bernard, H. D. O'Hara, C. G. Carruthers, L. C. Boustead, and R. de Lusignan ; Second-Lieutenant R. V. C. Corbet ; and Lieutenant and Quartermaster M. J. Kennedy.

Captain D. V. F. Anderson, who had proceeded some little time before to Bombay with a party of one sergeant and four privates to meet Territorials arriving there and escort them to Madras, followed the Battalion to England a month later, actually rejoining on February 3rd, 1915.

Battalion leaves India. The *Malda* and *Assaye*, forming part of a large convoy of transports and other ships, sailed from Bombay on the 19th, escorted by the French cruiser *Dupleix*, and, being joined on the 21st by seven more ships from Karachi, these made up a fleet of thirty-two ships in all.

The homeward voyage was wholly uneventful, the outstanding event being the meeting with the Australian Corps at Suez, where news was received of the sinking of the *Emden*.

HANDING OVER THE COLOURS TO SAFE CUSTODY OF
THE MAYOR OF TORQUAY, JANUARY 7TH, 1915.
LIEUT.-COLONEL R. A. ROOTH, COMMANDING, IN FRONT.

Plymouth was reached on December 21st, and, disembarking, the Battalion entrained for Torquay, where it was billeted, and from here all ranks were permitted to proceed on short furlough in small parties at a time.

While the Dublin Fusiliers were in India, and during their voyage to England, the British Army had been greatly expanded and many new organizations had been created. Among these was the 29th Division, the formation of which had been authorized in November, 1914, and which was now to be composed of the 86th, 87th, and 88th Brigades, made up, with two exceptions only, of infantry battalions which on the outbreak of war were serving in Eastern garrisons.

1915 In anticipation, therefore, of an approaching move from Torquay, where the Royal Dublin Fusiliers had already made themselves exceedingly popular, Lieut.-Colonel Rooth, on January 7th, 1915, handed over the Colours to the safe keeping of the Mayor, and in doing so said:—

"We are, as you know, an Irish Battalion, and we are far from home—we are a long, long way from Tipperary. I cannot conceive of a better temporary home for these Colours than this county of fair women and brave men. Some day some of us may come back, I hope, to claim these Colours at your hands, and I trust that by then we shall have gathered fresh honours to add to their record."

The orders for the Battalion to move to Nuneaton to join the 86th Infantry Brigade were issued on January 11th, and, parading that day at midnight, the companies left Torquay in two trains, and again went into billets on arrival at their new station. Here the Battalion joined the 86th Brigade, containing the 2nd Battalion Royal Fusiliers, 1st Battalion Lancashire Fusiliers, 1st Battalion Royal Munster Fusiliers, and 1st Battalion Royal Dublin Fusiliers—all battalions lately arrived from India; the Brigade Commander was Brigadier-General S. W. Hare, and the 29th Division was at this time in charge of Major-General F. C. Shaw (now Lieut.-General the Rt. Hon. Sir F. C. Shaw, K.C.B.).

Immediately prior to leaving Torquay Major C. R. L. Ronayne, M.B., R.A.M.C., reported his arrival, and was taken on the strength of the Battalion as Medical Officer.

From various signs and portents, it now really seemed that the time for the departure of the Division to an overseas theatre of war was at hand; all ranks were permitted the retention only of such scale of kit and baggage as might be taken on field service; furlough was now only given for very brief periods and under exceptional circumstances; all ranks underwent anti-typhoid inoculation; while identity discs were now invariably to be worn on the person.

On February 11th Major-General C. D. Cooper, C.B., the Colonel of the Regiment, came to Nuneaton and inspected the Battalion, which paraded by wings. In the course of the address which he made to the men of each half-battalion, the General said that he was glad to hear that the Battalion was reported as being so fit; he knew that all ranks would give a good account of themselves on active service, and add fresh honours to those already gained by " the Blue Caps "; he wished them Godspeed and a happy return to this country.

By the middle of February the 29th Division was completed in all respects, and it seems by this to have been an accepted belief among all ranks that the Division was shortly to go to the Dardanelles,* but the time was not yet, for on March 6th the Battalion marched to Kenilworth, and then early on the morning of the 12th proceeded by train to Brandon, in the neighbourhood of which the Division was inspected by His Majesty the King. On this day Major-General Shaw, who had been severely wounded in France and was not yet wholly recovered, handed over command of the Division to Major-General A. G. Hunter-Weston, C.B., D.S.O., described by General Sir Ian Hamilton as " a slashing man of action, an acute theorist."†

The 29th Division, immediately after this royal inspection,

---

* See Creighton, *With the 29th Division in Gallipoli*, p. 14.
† *Gallipoli Diary*, Vol. I., p. 3.

received orders to prepare for embarkation for an "unknown destination"; but it was an open secret that its destination was actually the Dardanelles, and something must now be said of the circumstances which had arisen calling for the necessity of the employment of large allied forces in this obscure corner of South-Eastern Europe.

When in the opening months of the European War—so soon, that is, as Turkey had entered into alliance with the Central Powers—the British Government decided in favour of the project of attempting to force the passage of the Dardanelles, it was confidently believed that success would bring about the collapse of the Ottoman Power and would lead to the capitulation of Constantinople, while an ice-free route to Russia through the Black Sea would at once be opened. It is to be noticed that those who pressed for the undertaking did not contemplate merely the *closing* of the Straits, which might have been effected by the military occupation of the Gallipoli peninsula, but the actual *opening* of the Dardanelles from the Mediterranean to the Black Sea—an operation for the complete and permanent success of which it was essential that naval command of the Straits should be established, and, further, that both the European and Asiatic shores should be held by military forces.

The operations, when finally initiated, opened not with a naval *attack*, but with a mere long-range bombardment of the forts at the western entrance of the Straits, carried out early in November, 1914. This served no useful purpose whatever, and did no more than put the Turks on the alert; and during the three and a half months that ensued, and during which no further offensive operations were taken in hand, the Turks and their German allies worked hard at the effective fortification of the Straits and the Peninsula. On February 19th and 25th, 1915, the naval bombardment was repeated, and on each of these days it appeared that the forts had been silenced; but on several successive occasions up to March 18th, when the allied squadrons attempted to move further in to the attack of the main fortifications, great difficulty was experienced in manœuvring so large a number of heavy ships of war in such narrow waters, while floating mines were encountered and several vessels were sunk or injured. The fleets were then withdrawn, and the attempt to force the Straits was not renewed.

Those members of the British Cabinet who had pressed for the purely naval attack now decided that military assistance on a tolerably large scale must be afforded. On March 12th General Sir Ian Hamilton was informed by Lord Kitchener :—" We are sending a military force to support the Fleet now at the Dardanelles, and you are to have command," adding later, " I hope you will not have to land at all ; if you *do* have to land, why then the powerful Fleet at your back will be the prime factor in your choice of time and place."*

The following were the troops placed at Sir Ian Hamilton's disposal :—

> The 29th Division.
> The 42nd East Lancashire Division
> The Royal Naval Division.
> An Australian Division.
> A Division of Australians and New Zealanders.
> Two French Divisions.
> Some Indian troops.

Of the above, Sir Ian remarks in his Diary :—" Of these the 29th Division are extras—*division de luxe.*"

" A military force of all arms, comprising seven divisions with a few additional units, ought to have represented a total of fully 140,000 men. But the divisions did not for the most part consist of the full number of units that a division is supposed to include. They were very weak in artillery. A proportion of the battalions were below war establishment when they started. From the nature of the enterprise on which they were about to embark, it was expedient for them to leave a large part of their impedimenta and animals in Egypt. The consequence was that the whole army numbered less than 100,000 officers and men, and it is well to

* *Gallipoli Diary,* Vol. I, pp. 1 and 7.

MEMORIAL TO THE 29TH DIVISION, NEAR DYMCHURCH, where they marched past the King before leaving for Gallipoli, on March 12th, 1915.

OFFICERS OF THE "BLUE CAPS," TAKEN IMMEDIATELY PRIOR TO EMBARKATION FOR GALLIPOLI, MARCH, 1915.

Back Row—2/Lieut. J. Hosford   2/Lieut. J. P. Walters   *Lieut. R. H. deLusignan   *2/Lieut. R. V. C. Corbet   *Lieut. H. D. O'Hara   *2/Lieut. W. Andrews
2/Lieut. C. W. Maffett   Lieut. & Qr.Mr. J. Kennedy   *Rev. Father Finn, C.F.   Lieut. H. de Boer, R.A.M.C.   *Capt. G. M. Dunlop
Lieut. F. S. Lanigan-O'Keeffe   *Lieut. R. Bernard   Lieut. C. G. Carruthers   *Lieut. L. C. Boustead.

Front Row—Capt. D. French   Capt. J. R. W. Grove   Capt. J. M. Mood   Capt. A. M. Johnson   *Capt. W. F. Higginson   *Major E. Fetherstonhaugh
*Lieut.-Col. R. A. Rooth   *Capt. C. T. W. Grimshaw, D.S.O.   Capt. E. A. Molesworth   Capt. H. C. Crozier   Capt. A. W. Molony
*Capt. D. V. F. Anderson   *Lieut. H. M. Floyd

* Killed in action.

remember that, throughout the campaign that was to follow, the expression 'division' was always a somewhat delusive one."*

General Hamilton and his staff left London on March 13th, and reached the base at Tenedos in time to witness the naval attack of the 18th, and as a result of what he saw he cabled to London that the whole of the troops which had been placed under his command would be needed to enable the fleet effectively to force the Dardanelles.

In the meantime the force intended to co-operate with the fleet had left England, and was making for the appointed rendezvous in the waters of the Ægean Sea.

On March 12th orders were received at the headquarters of the 86th Brigade at Coventry to entrain for the port of embarkation on the 14th, but on the next day the move was postponed for twenty-four hours, and it was not until the 15th that the Battalions finally left their stations. The 1st Battalion Royal Dublin Fusiliers proceeded to Avonmouth in three trains, the first at 5.30 p.m.; the port was reached between 9.50 p.m. on March 15th and 6.10 a.m. on March 16th, and the Battalion embarked in the *Ausonia* (hired transport), which also accommodated Brigade Headquarters and three companies of the Royal Munster Fusiliers. The rest of the Brigade embarked in the *Alaunia* and *Haverford*, while in the *Mercian* were all the horses and transport; the fleet then sailed at 7.30 p.m., escorted by two destroyers.

The following are the names of the officers of the 1st Battalion Royal Dublin Fusiliers who left England with it on this great adventure:—Lieut.-Colonel R. A. Rooth, Major E. Fetherstonhaugh; Captains E. A. Molesworth, W. F. Higginson (Adjutant), C. T. W. Grimshaw, D.S.O., A. M. Johnson, H. C. Crozier, D. French, A. W. Molony, J. M. Mood, D. V. F. Anderson, and J. R. W. Grove; Lieutenants H. M. Floyd, C. G. Carruthers, L. C. Boustead, F. S. Lanigan-O'Keeffe, R. Bernard, G. M. Dunlop, C. W. Maffett, H. D. O'Hara, R. V. C. Corbet, R. de Lusignan, J. Hosford, J. P. Walters,

* Callwell, *The Dardanelles*, p. 36.

and W Andrews; Lieutenant and Quartermaster M. J. Kennedy; Lieutenant de Boer, R.A.M.C., in medical charge; and the Rev. Father Finn, chaplain.

It is recorded in the Brigade Diary that the stores and vehicles were loaded under no particular system, while tents were put on board by the Ordnance Department and not by the troops. Helmets were issued on board the transports, as were also silk handkerchiefs to all ranks of the Battalion, these being a gift of the citizens of Madras.

The voyage was a very calm and peaceful one; the *Ausonia* put into Gibraltar on the 20th, and here Lieutenant Lanigan-O'Keeffe was landed by reason of ill-health; sailing on eastward, Malta was reached early on the morning of the 24th, and left again at 7.30 on the 26th.

In the early hours of the 29th the *Ausonia* reached the harbour of Alexandria, where the *Alaunia* had arrived, and where the Royal Fusiliers and Lancashire Fusiliers had already commenced disembarkation. Private Kavanagh, of the Royal Dublin Fusiliers, died of pneumonia on March 28th, and was buried at sea.

On the 30th the remaining battalions of the 86th Brigade began unloading baggage and disembarking, the *Mercian*, with horses and vehicles, having only come in that morning. The troops marched out to camp at Mex, where, however, owing to some insufficiency in the water-supply, only the 86th and 87th Brigades could be accommodated, the third Brigade of the 29th Division (the 88th) being camped at Mustapha, on the other side of Alexandria. Second-line vehicles only were taken to camp, the first line being left on board the transports.

The strength of the Battalion was now 25 officers, exclusive of the medical officer and chaplain, with 987 other ranks. On battalion charge were 220 rounds per man and 11,500 per machine gun, 11 riding horses, 53 draught horses, 19 wagons, 4 machine guns, and 16 tool-carts.

While lying in camp at Mex the two brigades there stationed

were practised in embarking and disembarking operations from small boats, and in forming up and advancing rapidly after a landing.

On April 16th the troops at Mex were reviewed by General Sir Ian Hamilton, and of this inspection he has recorded :—" There was a strong wind blowing which tried to spoil the show, but could not—that Infantry was too superb! Alexander, Hannibal, Cæsar, Napoleon: not one of them had the handling of legionaries like these. The Fusilier Brigade were the heavier. If we don't win, I won't be able to put it on the men."*

Everything was now ready for the important operations in which the Expeditionary Force under General Hamilton's command was about to take part, and on April 7th orders were issued to leave camp and march early that afternoon to the harbour.

At 4.30 p.m. the Battalion re-embarked in the *Ausonia* at a strength of 26 officers and 953 other ranks, while 1 officer and 38 men proceeded on board the *Marquette*, which carried 52 horses and 19 vehicles belonging to the Dublins. 4,800 gallons of drinking water in 1,200 kerosene tins in 600 boxes were taken on board, also timber and material for the construction of barrel piers.

At 11 a.m. on April 9th the *Ausonia* sailed from Alexandria, and on the afternoon of the 11th the transport came to an anchor in Mudros Harbour on the island of Lemnos.

---

* *Diary*, Vol I, p. 83.

CHAPTER II

THE GALLIPOLI LANDING

SOME description must now be given of the country in which the 1st Battalion Royal Dublin Fusiliers, with the other regiments of many races composing the Mediterranean Expeditionary Force, was to fight and die.

"The peninsula of Gallipoli is a tongue of hilly land, about fifty-three miles long, between the Ægean Sea and the Straits of the Dardanelles. At its north-eastern or European end it is four or five miles broad; then, a little to the south of the town of Bulair, it narrows to three miles in a contraction or neck which was fortified during the Crimean War by French and English soldiers. This fortification is known as the lines of Bulair. Beyond these lines, to the south-west, the Peninsula broadens in a westward direction, and attains its maximum breadth, of about twelve miles, some twenty-four miles from Bulair, between the two points of Cape Suvla, on the sea, and Cape Uzun within the Straits. Beyond this broad part is a second contraction or neck, less than five miles across, and beyond this, pointing roughly west-south-westerly, is the final tongue or finger of the Peninsula, an isosceles triangle of land with a base of some seven miles and two sides of thirteen miles each, converging in the blunt tip (perhaps a mile and a half across) between Cape Helles and Cape Tekke. . . . Bad roads, possible for wheeled traffic, wind in the valleys, skirting the hills, and linking up the principal villages. . . .

"The seashore, like the Straits shore, is mainly steep-to, with abrupt sandy cliffs rising from the sea to a height of from 100 to 300 feet. At irregular and rare intervals these cliffs are broken by the ravines and gullies, down which the autumnal and winter

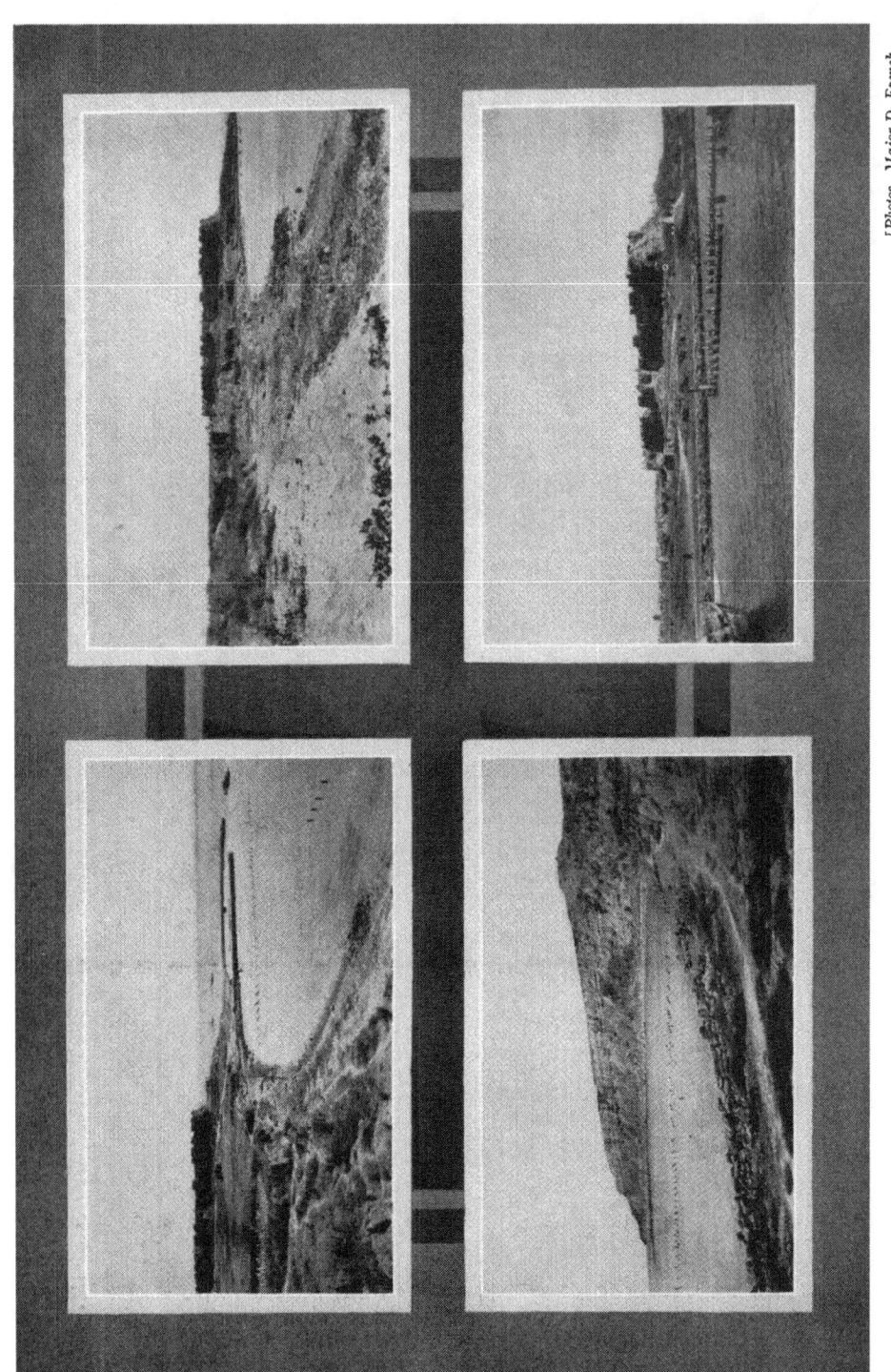

[Photos, Major D. French.

"V" BEACH, LOOKING FROM THE WEST, showing actual spot of the landing; where the *River Clyde* grounded; Fort Sedd-el-Bahr; and the Cemetery where the "Blue Caps" were buried.

"V" BEACH, LOOKING WEST. High ground in background was where Essex and Worcesters attacked. It was here that Tommy Frankland was killed—i.e., on the high ground.

"V" BEACH, LOOKING FROM THE WEST. It was at this spot (foreground) that Rooth was killed.

FORT SEDD-EL-BAHR. White Monument has been erected by the French.

rains escape; at the sea-mouths of these gullies are sometimes narrow strips of stony or sandy beach. . . .

"Those who look at the south-western end of the Peninsula, between Cape Suvla and Cape Helles, will see three heights greater than the rolling wold or downland around them. Seven miles south east from Cape Suvla is the great and beautiful peaked hill of Sari Bair, 970 feet high, very steep on its sea side and thickly fleeced with scrub. This hill commands the landing-place at Suvla. Seven miles south from Sari Bair is the long dominating plateau of Kilid Bahr, which runs inland from the Straits, at heights varying between 500 and 700 feet, to within two miles of the sea. This plateau commands the Narrows of the Hellespont. Five miles farther to the south-west and less than six miles from Cape Helles is the bare and lonely lump of Achi Baba, 590 feet high. This hill commands the landing-place at Cape Helles."*

"The plan of operations for securing a footing at the extremity of the peninsula was a somewhat elaborate one. Three main landings were to take place, and these were to be supplemented by a minor landing on either flank. The principal disembarkations were to be undertaken respectively at Beaches 'V,' 'W,' and 'X,' all three of which were in themselves favourable places, apart from the opposition that might be offered. Comparatively gentle slopes rose from the actual beaches in the case of 'V' and 'W,' and promised facilities for moving impedimenta forward as soon as a footing had been made good. In the case of 'X,' on the other hand, the ground abutting on the beach rose somewhat abruptly, giving it the character almost of a bluff; but this circumstance, coupled with the fact that the beach faced west, concealed the environs of the landing-place from Kum Kale, and gave reason to hope that the disembarkation at this point would not be interfered with by hostile artillery on the Asiatic side.

"The minor landings were to take place at Beaches 'S' and 'Y.' 'S' Beach was narrow, and was obviously much exposed to fire from across the Dardanelles. 'Y' Beach was situated at the

* Masefield, *Gallipoli*, pp. 4–7.

foot of the cliffs, was not for that reason adapted for the landing of troops other than infantry and mountain artillery, and was not the kind of spot that would naturally be selected to put troops ashore at. Sir Ian Hamilton hoped by means of these two secondary operations to protect the flanks, to disseminate the forces of the enemy, and to interrupt the arrival of hostile reinforcements."*

In Operation Order No. 1 issued to the 29th Division it was stated that the object of the expedition was to assist the fleet to force the Dardanelles by capturing the Kilid Bahr plateau and dominating the forts of the Narrows. The general plan to achieve this object included the following operations taking place simultaneously :—

(*a*) The bombardment of Bulair Lines, followed by a feint landing by the Royal Naval Division on the mainland north of Xeros Islands.

(*b*) The bombardment of the heights commanding the beach between Gaba Tepe and Nibrunesi Point, and the landing of the Australian and New Zealand Army Corps.

(*c*) The bombardment of the southern extremity of the Peninsula, and the landing of the 29th Division.

(*d*) Demonstration by the French Fleet at Besika Bay, and the landing of a portion of the French Expeditionary Force in the neighbourhood of Kum Kale.

"The task of the 29th Division," so runs the Order, "is the attack of the Kilid Bahr plateau from the south. The general plan to carry out this task is to land, under cover of the bombardment of the fleet :—

(*a*) A force on the coast west of Krithia ;
(*b*) A force on the coast near Eski Hissarlik ;
(*c*) The remainder on three beaches on the southern end of the Peninsula.

"The lines to be successively gained are :—
(*a*) The hills 141, 138, and 114 ;

* Callwell, *The Dardanelles*, pp. 61–63.

PLAN OF ATTACKS

(b) A line running from the hills at east of Old Castle, to join hands on the left with the force landing at ' Y ' Beach;

(c) A line from Eski Hissarlik, about half a mile east of Krithia—Hill 472—to the sea;

(d) The capture of Achi Baba and the spur running south from it;

(e) The occupation and fortification of a line running east from Achi Baba to the sea about the level of 300, and west from Achi Baba via Hill 472 to the sea."

Briefly stated, the following was the general plan to be carried out by the 29th Division as the " covering force " of General Hamilton's army: The Hampshire Regiment, Royal Munster and Royal Dublin Fusiliers were to land at Beach " V," the Lancashire Fusiliers at Beach " W," and the Royal Fusiliers at Beach " X." To the South Wales Borderers was allotted Beach " S," the King's Own Scottish Borderers and the Plymouth Battalion of Marines of the Royal Naval Division were to disembark at Beach " Y," while the remaining battalions composing the 29th Division were to land at Beaches " W," " V," or " X," as circumstances might dictate.

The ten days following the arrival of General Hunter-Weston's command at Mudros Bay were passed by the brigade and battalion leaders in reconnoitring the coast, and by the troops in practising getting up and down rope ladders, and in rowing and landing from boats. On April 18th the wind and sea got up, and the move from the island of Lemnos to the rendezvous at Tenedos, which had been arranged for the 21st, had to be postponed by reason of the storm; but at 6 p.m. on the 23rd the transports *Alaunia*, *Ausonia*, and *Caledonia* finally sailed.

The following is the text of the various orders, messages, and addresses with which the vanguard of the invading army was speeded on its way:—

On the 22nd the following gracious message was received from His Majesty the King, and was duly promulgated:—

"*The King wishes you and your Army every success, and you are constantly in His Majesty's thoughts and prayers*"

The Commander issued the following General Order to his troops:—

"*Soldiers of France and of the King!*

"*Before us lies an adventure unprecedented in modern war. Together with our comrades of the Fleet, we are about to force a landing upon an open beach in face of positions which have been vaunted by our enemies as impregnable.*

"*The landing will be made good by the help of God and the Navy; the positions will be stormed, and the war brought one step nearer to a glorious close. 'Remember,' said Lord Kitchener when bidding adieu to your Commander, 'Remember, once you set foot upon the Gallipoli Peninsula, you must fight the thing through to a finish.'*

"*The whole world will be watching your progress. Let us prove ourselves worthy of the great feat of arms entrusted to us.*"

What is very suitably described as "a personal note" was addressed by Major-General Hunter-Weston to each man of the 29th Division on the occasion of their first going into action together:—

"*The Major-General Commanding congratulates the Division on being selected for an enterprise the success of which will have a decisive effect on the War.*

"*The eyes of the world are upon us, and your deeds will live in history.*

"*To us now is given an opportunity of avenging our friends and relatives who have fallen in France and Flanders. Our comrades there willingly gave their lives in thousands and tens of thousands for our King and Country, and by their glorious courage and dogged tenacity they defeated the invaders and broke the German offensive.*

"*We also must be prepared to suffer hardships, privations, thirst, and heavy losses by bullets, by shells, by mines, by drowning. But if each man feels, as is true, that on him individually, however small or however great his task, rests the success or failure of the Expedition, and therefore the honour of the Empire and the welfare of his own folk at home, we are certain to win through to a glorious victory.*

[Photo, W. T. Munns, Gravesend.

LIEUT.-COLONEL R. A. ROOTH,
COMMANDING THE "BLUE CAPS."
Killed at the head of the Battalion on April 25th, 1915,
at Gallipoli.

"*In Nelson's time it was England, now it is the whole British Empire, which expects that each man of us will do his duty.*"

And then in a Special Brigade Order Brigadier-General Hare sought to prepare all ranks of the 86th Brigade for the full magnitude of the effort that was now demanded of them. He wrote :—

"*Fusiliers!*

"*Our Brigade is to have the honour to be the first to land and to cover the disembarkation of the rest of the Division. Our task will be no easy one. Let us carry it through in a way worthy of the traditions of the distinguished regiments of which the Fusilier Brigade is composed; in such a way that the men of Albuhera and Minden, of Delhi and Lucknow, may hail us as their equals in valour and military achievement, and that future historians may say of us as Napier said of the Fusilier Brigade at Albuhera—'Nothing could stop this astonishing Infantry.'*"

And so, thus fortified, heartened and speeded on their way the battalions of the 29th Division sailed from Mudros harbour; the men were heavily laden, since the difficulty of supplying troops on such a coast had been foreseen and fully appreciated. Three days' rations were carried on each man, and the soldiers had been earnestly warned that under the conditions likely to prevail this food-supply might have to last them for four or even five days.

Every infantryman had on him 200 rounds of ammunition, while for each machine gun with the force 3,500 cartridges in belts were also landed.

"On Friday, April 23rd, the weather cleared so that the work could be begun. Ship after ship, crammed with soldiers, moved slowly out of harbour in the lovely day, and felt again the heave of the sea. No such gathering of fine ships has ever been seen upon this earth, and the beauty and the exultation of the youth upon them made them like sacred things as they moved away. All the thousands of men aboard them gathered on deck to see, till each rail was thronged. These men had come from all parts of the British world—from Africa, Australia, Canada, India, the Mother Country, New Zealand, and remote islands in the sea.

They had said good-bye to home, that they might offer their lives in the cause we stand for. In a few hours at most, as they well knew, perhaps a tenth of them would have looked their last on the sun, and be a part of foreign earth or dumb things that the tides push. . . . As they passed from moorings to the man-of-war anchorage on their way to the sea, their feeling that they had done with life and were going out to something new welled up in those battalions; they cheered and cheered till the harbour rang with cheering. . . . They left the harbour very, very slowly; this tumult of cheering lasted a long time; no one who heard it will ever forget it, or think of it unshaken. It broke the hearts of all there with pride and pity. . . . **Presently all were out, and the fleet stood across for Tenedos, and the sun went down with marvellous colour, lighting island after island and the Asian peaks, and those left behind in Mudros trimmed their lamps, knowing that they had been for a little brought near to the heart of things."***

The following was at this time the distribution of the Battalion:—

Lieut.-Colonel R. A. Rooth, in command.

Major E. Fetherstonhaugh, second-in-command.

Captain W. F. Higginson, adjutant.

Captain J. M. Dunlop and Lieutenant R. V. C. Corbet, machine-gun officers.

Captain J. R. W. Grove, signalling officer.

Lieutenant G. M. Kennedy, quartermaster.

Lieutenant de Boer, R.A.M.C., medical officer.

Regimental Sergeant-Major W. O'Mahoney.

Regimental Quartermaster-Sergeant J. Thurlow.

Orderly-Room Sergeant P. Bonyage.

"*W*" *Company:* Captains H. C. Crozier and A. W. Molony, Lieutenants H. D. O'Hara and L. C. Boustead, Company Sergeant-Major C. Smith, and Company Quartermaster-Sergeant P. Curran.

"*X*" *Company:* Major E. A. Molesworth, Captain D. V. F. Anderson, Lieutenant C. W. Maffett, Second-Lieutenants J. P.

* Masefield, pp. 32–36.

[Photo, Imperial War Museum.

S.S. *RIVER CLYDE*, TAKEN FROM BELOW THE WALLS OF SEDD-EL-BAHR FORT.

[Photo, Imperial War Museum.

INHABITANTS OF TENEDOS FOLLOWING IN VARIOUS SMALL CRAFT THE BOAT WHICH CONVEYED M. VENIZELOS TO H.M.S. *TRIAD*, OCTOBER 24th, 1917. Behind is seen the town of Tenedos with the Castle.

Walters and J. Hosford, Company Sergeant-Major H. Fox, and Company Quartermaster-Sergeant H. Baker.

"*Y*" *Company*: Captains A. M. Johnson and D. French, Lieutenants F. S. Lanigan-O'Keeffe,* R. Bernard, and W. Andrews, Company Sergeant-Major G. Baker, and Company Quartermaster-Sergeant J. Bedding.

"*Z*"† *Company*: Major C. T. W. Grimshaw, Captain J. M. Mood, Lieutenants R. de Lusignan and C. G. Carruthers, Company Sergeant-Major M. O'Keefe, and Company Quartermaster-Sergeant F. Brennan.

Lieutenant H. F. Floyd remained on the *Marquette* with the transport.

The following "landings" were projected on the Gallipoli peninsula :—

1. The landing in four trips of two and a quarter battalions on Beach 'Y' and the bombardment of Helles Beaches by the fleet.

2. The landing in one trip of 2,900 troops at Beaches "S," "V," "W," and "X."

3. The landing of 2,100 troops in the steam collier *River Clyde*, to be run ashore on Beach "V."

4. The landing in one trip of the remainder of the covering force on Beaches "V," "W," and "X."

The rendezvous at the island of Tenedos was reached early on the morning of the 24th, when the wind was getting up and the sea was very choppy, but during the day the wind dropped, and the night that followed was very still. "The three-quarter moon set soon after 3 a.m., and there was total darkness over sea and mountains, until a cold and windless dawn gradually appeared. The water was smooth as a mirror, and a thin veil of mist covered the shore. Just before the sun rose in a blaze of gold, four of the battleships and four cruisers opened fire upon the defences at the main landing-places round Cape Helles, and continued a heavy bombard-

---

* This officer rejoined the Battalion at Lemnos about April 15th.

† This designation was adopted in lieu of A, B, C, D, or 1, 2, 3, 4 in Battalion Orders of March 19th.

ment. At the same time the landing of the covering parties at the five selected points round the end of the Peninsula began."*

The following is the detail of the troops to be set on shore at Beach " V " :—

>1st Battalion Royal Munster Fusiliers.
>1st Battalion Royal Dublin Fusiliers.
>Wing, 2nd Battalion Hampshire Regiment.
>Part of the Anson Battalion, Royal Naval Division.
>A Signal Section.
>West Riding Field Company, Royal Engineers.
>Three Bearer Subdivisions.

The Landing at Helles. Of the above troops, three companies, with the headquarters, of the Dublin Fusiliers and a party of the Anson Battalion were told off to proceed from Tenedos to the neighbourhood of the landing-place on the Dardanelles in two minesweepers—the *Newmarket* and *Clacton*—while the rest of this force embarked on the steam collier *River Clyde*. These troops were all on board their respective ships on the night of April 24th-25th. On the *River Clyde* was " W " Company of the Royal Dublin Fusiliers, with Captains Crozier and Molony, Lieutenants O'Hara and Boustead.

The *River Clyde* had been specially prepared for the rapid disembarkation of the troops on board her, and large openings had been cut in her sides from which the soldiers could pass to the lighters which she towed with her, by a hopper, and which it was hoped, on nearing the shore, to so place in position beyond the bows as to form a pier. To cover this landing, machine guns, protected by sandbags, were mounted in the bows of the *River Clyde* and also on the bridge. While lying in Mudros harbour, the troops had frequently been exercised in hasty landings from this vessel.

The headquarters staff of the 29th Division was at the first accommodated in H.M.S. *Euryalus*, and was eventually landed on Beach " W," where also the commander and staff of the 86th Brigade

* Nevinson, *The Dardanelles Campaign*, pp. 90 and 91.

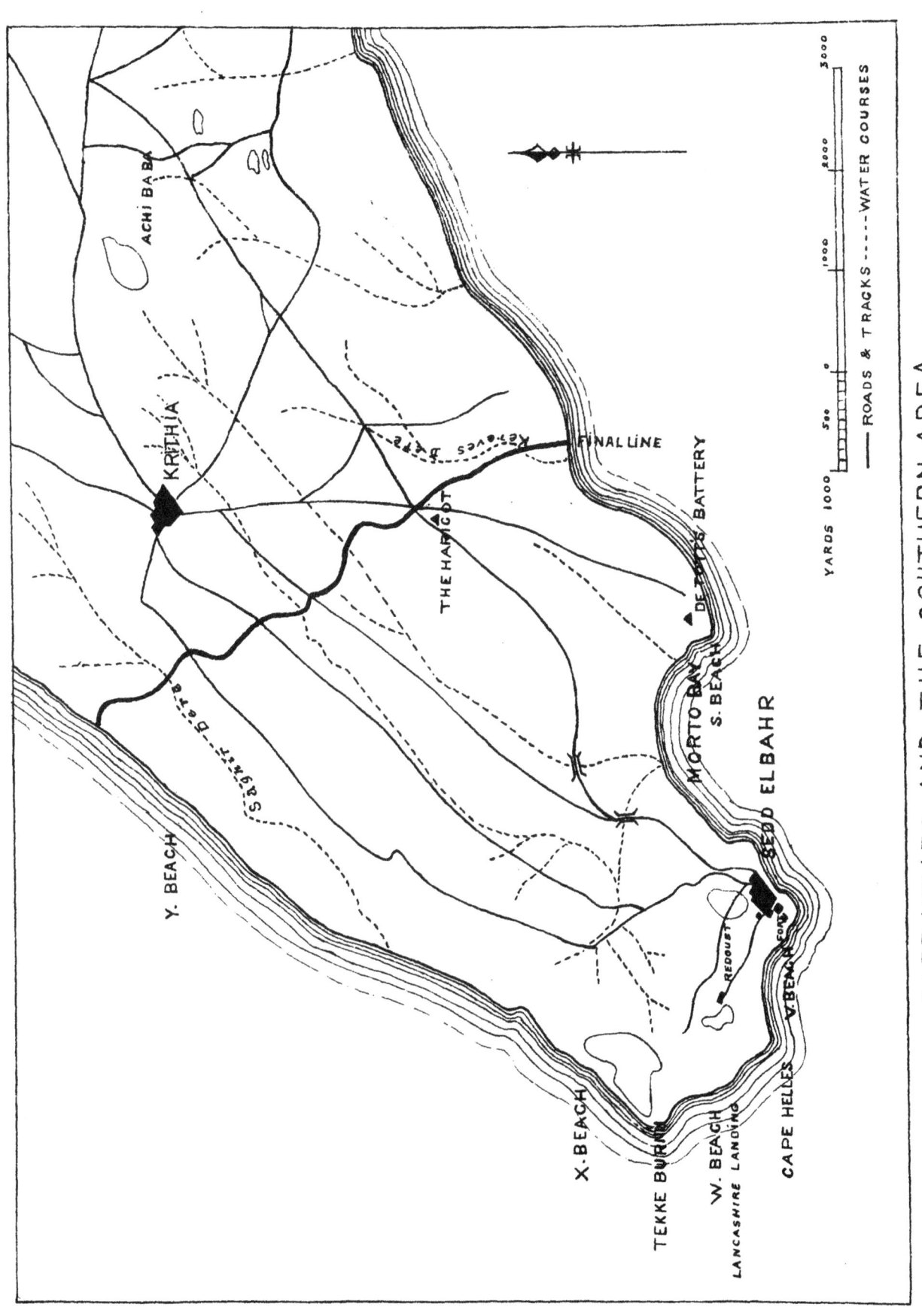

CAPE HELLES AND THE SOUTHERN AREA

- H.M. "H.T. RIVER CLYDE -

S.S. RIVER CLYDE BEACHED AT SEDD EL BAHR

DESCRIPTION OF "V" BEACH

were put on shore from the mine-sweeper *Whitby Abbey*. Owing to this, and to the very heavy casualties sustained by the troops which landed on Beach "V," it is almost impossible to get any very clear account of all that there happened.

General Sir Ian Hamilton gives in his despatch of May 20th, 1915, the following description of the place where " the Blue Caps " were to land :—

" ' V ' Beach is situated immediately to the west of Sedd-el-Bahr. Between the bluff on which stands Sedd-el-Bahr village and that which is crowned by No. 1 Fort the ground forms a very regular amphitheatre of three or four hundred yards' radius. The slopes down to the beach are slightly concave, so that the whole area contained within the limits of this natural amphitheatre, whose grassy terraces rise gently to a height of a hundred feet above the shore, can be swept by the fire of a defender. The beach itself is a sandy strip some 10 yards wide and 350 yards long, backed along almost the whole of its extent by a low sandy escarpment about 4 feet high, where the ground falls nearly sheer down to the beach. The slight shelter afforded by this escarpment played no small part in the operations of the succeeding thirty-two hours.

"At the S.E. extremity of the beach, between the shore and the village, stands the old fort of Sedd-el-Bahr, a battered ruin with wide breaches in its walls and mounds of fallen masonry within and around it. On the ridge to the N., overlooking the amphitheatre, stands a ruined barrack. Both of these buildings, as well as No. 1 Fort, had been long bombarded by the Fleet, and the guns of the fort had been put out of action ; but their crumbled walls and the ruined outskirts of the village afforded cover for riflemen, while from the terraced slopes already described the defenders were able to command the open beach, as a stage is overlooked from the balconies of a theatre. On the very margin of the beach a strong barbed-wire entanglement, made of a heavier material and longer barbs than I have ever seen elsewhere, ran right across from the old fort of Sedd-el-Bahr to the foot of the north-western headland. Two-thirds of the way up to the ridge a second and even stronger entanglement crossed the amphitheatre, passing in front of the old barrack and ending in the outskirts of the village. A third transverse entanglement, joining these two, ran up the hill near the eastern end of the beach, and almost at right angles to it. Above the upper entanglement the ground was scored with the enemy's trenches, in one of which four pom-poms were emplaced; in others were dummy pom-poms to draw fire, while the débris of the shattered buildings on either flank afforded cover and concealment for a number of machine-guns, which brought a cross-fire to bear on the ground already swept by rifle fire from the ridge."

The operations connected with the landing at Beach " V," with which this history is specially concerned, commenced at daybreak with a very heavy bombardment of the beach, the old castle, and the village of Sedd-el-Bahr by the guns of the *Queen Elizabeth*, *Albion*, and other warships; but to this the defence made no reply whatever, and there seemed reason to hope that the Turkish works had been abandoned.

The three companies of the Royal Dublin Fusiliers and the party from the Anson Battalion thereupon transhipped rapidly from the mine-sweepers into boats forming six tows, each made up of a pinnace and four cutters, and carrying 125 men apiece.* Captain Unwin, R.N., in command of the *River Clyde*, had been ordered to run his ship hard aground so soon as the tows had landed their first party, but actually the ship and the tows touched the shore practically at the same moment, and it was then that the defence first showed any sign of life, the assailants being greeted with a terrific fire as the troops scrambled out of the boats or endeavoured to reach the shore from the *River Clyde*. "A tornado of fire swept over the beach, the incoming boats, and the collier."

In his address before action, Brigadier-General Hare made use of one quotation from Napier's matchless prose; there is another which comes naturally to the minds of those who read of the landing on " V " Beach—" Many died, and there was much glory."

* Nevinson, p. 94. Callwell, p. 80, says there were five tows only.

"Only a very few of the Fusiliers succeeded in reaching the cover of the four-foot escarpment, mentioned in General Hamilton's despatch, where they found shelter. The majority were either shot down in the water or else as they reached the shore, or they were placed *hors de combat* while still in the boats. Many of these were seriously damaged, and most of them were rendered unmanageable owing to the sailors in charge being struck down or else by the rowers being killed or wounded. Within a few minutes this portion of the attack had been, to all intents and purposes, defeated, the troops detailed for the operation were almost wiped out of existence, and the few survivors were at the water's edge under the inadequate cover of the lip scooped by the waves."*

In a letter home from Captain Molony, of the Battalion, who was with the party in the *River Clyde*, and who seems to have been in a good position to see much that was transpiring on this beach, he wrote:—

"The boats came in; they were met by a perfect tornado of fire, many men were killed and wounded in the boats, and wounded men were knocked over into the water and drowned, but they kept on, and the survivors jumped into the water in some cases up to their necks, and got ashore; but the slaughter was terrific. Most of the officers were killed or wounded. Colonel Rooth, the C.O., was shot dead at the edge of the water; Major Fetherstonhaugh, second-in-command, was mortally wounded in his boat; Captain Johnson badly wounded while still in his boat; Captain French, the biggest man in the Battalion, got ashore with a bullet through the arm; Captain Anderson was shot dead on the beach, and many others were wounded. The machine-gun detachment worked desperately to get their guns ashore, but they were nearly all killed or wounded; both the officers, Captain Dunlop and Lieutenant Corbet, were killed. It was a terrible affair, and a few minutes of such fire decimated the Battalion. The people who got ashore established themselves on the beach as best they could under a bank which ran along the shore for some distance and was from four to five feet high."

* Callwell, p. 80.

Those who gained this cover were out of immediate danger, but they were no more than a handful.

Lieutenant Maffett, who landed with the companies from the mine-sweeper, has given the following account of his experiences:—

"When the picquet boat cast us off we all rowed for the shore as hard as we could. The Turks let us get very close, and then they opened a terrible fire on us with machine guns and pom-poms, the shells of which contained an incendiary mixture. They began to hit the boat I was in very frequently, and killed many of my men as we were rowing ashore. We were also unlucky enough to lose several of the blue-jackets who were rowing us in, and the men had to take over their oars, and as they did not know much about rowing the result was that we often got broadside on to the shore and presented a better target to the enemy. Just before we grounded the boat got hit once or twice with incendiary shells, and commenced to go on fire. She was also half full of water from the many holes in her by this time. Several of the men who had been wounded fell to the bottom of the boat, and were either drowned there or suffocated by other men falling on top of them; many, to add to their death agonies, were burnt as well.

"We then grounded, and I jumped out of the bows of the boat and got hit in the head by a machine-gun bullet, others going into a pack that I was carrying on my shoulders. I went under water and came up again, and tried to encourage the men to get to the shore and under cover as fast as they could as it was their only chance. I then went under again. Someone caught hold of me and began pulling me ashore, and as I got to dry land a blue-jacket joined him. When I recovered a bit I found it was my platoon-sergeant, Sergeant Willis. I did not see him again that day as far as I remember. Two men got ashore beside me, and then two more that were wounded. We took cover under a low sort of bank that was about ten yards from the water's edge, and bound each other up as best we could. Looking out to sea I saw the remnants of my platoon trying to get to the shore, but they were shot down one after another, and their bodies drifted out to sea or lay immersed a few feet from the shore. I found myself at the extreme left of the beach, and put the men I had around me on the alert for a rush from the enemy : of course we could not have done any good. . . .

"I lay under cover for the greater part of the morning, and tried to get into touch with some of the others. After a bit I crawled along towards the fort at Sedd-el-Bahr, and there found Captain French. He had been hit in the wrist with a bullet which had driven bits of his wrist-watch into him. I lay under cover with him for a time. . . . I then went to the left of the beach to see if I could collect any men there, but all I found were either wounded or dead. At the part almost under the lighthouse I found a boat that was nearly all submerged, and in it were some of our machine-gunners under Lieutenant Corbet ; they were all dead as far as I could see, and the machine guns useless. I then went back to where Captain French was lying, and spent the rest of the afternoon under cover beside him. We had a man near us with a pocket periscope, which we put over the top of the bank from time to time to see if the Turks were coming down on us, but there was no move on their part. We had no food or water with us, as the sea water had destroyed it all. . . The whole beach was strewn with dead, and there were very few hale men amongst us. One had to keep down the whole time, as the Turks were firing at us all the day . .
Night fell at length, and shortly after a large number of men came off the *River Clyde* without mishap ; these joined us on the beach, and we formed a sort of defensive line for the night."

The landing from the *River Clyde* had progressed no more favourably than had that from the boats.

The collier had taken the ground rather nearer to Sedd-el-Bahr than had been intended, and the water at the bows of the ship being too deep for the men to land, the lighters which had accompanied her had to be brought into position to establish a pier. A strong current, however, hindered the work, and the enemy's fire was so intense that almost every man engaged upon it was immediately shot Owing, however, to the splendid gallantry of the naval working party, the lighters were eventually placed in position, and then the disembarkation began, the companies of the Munsters leading, but incurring very heavy losses.

The following account is taken from a letter by Lieutenant O'Hara :—

" The idea in the case of our ship, the *River Clyde*, was that she was to be run ashore at full speed, and then the sides were partly arranged on hinges which were to open, and then we were to get ashore and dig ourselves in. The rest of the Regiment was to be towed ashore by steam pinnaces in boats. The latter arrived before we did, and you never saw such a shambles as that beach was when the boats got in. The whole of the high ground round was honeycombed with the enemy's trenches, and they waited till the boats, which were crammed full, got about five yards from the shore, when they let drive at them with rifles, machine guns, and pom-poms. Numbers of men were killed in the boats, others as they waded ashore, and more on the sand before they could take cover behind a sandbank some twelve or fifteen yards from the shore. . . . Meanwhile, our ship, instead of grounding as had been arranged, struck about fifteen yards from the shore, and it was that that saved our lives, as we had to stay where we were. Colonel Carington-Smith,[*] Hampshire Regiment, was killed on the bridge as he was looking through his field-glasses. Eventually Crozier, Boustead, and I got our company ashore about twelve o'clock that night by means of a gangway along the ship's side which connected with some lighters. Crozier went first and got his platoon on shore ; Boustead got his into the lighters ; and I was on the gangway with mine when suddenly the Turks opened fire, bullets simply whizzing up against the sides of the ship. Crozier shouted to me to take my platoon back into the ship, which I did, though not before three men had been hit, including Redmond, my soldier servant, who was standing beside me : the bullet caught him under the ear and came out just behind the nose without doing him much damage."

[*] An ex-officer of the Royal Dublin Fusiliers.

LANDING FROM THE *RIVER CLYDE*

Lieutenant C. McCann, who at the time of the landing was a sergeant in "W" Company, writes :—

"It was about 4.30 a.m. on the 25th when we were beached; then came the dreary wait for orders; several times the order was passed down to get dressed and immediately countermanded. At about 10 a.m. someone came aboard from the beach with the sad news that our Colonel, Adjutant, and most of our officers were killed. The effect of the news of Colonel Rooth's death could be read plainly on the faces of all ranks, as they had such faith in him as their commanding officer, and would have followed him to the ends of the earth.

"It must have been about 7 p.m. that the final order came to get dressed. We filed up out of the hold, where we had been in semi-darkness all this time, Captain Crozier leading, followed by Company Sergeant-Major C. Smith (who did splendid work all through the landing), myself, and No. 1 Platoon, of which I was in command, there being no officer with the platoon. As we filed out of the holes cut in the side of the old *Clyde* and down the gangway, machine guns opened fire, and we threw ourselves flat where we stood; two of my platoon were hit, and one of them fell headlong into the sea. After about ten minutes we moved on, but had only reached the two barges that formed the landing stage when we came under heavy rifle and machine-gun fire again.

"We threw ourselves flat on the barges and lay still for some time; I was between two men of the Munster Fusiliers who were dead, but I did not realise this until I asked one of them to make more room, and as he did not move I pushed him with my hand, and then found that his head was blown away.

"Captain Crozier now passed the word to get ashore; we moved off the barges over the small rowing boat, scrambled ashore through the water, and lined up along the beach. All this time we were under a very heavy rifle and machine-gun fire, several of the company being hit.

"I was then posted by Captain Grimshaw with six men as a look-out post till morning, when we attacked the fort and village of Sedd-el-Bahr."

To quote again from Captain Molony:—"Meanwhile the men on shore had attempted to advance, but any movement was impossible, for as soon as a man showed himself he was bowled over. Captain Higginson was shot through the head while endeavouring to knock out a Turkish sniper, and died instantly. By this time the beach was a harrowing sight; bodies were lying all over it, in some places in little clumps, in others half in and half out of the water. Wounded men were all over the place, and it was impossible in most cases to bring them aid."

An historian* tells us that "nearly all the boats in the tows had been destroyed, and some were idly drifting, manned only by the dead. The dead lay upon the lighters, and below the water, and awash upon the edge of the beach. The ripple of the tormented sea broke red against the sand."

"One of the tows had taken half a company of the Dublin Fusiliers" [under Captain Mood, with Lieutenant de Lusignan] "to a point called 'the Camber Beach,' just N.E. of the Sedd-el-Bahr castle. Perhaps they were intended to threaten the enemy's position from his left flank by creeping round the castle and attacking the village streets. This they proceeded to do, and, as the Turks had not entrenched this position, the Irishmen with great skill crawled from cover to cover till they reached the village windmills and the entrance to the houses. There they were overwhelmed by the crowd of snipers. Many were killed, some cut off, and twenty-five returned."†

When that Sunday evening closed—one wonders on how many occasions in the long history of the British Army have our most desperate battles taken place on this day—the general situation was briefly as follows:—The landing at "V" Beach had failed, all attempts to effect any further landing had been abandoned, and the main body of troops which was to have followed the covering force on shore had been diverted to "W" Beach; "W" Beach was held, though the position of the partially entrenched troops on the plateau above it was precarious; "X" Beach was fairly safe; at

* Nevinson, p. 97. † Nevinson, p. 98.

" Y " and " Z " Beaches the diminishing companies clung desperately to their gains against almost irresistible numbers and persistent onsets; while at Kum Kale the French were fulfilling their task, but were under orders to withdraw.

During the night of the 25th-26th the Turks became more daring, and at midnight they gathered in numbers unobserved, came down from their high ground to the beach, and in the darkness much hard fighting took place, when quarter was neither asked nor given. Then the attack would melt away and the Turkish machine guns would reopen; but while fighting went on during nearly the whole of that night, it had been found possible to get many wounded off the beach and back to the *River Clyde*, whence they were evacuated to the hospital ships. When day dawned on the 26th the survivors of the landing party were still crouched under the shelter of the sandbank; they had had no rest, food, or water; the majority of them had been fighting all through the night; the 29th Division had lost all three brigadiers—one killed and two wounded—while two of the commanding officers of the three battalions concerned in the landing at " V " Beach had been killed.

Retreat was unthinkable, while to stay on the beach was hopeless, and Lieut.-Colonel Doughty-Wylie of the staff, the senior officer on the beach, set about to organize an attack on the fort and village and the entrenchments of the Turks. The ships of the Fleet, so soon as visibility permitted, opened a heavy bombardment upon the old fort, Sedd-el-Bahr village, upon the castle north of the village, and upon the ground leading up from the beach.

" The naval gunners having done their work, the remnants of the three Battalions, their spirits wholly unsubdued by what they had gone through, rushed the castle, and by 9 a.m. they were already beginning to force their way into the village. It was only by slow degrees, and after gaining the mastery in an infuriated house-to-house contest, that the assailants had by about noon succeeded in gaining possession of the place. The triumph had, moreover, been somewhat dearly purchased in respect to killed and wounded."*

* Callwell, pp. 107-108.

Of the attack on the village Company Sergeant-Major Baker wrote:—" Lieutenant Bernard and Second-Lieutenant Andrews were together with about 20 men of ' X ' and ' Y ' Companies, and they took cover behind a wall 5 ft. 6 in. high. They were being fired at from a house in the village. Andrews stood in a gap made by a shell, and was directing the fire when he was shot through the heart. Lieutenant Bernard called on the others to follow him, and saying ' Come on, boys,' he dashed through the gap when he was shot. . . . On the left flank poor Grimshaw was leading a party when he got a bullet through the brain."

In the attack on the village, conspicuous where all showed great gallantry, were Corporal Cummins, Privates Oliver and O'Toole, also Company Sergeant-Major Fergusson and Sergeant Doyle.

No. 10113 Private T. Cullen, of the Battalion, was the first man into the fort at Sedd-el-Bahr, and was awarded the medal for Distinguished Conduct in the Field. Here, too, Lieutenant Boustead distinguished himself. Leaving the men, who had momentarily taken cover from the heavy machine-gun fire, he ran fearlessly to the opening in the fort, repeatedly firing his revolver at the enemy within and causing their fire to slacken.

Major Farmar, staff captain, and, on the death of Major Frankland, Brigade-Major 86th Brigade, has given an account of the landing and of the operations that immediately followed,* and writes of the attack of the 26th as follows:—" The Royal Munster Fusiliers and Royal Dublin Fusiliers, with a half-battalion of the Hampshire Regiment, organized by Colonel Doughty-Wylie, and led by him and such officers as Majors Grimshaw and Molesworth, Tomlinson, Nightingale, and Waldegrave, did magnificently. Their force of arms drove back superior numbers of the Turks from their points of vantage and into headlong rout. The fallen Grimshaw was spoken of as might have been Roland of Charlemagne's day by the witnesses of his deeds in the throes of close combat. The position won was quickly secured and consolidated under the direction of Sir Ian Hamilton's staff and the Brigade-Major of the 86th Brigade,

---

* In an " additional chapter " to Creighton's *With the 29th Division in Gallipoli*.

[Photo, Wiele & Klein, Madras

MAJOR C. T. W. GRIMSHAW, D.S.O.
1ST BN. ROYAL DUBLIN FUSILIERS

Major Molesworth and a few remaining officers doing the work of a score in reorganizing. The men, though deprived of their accustomed leaders, worked quietly according to their thorough training."

By the evening of the 26th the situation of the invading army was decidedly better than it had been on the preceding night; in every direction a footing had been gained, and the Allies now held all the ground near the coast from " X " Beach to De Tott's battery; the whole of the infantry of the 29th Division was ashore, as were also several French battalions, some guns had been landed, and a considerable amount of stores was already collected and collecting on " W " and " V " Beaches.

On the 27th there was a general advance, the opposition met with was of a half-hearted character, and by the evening of this day the landing at Helles might be regarded as consolidated, a front having been secured that extended from near De Tott's battery across to the mouth of the Zighin Dere about two miles north of Cape Tekke, the allies now occupying the toe of the Gallipoli peninsula for a depth of about two miles, while the Beaches " V " and " W " were at least safe from musketry and machine-gun fire.

In his despatch on these operations Sir Ian Hamilton states that " it was so vital to make what headway we could before the enemy recovered himself and received fresh reinforcements that it was decided to push on as quickly as possible. Orders were therefore issued for a general advance to commence at 8 a.m. next day " [the 28th]. " The 29th Division were to march on Krithia, with their left brigade leading, the French were directed to extend their left in conformity with the British movements, and to retain their right on the coast-line south of the Kereves Dere."

The following extracts are taken from Major Farmar's account of the events of this day—an account from which quotation has already been made :—" On April 28th the 86th Brigade, having reorganised, was at first employed in reserve. At 8 a.m. they entrenched a position in support of the main attack, which was being pressed forward by the French on the right, the 88th Brigade in the centre and 87th Brigade on the left. . . . The attempt, in spite of slender numbers, achieved much success. At 11.30 a.m. Major-General Marshall, temporarily commanding the three brigades of British infantry, gave orders for the 86th Brigade to join in the main attack. The 88th Brigade were in difficulties, and were short of ammunition. The 86th Brigade received orders to take forward ammunition for the 88th, and to carry the latter on in the advance to the objective given. This was a spur lying N.E. of Krithia, and involved the capture of this village. . . ." The Royal Fusiliers and Lancashire Fusiliers formed the firing line and supports; the Royal Munster and Royal Dublin Fusiliers formed the reserve.

When the advance began it was seen that the French appeared to be retiring from the ground they had taken earlier in the day. "The 88th Brigade were in difficulties, and a staff officer sent back for assistance. Unluckily the message did not reach Headquarters, but did reach some portions of both the Royal Munster and Royal Dublin Fusiliers, and some of these were diverted, unorganised, into the 88th Brigade, and lost touch with their own. These battalions had lost many officers on the 25th and 26th, and were moving in small parties, in artillery formation, to avoid the effect of shrapnel fire. In consequence, the 86th Brigade lost the power of giving effect to their movement. . . .

"Major Pearson had now got up some ammunition on pack animals. . . . Major-General Marshall gave orders for the ammunition to be taken forward and for the 86th Brigade to push on. Some fifty of the Royal Dublin Fusiliers loaded themselves with bandoliers full of ammunition, and were led to the firing line by the Brigade-Major. . . The ammunition was passed down the line and the party sent back under Sergeant Fergusson, Royal Dublin Fusiliers, whose services were most valuable. . . . When the Brigade-Major went to arrange for the consolidation of the position, only one officer of the Royal Dublin Fusiliers was left, Lieutenant O'Hara, who rose to every occasion with the greatest coolness and competence, from commanding a platoon at the terrible landing from the *River Clyde* to the command of a company the next day, and after April 28th to commanding the Battalion."

[Photo, Swaine]

CAPTAIN HENRY DESMOND O'HARA, D.S.O.
1ST BN. ROYAL DUBLIN FUSILIERS.
(The youngest Officer to obtain that honour at that period.)

Lieut. H. D. O'Hara, D.S.O.—"On April 25th, 1915, at Sedd-el-Bahr, he took command of his Battalion when all the other officers had been killed or wounded At night, when the enemy broke through the line, he displayed great initiative and resource in organizing a successful counter-attack, restoring the line and causing great loss to the enemy."—*London Gazette*, 3/6/15.

THE CASUALTIES

Here is this highly-tried young officer's own brief story of the happenings on April 28th and following days and nights :—

"It was an awful time, and at the end I was the only officer left in the battalion, as Grove and Molesworth were both wounded though only slightly. The Turks made no attempt to follow up their advantage, and we were able to dig in. We remained there for two nights, and on the third the Turks advanced, 20,000 strong, and tried to break through the line. The fight went on from 10.30 at night till 5 o'clock next morning—a desperate fight the whole time. My regiment alone got through 150,000 rounds, and they were only 360 strong. The Turks were simply driven on to the barbed wire in front of the trenches by their German officers, and shot down by the score. At one point they actually got into the trenches, but were driven out by the bayonet. They must have lost thousands. The fighting is of the most desperate kind—very little quarter on either side. The men are absolutely mad to get at them, as they mutilate our wounded when they catch them. For the first three nights I did not have a wink of sleep, and actually fell asleep once during the big night attack. We had no food for about 36 hours after landing, as we were fighting incessantly. My remnants have joined up with the Munsters as a composite battalion."

The Royal Munster Fusiliers and Royal Dublin Fusiliers were temporarily amalgamated into one battalion under Major W. A. Hutchinson, of the first-named regiment, and now held the right of the section allotted to the Brigade, the strength of which had by this time been very greatly reduced, that of battalions being as under :—

2nd Battalion Royal Fusiliers—12 officers, 481 other ranks.

1st Battalion Lancashire Fusiliers—11 officers, 399 other ranks.

1st Battalion Royal Munster Fusiliers—12 officers, 596 other ranks.

1st Battalion Royal Dublin Fusiliers—1 officer, 374 other ranks.

The casualties in the "Blue Caps" had been terribly heavy, for in the operations ending on the last day of April there had been killed or died of wounds 10 officers and 152 other ranks, the officers being Lieut.-Colonel R. A. Rooth, Majors E. Fetherstonhaugh and C. T. W. Grimshaw, Captains W. F. Higginson, D. V. F. Anderson, and G. M. Dunlop, Lieutenants R. Bernard, R. de Lusignan, and R. V. C. Corbet, and Second-Lieutenant W. Andrews; while the following 13 officers and 329 non-commissioned officers and men were wounded :—Major E. A. Molesworth, Captains A. M. Johnson, H. C. Crozier, D. French, A. W. Molony, J. M. Mood, and J. R. W. Grove, Lieutenants Lanigan-O'Keeffe, C. G. Carruthers, and L. C. Boustead, Second-Lieutenants C. W. Maffett, J. P. Walters, and J. Hosford; 21 non-commissioned officers and men were also reported missing.

This does not exhaust the list of those who fell with the 1st Battalion Royal Dublin Fusiliers, for the Rev. Father Finn, chaplain to the Battalion, was one of the first to give his life in the landing. In answer to the appeals that were made to him not to enter the boats, but to remain on board the ship, he replied: "The priest's place is beside the dying soldier," and, embarking in one of the first boats, he was shot immediately on setting foot on the shore. "The men never forgot him, and were never tired of speaking of him. I think they felt his death almost more than anything that happened in that terrible landing off the *River Clyde.* . . . It seemed to me that Father Finn was an instance of the extraordinary hold a chaplain, and especially perhaps an R.C., can have on the affections of his men if he absolutely becomes one of them and shares their dangers."*

Lieutenant de Boer, R.A.M.C., the medical officer, was among the wounded.

May 1st was spent in consolidating the ground gained, in resting the men, and in landing reinforcements, stores, and guns. On that day Lieutenant O'Hara wrote home :—"We are now back in the reserve trenches about 1½ miles from the firing line." But the respite was only a very brief one, for on the 9th he wrote again :— "We have made some 5 miles of ground and have had a most awful

* Creighton, *With the 29th Division in Gallipoli,* p. 67.

FORT SEDD-EL-BAHR, SHOWING TROOPS TAKING SHELTER FROM TURKISH FIRE.

time—fighting by day and night—appalling casualties. Ourselves and the Munsters are a composite battalion—strength 400 in all and hardly an officer left. We are absolutely worn out, mind and body. They are up against a big proposition here, and are pouring in reinforcements. Our Brigade has been merged into the 87th Brigade. We have 1,400 left out of 4,000. We have been with the firing line for the last fortnight, and it is rumoured that we go into reserve to-night."

But even this remnant of a regiment was still able to give a good account of itself, for Major Farmar describes how, during some very fierce fighting of these latter days, when, from copies which were found of the Turkish orders for the attack, it was learnt that this had been made by 16,000 of their best troops with 2,000 in reserve, " the fiercest fighting was against the Irish regiments who were defending the weakest part of the line and bore the greatest weight of the attack. When the masses were checked close to the British line, the Germans could be heard cursing, and the sound of blows as they tried to urge on the Turks. In the morning there were dead in piles close to the British trenches."

Of the share of the Battalion in this fighting Captain Devoy writes :—" The 21 men who garrisoned one particular bit of trench died to a man in the trench. One man, I recollect, a signaller, had as many as nineteen wounds. Of course, it was hand-to-hand fighting—no quarter was asked or given. Towards morning several of us were using Turkish rifles and ammunition, our own from overwork refusing to function. The following morning a patrol of twelve of us, under Company Sergeant-Major Fergusson, sallied out [it was Fergusson's own idea] to chase away one or two snipers, and if my memory serves me rightly, our total bag of live captives was 38, gleaned from all sorts of holes and corners."

And so, when after fifteen days and nights of hard fighting all that was left of the Battalion was at last withdrawn from the immediate front into what was at Gallipoli regarded, for want of a better name, as a back area, the Divisional General expressed his admiration of the valour of the Dublin Fusiliers in the following address :—

"*Well done, 'Blue Caps'!*

"*I now take the first opportunity of thanking you for the good work you have done. You have achieved the impossible. You have done a thing which will live in history. When I first visited this place, with other people of importance, we all thought a landing would never be made, but you did it, and therefore the impossibilities were overcome—and it was done by men of real and true British fighting blood. You captured the fort and village on the right that were simply swarming with Turks with machine guns, also the hill on the left where the pom-poms were. Also the amphitheatre in front which was dug line for line with trenches, and from where there came a terrific rifle and machine-gun fire. You are indeed deserving of the highest praise. I am proud to be in command of such a distinguished regiment, and I only hope that when you return to the firing line after this rest, which you have well earned, that you will make even a greater name for yourselves. Well done, the Dubs! Your deeds will live in history for Time Immortal. Farewell!*"

On May 9th the Commander-in-Chief issued the following Special Order to his troops:—

"*Sir Ian Hamilton wishes the troops of the Mediterranean Expeditionary Force to be informed that in all his past experiences, which include the hard struggles of the Russo-Japanese Campaign, he has never seen more devoted gallantry displayed than that which has characterised their efforts during the past three days. He has informed Lord Kitchener by cable of the bravery and endurance displayed by all ranks here, and has asked that the necessary reinforcements be forthwith dispatched. Meanwhile, the remainder of the East Lancashire Division is disembarking, and will henceforth be available to help us make good and improve upon the positions we have so hardly won.*"

The following appeared in Battalion Orders of May 22nd:—

"*Major-General Cooper, C.B., Colonel of the Regiment, wishes to express to all ranks his very sincere sympathy at the terrible losses of the Battalion. He knows very well how all ranks must have fought, and how they kept up the great traditions of the 'Blue Caps.' He again wishes to convey his heartfelt sympathy and condolences to all the relatives who may have lost their dear ones."*

On the body of a dead Turkish officer was found a letter which contained this sentence:—" These British are the finest fighters in the world. We have chosen the wrong friends."

CHAPTER III

GALLIPOLI

THE LONG STRUGGLE—THE EVACUATION

ON May 12th the following Special Order was issued by the General :—

"For the first time for eighteen days and nights it has been found possible to withdraw the 29th Division from the fire fight. During the whole of that long period of unprecedented strain the Division has held ground or gained it, against the bullets and bayonets of the constantly renewed forces of the foe.

"During the whole of that long period they have been illuminating the pages of military history with their blood. The losses have been terrible, but mingling with the deep sorrow for fallen comrades arises a feeling of pride in the invincible spirit which has enabled the survivors to triumph where ordinary troops must inevitably have failed.

"I tender to Major-General Hunter-Weston and to his Division at the same time my profoundest sympathy with their losses and my warmest congratulations on their achievement."

The rest was for five days only, and it was used by the Division and the Brigades in general, and by the 1st Battalion Royal Dublin Fusiliers in particular, for purposes of much-needed reorganization and reconstruction, for the collection and distribution of such scanty reinforcements as during these early days reached the attenuated battalion holding the lip of the beaches of the Gallipoli peninsula, and in making appointments for the command and administration of the units which had been so continuously engaged, and which had suffered so many and such heavy casualties.

Brigadier-General Hare had been wounded in the early hours of the landing, and Lieut.-Colonel D. E. Caley, Worcestershire Regiment, had on April 27th been appointed to the temporary command of the 86th Brigade; but three days later this officer was relieved by Colonel H. G. Casson, C.M.G., of the South Wales Borderers.

On May 4th, however, the Brigade was temporarily split up, when the above appointment naturally and automatically lapsed, as did those minor ones which had been made to the Brigade staff; and the battalions of the Royal and Lancashire Fusiliers were attached to the 88th, and those of the Munster and Dublin Fusiliers —already, as stated in the last chapter, merged into one battalion— were posted for duty to the 87th Brigade. The amalgamated Battalion was known among the rank and file composing it as " the Dubsters."

The operations at the outset of the Dardanelles campaign had left only three officers with the Royal Dublin Fusiliers—Lieutenant O'Hara in command; Lieutenant Floyd, who was promoted Captain from April 28th, and who had remained at sea in charge of regimental transport; and Lieutenant and Quartermaster Kennedy— but during May certain rather meagre reinforcements joined. Of the Regiment there came three officers—Captain C. B. J. Riccard, A. A. C. Taylor, and W. F. Stirling—with 1 sergeant, 2 corporals, and 43 privates—while during the early part of the month five officers of other regiments were attached to the Battalion for duty; from the 3rd Battalion, Captain G. E. Bruce; and from the 9th Battalion Somerset Light Infantry, Captain L. E. George, Lieutenant A. G. Cripps, Second-Lieutenants H. G. Rogers and F. G. Young.

On May 19th the Battalion was reconstituted as a separate unit.

While the 29th Division was " resting "—the Dublin Fusiliers at Gully Beach—its place in the front line was taken by the 29th Indian Brigade and by the 42nd Division, which had arrived two days previously; but the 29th Division was soon back at the front, though during the remainder of the month of May and until the middle of the first week in June the operations were confined to minor raids and to methodical sapping work, in which the Allies contrived from time to time to gain a little ground. About May 22nd there intervened a four-days' suspension of arms, while both sides buried the dead lying out between the front-line trenches.

On June 5th the 29th, the 42nd, and the Royal Naval Divisions were formed into the VIIIth Army Corps, under Major-General Hunter-Weston, Major-General H. de B. de Lisle, who had just arrived from France, taking over command of the 29th Division. On this day the 86th Brigade was re-formed, and Colonel O. C. Wolley-Dod, D.S.O., was placed in charge, with the rank of Brigadier-General. At this date the Royal Dublin Fusiliers were 750 strong, a strength which was raised on the following day to 830, with 19 officers, many officers of the New Armies having arrived for attachment.

On June 9th the Battalion was moved to "X" Beach; three days later, on the 12th, it was again in the first-line trenches, and held the so-called "Turkish Trench," repulsing one serious attack made by the enemy, but being driven slightly back by a second, which immediately followed the first. Casualties were daily, hourly, incurred; thus, on June 7th the "Blue Caps" had 6 men wounded and 5 missing; on the 16th 12 were killed, 31 were wounded and 4 men were missing; on the 23rd Captain Bruce was wounded, as was three days later Lieutenant Sellars, of the King's Own Scottish Borderers, who was attached for duty to the Battalion.

At the end of June some important operations were projected and carried out, and in these the Dublins were engaged and suffered heavy losses in officers and men. General Hunter-Weston had " formed a scheme for pushing forward on the left, so as to clear the obstacles which had hitherto checked our advance along the coast, and so reduce the salient in the centre. . . . While the centre remained steady about a mile from the sea, the left was to swing forward upon it as upon a pivot, covering less ground as the pivotal point was approached. Thus five Turkish lines had to be captured by the 29th Division on the extreme left, and two by the 156th Brigade (52nd Division), which had been inserted on their right."*

The operations which began on the 28th were entirely successful,

* Nevinson, p. 182.

and marked perhaps the most distinct advance which so far had been made on the peninsula; the Dublin Fusiliers were at the commencement in brigade reserve, and, the objective having been gained, went back on the 29th into bivouac in Gully Ravine. But on the two following nights the Turks attacked with great fury and desperation, and on the 30th the Battalion was ordered to remain on Geoghan's Bluff as a reserve to the 87th Brigade. During the 28th and 29th the casualties in the Battalion amounted to 9 officers and 45 other ranks killed, 1 officer and 138 non-commissioned officers and men wounded, 1 officer and 42 men missing. By June 30th the strength of the 1st Battalion Royal Dublin Fusiliers had fallen again to 8 officers and 595 other ranks.

The names of the eleven officers above mentioned are as follows: Killed—Capts. L. E. George (9th Somersets), E. Dickenson (11th Yorks), R. J. Rogers (14th Rifle Brigade), H. M. Floyd (Dublin Fusiliers); Lieutenants L. C. Boustead (Dublin Fusiliers), H. G. Rogers (9th Somersets), A. L. Halsted (15th Rifle Brigade); died of wounds—Lieutenants A. K. Kingcombe (11th Yorks), A. E. Knight (14th Rifle Brigade); wounded—Lieutenant C. E. S. Rucker (15th Rifle Brigade); and missing—Captain A. A. C. Taylor (Dublin Fusiliers).

On the first day of this action a message from General de Lisle ran:—

"*General de Lisle sends congratulations to the Brigade, and says they have done splendidly. Keep it up!*"

On June 29th the following Special Force Order was published:—

"*The General Officer Commanding feels that he voices the sentiments of every soldier serving with this Army when he congratulates the incomparable 29th Division upon yesterday's splendid attack, carried out, as it was, in a manner more than upholding the best traditions of the distinguished regiments of which it is composed.*

"*The 29th Division suffered cruel losses at the first landing. Since then they have never been made up to strength, and they have remained under fire every hour of the night and day for two months on end.*

Opposed to them were fresh troops holding line upon line of entrenchments flanked by redoubts and machine guns.

"But when, yesterday, the 29th Division were called upon to advance, they dashed forward as eagerly as if this were only their baptism of fire. Through the entanglements they swept northwards, clearing our left of the enemy for a full thousand yards. Heavily counter-attacked at night, they killed or captured every Turk who had penetrated their incomplete defences, and to-day stand possessed of every yard they had so hardly gained.

"Therefore it is that Sir Ian Hamilton is confident he carries with him all ranks of his force when he congratulates Generals Hunter-Weston and de Lisle, the Staff, and each officer, non-commissioned officer and man in this Division, whose sustained efforts have added fresh lustre to British arms all the world over."

Since the landing of the vanguard of the Expeditionary Force on the Gallipoli peninsula at the end of April certain reinforcements had arrived; thus, the 29th Indian Brigade had joined from Egypt, under Major-General Sir Herbert Cox, on May 1st; a few days later the 42nd Division was landed, under the command of Major-General Sir William Douglas; early in June Major-General Egerton brought out the 52nd Division; while the 13th Division arrived under Major-General Shaw, the one-time commander of the 29th Division, the 11th under Major-General Hammersley, and the 10th commanded by Lieut.-General Sir Bryan Mahon, all at intervals of some ten days in July. But these reinforcements, satisfactory as they seemed on paper, and all-sufficient as they doubtless appeared to the authorities at home who had the providing of them, hardly did more than replace the wastage incurred by the divisions which formed the original expeditionary force.

On July 17th Lieut.-General Hunter-Weston, commanding the VIIIth Corps, left the peninsula for a few days' rest, and was subsequently invalided to England, the command of his corps being assumed first by Lieut.-General Sir Frederick Stopford, and later by Major-General Douglas.

After the action of the latter half of June, it was decided to withdraw the brigades of the 29th Division by turns to Lemnos for a brief rest, and accordingly, on July 16th, the 86th Brigade sailed for Mudros harbour, and on arrival there disembarked and went into bivouac near the beach.

The battalions comprising the 86th Brigade had been a bare four days on the island of Lemnos when a telegram was received warning them to be ready to return to the peninsula next day should their presence there be required; and accordingly they were, on July 21st, directed to commence embarkation at 11 a.m. The Royal Dublin Fusiliers went on board their ship at 2 p.m., and the different battalions of the Brigade landed on " V " Beach between 11 p.m. on the 21st and 4 a.m. on the 22nd, and marched thence to Gully Beach. During the afternoon of July 22nd intelligence came in that the enemy was preparing a supreme effort to drive the British into the sea during the ensuing forty-eight hours, and that he had concentrated a force of 100,000 men for this purpose.

The 86th and 87th Brigades were now in Corps Reserve.

With the troops already at his disposal, the reinforcing divisions now on their way, and with those which had been promised him, Sir Ian Hamilton should have had available for future operations an infantry force of thirteen divisions and five independent brigades, representing on paper a strength of approximately 160,000 bayonets. But not only were the units nearly always below establishment on landing, but drafts in replacement of wastage were invariably seriously in arrear, and actually the Commander of the Mediterranean Expeditionary Force had never more than 110,000 bayonets under his orders, and could never reckon upon the employment of even this number for more than a very few days at a time. Further, it had for some weeks past been abundantly clear that no help from the direction of the Black Sea was to be expected from Russia, and that thus several extra Turkish divisions would be set free for the Dardanelles—that the Mediterranean Expeditionary Force must face Turkey on its own resources alone.

So far from the British forces having to await a serious attack, as rumour seemed to suggest at the moment when the 86th Brigade

rejoined from Mudros, it was the invaders who were to make an attack upon the Turks, and General Hamilton had decided upon the reinforcement of the Australian and New Zealand Army Corps, combined with a landing in Suvla Bay. Then, with a strong push to capture Hill 305, or Khoja Chemen Tepe, the culminating point of Sari Bair, and working from that dominating point, to grip the waist of the peninsula. The main strategical conception was then :—
" (1) To break out with a rush from Anzac and cut off the bulk of the Turkish Army from land communication with Constantinople. (2) To gain such a command for my artillery as to cut off the bulk of the Turkish Army from sea traffic, whether with Constantinople or with Asia. (3) Incidentally, to secure Suvla Bay as a winter base for Anzac and all the troops operating in the northern theatre."*

August 6th was the day fixed for the new enterprise, and on this date the troops of the Expeditionary Force were thus distributed :—

> At Anzac : The Australian and New Zealand Corps, the 13th Division, the Indian Brigade, and a brigade of the 10th Division.
> At Helles : The 29th, 42nd, 52nd, and Royal Naval Divisions, with two French divisions.
> At Mitylene : The 31st Brigade and half the 30th Brigade.
> At Lemnos : The other half of the 30th Brigade.
> At Imbros : The 11th Division.

The infantry of the 53rd and 54th Divisions, the last reinforcements now due, were then at sea approaching Mudros, and were intended to be kept as a general reserve, but on reaching Mudros harbour they were hurried on to Suvla without disembarking.

On August 5th Sir Ian had issued a characteristic Order calculated to stir the spirit of his troops ; it ran as under :—

"*Soldiers of the Old Army and the New !*

"*Some of you have already won imperishable renown at our first landing, or have since built up our footholds upon the Peninsula, yard*

---

* Final Despatch by General Hamilton, dated December 11th, 1915.

GALLIPOLI TROPHIES AND PICTURE OF THE s.s. "RIVER CLYDE."

On the *left*—STARBOARD LIGHT } Both presented to the "BLUE CAPS" by Admiral Sir J. DE ROBECK.
On the *right*—BINNACLE STAND

[*Photo, Gale & Polden, Ltd.*

by yard, with deeds of heroism and endurance. Others have arrived just in time to take part in our next great fight against Germany and Turkey, the would-be oppressors of the rest of the human race.

"*You, veterans, are about to add fresh lustre to your arms. Happen what may, so much at least is certain.*

"*As to you, soldiers of the new formations, you are privileged indeed to have the chance vouchsafed you of playing a decisive part in events which may herald the birth of a new and happier world. You stand for the great cause of freedom. In the hour of trial remember this, and the faith that is in you will bring you victoriously through.*"

The primary purpose of the attack to be delivered by the Anglo-French force at Helles was to hinder the enemy from sending any troops from that area to aid those defending Sari Bair; but the Higher Command also hoped that ground would be gained by the attack, and that the front would be improved locally in consequence.

When on August 6th the attack commenced against the Turkish trenches, the Dublin Fusiliers were commanded by Lieut.-Colonel T. Ward, of the Reserve of Officers of the West Yorkshire Regiment; the first assault failed, and various orders for its renewal were issued and as often cancelled. Then, at 2 a.m. on the 7th, the order was finally cancelled, and then an hour later the Battalion was directed to take over the whole firing line allotted to the 86th Brigade. This was done, and just before daybreak the Adjutant of the Essex Regiment (belonging to the 88th Brigade) reported to Colonel Ward that a party of the Essex were still holding the enemy's communication trenches leading from our southern barricade. Lieutenant Hannen and two platoons were passed through the barricade, and the party of the Essex Regiment was relieved and withdrawn. Later, however, a heavy shrapnel fire and bombing was opened on Lieutenant Hannen's party, which was driven back, followed up by the Turks, leaving about thirty dead and badly wounded in the trench they had held. Some twenty Turks got into the British trenches, and were at once bombed out, good work being done by Captain Carruthers. The following casualties were incurred by the Battalion :—25 non-commissioned officers and men were killed ; 3 officers—Captain N. P. Clarke, Lieutenant W. F. Hannen, and Second-Lieutenant C. A. Copland—and 150 other ranks wounded, with 30 missing.

The Battalion remained in the firing line until it was withdrawn to " Y " Beach, preparatory to transfer to another part of the peninsula, where the situation seemed to demand the services of the 29th Division and other reinforcements.

The force to be landed in Suvla Bay, the third of the three operations designed by General Hamilton, was composed of the 10th and 11th Divisions commanded by Lieut.-General Stopford. At the outset everything went as well as could have been hoped ; the actual landing was the most successful operation of its kind which up to this had been attempted, and since the Turks had been largely taken by surprise the losses were comparatively trifling ; but the ground was very difficult, there was great lack of water, and while the divisional commanders and brigadiers were as anxious to press on as was General Stopford himself, the exhaustion of the troops and the lack of artillery support seem to have combined to induce the leaders to decide that it was better to make good the ground gained rather than at all hazards to push on. The day of the 8th, then, was lost, and when next morning the advance was resumed it was clear that important Turkish reinforcements had arrived, and the British force was thrown back with very severe losses from the attempt on the Anafarta Ridge.

On the morning of the 9th the 53rd Division was disembarked to reinforce the 11th Division, and on the 11th the 54th Division also arrived at Suvla, and it was now intended that the 11th and 54th Divisions should move on Ismail Oglu Tepe, while the troops from Anzac made a fresh attack upon Sari Bair ; but for reasons which need not here be gone into these good intentions did not materialize. At Suvla there was now the greater part of four infantry divisions, but these did not number more than at most 30,000 bayonets by reason of the casualties sustained, and Sir Ian now called up the 29th Division and a division just arrived from

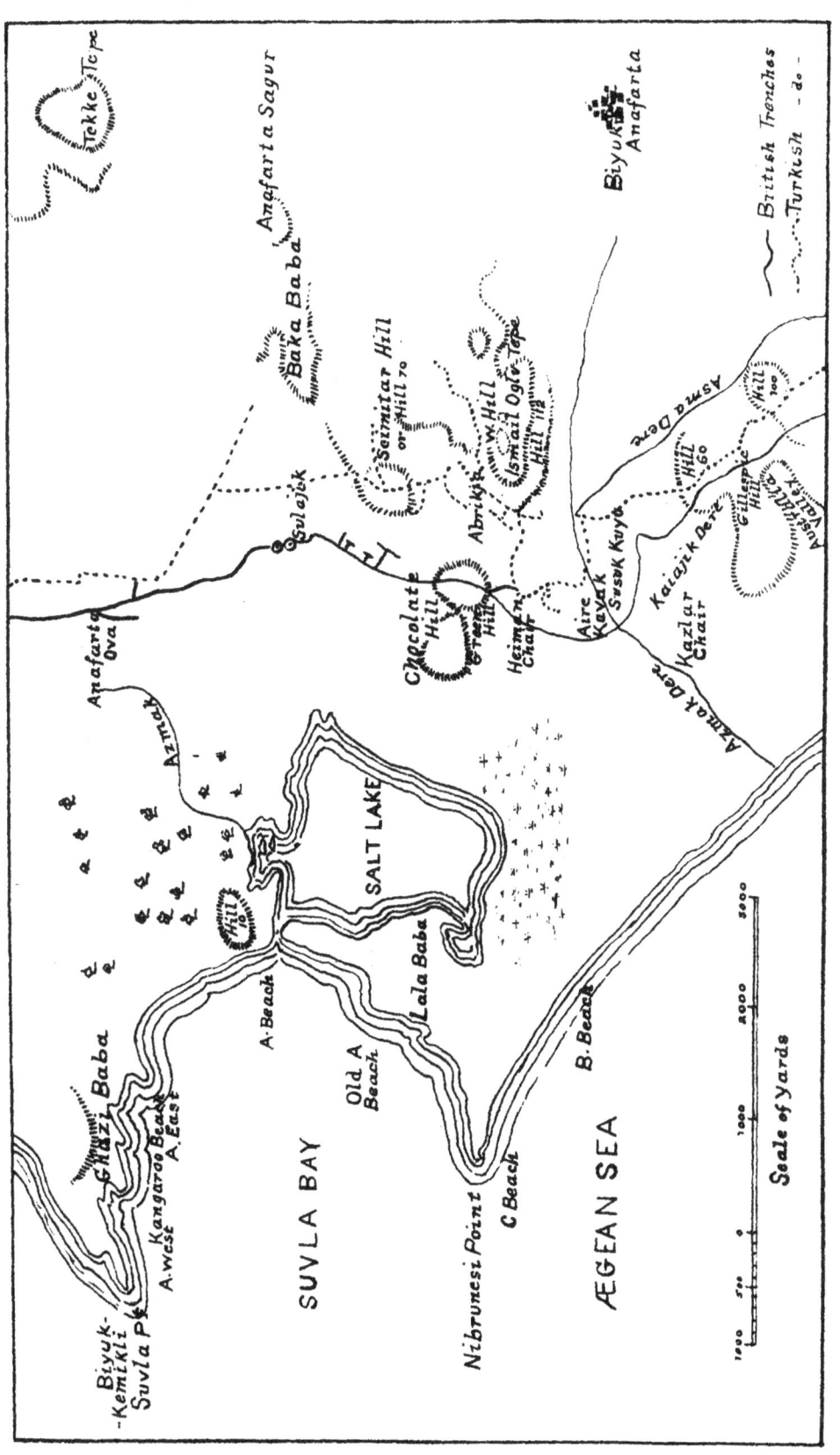

Egypt, and placed the force at Suvla under the command of Major-General de Lisle.

In his final despatch General Hamilton wrote :—" It was not until the 21st that I was ready to renew the attack. . . . I decided to mass every available man against Ismail Oglu Tepe. . . . The scheme for this attack was well planned by General de Lisle. The 53rd and 54th Divisions were to hold the enemy from Sulajik to Kiretch Tepe Sirt, while the 29th and 11th Divisions stormed Ismail Oglu Tepe. . . . I arranged that General Birdwood should co-operate by swinging forward his left flank to Susuk Kuju and Kaiajik Aghala."

Ismail Oglu Tepe is thus described :—" The hill rises 350 feet from the plain, with steep spurs jutting out to the west and south-west, the whole of it covered with dense holly-oak scrub, so nearly impenetrable that it breaks up an attack and forces troops to move in single file along goat-tracks between the bushes."

On August 18th the 1st Battalion Royal Dublin Fusiliers embarked from " W " Beach in H.M. transport *Prince Abbas*, and landed therefrom at Suvla Bay on the early morning of the 19th, moving at once to Chocolate Hill and thence into the first-line trenches on Hill 53, where all ranks were busily employed in improving the firing and communication trenches. This position was held during the assault on Hill 112 by the other battalions of the brigade, the casualties in the Battalion being 5 men killed, Lieutenants G. S. Fenning and E. Osborne and a few men wounded. The Dublins were relieved at night by the 5th Battalion Royal Irish Fusiliers, and then proceeded to fire-trenches two miles north at Kuchuk Anafarta Ova.

On August 21st the 29th Division was detailed to storm Scimitar Hill, the possession of which was essential to the attack on the main Turkish positions. " The 29th Division," says an historian,[*] " now contained far less than half of the troops who landed in April. Few indeed of their original officers were left,

---

[*] Nevinson, pp. 342 *et seq.*

few of the trusted sergeants and corporals whom they knew. They had been brought hurriedly into the midst of an unknown scene, and found themselves included between lines of unknown and untried battalions. . . . None the less, this indomitable Division, in this its last battle upon the Peninsula, displayed to the last the indomitable spirit habitual to its nature, and fought with the same proud self-sacrifice and confident enthusiasm as had distinguished it at the landing."

The 87th Brigade attacked the left front of Scimitar Hill, while the 86th was intended to storm the position from the right. "But as they advanced they found their progress hindered by battalions of the 32nd and 33rd Brigades, which had edged off to their left instead of keeping their direction straight forward and working on parallel lines with the 29th Division. Battalions in the three brigades thus converged and became confused. . . . Instead of being covered by the 11th Division as intended, the right flank of the 29th Division was hampered and almost paralysed. . . . The confusion was increased by a raging fire, which with long tongues of flame consumed what was left of the bush . . . and entirely cut off co-operation with the 87th Brigade. Such parties as reached the broad bare patch of ravine from which the name of 'Scimitar' was derived became at once exposed to the storm of shrapnel and rifle fire. . . . The leading troops were simply swept off the top of the spur, and had to fall back to a ledge S.W. of Scimitar Hill, where they found a little cover. . . . This unsuccessful attempt to capture the hill so ominously known as 'Scimitar' cost little less than 5,000 casualties."

During these operations excellent work was done by Captain de Wolf, Lieutenants Tooth and Hawes, Sergeant O'Connor (killed), and Corporal Doyle, of the Battalion. During the latter part of the time the Battalion was commanded by Lieut.-Colonel O'Dowda, West Kent Regiment, who had relieved Colonel Ward.

The "Blue Caps" remained at Suvla until September 8th, when at night they marched to the beach for embarkation to Imbros, one man being killed by shell-fire during embarkation. Imbros was reached during the 9th, and the Battalion, having landed, went into camp at Kephalos for rest.

On September 18th, while at Imbros, the following was received from H.R.H. the Duke of Connaught, Colonel-in-Chief of the Regiment :—

"*His Royal Highness is proud of the magnificent behaviour of the Royal Dublin Fusiliers, and hopes you will on the first opportunity convey to the Regiment his appreciation of all they have done at the Dardanelles and in France, and his sincere sympathy at the sad losses sustained.*"

Next day it was announced in Battalion Orders that a return to Suvla would take place on the following night, and the baggage was taken down to the beach to be put on board, but was sent back again, as it was then considered too stormy to embark for the Peninsula. But on the afternoon of the 21st embarkation took place, the Battalion landing again at Suvla at 11 at night and marching to Reserve Nullah, where the night was passed. Next evening the Battalion relieved the 1st Battalion King's Own Scottish Borderers in the fire trenches, and at once set to work to improve and extend them. During the next few days there was very little rifle fire from the Turks, simply intermittent shelling and persistent sniping, Second-Lieutenant J. A. H. Taylor being killed by a sniper on the night of the 23rd-24th. The plague of flies was very distressing, dysentery was rife, and men went sick daily, and by the end of September the strength of the Battalion was down to 15 officers and 608 other ranks, despite the fact that during the last two months upwards of 300 non-commissioned officers and men had reached the Battalion in drafts from home.

The Battalion remained in the front line, work went on, there were days of quiet, days of outbursts of heavy fire and accompanying losses. On October 2nd Corporal Byrne, Privates Irwin and McGuire behaved in a very gallant manner, and brought in two wounded men from the open under a very heavy fire.

On October 11th Lord Kitchener cabled to General Hamilton asking for an estimate of the losses which would be involved in an evacuation of the peninsula, and Sir Ian replied estimating these at 50 per cent., and giving his opinion that such a step as evacuation was " unthinkable." Five days later—on the 16th—Lord Kitchener again telegraphed saying that the War Council wished to make a change in the command, and later he was informed that General Sir Charles Monro had been appointed to relieve him, and that, pending this officer's arrival, General Birdwood was to assume command on the Peninsula ; and on the 17th General Sir Ian Hamilton issued the following farewell order :—

" On handing over the Command of the Mediterranean Expeditionary Force to General Sir C. C. Monro, the Commander-in-Chief wishes to say a few farewell words to the Allied troops, with many of whom he has now for so long been associated. First, he would like them to know his deep sense of the honour it has been to command so fine an Army in one of the most arduous and difficult campaigns which has ever been undertaken ; secondly, he must express to them his admiration at the noble response which they have invariably given to the calls he has made upon them. No risk has been too desperate, no sacrifice too great. Sir Ian Hamilton thanks all ranks, from Generals to private soldiers, for the wonderful way they have seconded his efforts to lead them towards that decisive victory which, under their new Chief, he has the most implicit confidence they will achieve."

General Monro reached the Peninsula on October 30th with orders (1) to report on the military situation ; (2) to give an opinion whether on purely military grounds the Peninsula should be evacuated, and, in the event of his deciding against this last, to estimate the number of troops required to carry the Peninsula, to keep the Straits open, or to take Constantinople. For many and cogent reasons which will be found set out in detail in Sir Charles Monro's despatch of March 6th, 1916, but which need not here be repeated, he condemned the whole expedition root and branch ; but before coming to any conclusion as to the military policy to be adopted, the Cabinet commissioned Lord Kitchener to visit the Dardanelles in person and assume the responsibility of decision.

The Field-Marshal left England on November 5th, and on

reaching Mudros consulted with Sir Charles Monro, who meantime had visited Egypt, and now returned accompanied by General Maxwell, commanding the forces in Egypt. "Purely military considerations apart, Kitchener was an opponent of immediate evacuation. He thought, too, there was still room for further resistance, and before leaving London had even urged Mr. Balfour to consider the possibility of another enterprise by the Navy to force the Straits." * But on talking the matter over with the senior officers on the spot, Lord Kitchener finally and reluctantly decided in favour of evacuation, and the necessary orders were accordingly given.

While on the Peninsula the Field-Marshal visited Helles, Anzac, and Suvla, and on November 11th caused the following to be published :—

"At the conclusion of his visit to Suvla to-day Field-Marshal Lord Kitchener instructed the Corps Commanders to express to all ranks of the corps and troops attached, His Majesty the King's deep appreciation of the ceaseless and arduous work performed by them during the past three months in the face of a determined enemy. His Majesty graciously directed Lord Kitchener before he left England to convey this message to the troops concerned."

On November 19th Lieut.-Colonel O'Dowda was appointed to act in command of the 38th Brigade, 13th Division, and Captain de Wolf assumed command of the Battalion in his place.

During the remainder of the stay of the Royal Dublin Fusiliers on the Peninsula there were no more desperate actions such as were some of those in which the "Blue Caps" had earlier been engaged; but there was a ceaseless round of hard work in preparing new defences and in the improvement of those already existing, and the troops were always opposed to, and under the fire of, a brave and untiring foe. Casualties were occurring daily—almost hourly—not, indeed, in any large numbers, but there was a constant drain or wastage which such drafts as at long intervals arrived did little to make good. By the end of November the strength of the Battalion had fallen to 12 officers and 332 other

* Arthur, *Life of Lord Kitchener*, Vol. III, pp. 187, 188.

ranks, but there was no withdrawal to rest-quarters, and the men, if taken from the fire trenches in one part of the line, were merely transferred to others where equal vigilance was called for.

To the end of November the weather remained generally fine, but on the 27th and the four following days there was a heavy south-west gale and torrents of rain; piers and landing-stages were destroyed, light craft were driven ashore, trenches were filled with water, and streams roared down the gullies. At Suvla the havoc wrought was exceptionally heavy. " Across a long and deep ravine leading obliquely down from the whale-back ridge of Kiretch Tepe Sirt, high parapets had been constructed by Turks and Britons alike. Against these parapets the water was dammed up as in a reservoir. They gave way, as when a reservoir's embankment bursts, and the weight of accumulated water swept down the ravine into the valley, and from the valley into the Salt Lake and the shore, bearing with it stores and equipment, mule-carts and mules, and the drowning bodies of Turks and Britons, united in vain struggles against the overwhelming power of nature. Along the other sections of the lines the men stood miserably in the trenches, soaked to the skin, and in places up to their waists in water.

" Then, of a sudden, the wind swung round to the north and fell upon the wrecked and inundated scene with icy blast. For nearly two days and nights snow descended in whirling blizzards, and two days and nights of bitter frost succeeded the snow. The surface of the pools and trenches froze thick. The men's great-coats, being soaked through with the rain, froze stiff upon them. Men staggered down from the lines numbed and bemused with the intensity of the cold. They could neither hear nor speak, but stared about them like bewildered bullocks. The sentries and outposts in the advanced trenches could not pull the triggers of their rifles for cold. . . . Few can realise the suffering of those four days.

" As though to test their power of endurance up to the very last, the full weight of misery fell upon the 29th Division, detained at Suvla since their final battle of August 21st. . . . The dead in the IXth Army Corps alone numbered over 200. From the Peninsula about 10,000 sick had to be removed. Many were frost-bitten; many lost their limbs; some, their reason."*

In the 1st Battalion Royal Dublin Fusiliers several men died of exposure, and the Battalion War Diary says, under date of November 29th:—" Many men went to hospital and a few returned. Impossible to estimate number of sick." Indeed, by the end of November the Battalion was, as has been stated, so seriously reduced in numbers that it is difficult to see how it could have kept the field as a serviceable unit had it not been for the opportune arrival on December 2nd of a draft of three officers—Second-Lieutenants G. B. Hollom (5th Middlesex), R. G. S. Durward (14th Royal Scots), and C. F. Greenlees (9th Queen's)—and 168 non-commissioned officers and men.

By many people the mere landing on the Peninsula had been looked upon as an operation almost impossible of achievement, but to bring away an army from open beaches in the face of a resolute enemy seemed a task of even greater difficulty, involving risk of the heaviest losses, or even of disaster. It has been done before in military history, but only after the enemy has suffered serious defeat, and here there was of this no question. Competent authorities had estimated that the loss might be anything from 15 to 50 per cent., and at Mudros preparation had been made for 10,000 wounded. It must be remembered that at Suvla and Anzac alone more than 83,000 men had to be embarked, with some 5,000 horses and mules, 2,000 carts, 200 guns, and 30 days' supply for the troops, with great quantities of engineering and medical stores; and all this had to be done under the very nose of a brave and vigilant enemy who was nowhere more than 300 yards distant from our front, and at many points no more than 10 or 20 yards!

It was decided that Anzac and Suvla should be the first places on the Peninsula to be evacuated, and when definite instructions to this end were issued there were no fewer than five divisions then at Suvla, all now under the command of General Byng. These were,

* Nevinson, p. 383 *et seq.*

counting from left to right, the 11th, the 29th, the 53rd, the 13th, and the 2nd Mounted Division, and it was decided that of these the 29th and 53rd should first be sent away, the 29th returning to the scene of its early triumphs at Helles.

On December 13th, then, orders were received by Captain de Wolf that the Battalion was to leave next day, and accordingly, about 7.30 on the night of the 14th, a start was made from Reserve Nullah, and, embarking in H.M. transport *Hazel* at midnight, they reached Mudros harbour the next morning. The Battalion remained all that day on board the ship, which sailed again at 7.30 p.m. for Helles; this was reached about midnight, and the troops, at once landing, marched to and bivouacked at the old French Headquarters; but in the course of the next forty-eight hours they moved, first, to the lines of the Royal Fusiliers above " X " Beach, and then to those which had been previously occupied by the Royal Marines. From here the Battalion moved up to the firing line, its effective strength being now 590 all ranks, and at once came under heavy rifle fire, the support and reserve trenches being also continuously shelled, though casualties were happily few in number.

On December 22nd there was again a very heavy rain-storm, resulting in the trenches becoming 2 to 3 feet deep in mud and water; the front and communication trenches were shelled intermittently during the day, and just before dawn on the 23rd " the Turks bombed us out of two saps in ' Z ' Company's lines, but were at once again driven out by a bombing party under Lieutenant H. L. Ridley, who behaved with great gallantry. Casualties: 12 killed and 18 wounded; enemy—20 dead bodies either brought in or seen in No Man's Land."

On this day Major H. Nelson, 1st Battalion Border Regiment, arrived and took over command of the Battalion, with the temporary rank of Lieutenant-Colonel.

By 5.30 a.m. on December 20th every single soldier had been withdrawn from Suvla and Anzac, and four days later General Birdwood was directed to make all preliminary preparations for the immediate evacuation of Helles in the event of orders to this effect

THE EVACUATION

being received. These orders arrived on the 28th, and General Birdwood proceeded immediately to carry them into effect.

The troops at Helles on this day consisted of the 29th, 42nd, 52nd, and Naval Divisions, with a comparatively small body of French troops; but on December 29th the 13th Division, which had moved to Imbros from Suvla, was shipped across in relief of the 42nd. To make sure of rapid embarkation, it was proposed to use four beaches—Gully Beach, " X," " W," and " Y " Beaches—and at each of these many piers had been placed in position, while defensive positions were selected and prepared for covering the embarkations at each beach.

1916 It had been intended that the 13th and 29th Divisions should be the last troops to leave, but with the New Year the weather showed signs of breaking, and certain modifications had to be made in the arrangements; so that while the rearguards of these two divisions did not actually leave the Peninsula until the night of January 8th-9th, when the evacuation was finally and most successfully completed, the 1st Battalion Royal Dublin Fusiliers sailed away just a week earlier.

Battalion leaves Gallipoli. It was on January 1st, 1916, that the Battalion, when working on the defences, suddenly received orders to embark at " V " Beach at midnight. Here, after considerable delay, the Battalion was placed on board the *River Clyde*, and thence on tugs which took the troops to the *Ausonia*, the usual difficulties of transhipping at night being aggravated by a choppy sea. All, however, were safely on board the transport just as day was breaking. Mudros harbour was reached about noon on January 2nd, when the Battalion disembarked and marched to camp at Mudros East.

On the 5th Captain Carruthers, with 10 officers and 100 other ranks, sailed for Egypt as an advance party in the *Caledonia*, being followed by the rest of the Battalion in the *Serangbee* on the 8th. During the voyage a zig-zag course was pursued from fear of submarines, some of which were known to be in these waters; but Alexandria was safely reached on the afternoon of the 10th, the troops disembarking next day and entraining during the afternoon for Suez. On arrival at a railway siding some three miles from Suez, the train was left, and the Battalion moved into a camp which had been pitched in readiness for its arrival by the advance party under Captain Carruthers.

During the comparatively brief stay of the Fusiliers in Egypt they were a good deal moved about. On February 13th they moved across the Suez Canal to El Kubri; on the 20th they relieved the Lancashire Fusiliers in the front-line trenches at Darb-el-Haj; on March 3rd, during a very heavy sandstorm, they marched back again to El Kubri, and on the next day to their first camp near Suez. Here orders were received for the 29th Division to prepare to proceed to an "unknown destination," and on March 11th the Battalion entrained at Suez, and travelled right through to Alexandria in two parties. The port was reached at daybreak on the 12th, and embarkation took place forthwith on the transport *Minominee*. Alexandria was left on the 13th, and, pursuing the usual zigzag course, the ship sailed for a port in Southern France.

The following are the names of the officers who appear to have landed in the new theatre of war with the Battalion:—Lieut.-Colonel H. Nelson; Captains A. S. Trigona, C. G. Carruthers, C. E. Hawes, G. M. Moffatt, H. L. Ridley, and C. Maffett; Lieutenants G. C. Jacobs and F. H. McCormack; Second-Lieutenants C. F. Greenlees, D. F. Scott, T. W. R. Neill, F. R. Oxley, A. M. B. B. Rose-Cleland, W. J. Robertson, H. V. Spankie, R. G. S. Durward, J. Trotter, D. R. Warner, G. B. Hollom, A. J. W. Pearson, A. G. Tooth, and C. A. Copland; Second-Lieutenant and Adjutant F. A. Wilson; Lieutenant and Quartermaster C. W. Armstrong; Captain the Rev. D. Power, Roman Catholic chaplain; and Lieutenant L. D. Shaw, R.A.M.C., in medical charge of the Battalion.

The strength of the Battalion on February 29th, the nearest date for which any return appears to be forthcoming, was 1 warrant officer, 30 sergeants, 40 corporals, 9 drummers, and 1,335 privates, so that the "Blue Caps" were once again a really strong unit; but the personnel of the Battalion had undergone an almost complete

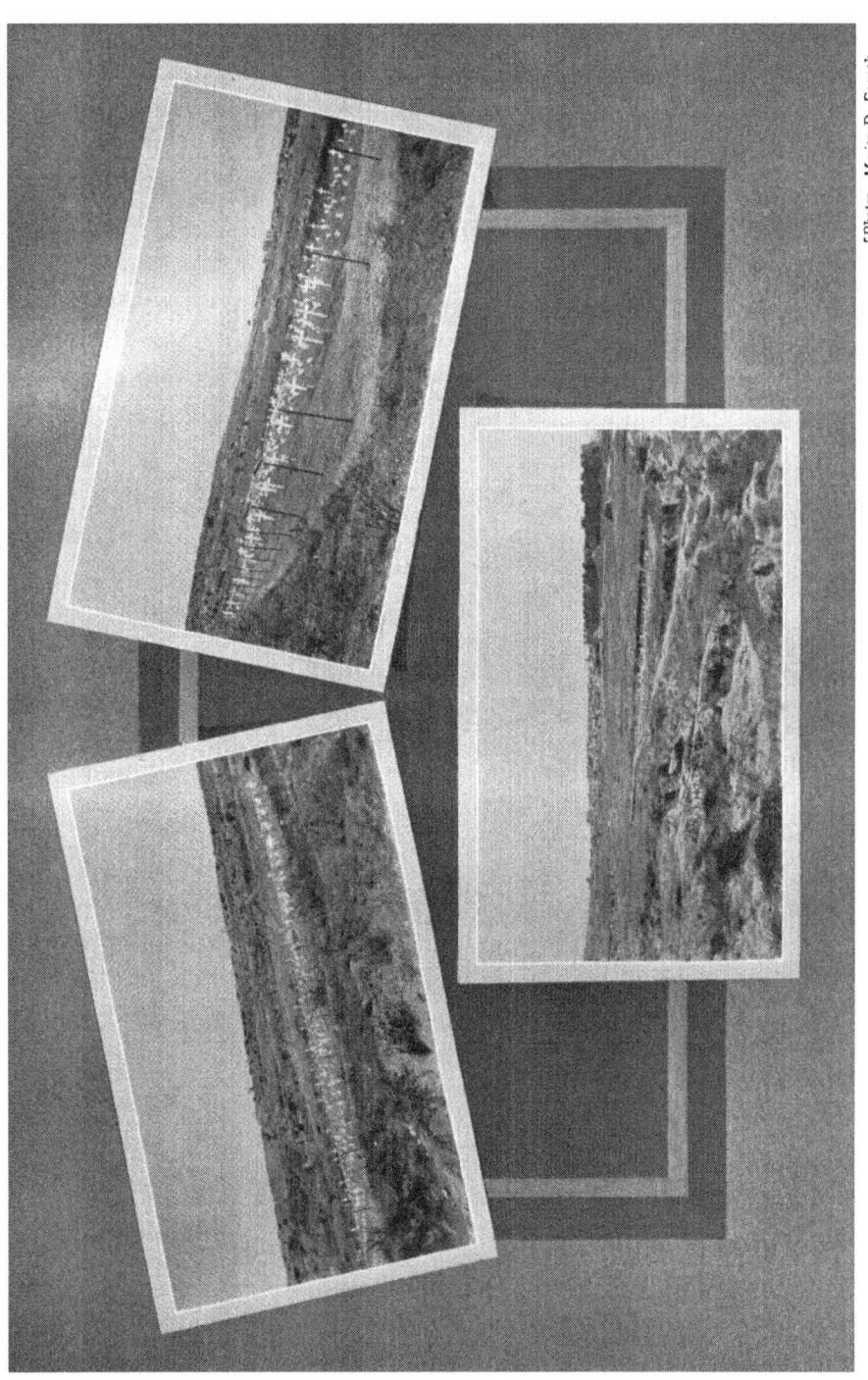

[Photos, Major D. French.

CEMETERY WHERE "BLUE CAPS" WERE BURIED (who fell at the Landing). Turkish Position in the background. (Two views.)

CEMETERY AND SEDD-EL-BAHR FROM HIGH GROUND WEST OF BEACH.

change since it had landed in Gallipoli rather less than eleven months previously. Of those who had then stormed ashore from the boats or from the *River Clyde*, there remained at the final evacuation no more than *eleven* non-commissioned officers and men who had served continuously throughout the campaign without having been invalided by reason of wounds or sickness; while of those who, having landed with the Battalion, had been invalided, but had returned to duty in time to leave the Peninsula on evacuation, there were but 1 officer and 78 other ranks. Lieutenant O'Hara, who was the only officer left after the fierce fighting of the early days, had died on August 29th, 1915, of wounds received in action.

Of those of the Battalion who died we can hardly more fittingly take leave than in the words with which the Commander of the Mediterranean Expeditionary Force, in the concluding paragraph of his final despatch, pays his tribute " to the everlasting memory of my dear comrades who will return no more." Of them Sir Ian writes :—

" *So I bid them all farewell, with a special Godspeed to the campaigners who have served with me right through from the terrible yet most glorious earlier days—the incomparable 29th Division; the young veterans of the Naval Division; the ever-victorious Australians and New Zealanders; the stout East Lancs, and my own brave fellow-countrymen of the Lowland Division of Scotland.*"

CHAPTER IV

MARCH, 1916—OCTOBER, 1917—FRANCE.

THE BATTLES OF THE SOMME, 1916; BATTLES OF ARRAS, 1917; THE BATTLES OF YPRES, 1917.

Battalion arrives in France. March, 1916. THE voyage through the Mediterranean was eventless, and Marseilles was reached early on the morning of March 19th. Here the Battalion was landed during the afternoon and entrained, leaving Marseilles very early in the morning of the 20th. Travelling steadily northward for forty-eight hours the Royal Dublin Fusiliers arrived at Pont Rémy just before daylight on the 22nd, detrained and marched to Domqueur, where they went into billets : battalion training was at once commenced, and leave was for the first time opened to the United Kingdom. On the last day of the month the whole of the 86th Brigade moved up to Beauval, whence on April 4th the Battalion marched to Acheux preparatory to going up into the front line.

During the past winter considerable reinforcements had reached the British Army in France, while the incessant strain of the recruiting service had been eased by the recent introduction in the United Kingdom of compulsory service. At the time when the 29th Division was brought over to France from Egypt there were four British armies in the field, the Second (Plumer) in the Ypres district, the First (Monro) opposite to Neuve Chapelle, the Third (Allenby) covering the new French sector down to Arras, and the Fourth (Rawlinson) from Albert to the Somme, where the British line joined on to that of the French. The 29th Division was still in the VIIIth Corps, which had, however, been re-constituted, and it was now composed of two regular divisions, the 4th and 29th, with the 31st Division of the New Army, and the 48th South Midland Territorial Division.

The spring of the year had witnessed a most determined attack by the Germans upon the Ypres salient, while in the middle of March the pressure upon the French at Verdun had become very severe, and in order to afford some easement to our Allies a French army—the Tenth, under Foch—had been drawn out of the line and twelve miles had been added to the British front. At the end of March there was heavy fighting about St. Eloi, and in April about the dangerous Loos salient, but it seemed that all the activity exhibited by the enemy was partly to hold us to our ground while they dealt with the French at Verdun, and partly— since the Germans had a shrewd suspicion that some great movement by the British was in contemplation—to try to provoke a premature offensive on our part.

At this time the southern end of the whole British line was held, as has been stated, by Rawlinson's Fourth Army. This consisted of five corps, each of from three to five divisions, his infantry numbering about 200,000 first class troops. The five corps, counting northwards from the junction with the French, were the XIIIth (Congreve), the XVth (Horne), the IIIrd (Pulteney), the Xth (Morland), and the VIIIth (Hunter-Weston); and when the preparations were set on foot for the Battle of the Somme, whereby it was intended to break or shift the western end of the German line and so relieve the pressure on Verdun, the front of the VIIIth Corps extended from Hébuterne in the north down to a point just north of the Ancre, and faced the very strong German positions of Serre in the north and of Beaumont Hamel in the centre.

The Battalion spent the time between its arrival at the front from the port of disembarkation and the commencement of the operations known as the Battle of the Somme either in the front line about Auchonvillers, in the brigade or divisional reserve at Mailly Maillet, or in corps reserve near Louvencourt. There was much good work done in digging new trenches and in repairing existing ones. The weather was for the most part wet and stormy, and there was a certain amount of sickness, but the drafts were strong and provided at regular intervals; and when on June 27th orders were received to move up next day, ready for the attack, to the portions of the line known as "88th Trench" and "Essex Street," the strength of the Battalion was probably at its highest, containing, as it did, 43 officers and 1,066 non-commissioned officers and men. A new second-in-command had joined ten days previously, Major E. F. E. Seymour, of the Regiment, displacing Captain Trigona, who now reverted to the command of "Z" Company.

Battle of the Somme. The opening of the battle had been planned for June 28th, but the weather was so tempestuous that it was put off until it should moderate, but on moving up to the position detailed the Royal Dublin Fusiliers were ordered to make a raid on the German trenches either on the night of the 28th or early morning of the 29th, and a party of two officers —Lieutenant Gun-Cuninghame and Second-Lieutenant Devoy— and eighty other ranks was told off for this duty. The raiding party reached the front line very early on the 29th, and Second-Lieutenant Devoy laid the tape on the enemy's wire before our barrage lifted, but was wounded on his way back, Second-Lieutenant Pearson taking his place. On arriving near the enemy's wire fire was opened upon the party with bombs, rifle grenades, rifles, machine guns, guns and trench mortars, and the party was forced to retire. All ranks behaved admirably, and some with conspicuous gallantry in bringing in the dead and wounded. The casualties were 3 men killed, 2 officers (Cuninghame and Devoy), and 7 other ranks wounded, while 19 men were at first reported missing, but next day 6 of these reported themselves, having remained hidden from the enemy in shell-holes in No Man's Land.

The order of battle of the VIIIth Corps was as follows:— Counting from north to south were the 31st Division, having Serre for its objective; the 4th Division, opposite Beaumont Hamel; and south of this again the 29th; while the 48th Division was in reserve. "Such was the force, comprising nearly 50,000

[Photo, Imperial War Museum.

MINE CRATER BLOWN UP ON JULY 1st, 1916, BEAUMONT HAMEL.

[Photo, Imperial War Museum.

GERMAN BARBED WIRE AND SHELL-HOLES AFTER RAIN,
BEAUMONT HAMEL, END OF NOVEMBER, 1916.

excellent infantry, who set forth upon the formidable adventure of forcing the lines of Beaumont Hamel. They were destined to show the absolute impossibility of such a task in the face of a steadfast, unshaken enemy, supported by a tremendous artillery, but their story is a most glorious one, and many a great British victory contains no such record of tenacity and military virtue."*

Beaumont Hamel has been described as an exceptionally difficult place, for it contained enormous quarries and excavations in which masses of Germans could remain concealed, almost immune to shell fire and ready to sally out when needed. In spite of the terrific bombardment the actual danger done to the enemy was not excessive, and neither his numbers, his *morale*, nor his guns had been seriously diminished.

On the day that the battle commenced the 86th and 87th Brigades of the 29th Division formed the first line, with the 88th Brigade in support.

The following is the account of the attack as given in the Battalion diary:—"Reached our allotted positions in the trenches via Broadway at 1 a.m. on July 1st, 'W' Company on right and 'X' Company on the left in Essex Street, with 'Y' Company on the right and 'Z' on the left in 88th Trench. Casualties during move two other ranks slightly wounded. Bombardment became more intense from 6.30 to 7.30, at which hour the attack was launched. The 2nd Royal Fusiliers on right and the 1st Lancashire Fusiliers on left advanced against the German first-line trenches. In front of the Lancashires a large mine was exploded by us near Beaumont Hamel at 7.30. Immediately the 2nd Royal Fusiliers and 1st Lancashire Fusiliers advanced we commenced to move up to our front-line trenches, 'W' Company, with 'Y' Company in support, up F. Street and Broadway, and 'X' Company, with 'Z' in support, up Bloomfield and Second Avenue ready to move out against the German second-line system of trenches on Beaucourt Ridge, S.E. of Beaumont Hamel. The Battalion was supposed to move out

*Conan Doyle, *The British Campaign in France and Flanders*, Vol. III, pp. 46, 47.

behind the 2nd Royal Fusiliers by companies and reform at Station Road, also by companies, ready for the assault of the enemy second-line system; but this could only be done after the 2nd Royal Fusiliers had gained their objective, the enemy front-line system, and this the 2nd Royal Fusiliers were unable to accomplish. It was very difficult for companies to move up to the front line owing to the trenches being blocked by a number of men of the Battalion in front, 86th Brigade Machine Gun Company, and consolidating parties. Consequently it was 8 o'clock before 'W' and 'X' Companies were able to begin moving out over the parapet. Our own barbed wire was cut only at intervals of about forty yards, and by this time the Germans had machine guns trained on these gaps, the result being that our casualties were very heavy, and only a few of our men ever got through our own wire, and still fewer of these succeeded in advancing more than fifty or sixty yards before being shot down. 'W' and 'Y' Companies both behaved exceptionally well under fire. At noon the attack here was abandoned, and we were ordered to hold and consolidate our own front line."

An historian of the war recounts in confirmation of the above that " parties of the leading regiments were speedily up to the German front-line trench, but their advance beyond it was delayed by the fact that the dug-outs were found to be full of lurking soldiers who had intended no doubt to rush out and attack the stormers in the rear, but who were discovered in time and had to fight for their lives. These men were cleared out upon the right, and the advance then made some progress, but on the left by 9 o'clock the 86th Brigade had been completely held up by a murderous machine-gun fire in front of Beaumont Hamel, a position which presented peculiar difficulties. . . . By half-past ten the action had resolved itself into a bombardment of the German front line once more, and the assault had definitely failed. There was an attempt to renew it, but when it was found that the 86th and 87th Brigades were equally reduced in numbers it was recognized that only a defensive line could be held.

"All the troops of the 29th Division had lived up to their fame. . . . There was no slackness anywhere, either in preparation or in performance, and nothing but the absolute impossibility of the task under existing conditions stood in the way of success." *

The losses of the Division were heavy, and in the Royal Dublin Fusiliers they amounted to:—Killed, 4 officers (Captain E. R. L. Maunsell, Second-Lieutenants A. J. W. Pearson, 14th Royal Fusiliers, C. F. Greenlees, 9th Queen's, and A. M. B. B. Rose-Cleland) and 18 non-commissioned officers and men; wounded, 7 officers (Lieutenant R. Elphick, Second-Lieutenants T. W. R. Neill, 9th Royal Scots Fusiliers, W. J. Robertson, 9th Royal Scots Fusiliers, H. V. Spankie, R. G. S. Durward, 14th Royal Scots, J. E. B. Maunsell, and M. H. Tighe), and 125 other ranks, while 1 officer (Second-Lieutenant D. R. Warner) and 63 men were missing.

Second-Lieutenant Neill died of his wounds on July 3rd.

On the 3rd the following telegram was received in the 29th Division:—

"*Sir Aylmer Hunter-Weston desires all ranks to know that General Joffre has expressed his appreciation of the hard fighting carried out by our troops on the English left. It is greatly due to the fact that the Germans were so strong and so well provided with guns in front of the VIIth and VIIIth Corps that the French and the British troops in touch with them on the right of the Fourth Army were able to make our brilliant and successful advance. Sir Aylmer Hunter-Weston congratulates all officers, non-commissioned officers and men of the VIIIth Corps on the magnificent courage, discipline and determination displayed by the troops who carried out the attack. No words of praise can be too high, and Sir Aylmer Hunter-Weston considers it an honour to be the comrade of such heroes.*"

* Conan Doyle, Vol. III, pp. 54-57.

On July 4th* the Corps Commander published the following message to all officers, non-commissioned officers and men of the VIIIth Corps:—

"*In so big a command as an Army Corps of four Divisions (about 80,000 men) it is impossible for me to come round all front trenches and all billets to see every man as I wish to do. You must take the will for the deed, and accept this printed message in place of the spoken word.*

"*It is difficult for me to express my admiration for the splendid courage, determination and discipline displayed by every officer, N.C.O. and man of the Battalions that took part in the great attack on the Beaumont Hamel-Serre position on July 1st. All observers agree in stating that the various waves of men issued from their trenches and moved forward at the appointed time in perfect order, undismayed by the heavy artillery fire and deadly machine-gun fire. There were no cowards or waverers, and not a man fell out. It was a magnificent display of disciplined courage worthy of the best traditions of the British race.*

"*Very few are left of my old comrades, the original 'Contemptibles,' but their successors in the 4th Division have shown that they are worthy to bear the honours gained by the 4th Division at their first great fight at Fontaine-au-Pire and Ligny during the great retreat and greater advance across the Marne and Aisne, and in all the hard fighting at Ploegsteert and at Ypres.*

"*Though but few of my old comrades, the heroes of the historic landing at Cape Helles, are still with us, the 29th Division of to-day has shown itself capable of maintaining its high traditions, and has proved itself worthy of its hard-earned title of 'the Incomparable 29th.'*

"*The 31st New Army Division and the 48th Territorial Division, by the heroism and discipline of the units engaged in this their first big battle, have proved themselves worthy to fight*

---

* General Hunter-Weston had reassumed command of the VIIIth Corps on March 7th, 1916. General de Lisle was still commanding the 29th Division.

by the side of such magnificent regular divisions as the 4th and 29th. There can be no higher praise.

"We had the most difficult part of the line to attack. The Germans had fortified it with skill and immense labour for many months, they had kept their best troops here, and had assembled N.E. and S.E. of it a formidable collection of artillery and many machine guns.

"By your splendid attack you held these enemy forces here in the north and so enabled our friends in the south, both British and French, to achieve the brilliant success that they have. Therefore, though we did not do all we hoped to do, you have more than pulled your weight, and you, and our even more glorious comrades who have preceded us across the Great Divide, have nobly done your duty.

"We have got to stick it out and go on hammering. Next time we attack, if it please God, we will not only pull our weight but will pull off a big thing. With such troops as you, who are determined to stick it out and do your duty, we are certain of winning through to a glorious victory.

"I salute each officer, N.C.O. and man of the 4th, 29th, 31st and 48th Divisions as a comrade in arms, and I rejoice to have the privilege of commanding such a band of heroes as the VIIIth Corps have proved themselves to be."

A telegraphic message from His Majesty the King to General Sir Douglas Haig was briefer, but not one whit less appreciative. It ran :—

"Please convey to the Army under your command my sincere congratulations on the results achieved in the recent fighting. I am proud of my troops. None could have fought more bravely."

For full three weeks the Battalion remained in the same neighbourhood, when in the front line holding grimly on, and when withdrawn to the reserve position about Mailly Wood reorganizing and cleaning up, while providing large and frequent working parties for making, enlarging and repairing the communication trenches. During these three weeks reinforcements were received, but these came from all corps, and only a comparatively insignificant proportion of them came from the *Regiment,* which was regrettable, but possibly unavoidable under the circumstances and in view of the pressing need of relieving the daily wastage incurred; thus of the reinforcements received in "other ranks" only 54 were provided by battalions of the Royal Dublin Fusiliers, while 52 came from the Royal Munster Fusiliers, 63 from the Royal Irish, 18 from the Leinsters, 9 from the Royal Irish Fusiliers, 4 from the Royal Irish Rifles, 4 from the Royal Inniskilling Fusiliers, and 2 from the Connaught Rangers. Eleven young officers also joined the Battalion at the same time.

A good deal of spasmodic shelling was done by the enemy, especially at night, with gas shells, heavy howitzers, field guns and Minenwerfers, and casualties, of course, were daily incurred, these amounting by June 24th to 11 non-commissioned officers and men killed, 2 officers (Lieutenant McCormack and Second-Lieutenants Addis) and 33 other ranks wounded.

There were orders given at one time to prepare for another "push," but nothing happened, and the Battalion moved down on the 23rd to Warnimont Wood on relief, and on the next day was directed to move to Beauval. Here, on the 26th, three more young officers joined.

The reason for the move of the Battalion from the Beaumont Hamel front was that it had now been decided to create a Fifth Army, under Lieut.-General Sir Hubert Gough, the functions of this army being to hold the line from La Boisselle to Serre, and to form a defensive flank and pivot for the IIIrd, XVth and XIIIth Corps to the south. The new Fifth Army was created by the detachment of the two northern corps of General Rawlinson's army, the VIIIth Corps (Hunter-Weston) and the Xth Corps (Morland).

On July 27th the 1st Battalion Royal Dublin Fusiliers marched from Beauval to Doullens, whence it proceeded by train to Esquelbecq, which was reached next morning, and from where the Battalion moved by road to Wormhoudt, and here remained in billets until the 30th, when it went into Camp "J" at Poperinghe, relieving the 14th Battalion Durham Light Infantry. First impressions appear to have been good, for the Battalion diary for July 31st ends with the jubilant remark: "Best camp the Battalion has yet moved into," but on the next day this favourable opinion is qualified, for we read: "Most convenient camp we have yet been in, but does not seem particularly sanitary." It was possibly for the reason here given that on August 3rd a fresh move was made, this time to Camp "O," on the E. of Poperinghe, but the Battalion was not long left here in peace, for on the 8th it marched to the railway a mile distant and travelled to Ypres, "where guides from the 2nd South Wales Borderers met us and conducted us to the dug-outs on the canal bank, where we were to spend the night in brigade reserve."

On the 9th the Battalion went up to the front trenches, two companies in the firing line, one in support, and one in reserve in St. Jean, where was also the Battalion Headquarters. "We are the left sub-sector on the left sector of the divisional front. Our front is known as the Wieltje Salient." Allowing for the natural tendency to depreciate the condition of any trenches taken over from another corps, those in which the Dublins now found themselves seem to have been about as bad as they could be. "There was no parados, the parapet too low and not bullet-proof, no dug-outs to speak of, and the line littered with old tins and rubbish, which had been accumulating for months. The wire in front was very poor. Owing to the state of the trenches work is only possible by night, and during the day it is necessary to avoid as much movement as possible."

The Regiment remained in the firing line, incurring only very few casualties, until August 19th, when it was withdrawn to the town of Ypres, part of it being at the Convent near the Cloth Hall, part in billets in very dark and damp cellars, while half of "Y" Company was on detachment at Vlamertinghe. This distribution was maintained until the 29th—large fatigue parties being daily furnished to all parts of the line—when the Battalion was relieved by the 16th Middlesex, and proceeded by train and march route to Camp "O" at Poperinghe, with a small detachment at Reigersburg. But the "rest" was only a very brief one, for on the evening of September 8th it came to an end, and the Battalion moved back again to the canal bank at Ypres and resumed the former routine.

The Battalion remained in the Ypres area, moving from the canal bank to the firing line and back again, in turn to the neighbourhood of Ypres or to Poperinghe, until the end of the first week in October, when the orders to be ready to move again to the south, which had some days before been received, were put into execution. The Royal Dublin Fusiliers were on October 7th at Wormhoudt, and leaving this place early on the morning of the 8th the Battalion proceeded by train via Poperinghe, Hopoutre, Longuereau near Amiens, Neuville to Dernancourt, which was reached early on the afternoon of the 10th. On the 13th the journey was resumed, and the Dublin Fusiliers finally found themselves established in trench shelters, bivouacs and a few billets at the S.E. corner of Mametz Wood. An unfortunate accident, the cause of which was never really satisfactorily explained, occurred here two days after arrival. During bombing practice by "X" Company in the course of the morning, a Mills rifle grenade exploded in the middle of a party of officers and men under instruction, and injured more or less seriously Captain Carruthers, Lieutenant Barry, Second-Lieutenant Trotter and twelve other ranks.

The 29th Division, on proceeding to the south from the Ypres area, at last severed its connection with the VIIIth Corps and with General Sir Aylmer Hunter-Weston, under whom the 29th had so long served as divisional and corps commander; and during the remainder of the year 1916 the 29th Division formed part, first, of the XVth and later of the XIVth Corps.

During the many weeks that the battle of the Somme had lasted the success of the Allies had been general, but it had been very dearly and slowly gained. During July and August positions

VLAMERTINGHE.

A CONVENT IN YPRES.

had been taken, re-taken and captured again; the ground had to be contested inch by inch, and it took many weary days to win. Villages and woods all along the front were only captured by fragments, and most of the fragments were lost again more than once before they finally passed into our hands. In September matters improved. Guillemont, the possession of which had been disputed for six weeks, was at length carried, while the French seized the German lines up to the outskirts of Combles. Two days later the British had some further successes, while the French pushed their advance north and south of the Somme, and the German counter-attacks were singularly unsuccessful. Ginchy was captured on September 9th, and we were now half-way to Bapaume.

On October 3rd Eaucourt l'Abbaye was taken, Le Sars on the 7th, and the "Stuff" and "Regina Redoubts," between it and Thiepval, on the 21st. The French also had been at least equally fortunate, and only the bad weather then experienced in this month, which made transport almost impossible across the mangled soil of the Somme battlefield, prevented the Allies from reaping the full benefit of the heavy sacrifices which had been made.

It was at this juncture that the 29th Division came back again to the more southerly portion of the long British line, but while too late to take any very active part in the concluding operations of the Somme battle, which may be said to have finally ended on November 14th, the Dublin Fusiliers had plenty of heavy work in the trenches, varied by brief periods of so-called "rest," when the worn-out men were ceaselessly engaged on working parties and fatigues of all kinds.

The condition of the trenches on first taking over is described as "appalling—poor, shallow and very muddy, up to the knees in mud, and during the relief many men became stuck fast in the mud—the ground all round covered with shell-holes—difficult to send rations and water up to the front line as it can only be done at night." In this part of the line the Battalion remained during the remainder of the year, moving back at times to Delville Wood, to Ville-sur-Corbie, to Meaulte, to Carnoy or Bernafay Camps, and then being sent in the middle of December via Condé to Saisseval, where the officers and men were billeted in barns and houses about the village, in which a certain degree of rest could be enjoyed, and where a much-needed draft joined the Service companies.

On December 31st, 1916, the strength of the 1st Battalion Royal Dublin Fusiliers was 39 officers and 731 other ranks. The following are the names of the officers actually serving on that date with the Battalion in the field:—Lieut.-Colonel H. Nelson, D.S.O.; Major N. P. Clarke; Captains W. P. Oulton, M.C., F. A. Wilson, A. B. Bagley and C. O. Matthews; Lieutenants H. M. B. Gun-Cuninghame, W. B. St. G. Cameron, C. M. Tweedy and A. G. Tooth; Second-Lieutenants A. V. G. Killingley, M. F. Healy, A. F. Hernon, J. L. A. Gibbs, T. H. L. Addis, I. D. McKenzie, B. B. Murphy, G. F. Gradwell, J. H. Blair-White, F. Mooney, W. T. O'Carroll, W. P. Kinneen, A. R. Holman, A. M. Kneafsey, E. H. Robertson and T. W. H. Mason; Lieutenant and Adjutant H. L. Ridley; Lieutenant and Quartermaster J. A. Clarke; the Rev. D. Power, R.C. Chaplain; and Captain D. Kelly, R.A.M.C., in medical charge of the Battalion.

"In the latter days of 1916 and the beginning of 1917 the British Army, which had in little more than two years expanded from seven divisions to over fifty, took over an increased line. The movement began about Christmas time, and early in the New Year Rawlinson's Fourth Army, side-stepping always to the south, had covered the whole of the French position occupied during the Somme fighting, had crossed the Somme, and had established its right flank at a place near Roye. The total front was increased to 120 miles."* The general disposition of the British forces after this prolongation to the south was as follows: Plumer's Second Army was about the Ypres Salient; south of

* Conan Doyle, Vol. IV, p. 1.

A VIEW ON THE OUTSIDE OF DELVILLE WOOD, SEPTEMBER, 1916.

VIEW OF CORBIE FROM THE CHURCH STEEPLE.

H.M. THE KING VISITS QUESNOY, DECEMBER 2nd, 1918.

SAILLY-SAILLISEL.

Plumer, in the Armentières district, was the First Army, under Horne; and Allenby's Third Army carried the line onwards to the south of Arras. From the point upon which the British line had hinged during the Somme operations Gough's Fifth Army took over the front, and this joined on to Rawlinson's Fourth Army near the old French position.

1917 As soon as active operations again became possible when the worst of the winter seemed to be past, the enemy was driven in the first half of January from that portion of the Beaumont Hamel spur, which he was still holding; and during the early days of February the success of some hard fighting brought the British forward north of the Ancre to a point level with the centre of Grandcourt, a success which obliged the enemy to evacuate the last remaining portion of the German second-line system between Grandcourt and the "Stuff Redoubt." Further British offensives towards the middle of February led to the evacuation of Miraumont and Serre. Between February 25th and March 2nd a series of attacks were carried out against "a strong secondary line of defence which, from a point in the Le Transloy-Loupart line due west of the village of Beaulencourt, crossed in front of Ligny-Tilloy and Le Barque to the southern defences of Loupart Wood."* It was in the course of these operations that the "Blue Caps" were concerned in, and suffered heavy losses during, the attack on and capture of Sailly-Saillisel.

During January and February the Battalion had occupied very much the same positions as during the previous months—about Saisseval, Quesnoy, then back to their old billets at Corbie. Thence to Meaulte, Carnoy, and Guillemont and trenches in the Morval sector, and, finally, about February 10th to La Neuville, where the officers and men carefully rehearsed the details of the attack which they had been warned they were very shortly to carry into practice. February 27th found the Battalion in Hardecourt, whence on the 28th at 5.45 a.m. it moved to the attack of Potsdam Trench and Palz Trench east of Sailly-Saillisel.

* Sir Douglas Haig's despatch of May 31st, 1917.

Lieut.-Colonel Nelson had gone home on leave early this month, having been in indifferent health all through a very trying winter, and the Battalion was at this time commanded by Major Clarke, from whose report the following account of the attack is drawn. The actual fighting strength of the Battalion this day was only 15 officers and 270 other ranks :—

"Previous to zero hour all the men got out of their trenches and lay on the forward parapet. On our artillery barrage falling all went forward. The line moved forward to the tape stretched out in No Man's Land, but struck this tape at an angle, and pushing on into our barrage did not correct its alignment. The whole line, from the Royal Fusiliers to the Lancashire Fusiliers, appears to have moved rather too much to its left, and struck its objectives rather to the left of where they should have been. The barrage lifted, and the first objective, 'Potsdam Trench,' was taken and occupied by moppers-up of the 16th Middlesex. A few Germans in it rushed out with hands uplifted and surrendered.

"The line advanced again, following the barrage, and arrived opposite the second objective, and then lay down outside the trench waiting for our barrage to lift, which it did not do for some time. The barrage at length lifted, and the line sprang forward into 'Palz Trench' through gaps in the enemy's wire E. and W. of 'Weimar' and 'Palz Trenches.' Many casualties had by now been caused by :—

(1) Our own barrage;
(2) Hostile machine guns from front and left flank.

"As the men on the left, where the going was bad, had not yet come up, those in 'Palz Trench,' headed by Lieutenant Tweedy and Lieutenant McFeely, turned up it to their left, where the enemy was encountered, and a fierce fight was carried out with bombs, rifles, and revolvers; the Lewis guns were choked with mud, and at first could not be used. Lieutenant Tweedy, who had showed conspicuous coolness and had accounted for some of the enemy, knocking down with his fist a German just about to throw a bomb, was here killed.

AMMUNITION UNDER CHURCH, LE NEUVILLE.

TANKS GOING THROUGH MEAULTE, CAPTURED BY US ON
AUGUST 23rd, 1918.

"After bombing the enemy back for about 15 yards no further progress could be made, but the position was maintained by firing down the trench until the Lewis guns were cleaned and bombs had been collected. Then, assisted by Lieutenant Gun-Cuninghame, who throughout the operations handled his company with great skill and gallantry, Lieutenant McFeely attacked again and bombed the enemy back for about another 50 yards. The trench bottom was now impassable for attack, being 18 inches deep in mud, while enemy snipers also commanded it from a sap running to the enemy's rear, and casualties were numerous. A block was accordingly made, and in the meantime 'Weimar Trench' was found to be unoccupied, full of water and blocked.

"The left company attacking 'Palz Trench' suffered from the heavy going, and was unable to keep up with the barrage, which got right ahead of them. Captain Bagley appears to have reached the trench on the right and in front of his men. He jumped into it and shot one of the enemy, but now noticed that his men were to his left standing just outside the German wire, apparently uncertain whether they had not over-shot their objective. Captain Bagley could not make them hear him, so rushed over and brought them towards 'Palz Trench.' By this time hostile machine guns were causing casualties, and on reaching the enemy wire our men were heavily bombed from the trench and could not get through the wire, which here was almost intact. Their bombs being exhausted and the German fire becoming heavier, Captain Bagley and his men were obliged to go back to 'Potsdam Trench.'

"No more bombs were here obtainable, three of the Lewis guns had been lost, and their detachments were killed or wounded, while the carrying waves had suffered heavily and had dumped their material outside 'Palz Trench.' Captain Bagley had lost all his officers, and could only find about twelve men of his company, so he made a strong point where he was, assisted by as many moppers-up as he could collect.

"Meanwhile a mixed body of Lancashire Fusiliers and

Dublins had entered the right communication trench and started bombing up it till held up by the enemy, who ran down it. Our men then held on, occupying their left objective and eventually both trenches."

Conflicting reports of what had happened had reached Battalion headquarters, so Second-Lieutenant McKenzie was sent out to ascertain the exact situation, and from his report it seemed that the strong point occupied by Captain Bagley must be held to prevent the enemy from cutting in between the Royal Dublin Fusiliers in " Palz Trench " and the Lancashire men in " Potsdam Trench." At 11.30 a.m. such moppers-up as could then be collected and spared were sent to join Gun-Cuninghame, and so the situation remained during the next thirty-six hours.

" At 2.55 p.m. a German bombing attack on the right caused the Royal Fusiliers to retire down the communication trench at the junction of the Dublins and Royal Fusiliers in ' Palz Trench,' and instructions were sent by telephone to Lieutenant Gun-Cuninghame to give the Royal Fusiliers all possible help in bombs, rifle grenades, Lewis guns and material of all kinds. This was done, and the attack was held in front, but the effect of it was to expose both flanks of ' W ' Company of the ' Blue Caps,' and both Gun-Cuninghame and McFeely reported that they feared they could hardly withstand a night attack, and that they considered a withdrawal necessary. They were, however, ordered to hang on at all costs; every available man was sent forward with stores, additional Lewis guns were sent up from Battalion headquarters, a protective barrage was asked for, as also reinforcements, for the O.C. Royal Fusiliers stated that he had only 125 men now left.

" At 7 p.m. there was an intense German bombardment and our barrage came down, but though no enemy attack developed bombardments continued at intervals all night."

On March 1st about noon two German aeroplanes came over and appeared to signal to the German artillery, which opened a very heavy fire on the British trenches and rearward communications, but on the early morning of the 2nd the Battalion was finally relieved and proceeded to Ville-sur-Corbie, which was reached at 6 p.m. on the 3rd.

The ground passed over during these operations had been so churned up by shell-fire that after the winter rains it was knee-deep in slimy mud, and the rate of advance of troops in the attack on the trenches varied from two to four minutes to the hundred yards, while the rate of the artillery supporting barrage was for this reason fixed at ten minutes to the hundred yards.

During these operations the casualties in the Battalion amounted to :—Killed, 4 officers (Lieutenant Tweedy, Second-Lieutenants Green, Mooney and Gradwell) and 22 other ranks; wounded, 3 officers (Lieutenants O'Carroll, Dunne and Burroughs, died of wounds) and 88 non-commissioned officers and men; and missing, 1 officer (Second-Lieutenant Kent) and 29 men, of whom 10 were known to be wounded.

Of the "wonderful gallantry" during these days of the Battalion stretcher-bearers, Captain Kelly, R.A.M.C., the Medical officer, writes in glowing terms :—" As my dressing station was some distance from headquarters I was given an orderly named Macintosh to keep in touch. On one of his perilous journeys Macintosh saw two men badly wounded in a shell-hole. He volunteered to go and get them, and he and my servant, Campbell, and I proceeded to the place. No sooner had we three left the old front line than a machine gun opened fire. Campbell and I were going very cautiously, but Macintosh cried out, 'Come on, that's only an old machine gun; he can't hit anything.' We got the two men, one of whom, with wounds in both legs, was nearly drowned in a shell-hole, and got them to safety. Not satisfied with this Macintosh advanced to the new front line, and soon came back to say there was a wounded man lying on the wire. At this point the Germans were only a few yards away. I forbade Macintosh to go out of the trench, but when my back was turned he jumped out, and when I looked over the parapet again he was lying dead over the wounded man, who was also by this time dead."

The following congratulatory messages were received by the G.O.C. 29th Division; from the Commander-in-Chief :—

"*Congratulate 29th Division on success of minor operations carried out on morning of February 28th.*"

From the General Officer Commanding the Fourth Army :—

"*Please convey to 29th Division, and especially to 86th Brigade, my congratulations on their successful attack yesterday. The tenacity in holding on to ' Potsdam Trench ' and the efficient support of the artillery are deserving of high praise. The plan of attack was well conceived by the Divisional Commander and Staff, and very gallantly executed by the 1st Royal Dublin Fusiliers and 2nd Royal Fusiliers.*"

From the Commander of the XIVth Corps, with which the Division was serving :—

"*Please convey to 86th Brigade my hearty congratulations and thanks for grit and tenacity during a trying day. The capture of ' Potsdam Trench ' was quite up to Gallipoli form. It is of the utmost importance, and I know the 86th Brigade will hold and keep it. Artillery support and barrage quite admirable.*"

The Battalion now had a succession of moves, consequent on the transfer of the 29th Division from the XIVth Corps of the Fourth Army to the XVIIIth Corps (Maxse) of the Third Army (Allenby), and to the region of Arras.

At this time the Third Army contained the VIth, VIIth, XVIIth and XVIIIth Corps, while the XVIIIth Corps was composed of the 17th, 29th, 33rd and 50th Divisions.

As a result the Battalion marched from Ville-sur-Corbie on March 20th and proceeded from there to Mericourt, thence to Belloy St. Léon; from there on the 29th to Soues, then to Halloy, and from there via Longuevillette, Beaurepaire, Beaudricourt, Bavincourt and Simoncourt in very heavy snow to Arras, which was reached on April 12th. Here the Battalion occupied quarters in the Citadelle, but was greeted with orders to move up into the line next morning, leaving behind ten per cent. of officers and men for reinforcing purposes.

[Photo, Imperial War Museum.

HOTEL DE VILLE, ARRAS.

THE BATTLE OF FLANDERS. SCENE ON THE BATTLEFIELD, ST. JEAN.
JULY 31st, 1917.

BATTLE OF ARRAS

Battle of Arras.

The Battle of Arras, which raged from April 9th to 23rd, and in which the 29th Division had been called to take a hand, was the result of a wide advance now intended by the British on a front of more than 12 miles, from Lens in the north to Arras in the south. Here very many guns had been collected, and four corps were waiting for the signal to advance—three corps of Allenby's Army and one of the First Army, now under Horne. Maxse's XVIIIth Corps was in reserve in rear of the Third Army. There was hard fighting from April 9th to 12th, by which latter date the British had captured Vimy Ridge and the village of Monchy-le-Preux, but the losses had not been inconsiderable, and on the evening of the 12th one of the divisions of the VIth Corps in the immediate front of Maxse's was drawn out and replaced by the 29th Division, and on the 13th this portion of the front was held by two divisions only, the 29th to the south and the 17th to the north, covering the whole broad area from the north of the Cojeul River to the south of the Scarpe.

During the next few days the Royal Dublin Fusiliers were constantly in the firing line, and supplied large parties daily, when, for brief periods, they were withdrawn, for consolidating the position and digging communication and other trenches. The position was almost incessantly shelled by the enemy, and even in Monchy it was found to be very dangerous to move about above ground, and by the 23rd the casualties incurred amounted to 16 non-commissioned officers and men killed, 4 officers (Captain Lanigan-O'Keeffe, Second-Lieutenants Baker, Kidson and Devoy) and 60 other ranks wounded, while 2 men were missing. But on the very next day still heavier losses were experienced. On the night of the 23rd orders had been issued for a general attack on the following evening. These were, however, cancelled later, but the Battalion was ordered to assault a certain hill at 4 p.m. However, owing to the brigade runner losing his way the orders as to a change in the time of barrage did not arrive, and the two companies detailed—'W' and 'X' of the Battalion—attacked with very great gallantry, unsupported by our guns. They were met by very heavy shell, machine-gun and rifle fire, and the attack failed, the companies being at last compelled to fall back on the original front line. Second-Lieutenant E. A. Byrne and 18 other ranks were killed; Lieutenants Tooth and Barry, Second-Lieutenants Rogers, Reilly and Hegarty and 98 non-commissioned officers and men were wounded, while 14 other ranks were missing.

The 12th Division now resumed its place in the line, relieving the 29th, which was withdrawn to behind Arras, the Dublins going until the end of the month of April to billets at Souastre and Gouy-en-Artois. For some weeks now the Battalion was not engaged in operations of any real magnitude, but during the latter part of May a good many casualties were incurred, between May 21st and June 1st 12 men being killed or died of wounds, while Lieutenant Gun-Cuninghame, Second-Lieutenants Hernon and Jones-Nowlan and 35 non-commissioned officers and men were wounded. The Battalion remained in the Arras area until June 3rd, when it proceeded by rail and march route to Pernois, where it was engaged in training of all kinds, remaining here until June 27th.

'At the end of June the 29th Division, now once more in the XIVth (Cavan's) Corps, was moved up to the north in readiness to take part in the great new attack projected against the ridges which dominate the region of Ypres from the north and north-east. The success of Messines had already relieved the pressure on the south of the great salient, and it was hoped that a similar flattening-out in the north would have the effect of advancing the British line towards Bruges, since the occupation of this town by the Allies would involve the abandonment by Germany of the Flemish coast.

"The British line of battle was formed by five corps, the XIVth (Cavan) to the north, the XVIIIth (Maxse) upon its right, the XIXth (Watts) upon the right of that, the IInd (Jacob) came next, and then upon the southern edge of the area, and hardly engaged in the main fighting, was the Xth (Morland). Each corps had two divisions in the line and two in reserve. . . . It should be noted that the four first corps made up Gough's Fifth Army, and that the Xth Corps was the only part of Plumer's Army to be engaged. . . . Cavan's XIVth Corps was next to the French, with the Guards in immediate touch with our Allies, and the 38th Welsh Division upon its right. The 20th and 29th Divisions were in support." *

Battle of Ypres, 1917. The Third Battle of Ypres, which is the official name of the operations in which the 29th Division was now to play its part, did not actually commence until July 31st, and as already stated the 29th Division was not at the outset in the forefront of the battle; but already before the date mentioned the 1st Battalion Royal Dublin Fusiliers had suffered no inconsiderable losses, with the result that while on moving into this area the strength of the Battalion was 47 officers and 935 other ranks, this had fallen by death, wounds and sickness to 40 officers and 855 non-commissioned officers and men when the battle opened. The actual casualties caused by the enemy in July amounted to 1 officer (Lieutenant Ridley) and 13 other ranks killed, 1 officer (Second-Lieutenant Blake) and 29 other ranks wounded.

At the outset of the battle the Battalion was not required, and it remained until August 6th in Forrest Area Camp 13, experiencing very wet weather, but taking no active part in the operations. At 8.30 on the evening of this day, however, it moved up by White Hope Corner and Boesinghe Pontoon, and relieved the 4th Battalion Grenadier Guards in the left sector. The Battalion headquarters was at Saules Farm, the disposition of the companies being:—" W " at Saules Farm, " X " Company, one platoon at Abri Farm, half-platoon Major's Farm, one platoon and a half Blue Line, and " Y " Company the Blue Line. The Dublins remained in the front line until 1.30 a.m. on the 10th, exposed during these days to very heavy shelling, but managing to push out and establish several posts on the E. bank

* Conan Doyle, Vol. IV, pp. 137, 138.

of the Steenbeck. When at last relieved by the 16th Battalion Middlesex Regiment the losses were found to have totalled 42, of whom 4 were killed or died of wounds, while 1 man was reported missing.

Until the evening of the 15th the Royal Dublin Fusiliers remained in a tolerably comfortable camp at De Witte Cross Roads, reorganizing the companies and enjoying a brief period of rest and shelter from the rain. But " the ground was still very wet and the conditions deplorable, but the advance must be continued at all costs if the preparations were not to be thrown away and winter to find us still within the old pent-house of Ypres. By the end of the second week in August the higher ground was beginning to dry, though the bogs in between were already hardly passable. One more fortnight would be invaluable, but Sir Douglas could not afford to waste another day. Upon August 16th the advance was resumed . . . after the usual heavy bombardment the attack began at 4.45 in the morning. . . ."

" The front of Cavan's XIVth Corps was formed by the grand old 29th Division upon the left, and the 20th Light Division, the heroes of many fights, upon the right. Both divisions lived up to their highest that day, which means that many a brave man died at his highest to carry on the record. . . . The advance of the 29th Division was begun by crossing in the early dawn the bridges thrown over the Steenbeck. Starting from the line of the stream the advanced mud-beplastered lines, extending as they crossed country, coalescing as they concentrated upon any obstacle, moved swiftly forwards to their objectives, which were taken in their entirety. Passerelle Farm was carried by the veterans of the 29th, and so was Martin's Mill upon the right, many prisoners being sent to the rear. Another heave took them across the grass-grown lines of the abandoned railway, and on into the hamlet of Wijdendrift, the line being established well to the N.E. of that place." *

In this attack by the 29th Division the 87th and 88th Brigades

* Conan Doyle, Vol. IV, pp. 162-164.

formed the firing line, the 86th Brigade and the 1st Battalion Inniskilling Fusiliers being in reserve, but at night the "Blue Caps" moved up to the front line in relief of the 4th Worcesters, who were engaged in consolidating the third objective. The 17th, so the Battalion diary tells us, was a "fairly quiet day, though the four companies in the front line have casualties. 'X' Company fire on enemy patrol of three, who surrender; they belong to the 119th Infantry Regiment, 26th Division. Second-Lieutenant Hawtrey, on patrol, meets an enemy patrol of three, fires on them, two escape, one surrenders; another of the enemy leaves his lines and surrenders to 'X' Company."

The Battalion remained in the front line until the night of the 20th, sustaining very heavy enemy shell fire, but working hard on the consolidation of the trenches and patrolling the Broembeck River, with a view of setting up bridgeheads; but no crossing could then be effected as existing bridges had been destroyed by gun-fire. On relief by the Newfoundland Regiment the Battalion withdrew to camp near Elverdinghe, when the casualties during the operations of the 16th to 20th were found to be as follows:— Killed or died of wounds, 20 non-commissioned officers and men; wounded, 58. The Battalion was not further engaged in the month of August, during which it had had some 120 of all ranks killed and wounded, and the following letter from the Colonel of the Regiment, though received some weeks later, may well here be quoted as showing how closely friends at home were following the doings of the Regiment:—

"*I am indeed deeply grieved at the very heavy losses sustained by your Battalion, which have been brought to my notice from a Casualty List sent to me by the Officer in Charge of Records of the Royal Dublin Fusiliers, from August 5th to 31st, 1917, received this morning. Kindly convey to all ranks my sincere sympathy and very high appreciation of their splendid gallantry and devotion to duty, maintaining in such a brilliant manner the great traditions of our grand old Regiment. Bravo the 'Blue Caps!' Every good wish to you all.*"

During the latter part of September Brigadier-General Jelf, the commander of the 86th Brigade, had been ill, and Lieut.-Colonel Nelson had taken his place from the 16th to the 23rd, during which time Major Clarke again took charge of the Battalion. On September 24th Brigadier-General G. R. H. Cheape, M.C., was appointed to command the 86th Brigade, and on the 27th Lieut.-Colonel Nelson assumed that of the 88th Brigade, when Major Moore again commanded the Battalion.

During the month of September the Battalion was not seriously engaged, though in the last few days it sustained some 14 casualties, 1 man being killed. The Battle of Ypres of this year had not yet come to an end, and on the 20th of this month the British had made a fresh attack between Langemaarke and Hollebeck, but while the XIVth Corps still held the extreme north of the British line neither they nor the French on their left were really engaged in the advance. This corps covered the front as far as Schreiboom.

Then on October 4th the corps on the right attacked, one battalion of the 29th Division being ordered to co-operate. The 1st Battalion Royal Dublin Fusiliers had received instructions ere this to join the 16th (South Irish) Division, which found itself unable to maintain its strength without absorbing all other Irish units. Hearing of this single-battalion attack the "Blue Caps" sent a deputation to the divisional commander requesting permission to make one more attack for the honour of the 29th Division, which all ranks were so grieved to leave. This request was granted, and the account of the part played by the Battalion may here be given as recorded in the official narrative.

On the night of October 3rd-4th the Dublins relieved the 16th Middlesex in the right sector of the divisional front; the two leading companies for the assault—" Y " on the right and " Z " on the left—moved into Eagle Trench and put out covering posts. The section of the Trench Mortar Battery formed up in rear of " Y " Company, and in rear of that again was a flanking detachment of the Middlesex; " W " Company in support and " X " in

[Photo, Mora, Southsea.

10605 SERGEANT J. OCKENDEN, V.C.
1ST BN. ROYAL DUBLIN FUSILIERS.

reserve were behind one another in shell-holes to the left rear of the Trench Mortar Battery.

The companies moved forward very quietly and relieved the Middlesex Regiment, tools and battle stores were noiselessly issued, and the early hours of the 4th passed without enemy movement, the shelling becoming slightly more heavy at 5 a.m. One hour before zero all was ready, and on our barrage coming down in great accuracy and volume the leading companies left their positions and moved in lines of sections as close under the barrage as possible.

"W" Company was the first to report the capture of its objective and "Z" seized both its objectives, capturing 2 machine guns and 31 prisoners, as well as 20 others in shell-holes, but part of the company came under very heavy machine-gun fire from across the Broembeck. No report came in from "Y" Company, all the officers and the sergeant-major of which had become casualties, but it was found to be on its objective and in touch with the leading battalion of the 4th Division. As a matter of fact, the Battalion was the only unit engaged which reached its objective and maintained itself there, and as one of the men of the Battalion put it in a letter home when writing to his wife of the success of the "Blue Caps" attack, "We went through them like the way the Divil went through Athlone—in standing jumps!"

The Germans delivered a rather half-hearted counter-attack, but this was easily beaten off, and by the afternoon the companies of the Dublins had dug themselves in so well that though under tolerably heavy shelling they escaped excessive casualties.

Lieut.-General Sir H. de Lisle writes: "Sergeant Ockenden, who won his V.C. on this occasion, performed a very sensational act. He was officiating as company sergeant-major that day; seeing a platoon officer hit and the advance stopped by a machine gun, he charged it from a flank, killing all the detachment but one, who ran away. He chased this man across the whole front of the Battalion and bayoneted him, and in spite of the bullets the whole Battalion rose up and cheered him. Later in the day he attacked a farm, killing four of the enemy himself and accepting the surrender of sixteen others."

The official account of the act which won the Victoria Cross for No. 10605 Sergeant James Ockenden is given as follows in the *London Gazette* of November 8th, 1917, Supplement No. 30372 :—
"In the attack on the morning of October 4th, 1917, east of Langemaarke (Flanders), Sergeant James Ockenden was acting company sergeant-major. Noticing the right platoon held up by an enemy machine gun which was causing many casualties he, with absolute disregard for his personal safety, immediately rushed the gun, killed two of the gunners and followed and killed the third who was making his escape across No Man's Land. He then led a party to the attack on T. Gord Tervestern Farm. This party was heavily fired on as it advanced. Sergeant Ockenden dashed ahead and called upon the garrison to surrender. They, however, continued to fire, and with great boldness Sergeant Ockenden then opened fire himself. Having killed four of the enemy he forced the remaining sixteen to surrender. During the remainder of the day Sergeant Ockenden displayed the greatest gallantry, making many dangerous patrols and bringing back most valuable information as to the disposition and intentions of the enemy."

The night of the 4th-5th was calm, and the next morning was clear with considerable enemy aerial activity. By midday the German fire from the Broembeck—guns, machine guns and rifles—was heavy, but the companies succeeded in pushing posts well out towards the river so as to maintain better observation of the movements of the Germans.

During the night of the 5th-6th there was again heavy enemy gun-fire, and, owing to the relieving battalion not knowing the locality and the guides losing their way, the relief was not completed until 2 a.m. on the 6th when the "Blue Caps" withdrew to Eton Camp, "arriving in very good spirits."

On this day General de Lisle visited Battalion headquarters to express in person his congratulations on the great success of the operations, in the course of which many gallant deeds were done and brought to notice. Second-Lieutenant Devoy was wounded, but refused to go to hospital and remained with his company, while another subaltern, Second-Lieutenant Wallis, who was officer in charge of "dumps," was rendered unconscious by a shell-burst at 1 a.m. on the 4th, and remained so until found at 10 a.m., "not reported as casualty as he remained with unit."

The following were the losses in the Battalion:—Killed, Second-Lieutenants A. H. Allen and A. J. McCann and 30 other ranks; wounded, Acting-Captain McIntyre, Second-Lieutenants Smith, Seale, Hastings, Johnston and O'Carroll, and 127 non-commissioned officers and men, while 17 men were missing. Of Seale's wound Captain Devoy has a curious story to tell illustrating the complex character of the Hun:—"When I went back to have a wound dressed I found Seale lying in a shell-hole badly hit through an artery high up in the leg. Lying beside him was a young Boche, scarcely more than a boy, holding the severed ends of the artery tightly with his half-frozen fingers, which were blue with the cold. . . . He undoubtedly saved Seale's life."

The Divisional Commander received the following message from Lieutenant-General Lord Cavan, commanding XIVth Corps: *"My heartiest thanks and congratulations to you and all ranks. A very fine finish to your noble work in Flanders."*

The time had now come for the 1st Battalion Royal Dublin Fusiliers to leave the 86th Brigade and the 29th Division in which they had served since arrival in England from India on the outbreak of the war, with which they had seen such hard fighting, sustained so many losses, and had added so greatly to the high character which during so long a period the "Blue Caps" had maintained. On October 15th Brigadier-General Cheape took leave of the Battalion in a very complimentary speech, and on the 18th, when in camp at Beaumetze, the Dublins were inspected for the last time by General de Lisle, who, in bidding them farewell, called out all the officers of the Battalion, thanked them for the good work of the Regiment during the two and a half years it had served with the 29th Division, and expressed his deep regret at losing so fine a Battalion.

Only two of the original battalions now remained in the 86th Brigade, the 2nd Royal Fusiliers and the 1st Lancashire Fusiliers, and from both of these the kindliest messages were received. From the first-named regiment:—" We all most sincerely regret your leaving the brigade, and wish you the best of luck and glory "; while the O.C. the last-named corps wrote:—" Just a line to wish you all, on behalf of the regiment, the best of good fortune in your new division, and to tell you how much we regret your departure. Hoping to meet you again in the near future."

Played out by the bands of these battalions the " Blue Caps " marched from Beaumetze on the morning of October 19th and arrived the same evening at Armagh Camp in the Croisilles area, some 10 miles S.E. of Arras, and here joined the 48th Brigade.

CHAPTER V

The Last Year of the Great War.

FIRST BATTLES OF THE SOMME, 1918—THE BATTLE OF THE LYS.

THE 16th (South Irish) Division was at this time commanded by Major-General W. B. Hickie, C.B., and contained the 47th, 48th and 49th Brigades. It was then in the VIth Corps (Haldane), which, with three other corps, the IVth, Vth and XVIIth, formed the Third Army, under General Byng, and the VIth Corps was now holding a front from Monchy to rather beyond Bullecourt. The commander of the 48th Brigade was Brigadier-General F. W. Ramsay, C.M.G., D.S.O., and the Brigade consisted of the 1st, 2nd, 8th, 9th and 10th Battalions of the Royal Dublin Fusiliers.

The 1st Battalion reached its new unit at a strength of 32 officers and 812 other ranks, but within the next few days several officers joined, some on appointment, others in consequence of the amalgamation of the 8th and 9th Service Battalions of the Royal Dublin Fusiliers, so that by October 31st the strength of the 1st Battalion in officers was as high as 52, while that of other ranks was 823. The following were the officers who on this day appear to have been present at headquarters:—Lieut.-Colonel A. Moore, D.S.O., in command; Major W. T. Rigg; Captains W. P. Oulton, M.C., J. C. Bonnar, G. H. Chandler, M.C., P. J. Shears, G. E. Cowley, J. Devoy, and A. C. Lendrum; Lieutenants A. M. Kneafsey, L. A. King, W. B. St. G. Cameron, W. E. Caldbeck, W. Kee, M.C., and G. G. T. Browne; Second-Lieutenants D. P. Wagner, M.C., P. Laffan, M.C., G. H. Noblett, D. W. Wallis, W. F. Spiess, M. Layton, B. Ward, S. G. Crawford, J. St. J. G. Ervine, D. Mackillop, J. F. Williamson, T. Bedell-Sivright, J. J. Gyves, J. E. Johnston, R. S. Boles, D. W. Harris, R. H. Howell, A. Tumility, G. P. G.

Crawford, R. H. Burns, P. McCarthy, W. A. McWilliam, G. B. Barre, H. Burns, and E. W. Jackson; Acting Captain R. Maguire, M.C., adjutant; Lieutenant T. J. Considine, assistant adjutant; and Captain J. A. Clarke, quartermaster.

At the end of the month of October the distribution of officers by companies appears to have been as under:—

"*W*" *Company.*—Captains Oulton, Cowley and Shears; Lieutenants Cameron and Browne; Second-Lieutenants Wagner, Layton, Sidwell, Somers, Mackillop, Gyves, Howell and McWilliam.

"*X*" *Company.*—Captains Lendrum and Holman; Lieutenants Kneafsey and Kee; Second-Lieutenants Wallis, Ward, Spiess (Intelligence Officer), Laffan (Signalling Officer), Boles, Barre, H. Burns and Jackson.

"*Y*" *Company.*—Acting Captain Bonnar; Lieutenants Letchworth, Caldbeck and King (Lewis Gun Officer); Second-Lieutenants Bedell-Sivright, S. G. Crawford, Williamson, Johnston and R. H. Burns.

"*Z*" *Company.*—Captains Chandler and Devoy; Second-Lieutenants Walker, Noblett, Ervine, Harris, Tumility, G. P. G. Crawford and McCarthy.

During the month of October the 1st Battalion Royal Dublin Fusiliers remained quietly at Armagh Camp, engaged in battalion training, and was inspected by its new brigadier and divisional commander; but on the morning of November 1st it moved off and relieved the 2nd Battalion Royal Irish Regiment as right support in the sunken road about Croisilles, sending out working parties to the front, which were for the most part engaged in wiring the position held. Then on the 7th the Battalion relieved the 2nd Battalion of the Regiment in the right sub-section of the front line N.E. of Croisilles, "W" Company being on the right, "Y" in the centre, and "Z" on the left, with "X" Company in support.

On the night of the 9th-10th various patrols were sent out from the British lines, but Lieutenant Tumility and Sergeant Fenton, who had gone out from "Z" Company, failed to return, and two days later it was learnt that they had been surrounded by an enemy patrol, when Lieutenant Tumility had been killed and the sergeant wounded and taken prisoner.

By the 19th the "Blue Caps" had been again withdrawn, and were in rear at Railway Support, and on the next day took part, with the 16th Division, in an assault which was delivered in conjunction with some larger operations undertaken by the Third Army. The task allotted to the 16th Division was to carry out an attack on Dovis Tunnel and Tunnel Support trenches, the 47th Brigade being on the right, the 48th in the centre, and the 49th on the left. The order of attack by the 48th Brigade was as under :—On the right was the 10th, on the left the 2nd, and in support was the 1st Battalion Royal Dublin Fusiliers, the reserve at Ervillers being composed of the 8th/9th Battalion of the Regiment. Zero hour was 6.20 a.m. Battalion headquarters of the 1st Battalion, with "Y" and "Z" Companies, was in Railway reserve, while "W" and "X" were under cover adjacent to and immediately S.W. of Lincoln Support.

The orders issued to the Battalion directed that at zero hour "X" Company, with "W" in rear, was to move forward behind any infantry assembled in "Lincoln Trench" until the latter had taken up their positions in the front line, after which they were to follow the assaulting troops, collecting the wire *en route*. On the wiring material being dumped in forward position, "W" Company was to move back to company lines, the O.C. Company having previously satisfied himself that "X" Company did not need assistance in completing its task. On the wiring being completed "X" was to withdraw to Tunnel Support after reporting to the O.C. 2nd and 10th Battalions.

The Brigade assaulted with admirable dash and secured all objectives. "X" Company, under command of Captain Lendrum, followed closely behind the leading waves, and with remarkable rapidity put up a double belt of concertina barbed wire along the whole brigade front. "W" Company, under Captain Oulton, worked splendidly, making repeated journeys backwards and forwards from and to the captured position with wire for " X " Company. The G.O.C. Brigade expressed his entire satisfaction with the work done by the Battalion, and made very complimentary reference to the excellence of the wiring carried out by the two companies of the Battalion.

The 16th Division secured in all 670 unwounded prisoners, and caused very considerable loss to the enemy. The casualties in the Battalion were unusually light. Second-Lieutenant B. Ward, " X " Company, who behaved very gallantly, was killed, having been previously wounded in the wrist but carried on; Corporal Wall, D.C.M., of " X " Company, was also killed, while Captains Oulton and Lendrum, Second-Lieutenant McWilliam and 4 other ranks were wounded.

Before the end of the month of November Lieutenant Bedell-Sivright and 8 men were wounded.

On December 1st the Battalion was up again in the front line, headquarters in Hindenburg Tunnel, described as "quite a wonderful work about 40 feet deep and lit by electric light." On the next day, at 2 a.m., the enemy made a very successful raid on a post held by a small party of " X " Company. The post was at the end of a T sap, and the Germans must have got in behind the garrison. By blood and bits of clothing it would appear that the enemy must have suffered some casualties, but one non-commissioned officer and 4 men of the Battalion were missing. On patrols moving out no trace could be found of the raiders; two men of the post who at the time were off duty and were sleeping in a shelter beside the post heard nothing, and the only thing noticed by posts a short distance away on either flank was a shout of " Stand to." An officer had visited the post at 10 minutes to 2, when he found everything quiet.

The Battle of Cambrai had been raging since November 20th, and had at the outset resulted in considerable successes to the British, but by degrees the enemy had brought up new divisions and had grown so strong that by the end of the month the initiative had passed to the Germans, and there were everywhere signs that a great counter-offensive was about to be launched. This was eventually delivered on November 30th, with the unfortunate result that three British divisions had experienced very serious losses, while we had been obliged to withdraw from certain positions we had captured and held north of the Flesquières Ridge. The event was not without its effect upon units occupying other portions of the long line, and early in December the 16th Division was at short notice moved to the neighbourhood of Epéhy.

From Armagh Camp the Battalion marched to Rocquigny, where the Dublin Fusiliers Brigade found itself in camp together; next day, on receipt of urgent orders, the march was renewed to Templeur-la-Fosse, where the Battalion "embussed" and arrived very early on the morning of December 4th at St. Emilie. This was left again on the 11th for Hamel, and Hamel on the 17th by road and rail for Epéhy—"the weather very cold, ground covered with snow, some cases of frost-bite."

The 16th Division was now in the VIIth Corps, under General Congreve, this corps being the northern-most unit of Gough's Fifth Army.

Christmas Day, 1917, was passed by the Battalion in the front line, for on December 23rd it moved into brigade support, the headquarters being accommodated in cellars in the village of Lempire, and the companies being distributed as follows:—"W" Company in Malassise Farm and Old Copse, "X" Company in Lempire village, Enfer Wood and May Copse, "Y" Company in old "Support Trench," and "Z" Company in the sunken road near Battalion headquarters. Here all ranks were under very heavy shelling by the enemy of the forward and back areas, 2 men being killed on the 26th by a high explosive shell, while the weather was very cold, sleet or snow falling nearly every day that the Dublins were up in the line.

On December 29th the Battalion was relieved, and moved back to Villers Faucon, the accommodation here being Nissen huts for the officers and Adrian huts for non-commissioned officers and men, while Battalion headquarters were in one of the few houses left standing in the village.

During the latter part of this month Major Rigg had been in command owing to the absence on leave of Lieut.-Colonel Moore, but on the 27th Major Rigg proceeded to England to attend the Senior Officers' Course, and Major J. P. Hunt, 8/9th Battalion Royal Dublin Fusiliers, assumed temporary command.

1918 Christmas Day was celebrated on January 1st, 1918. The Battalion remained on this part of the front for some weeks, but as early as the middle of February persistent rumours began to circulate that the Germans were projecting an attack in force, though for some considerable time there did not seem to be any real foundation for such reports, since our patrols sent out to endeavour to secure prisoners for identification purposes could not establish any serious reinforcement of the enemy forces in the immediate front.

Later in the month, however, the Germans began to display a slightly increased activity, and on the early morning of the 23rd, when the Battalion was again up in the line, with its headquarters in "Sandbag Alley," the morning being dull and visibility indifferent, the enemy in force attempted to raid "Heythrop Post." They were, however, detected by a listening post of "X" Company, fire was opened upon them, and after a short engagement they were dispersed without reaching our trenches. The Dublins had 2 men killed and 2 wounded.

On the next morning, just before dawn, a patrol of "W" Company, under Second-Lieutenant Cox, met two of the enemy in No Man's Land—both Germans were wounded, but while one made his escape the other was captured in a dying condition, and valuable identification was secured.

For some little time past the great and increasing drain upon the man-power of the nation had been causing very considerable anxiety to the authorities, military and political, and it was finally resolved to effect a reorganization of the divisions of the British Army in France. This reorganization was completed during the month of February, 1918, the number of battalions in a division was reduced from 13 to 10, and the number of battalions in each brigade from 4 to 3. The effect of this reorganization upon the 16th Division was that the 8/9th and 10th Battalions Royal Dublin Fusiliers were practically disbanded and taken out of the division, and that the 48th Brigade was now composed of the 2nd Battalion Royal Munster Fusiliers—transferred from the 1st Division—and the 1st and 2nd Battalions of the Royal Dublin Fusiliers.

During the first fortnight of March there were many raids and counter-raids, those carried out by the British having the object of obtaining identifications of the new German divisions said to be moving up, while those by the enemy were no doubt undertaken with a view to restraining the inconvenient activities of the British. But it was by this time abundantly evident that the Germans were preparing for an offensive on a large scale, and that the attack was intended to fall upon that portion of the British front held by the Third and Fifth Armies, which were approximately of equal strength, each having 12 divisions in the line or in immediate support. This front was a long curve of some 50 miles from Arras in the north down to Barisis, 8 miles south of La Fère, and was strongly fortified throughout its length, but was the stronger in the north, which our troops had occupied for the longer period of time. In the southern sector the defence had less depth, but work had for some time past been carried out upon it, and by the end of the third week in March this part of the front was at least as well prepared as the number of men available would permit.

There were here not enough troops to man continuous lines of trenches; but under the system adopted there was an *advanced zone*—a thin line of infantry supported by numerous strong posts composed of infantry and machine guns; 1,000 yards in rear was the *battle zone*, where lay the main body of the infantry behind barbed wire and supported by isolated forts; and 2,000 yards in rear another zone was under preparation, but was not as yet completed. Behind the whole position in the south was the great bend of the Somme, which was also being organized as a reserve position, but this was equally incomplete.

On March 20th, in face of this 50 miles of British front held by 24 divisions or 200,000 British soldiers, there lay a German *first line* of 60 divisions or 500,000 infantry, and, further, while the Germans held another 30 divisions in immediate support, the British reserves, particularly as regards the Fifth or Southern Army, were few and distant. Finally, the German guns were here more than twice as numerous as those at the disposal of General Sir Hubert Gough.

The War Diary for March 20th of the 1st Battalion Royal Dublin Fusiliers contains the significant statement: " Enemy attack is expected any day now. It is now stated to be certain, although on many previous occasions it was given out that it was about to take place."

At this time the front of the VIIth Corps—14,000 yards—" went southward from a point about half a mile north of Gouzeaucourt, at the top of a hill about 400 yards west of Gonnelieu, through Gauche Wood to Vaucelette Farm, then south-eastward to Epéhy and Ronssoy. A few hundred yards south of Ronssoy the 16th (South Irish) Division, VIIth Corps, joined the 66th Division, XIXth Corps. Congreve had 3 divisions in line, the 9th, first under General Tudor, then under General Blacklock; the 21st, under General Campbell; and the 16th, under General Sir Amyatt Hull.* Reserves, 39th Division, under General Feetham."†

On the night of March 20th-21st the Battalion was holding the centre sub-section of the 48th Brigade front. Roughly, the front of the 1st Battalion Royal Dublin Fusiliers was from Malassise Farm exclusive to May Copse inclusive, the Battalion headquarters being in the old battery position about 200 yards in rear of the centre. " Y " was the right front company, in shelters

---

* Succeeded Major-General W. B. Hickie in February, 1918.
† Sparrow, *The Fifth Army in March*, 1918, p. 19.

along the Lempire road; " W " was on the left front about Old Copse; " Z " was in right support near May Copse, and " X " was in and in front of Malassise Farm.

In the event of attack, the orders were to hold the front line at all costs. Should Epéhy or Malassise Farm be taken, the Battalion was to be prepared to form a defensive flank against the enemy trying to turn the flank through Lempire.

Battle of the Somme, 1918. " The division had two brigades in the line, the 48th to the left and the 49th to the right, and it appears to have sustained an attack which was of a peculiarly crushing nature. . . . These brigades were desperately engaged during the day, as was the 116th Brigade of the 39th Division which came to the help of the Irish, while the other two brigades of this supporting division endeavoured to strengthen the line of defence in the rear zone with a switch line from Saulcourt to Tincourt Wood. . . . Especially fierce was the resistance offered by the 48th Brigade in the north, some units of which were swung round until they found themselves sharing with the 21st Division in the defence of Epéhy. . . . The general situation upon the front of the VIIth Corps on the night of March 21st was that the 16th Division, reinforced by the 116th Brigade, held the main battle positions, save on the extreme right, as far north as St. Emilie. Thence the line followed approximately the railway round and E. of Epéhy, in the region of the 21st Division."*

" Shortly before 5 a.m. on March 21st a bombardment of great intensity, with gas and high explosive shell from all natures of artillery and trench mortars, was opened against practically the whole fronts of the Fifth and Third Armies from the Oise to the Scarpe River, while road centres and railways as far back as St. Pol were engaged by high velocity guns. Violent bombardments were opened also on the French front in wide sectors E. and N.E. of Reims, and on portions of the British front between the Scarpe River and Lens. Our positions from S. of the La Bassée Canal to

* Conan Doyle, Vol. IV, pp. 90-93.

the River Lys were heavily shelled with gas, and battery areas between Messines and the Ypres-Comines Canal were actively engaged. Dunkirk was bombarded from the sea."*

The 48th Brigade was on March 20th, as already stated, holding the left front of the 16th Division, while the 1st Battalion Royal Dublin Fusiliers was posted in the centre of the brigade. We may now describe in as great detail as possible the part which the Battalion played in the great events which transpired, and which are known as "the First Battle of the Somme, 1918."

At 4.45 a.m. on March 21st an intense barrage with gas shells was opened by the enemy along our whole front and battery positions, and at the same time visibility was greatly limited by a very thick mist which hung over the battlefield. Both sides have claimed that the presence of this mist was a very serious hindrance to their operations, but General Gough discusses this point at much length, and sums up with the remark:—"On the whole, then, it may be said that the fog favoured our Fifth Army."†

The British batteries at once replied, but were speedily outmatched, or possibly the gun detachments were overcome by the gas. After an hour or so the gas barrage gave way to H.E., which continued for a couple of hours, and by then the gas seems to have cleared sufficiently to permit of the men taking off their box respirators.

At 10.45 and 10.55 respectively "Z" and "W" Companies of the Battalion, on the left and centre, reported the enemy infantry attacking but held, and then some half-hour later a message came from "Y" Company, on the right, that the 2nd Battalion, on the right, had withdrawn, and that this flank was exposed. "X" Company, in support, then sent up two platoons to reinforce the exposed flank, while its remaining two platoons moved up to help "Y" Company, which by this time had suffered heavily in casualties. About midday the centre company of the Battalion was again attacked in overpowering strength, and was

* Sir Douglas Haig's despatch of July 20th, 1918.
† Sparrow, p. 60.

compelled to fall back on the support line, the Germans being thereby able to obtain a footing on the Lempire-Epéhy road. The mist now lifted slightly, and some idea of the general immediate situation could be obtained. On the left the Munster Fusiliers still held the front line; on the right touch had been lost with the 2nd Battalion, which had withdrawn; while further to the right the 49th Brigade could be seen falling back through Ronssoy.

Brigade headquarters were apprised of the state of affairs, and it was decided that the "Blue Caps" should hold on as long as possible, if forced to withdraw making a defensive flank for the Munsters. The enemy was now advancing through Ronssoy, and Tanks were moving forward in counter-attack to cover the withdrawal of the British guns. Reports from the wounded made it clear that the men in the front line were very hard pressed, but at the same moment a very noble message came in from Acting-Captain Letchworth, commanding "Y" Company, that he "was surrounded, but would hold on to the end." Reinforcements there were none, but the whole *personnel* of Battalion headquarters was hurriedly collected to man the sunken road and defend the right flank.

At 1.50 the last of the defenders of the original front line were overwhelmed, the Germans could be seen along the Lempire-Epéhy road, the sunken road was swept by machine-gun fire at close range, and the enemy was noticed working round the right from Ronssoy Wood. At 2.5 p.m. the Brigadier ordered what was left of the Battalion to fall back to the railway embankment S.E. of the St. Emilie-Malassise road and protect the right flank of the Royal Munster Fusiliers. This was effected by 2.30, the Battalion, now only 70 strong, falling back by twos and threes, and a position was taken up commanding the Lempire-Epéhy road.

The party on the railway embankment effected touch with a battalion of the Leicestershire Regiment, which had moved up in support of the Munsters, but at 5 p.m. the enemy opened an intense barrage on our second line, attacking it S.E. of St. Emilie, and half an hour later this party, finding its right turned and that it was impossible longer to hold the position, fell back in good order through the Leicestershire Regiment, and at 6 p.m. joined up with the rest of the Battalion on the second line. Here at 8.45 p.m., the 47th Brigade having taken over the position, the Dublins were withdrawn, and having been reinforced with details of all kinds took up a line from the Quarry to the Sugar Factory at St. Emilie, being in touch on the right with the 11th Hampshires. Finally, at midnight, the Battalion retired to divisional headquarters at Tincourt, which was reached at 4 a.m. on March 22nd.

The general situation upon the front of the VIIth Corps on the night of March 21st was that the 16th Division, reinforced by the 116th Brigade, held the main battle positions, save on the extreme right, as far as St. Emilie.

At 10.30 on the morning of the 22nd the German attacks were renewed, and the Battalion, of which some 140 bayonets had now been collected, was ordered to occupy a line with the right resting on Hamel. Established here, a counter-attack developed about 3 p.m. by the 50th Division on the right in the vicinity of Roisel, but there was no infantry action on the Battalion front, and having maintained the Hamel position all the 22nd and following night, the 48th Brigade was ordered at 9 on the morning of the 23rd to fall back to the line Doingt-Bussu, a withdrawal made necessary by the retirement of the XIXth Corps on the right. The new line was reached at 11 o'clock without molestation, the retreat being covered by Tanks. The Battalion was at first placed in brigade reserve, but some two hours later moved S. of Doingt and took up to a position one mile S.E. of Peronne, with orders to cover the withdrawal of the brigade across the Somme should such retirement become necessary. About 2 o'clock this further retirement became inevitable by reason of the withdrawal of the 39th Division on the left, and the brigade was ordered across the river to La Maisonette, covered by the "Blue Caps," who followed through Peronne about 3.15 in the afternoon.

Some of the Battalion and details of the 48th Brigade took up a position on the La Maisonette line, while the remainder occupied one 2 miles east of Flaucourt, on to which the whole brigade fell back later in the day. About midnight the Battalion found itself in billets in Cappy.

By the evening on the 23rd, says an historian, " the remains of the 16th Division had been practically squeezed out of the line."

" The loss of the line of the Somme was a very serious matter, for the Germans now entered upon the zone in which were placed our depots, stores and hospitals. These had all to be abandoned or evacuated hastily, and consequently great quantities of war material of all kinds fell into the enemy's hands; much suffering was caused to the sick and wounded, of whom numbers had to be left untended and without shelter alongside the railway lines in the rear until the hospital trains could pick them up; the telegraph and telephone communications were disorganized, and the difficulties of organizing defence increased as the danger grew. It was clear that the main object of the Germans was to reach Amiens, and that the weight of their attack was falling upon the Fifth Army." *

From early morning on the 24th until 3 p.m. next day the Battalion was guarding the bridgehead at Froissy; it was then similarly employed at Eclusier, and at 9 a.m. on the 26th it had fallen back to a position in brigade reserve at the cross roads 2 miles E. of Mericourt, on a portion of the front in the Bray-Proyart line. This move was consequent on the decision which had been come to that such units of the Fifth Army as were now north of the Somme should become part of General Byng's Third Army, for it was considered that this arrangement would allow General Gough to devote his whole attention to the enemy advancing south of the river. The greater part of Congreve's Corps was then incorporated in the Third Army, but two divisions, the 16th and 39th, both greatly shattered and exhausted, remained with the Fifth Army, and were included in General Watts' XIXth

* Maurice, *The Last Four Months*, p. 42.

Corps, which, although it now contained six divisions, had no more than the normal strength of two.

At 2.30 p.m. on the 26th the attack developed on the divisional front, but the Battalion held on to its position until dark, when it withdrew to the heights just E. of Mericourt, and was placed in brigade reserve. On the next morning the enemy came on again in great strength from the direction of Proyart, but were beaten off by artillery, machine-gun and rifle fire, valuable co-operation being afforded by British aircraft. In the later hours the attack was renewed, and about 4 to 4.30 the 47th and 49th Brigades, on left and right respectively of the 48th, were forced back, while the Battalion held stoutly on in the centre to cover these withdrawals, and then, its mission accomplished, fell back and took up a fresh position in the sunken road about Morcourt-Cérisy, with the 11th Hampshires on the left. The Germans, however, were coming on full of fight and confidence; they now crossed the river at Cérisy, drove back the line of the Hampshires and attacked the 1st Battalion Royal Dublin Fusiliers on the left rear, thus necessitating their withdrawal to the main Amiens-Peronne road east of Lamotte. Once established here a counter-attack against the enemy was launched, supported on the left by men of the 16th, 39th and 66th Divisions, who had been hurriedly collected and organized by officers of the 48th Brigade. The counter-attack went forward for some 1,500 yards, temporarily checking the enemy, but being unsupported in rear or flank, and being enfiladed by enemy machine-gun fire, the troops were forced at 7 p.m. to fall back to the main Amiens road.

Communication had been lost with the remaining units of the brigade, and it appearing impossible to establish a defensive line, the Battalion retreated between 7.30 and 8 p.m. across country between Lamotte and Bayonvillers to Villers Bretonneux, which was reached somewhere about 11.30 p.m.

Throughout the pressure on the XIXth Corps had been exceptionally severe; reinforcements had, indeed, been sent to it from time to time, but they for the most part consisted of exhausted men from decimated divisions, and the 61st Division of the XVIIIth Corps sent to General Watts to help him form a new line numbered no more than 2,400 bayonets!

"The 16th Division," so writes an historian of the war, "was now rather a crowd of warlike particles than an organized unit"; at 10 a.m. on the 28th the "Blue Caps"—*forty-five strong!*—reached divisional headquarters at Fouilloy, and having been incorporated with other details were sent into billets at Aubigny. From there they moved early next morning to Hamel, and took up a position in the Bois de Vaire in support of our line in front of the Bois des Tailloux. Here soon after midday on March 30th they were heavily attacked again from the river to the south of Bois des Tailloux, following a violent bombardment, and what was left of the Battalion occupied with the so-called 'Aubigny details,' a position in front of the Bois de Vaire, and helped to beat off the attack.

"On this evening several of those heroic units which had fought themselves to the last point of human endurance from the beginning of the battle were taken from that stage where they had played so glorious and tragic a part. The remains of the 39th, 50th, 16th and 66th Divisions were all drawn back for reorganization. It was theirs to take part in what was a defeat and a retreat, but their losses are the measure of their endurance, and the ultimate verdict of history upon their performance lies in the single undeniable fact that the Germans could never get past them. Speaking of these troops an observer remarked: 'They had been fighting for nine days, but were very cheerful and full of vigour.' The losses of some units and the exertions of the individuals who composed them can seldom have been matched in warfare." *

On the 31st the "Aubigny details" joined their own units, and battalions were as far as possible reformed, when the Dublins, reinforced by 23 men who had been fighting with the

* Conan Doyle, Vol. IV, p. 150.

2nd Battalion, relieved a squadron of the Queen's Bays in front of Hamel.

The enemy continued their offensives up to April 5th, when the great Battle of the Somme may be said to have come to an end. During its progress Marshal Foch had assumed supreme control of the operations of the Allied Armies in France and Belgium.

The losses on either side had been exceptionally heavy, Congreve's Corps alone—the 9th, 16th, 21st, 35th and 39th Divisions—having lost 25,000 men and 135 guns, 27 of the latter being heavies.

The casualties in the 1st Battalion Royal Dublin Fusiliers were as under:—

Killed or Died of Wounds.—7 officers and 46 non-commissioned officers and men. The officers were Second-Lieutenants G. A. Clarke, R. C. W. Belas, W. S. Roberts, E. Murphy, S. Lowe, F. H. Howden and R. H. Howell.

Wounded.—9 officers and 253 other ranks, the officers being Captain and Adjutant R. Maguire, M.C.; Lieutenants G. W. Bolster, F. M. Kiernan and W. F. MacHutchinson; Second-Lieutenants J. Nolan, J. F. Williamson, R. F. A. Dickson, J. A. Greaney and D. MacKillop.

Missing, believed Killed.—5 non-commissioned officers and men.

Wounded and Missing.—7 officers and 6 other ranks. The officers were Captain G. E. Cowley; Acting-Captains G. H. Chandler, M.C., and W. Kee, M.C.; Second-Lieutenants G. P. G. Crawford, P. McCarthy and R. G. Hunter; and Lieutenant O. L. Milburn, R.A.M.C.

Missing.—4 officers and 290 non-commissioned officers and men. The names of the officers were Acting-Captain H. M. Letchworth; Lieutenant R. S. Peacey; Second-Lieutenants W. N. Gourlay and W. R. W. Briscoe.

The total casualties in the Battalion thus reached the grave total of 28 officers and 600 non-commissioned officers and men.

The Battalion remained at Hamel until the evening of April 3rd, receiving while there a reinforcement of 200 men, and then marched via Aubigny and the cross roads Blangy Thronville—main Amiens road, and thence by Saleux, Rambures, Feuquières, Moincourt, Wizernes and Assinghem by march route, train and omnibus to Campagne les Boulonnais, which was reached on the 11th, and where some few days were to have been spent in rest and reorganization. But on the afternoon of the 13th sudden orders were received for the Battalion to march within an hour and a half for "an unknown destination." Accordingly the whole brigade moved off at 3.30 p.m., and arrived at Cléty on the afternoon of the 14th.

Here the 1st and 2nd Battalions Royal Dublin Fusiliers were formed into a composite battalion, two companies being made up from each and the 2nd Battalion providing the headquarters and staff; Lieut.-Colonel K. Weldon, D.S.O., assuming command, and the new unit being described as the 1st/2nd Royal Dublin Fusiliers.

At 9 a.m. on the 15th the Composite Battalion marched to Boeseghem, where it was at once employed in digging and wiring a defensive line in front of Thiennes. The headquarters, staff and transport of the original 1st Battalion marched to and were billeted at Wavrans.

On the 18th there was a general move via Aire to Boeseghem of the cadre of the 1st Battalion, and at this last-named place fresh orders as to reorganization were received, and it was now given out that the 1st and 2nd Battalions of the Royal Dublin Fusiliers were to be amalgamated to make up a new 1st Battalion—strength 940 other ranks—under Lieut.-Colonel A. Moore, D.S.O., then commanding the 1st Battalion, with existing 1st Battalion staff, while the headquarters 2nd Battalion was to organize as a Battalion Training Staff, with 10 officers and 43 non-commissioned officers and men. All the units of the 16th Division were to reorganize on similar lines.

On the 21st an order was received by the 1st Battalion which gave the greatest pleasure to all ranks. This was to the effect that the Battalion was to proceed at short notice to rejoin the 29th Division, with which, except for a comparatively brief interval, the "Blue Caps" had served throughout the war, and accordingly, on April 26th, it marched to Hurdeghem and rejoined the 29th Division, being played in by the divisional band.

Here the Battalion found awaiting it the following message, which had been received two days previously from General Sir A. Hunter-Weston, the first commander of the 29th Division :—

"*On this the eve of the anniversary of the historic landing at Cape Helles your old Divisional Commander sends to every officer, warrant officer, non-commissioned officer and man who took part in that marvellous feat of arms his greetings and best wishes.*"

To this the Brigadier added : " The men who have joined the Brigade since that day have worthily upheld the reputation then established."

General de Lisle, the former commander of the division, was now in charge of the XVth Corps, and the division was commanded by Major-General D. E. Cayley, C.M.G. The 1st Battalion Royal Dublin Fusiliers now returned to the 86th Brigade, which was constituted much as when the Battalion left it, the other units being the 2nd Battalion Royal Fusiliers and the 1st Battalion Lancashire Fusiliers, with the 86th Trench Mortar Battery.

The commander of the Brigade was Brigadier-General Cheape.

On May 1st the Battalion was moved up to the front line, remaining here until the 9th. Its headquarters were on the western fringe of the Forest of Nieppe, near the village of Lamotte, the companies occupying what was really no more than an outpost line on the edge of the Bois d'Aval. Of the position Lieutenant O'Donnell writes :—" We had been given instructions to make as little movement as possible. This warning was, to my mind, unnecessary, as the trench we occupied was only about 3 feet deep, and we were told not to deepen or widen it, as new soil would give our position away to the enemy. The weather, fortunately, was very fine at this time; the Boche was holding Vieux Berquin and some farm-houses about 200 yards in front of our outposts. We got only one meal a day during our tour in the line, and this was brought to us at about 2.30 in the morning."

During these days the enemy artillery was very active, the front line and even the Battalion headquarters were repeatedly shelled, and the casualties in consequence were by no means light. Lieutenant Thompson was killed and Second-Lieutenant Boles died of wounds, 4 men were killed, while Second-Lieutenant Ervine and 28 other ranks were wounded, and even when the Battalion was relieved and withdrawn to brigade reserve at Papote the Germans sent many thousands of gas shells over the back areas.

While up in the line 11 officers and 138 other ranks joined. The officers were Second-Lieutenants Guret, McAllen, J. Kirwan, C. Kirwan, Condron, Cooney, McGowan, Martin, Ross, Lennon and Chudleigh.

On the night of the 11th direct hits were obtained on numerous company billets, causing the following heavy casualties :—6 killed, 11 wounded and 231 " gassed," some of the latter dying later from the effects of the gas, in spite of the fact that all the usual precautions were taken; but owing to the nature of the gas used (yellow cross, mustard) many men were severely burnt and blistered about the body. Immediate orders were given for the evacuation of the gas-affected areas, and the Battalion was moved to billets S.W. of Papote.

During the early hours of May 15th the Marquette area was badly gas-shelled, and 39 men were " gassed." Even this does not exhaust the number of those who suffered from this form of warfare, for when on the 19th the 86th Brigade moved back into divisional reserve, the Battalion to hutments by the cross roads Grand Hazard on the main Hazebrouck-Morbecque road,

43 more men were evacuated who had developed symptoms of gas at different times after the gas attacks.

At the beginning of June the Battalion was in the Petit Bois Sec sector, and was ordered to take part in certain minor operations, the general scheme of which was as follows:—The 2nd Royal Fusiliers were to attack and capture Lug Farm, while the 1st Royal Dublin Fusiliers were to advance the front to the line of the Becque on the western bank between certain points which were specified; while on the night of June 3rd-4th posts were to be established along the remainder of the line of the Becque on the 86th Brigade front. Zero hour was 1 a.m. on the 3rd, and the attack was to be supported by artillery, trench-mortar and machine-gun barrages.

In order to assemble the necessary troops in the line a slight re-adjustment had to be effected, but this was completed by 11 p.m. on June 2nd. The two platoons each of "Y" and "Z" Companies in the support line, rejoined their companies in the front line, while "W" Company moved out of the Petit Bois Sec defences and occupied the positions vacated by the above-mentioned four platoons. Four Lewis guns manned by "W" Company took up positions behind the assembly trench of "Y" and "Z" Companies with orders to occupy it when these companies left it to form up outside their wire at zero, less fifteen minutes, and to become its permanent garrison.

Fifteen minutes before zero hour "Y" and "Z" Companies began to form up outside their wire, which they had great difficulty in negotiating owing to its dimensions and the long grass and many fallen trees in No Man's Land. At 1 a.m. on the 3rd the barrage came down and companies moved forward as close under it as possible. On the front of "Y" Company on the left the artillery had previously made good gaps in the hedges, but "Z" experienced more trouble. The attack progressed excellently from the start, and despite the difficulties of the ground the barrage was never lost, but the companies were nevertheless somewhat late in reaching their objectives owing to the amount of "mopping up" required by reason of the machine-gun and rifle fire from Germans in camouflaged shell-holes.

The companies then at once commenced consolidation of posts and establishment of touch on the flanks, while the original front line was used as a line of support to afford more depth to the defence.

During the early morning of the 3rd consolidation by "Z" Company was harassed by the activities of an enemy machine gun, but this was silenced by Second-Lieutenant McGowan, who, taking out a party to a flank, bombed a dug-out, killed two German officers and some men, and caused the withdrawal of the machine gun, which he could not reach.

Second-Lieutenant Gyves, commanding "Y" Company, had been killed on the objective after gallantly leading his company to it, and one of his subalterns, Second-Lieutenant Kirwan, was missing, while Second-Lieutenant Montgomery, M.C., commanding "Z" Company, had been wounded. Second-Lieutenants Alexander and Ross now assumed command of these companies respectively, and effectually carried out the scheme of consolidation.

Our barrage had by this died down, and the Germans, evidently believing that the operation had been nothing more than a mere raid, tried to cross over from the east side of the Becque and return to their old positions, but were met by heavy Lewis-gun and rifle fire and dispersed. Orders were received to establish posts all along the brigade front on the Becque, and this was comparatively easily effected. Only in front of "Y" Company was any trouble experienced, and this was from an enemy post which had entered the line through a gap and established itself in a slit trench. It was, however, quickly ejected by Second-Lieutenant Alexander with a smart co-operation of Lewis gun, Stokes mortar and rifle grenades.

Early on the morning of the 4th the enemy attempted something of a counter-attack, but was driven back with loss, and later the Battalion withdrew to brigade reserve, having during the operations had 1 officer and 7 men killed, 1 officer and 44 other ranks wounded, and 1 officer missing.

The Battalion remained generally in this sector of the front until the afternoon of June 29th, when it moved a short distance to the Campagne area, where the accommodation was good, while the weather was fine and warm. On this date the strength of the Dublins was 42 officers and 939 non-commissioned officers and men.

In this area the Battalion remained throughout the month of July, training for the general advance or war of movement which it was expected would shortly commence, and also taking part in boxing and other competitions, in which the "Blue Caps" more than held their own. On July 4th there was a brigade ceremonial parade, at which General Sir Herbert Plumer, commanding the Second Army, presented decorations which had been awarded for gallantry and good work during the recent operations. Of the 1st Battalion Royal Dublin Fusiliers 2 officers and 8 warrant, non-commissioned officers and men were thus decorated.

Towards the end of July the 29th Division left the Campagne area and the XVth Corps, and moved in great heat to Noordpeene by march route, coming here into the Xth Corps, and from Noordpeene, on August 1st, the Battalion marched to Hazebrouck, having several bombs dropped very close to it from enemy aircraft, whereby 2 men were slightly wounded. At Hazebrouck, where the 29th Division again reverted to the XVth Corps, the Battalion was accommodated in tents and shelters.

On August 6th, when the Battalion was up in the front line, patrols sent out met with varying fortune: one from "Z" Company, under Second-Lieutenant Reilly, rushed an enemy post, killed three of the enemy and captured a machine gun; but another from "Y" Company, under Captain Hughes, M.C., taking a Lewis gun, went out to Célery Copse. Here it unexpectedly encountered heavy machine-gun fire and bombs, and Captain Hughes was killed, Company Sergeant-Major Kavanagh died of his wounds, 2 men were wounded and 2 missing.

[Photo, Gale & Polden, Ltd.

REGIMENTAL DOG "JACK"

Found wounded in a German dug-out beside a wounded German Sergeant-Major at Festubert on April 12th, 1917. Wounded again at Locre, July 12th, 1918. Brought home by Pte. Carroll to Neath Hospital, South Wales; and, on the re-enlistment of this soldier into The Royal Dublin Fusiliers, became the mascot of the "Old Toughs." Given over to the "Blue Caps" when the "Old Toughs" proceeded to Constantinople on December 4th, 1919.

This attack had taken place early in the afternoon, and about midnight a youngster of "Y" Company reported at Battalion headquarters, bringing with him a note from a captain of the Middlesex Regiment, which was holding the line about a mile to the south, and explaining that the lad had entered the line in his area. This young soldier had been cut off during the attack, and in the attempt to get back had lost his direction and got into and behind the enemy lines. He was repeatedly challenged and pursued by the Germans, but escaped, holding on to his rifle throughout, and was able to give accurate and valuable information as to various enemy dispositions and strong points. This boy—for he was only 17—was complimented by Brigadier-General Cheape, particularly for having stuck to his rifle throughout, and was recommended for and received the Military Medal.

During the remainder of the month of August there were raids almost nightly from the British trenches, and the divisional line was everywhere advanced, the enemy appearing to be retiring on this front. The advances were usually made by whichever battalion of the brigade happened to be up in the front line, the remaining units finding large parties for carrying up stores and rations and supplies of all kinds.

Battle of the Lys. On September 2nd the Battalion moved to the Outtersteene area, on the front of which the enemy was reported to be retiring, and on the night of the 3rd-4th moved up into position ready to attack the village of Ploegsteert. The following is an account in detail of the operations which ensued :—

The Battalion was in position at Romarin Camp at 11.15 p.m. on the 3rd, "Z" Company sustaining 7 casualties from heavy gas shelling on the march to the position of assembly. The distribution of the "Blue Caps" was as follows :—Two companies were in front, "W" on the right, its left flank resting on the main Ploegsteert road, in touch with "X" Company on the left, with its right on the road. "Y" Company was in support on

Neuve Eglise road, while "Z" Company was in reserve on Neuve Eglise road N. of Ploegsteert road.

The 1st Lancashire Fusiliers were on the left, and the 31st Division on the right.

At 3 a.m. on September 4th "W" and "X" Companies moved forward, closely supported by "Y," but the attack progressed only with difficulty, as very strong opposition was experienced. Several casualties occurred, and it was clear that the ground to the front was strongly held and thick with enemy machine guns. At 4 a.m., as casualties increased and it seemed impossible to reach the "jumping off" place by 6 a.m. as ordered, an artillery barrage was asked for, but this could not be afforded, and the Battalion was directed to proceed according to plan.

A further advance was made with great difficulty and loss, but was again held up about 9 a.m., a barrage which had been now put down on Ploegsteert village having but little effect on the enemy in the immediate front of the Dublins; and owing to heavy casualties "W" and "Y" Companies had been amalgamated, and "Z" was held in readiness to move up in support, its place in reserve being taken by a company of the Royal Fusiliers.

The Battalion was now ordered to remain in its position until artillery assistance could be arranged, and was finally directed to attack again at 3 p.m. under a creeping barrage. At that hour the advance was accordingly renewed and carried through with complete success, all objectives being taken by 4.10 p.m. and a line established along the narrow gauge railway. In this final attack the casualties in the Battalion numbered 17 only, the majority of these occurring prior to 3 p.m. One who took part with the Battalion in the attack thus describes the advance:—
"We moved off before dawn, and had not proceeded far when we were trench-mortared by the Boche. Our right was in the air as no other troops appeared when dawn broke. On we pushed, suffering severely, but never wavering until we got to a dyke about 900 yards from Ploegsteert about 8.30 a.m. The enemy

shelling was very heavy, and machine-gun fire was played mercilessly on us. Lieutenant McNulty was in command of the leading platoon of " Y " Company forming the defensive flank to " W " Company, under Captain Darling; Second-Lieutenant O'Donnell was in command of the second platoon forming the defensive flank, and the fourth platoon was under a non-commissioned officer.

"The leading company had suffered severely prior to being held up, and the going at this point seemed rather sticky. O'Donnell went forward to the leading company commander, who was sending back a message for reinforcements, and discovered McNulty out in front, who had captured two enemy machine guns. The company commander asked me to go to McNulty's assistance, he being some 40 yards out in front in a good-sized house on the main road to Ploegsteert, which divided the attacking companies.

"As soon as he saw me McNulty shouted, 'are there any stretcher-bearers there?' and on running towards him with my runner McNulty had fallen, wounded in the throat by a machine-gun bullet, and when kneeling over him to ask if he had any request to make, my runner, Private Coffee, was wounded in the wrist beside me. Poor McNulty never spoke. He had only five men left in his platoon, the rest were casualties.

"I took over the remnants of his platoon, and we sheltered in the drain which was about 5 feet deep and contained some 18 inches of water, and we got touch with Captain Noblett in command of " X " Company on the left. Here we reorganized, formed a line and awaited orders. At 3 p.m. a message was received that a barrage would be sent down, and that we were to advance under this until Ploegsteert was taken. Meanwhile the 31st Division was to be seen on our right, but at least 500 yards behind the leading company of the Dublins, and I do not think the Lancashire Fusiliers had made much progress on our left, for they were held up.

"Under the barrage the Dublins advanced. The Germans

had very thick wire erected in front of their position; machine guns seemed to spring up from everywhere, chiefly on our right flank. We hacked our way through the wire and got in among the enemy, who failed to meet us, and surrendered rather too willingly. We reached Ploegsteert, consolidated, and were relieved that night by the Royal Fusiliers, all the Battalion, that is, except Captain Noblett's Company, which by some mistake was not relieved at that time and remained in the line for a further twenty-four hours."

Of the success of these operations Sir Douglas Haig writes, in his despatch of January 7th, 1919 :—" Thereafter the enemy's withdrawal continued rapidly. At certain points, indeed, his rear guards offered vigorous resistance, notably about Neuve Eglise and Hill 63, captured with a number of prisoners by the 36th and 29th Divisions; but by the evening of September 6th the Lys salient had disappeared. Kemmel Hill was once more in our hands, and our troops had reached the general line Givenchy, Neuve Chapelle, Nieppe, Ploegsteert and Voormezeele."

The 1st Battalion Royal Dublin Fusiliers captured 4 field guns and 170 prisoners, including 6 officers, but their own losses were by no means light. Lieutenant McNulty and 23 other ranks were killed, Second-Lieutenants Darley (Royal Irish Regiment, attached) and Cooney and 89 other ranks were wounded, while Second-Lieutenant Owen and 14 men were missing.

On relief by the 2nd Royal Fusiliers the Battalion marched back to Bailleul, and was accommodated in tents and bivouacs hurriedly pitched and prepared beside what had been old Swindon Camp, and here on the night of September 6th-7th the camp was shelled by high velocity guns, when 2 men were killed and 10 wounded. In consequence, no doubt, of the exposed position of this camp the brigade marched on the 11th to Hazebrouck, where the officers and men found shelter in the badly damaged and deserted houses of the town.

CHAPTER VI

THE END OF THE WAR AND THE OCCUPATION OF GERMANY.

THE 29th Division was now transferred from the XVth to the IInd Corps, and on September 19th the 1st Battalion Royal Dublin Fusiliers left Hazebrouck by rail and march route for Brake Camp in the Poperinghe area. The camp itself was new and comfortable enough, but the weather was overcast and showery.

The IInd Corps was in General Plumer's Second Army, and was at this time commanded by Lieutenant-General Sir C. W. Jacob.

During the first few days in this new camp the Battalion was engaged in practising the attack in view of pending operations, and on the night of September 27th-28th a very heavy and continuous bombardment was opened on the whole front, the attack commencing at 5.30 a.m. on the 29th. The advance this day was made on a one-battalion front of 800 yards; the Lancashire Fusiliers in the front line, the Dublins in support, and the Royal Fusiliers being in reserve. The supporting battalion was to pass through the leading battalion when this should have reached the first objective, and then capture the second and push on towards the third, the Dublin Fusiliers attacking on a two-company front, the remaining two companies in support, while the whole advance was to be covered by an intense artillery barrage of high explosive and smoke.

The move forward to the assembly position was very successfully accomplished and without excessive casualties, but when the actual advance to the first objective began the losses increased, for the reason that the troops of the brigade had never before moved forward under a high explosive barrage, and owing to their eagerness to get to grips with the enemy, and one of the British batteries firing very short, many casualties were caused by our own barrage. The Germans in front did not put up so good a fight as usual, and by the time that the third objective was reached the enemy opposition had been completely broken.

Here the 88th Brigade took the place of the 86th, which re-organized, and then followed on in rear.

On the 29th the advance was renewed with vigour, and the 86th Brigade attacking again energetically by dusk the line was within a few hundred yards of the Dadizeele-Gheluvelt road. During the two following days, however, but little progress could be made, the enemy resistance stiffening appreciably and the Germans offering strong opposition by machine-gun fire from many "pill-boxes," while no artillery support was at the time available from the British guns. On the night of October 2nd-3rd the 86th Brigade was relieved by the 87th, and on the afternoon of the 3rd the 29th Division having been relieved in the front line by the 41st, the Battalion moved back to billets in Ypres.

The casualties sustained were as follows :—Killed or died of wounds, Lieutenant Blackwell, Second-Lieutenant Nolan, M.C., D.C.M., and 17 non-commissioned officers and men; wounded, Captains Ryan and Noblett, M.C., Lieutenant Wagner, M.C., Second-Lieutenants Spiess, Stewart, and Semmence, and 91 other ranks, while 10 men were missing.

On October 5th the 86th Brigade moved by train to the Ledeghem area, relieving troops of the 107th Brigade, 36th Division, and the Battalion taking the place in the line of the Royal Scots; during the next two nights there was very heavy enemy shelling, and an attack was expected but did not materialize. The shell fire occasioned, however, some regrettable casualties, 5 men being killed, while Lieutenant Layton, Second-Lieutenants Burke-Savage, M.C., and Conerney, and 37 other ranks were wounded. On the 10th the Battalion marched back to Ypres, where it was in divisional reserve, and

[Photo, Imperial War Museum.

THE HINDENBURG LINE. TUNNEL WHERE THE ST. QUENTIN CANAL RUNS UNDERGROUND, NEAR BELLICOURT. OCTOBER 4th, 1918.

theoretically "rested," but the town and neighbourhood were constantly under enemy shell-fire.

On October 13th, at 1 p.m., the Battalion proceeded by train to an assembly position near Ledeghem in readiness for an attack on the following day by the 29th Division, with the 9th Division on the left and the 36th on the right, the 29th being directed to attack on a two-brigade front, the 86th Brigade on the left and the 88th on the right. The disposition of the Battalion was as follows:— "Z" Company, under Captain McFeely, who at the time was actually acting as brigade-major but rejoined the Battalion to lead his old company into action, was on the left; "Y" Company, commanded by Second-Lieutenant O'Donnell, was on the right, while "X" and "W" Companies, under Lieutenant Blake and Captain Darling, were in rear of "Z" and "Y" respectively. The attack commenced at 5.30 on the morning of October 14th, and was to prove especially costly for the "Blue Caps." It progressed very favourably, although a thick fog greatly enhanced the difficulty of maintaining direction, and the Battalion objective some 2,500 yards east of Ledeghem was taken, but Lieut.-Colonel Moore was killed by shell-fire some 300 yards from the position captured. He had held command of the Dublins since October, 1917, and his death cast a gloom over what was otherwise a splendid day of achievement for the Battalion. The objective having been taken the Dublin Fusiliers halted, and the Lancashire Fusiliers passed on through them. Several prisoners and machine guns were captured, and at 6 p.m. the Battalion withdrew to billets in brigade reserve south-east of Rolleghem Cappel.

In this attack 8 non-commissioned officers and men of the Royal Dublin Fusiliers met the same fate as their commanding officer, while Second-Lieutenants Breakell, Chadwick, and Coldwell and 47 other ranks were wounded; there was 1 missing.

On the 16th the Battalion moved forward in support near Heule, and was heavily bombed that night in its billets by enemy aircraft, and then on the 19th orders came in that the advance would be continued next morning, the 88th Brigade forcing the crossing of the Lys on the divisional front. The Germans were now everywhere falling rapidly back, and it was intended to give them no rest.

On October 20th the Battalion moved from its billets early in the morning and proceeded to the assembly position. The barrage opened at 6 a.m., and covered by it the 88th Brigade forced a crossing, and the Battalion following after got over the Lys at Courtrai by a temporary bridge thrown over it by the Engineers, the men crossing in single file at intervals of 15 paces to reduce loss. The "Blue Caps" were soon over the river without mishap, and found themselves speedily in action under a heavy machine-gun fire from the right. "W" and "X" Companies formed the firing line, with "Y" and "Z" in support; the Royal Fusiliers were in support of the Dublins, while the Lancashire Fusiliers formed the reserve. The attack was not altogether successful, for the divisions on the flanks were held up by very strong opposition, and on the 21st the Battalion withdrew to a position in support in St. Louis, and later to billets near Steenbrugge.

During these operations 7 men were killed and 4 officers and 50 other ranks were wounded. The wounded officers were Major Rigg, who had assumed command on the death in action of Colonel Moore, Second-Lieutenants O'Donnell, Hawtrey and Stewart. Captain McFeely now assumed temporary command of the Battalion, which moved by march route via Cuerne and Roncq to Bondues, which was reached on the 26th, and here the division passed again from the IInd to the XVth Corps.

Lieut.-Colonel Meldon now relieved Captain McFeely in command.

It was becoming increasingly evident that the end was very near, that Germany, deserted by her Allies, was virtually beaten to the ground, and that the four years' war was practically over.

In the rest area of Bondues the Battalion no longer practised the attack—rather was "ceremonial" the order of the day, while the evenings were enlivened by concerts provided by talent, local or imported.

On November 9th the Battalion moved to Luigne, on the next day to St. Genois near Ruddervoorde, hearing rumours that the enemy was in full retreat—that the Kaiser had abdicated. The 29th Division was now in the Xth Corps, under Lieutenant-General R. B. Stephens.

Confirmation of all that the reports had meant was received in camp on November 11th, when at 10.10 a.m. the following wire from the Brigadier was handed to the commanding officer of the Dublins:—

Hostilities Cease. *"29th Division wire begins. Hostilities will cease at 11 a.m. 88th Brigade will establish outposts on line of River Dendre, 87th and 86th will stand fast in present positions. Defensive precautions will be maintained. There will be no intercourse of any description with enemy. C.R.E. will concentrate all energies on communications indenting on this office for any infantry required. Ends."*

During the night strong rumours had been current that the enemy had accepted Marshal Foch's terms for an armistice, so that the news contained in the above-quoted telegram did not come altogether as a surprise, but the announcement that the war was really over was received by the Battalion with extraordinary calm, for nobody seemed able altogether to realize that the war was finished and done with, and that all fighting had really ceased.

"Men were too weary and deadened for their imaginations to rise to the great moment, for it is not at the time but long afterwards that the human mind grasps the drama of a crisis. Suddenly as the watch-hands touched eleven there came a second of expectant silence, and then a curious rippling sound which observers from behind the front likened to the noise of a great wind. It was the sound of men cheering from the Vosges to the sea. After that peace descended on the long battlefield. A new era had dawned and the old world had passed away."[*]

[*] Buchan, *History of the War*, Vol. XXIV, p. 82.

The commander of the British Army in France has stated that : *" In the fighting since November 1st our troops had broken the enemy's resistance beyond possibility of recovery, and had forced on him a disorderly retreat along the whole front of the British Armies. Thereafter the enemy was capable neither of accepting nor refusing battle. The utter confusion of his troops, the state of his railways, congested with abandoned trains, the capture of huge quantities of rolling stock and material, all showed that our attack had been decisive. It had been followed on the north by the evacuation of the Tournai salient, and to the south, where the French forces had pushed forward in conjunction with us, by a rapid and costly withdrawal to the line of the Meuse."

On the date when the Armistice granted to Germany by the Allies took effect, the British front extended over a distance of about 60 miles from the neighbourhood of Montbliart, east of Avesnes, to just north of Gramont. This front from south to north was held by troops of the Fourth, Third, First, Fifth and Second British Armies, all of which were in hot pursuit of the enemy at the moment when the Armistice came into operation.

It may be of future historical interest to state that on the date when hostilities actually ceased there were serving with the 1st Battalion Royal Dublin Fusiliers 41 officers and 776 non-commissioned officers and men. The names of the officers were as under: Lieut.-Colonel J. A. Meldon; Captains T. J. Considine, C. M. McFeely, D.S.O., M.C., S. G. Darling, M.C., W. P. Oulton, M.C., J. C. Bonnar, C. Bailey, M.C., and A. S. Delany; Lieutenants C. J. O'Carroll, C. Neill, N. A. Arnold, M.C., D. P. Wagner, M.C., H. M. Blake, R. E. Tighe, L. R. Elliott, J. Cassidy, M.C. (Lancashire Fusiliers, attached), W. J. Riordan, G. Lord, and J. G. D. B. Dunne; Second-Lieutenants H. McAllen, F. G. Ross, M.C., E. C. Bourke, T. S. Clarke (Royal Irish, attached), J. F. Williamson, M. J. Sheehan, W. Martin, M. A. Condron, R. C. H. Chudleigh, C. J. Brown, G. G. Holmes, C. J. G. Conerney, A. R. Holman, D. S. Norman, J. P. O'Reilly,

* Despatch of December 21st, 1918.

G. A. Hinkson, and A. H. Hamilton; Second-Lieutenant and Adjutant C. G. C. Fisher, M.C., Lieutenant and Quartermaster J. Merry; Captain G. M. Morris, M.C., R.A.M.C., in medical charge; and the Rev. D. Power, R.C. Chaplain. No. 26248 Sergeant G. Cullen was acting as regimental sergeant-major.

Under the terms of the Armistice no advance into Germany was to commence before December 1st, but there was much to be done, and the troops at once began to distribute themselves in less close quarters than had been demanded by the exigencies of active warfare. On the 12th then the Battalion marched to Pottes, thence on the 13th to Baureux, on the 14th to Flobecq, and from there again by way of Fouleng and Rebecq-Rognon to Court St. Etienne, which latter place was reached on the afternoon of the 24th, the Battalion being played in by civilian bands and given a most enthusiastic reception by the inhabitants.

No stay was made here, for on the 25th the march was resumed, and the Dublins proceeded, via Walhain St. Paul, Egbezee, Maha and Warzee, to Aywaille, which was reached by very muddy roads on the last day of November.

Advance into Germany. The 1st of December opened, and the armies moved forward into Germany. On this day the Battalion made a short march of some three hours only to Basse Desnie, where two days were spent in "cleaning up." On the 4th the march was resumed by way of Spa to Ster, but December 5th was really of all preceding and future ones the momentous day, for at 8.30 a.m. the frontier was crossed into Germany, and billets were provided for the Dublins at Weywertz, where the inhabitants were found, contrary to expectation, to be "friendly."

"The people," wrote an officer then serving with the Battalion, "are extraordinarily friendly, everything considered. I arrived in my first billet yesterday, armed with a loaded revolver and accompanied by an armed orderly, and the first thing my ' Frau ' did was to light a fire in my bedroom and bring me coffee. All the demobilized soldiers are back in their homes again. One fellow told me he was last fighting at a place near Courtrai, and when he discovered that we were the people against whom he had been fighting he could not do enough for us. . . . The high standard of living here strikes one very much after Belgium. We arrived here ready for any form of unfriendliness, but we are met with hot coffee and cigarettes."

Then by long and hilly marches and in fine weather and amid beautiful scenery the Battalion tramped on by Simmerath, Embloen and Lechenich until, on December 9th, Cologne was reached, and the Royal Dublin Fusiliers moved on to billets in the suburb of Sulz.

To quote again from the letters home of the same officer:— "We arrived to-day on the outskirts of Cologne; the people generally are extraordinarily friendly and cannot do enough for us —a good deal of it, I think, is policy. I went with another fellow last night to the local cinema. A Boche came in and sat down beside us, and after bidding us good evening insisted on presenting us with cigars. We enter Cologne the day after to-morrow. . . .

"To-day we marched through Cologne. The rain was pouring down in sheets. We marched by the giant cathedral, with the towers, swathed in mist, standing out majestically and towering high above the city. We marched past the Army Commander, General Plumer, who took the salute near the Hohenzollern Bridge as the 86th Brigade was about to cross the Rhine. Though the weather was so unfavourable, a very large and orderly crowd of civilians had assembled to witness the entry of the troops, but none made any remark, disparaging or otherwise."

On December 13th the Brigade left Sulz and marched to Bensberg, where all the battalions composing it were accommodated in the large local military college or cadet school; and here on the 16th the Commander-in-Chief, Field-Marshal Sir Douglas Haig, paid them a visit and inspected the battalions drawn up round the square to receive him.

The Battalion moved from Bensberg on the 21st, but only a short distance—to Berg Gladbach—where it was distributed in comfortable but very scattered billets; but after a stay here of little more than a week the "Blue Caps" relieved the Lancashire Fusiliers in the so-called "outpost area," when the Battalion headquarters was at Kurten; "X" Company was on the right at Forsten, "Z" in the centre at Junkermühle, "W" on the left at Wipperfeld, while "Y" was in support at Bechen.

But while the Battalion had been almost daily on the march the work—which could not wait—had already commenced for effecting and expediting the demobilization of the huge armies which the British Empire had created for the war, and for taking the initial steps towards the resumption of the peace-time life of the nation. Even in the early days of the cessation of arms many men, and especially those concerned in the coal-mining industry of the United Kingdom, had been sent home for discharge. The number of these was daily increasing, and the office work in connection with this was now so heavy and absorbing that it had been found necessary to set aside a special and separate staff to deal with it under Second-Lieutenant Cassidy, M.C.

1919 The Battalion remained in the outpost area until January 14th, 1919, when it was relieved by the Royal Fusiliers and moved back to Berg Gladbach, where on the 16th a ceremonial parade was held for the official reception of the Colours, which had arrived from England, and Brigadier-General Cheape, commanding the 86th Brigade, inspected the Battalion. This ceremony was repeated on the 20th, when the inspection by the divisional commander, Major-General Cayley, took place, and this officer took the opportunity of presenting to officers and men the decorations they had won for gallantry in the field. He also handed over to the Dublins the silver bugle won by their drummers in the previous July in the Divisional Drums Competition.

During this month men were leaving the Battalion almost daily for demobilization; while other men with two years or more Colour service to complete were sent to England on twenty-eight days' leave. The numbers thus sent away under these two categories during January amounted to 150, but there had been changes in the demobilization arrangements as originally announced, and many false hopes in regard to early and rapid discharge had been raised. These it was not in all cases possible to gratify, and a good deal of difficulty was experienced in making those men understand who were unavoidably detained with the Army of Occupation that a state of war still existed, that peace had not yet been declared, and that an army had still to be maintained in the field.

During the month of February company training was proceeded with, and musketry instruction and practice was carried out; competitions of all kinds were instituted; the Battalion band rejoined from the Depot at Naas, County Kildare, under Bandmaster Caulfield; and the Rev. D. Power, R.C. Chaplain, who had served with the Dublins for three years or more, left the Battalion for good, and was succeeded by the Rev. E. Kelly, M.C.

The Royal Dublin Fusiliers were still very strong in officers, for this rank was only very slowly demobilized, but the numbers of other ranks were being almost daily reduced, and on the last day of February, 1919, there were no more than 659 non-commissioned officers and men left in the Battalion. But in the month of March the processes of demobilization made very great strides, and it was not long before the Battalion had been reduced to little better than a skeleton of what it was when the Armistice was announced.

The reduction in actual numbers was not at first very apparent, since although officers and men were almost daily proceeding to the United Kingdom on demobilization, drafts of officers and men were also arriving from the Depot and from the 2nd Battalion of the Regiment. Thus on March 2nd a draft of 9 young officers and 79 other ranks joined the 1st from the 2nd Battalion, the names of the officers being Second-Lieutenants Morris, Gibbons, Buckley, Tully, Cooke, Wood, Conran, Horrell, M.C., and Coakley. On the other hand, on the 8th and 9th

Second-Lieutenant Allen and Major Dickie went home to be demobilized, and on the 20th 16 more officers and 245 non-commissioned officers and men left the 1st Battalion Royal Dublin Fusiliers, they having been drafted to the 5th Battalion Royal Irish Regiment, which was detailed to remain in Germany as part of the Army of Occupation. These 16 officers were Captains Delany and Darling; Lieutenants Neill, Arnold, Blake, Lord, Elliott, and Savage; Second-Lieutenants McGowan, M.C., Ross, M.C., Chudleigh, Bourke, Holmes, Conerney, Williamson, Sheehan, Dundon, Brown, Hickey, Gibbons, Buckley, Tully, Cooke, Wood, Conran, Horrell, M.C., and Coakley.

On the 21st Second-Lieutenant Scott proceeded to England for demobilization.

On this day the 1st Battalion Royal Dublin Fusiliers was relieved by one of the newly-raised young-soldier units, the 53rd Battalion Royal Warwickshire Regiment, and proceeded to the cadre area, Mulheim, near Cologne, whence all releasable and re-engaged men were to be dispersed, and on the departure of the Battalion from Berg Gladbach all correspondence, mobilization stores, and transport were handed over to the relieving corps.

As a consequence of all these movements of *personnel* during March the strength of the Battalion at the end of the month was only 12 officers and 352 non-commissioned officers and men, despite the fact that during the same period 11 officers and 126 other ranks had been taken on the strength. The 12 officers present with the Battalion on March 31st appear to have been Lieut.-Colonel Heffernan, M.C., in command; Captains Considine and Holman, Lieutenant Morris, Second-Lieutenants Norman, Martin, Wallis, and Condron, Captain and Adjutant Fisher, M.C., Captain and Quartermaster Williams, and the Rev. E. Kelly, M.C., chaplain. The regimental sergeant-major at this time was Sergeant-Major C. Anderson.

During the month of March the 29th Division was broken up, as was also the 86th Brigade, of which the Battalion had for so long formed part, and the following is the text of the addresses made respectively by the acting Brigadier, Lieut.-Colonel Ellis, and by Major-General Cayley, the divisional commander, on quitting their commands. Colonel Ellis said:—

"*Now that the time has come for you to leave the Army and go back to civil life, I wish, both personally and officially, to thank you for the service you have given.*

"*You take away with you the priceless knowledge that you have played a man's part in this great war for freedom and fair play. You will take away with you also your remembrances of your comrades, your pride in your Regiment, and your love for your Country.*

"*You have played the game; go on playing it, and all will be well with the great Empire which you have helped to save.*

"*I wish you every prosperity and happiness.*"

The address made to the Battalion by General Cayley ran as follows:—

"*On leaving the 29th Division at the time of its being broken up, I wish to place on record their splendid services during the war. Their fighting has always been magnificent from the first day they were in action on April 15th, 1915, to the final victorious finish on November 11th, 1918. In good times and bad their spirit and discipline have been constantly maintained at the highest level. They can look back with the utmost pride at their splendid record throughout nearly four years of strenuous fighting. They have helped to bring to the 29th Division the incomparable reputation attained by it during the war.*

"*In bidding the 1st Royal Dublin Fusiliers good-bye, I offer everyone of all ranks my heartiest thanks for their splendid services and wish all a prosperous future.*"

Demobilization had by this time progressed so far, and the Battalion had on this date been reduced to but little more than a mere cadre, so that it may here be profitable to attempt some brief description of the measures which had been adopted for the expeditious and orderly dispersal of the very large number of men contained in the British armies operating in many widely separated theatres of war on the cessation of hostilities.

It had early become abundantly evident that more must be done than had ever before been attempted to minimize the possible distress and confusion which might easily be occasioned by the sudden disbandment of men having little means and no immediate prospect of earning money. Still less could the ancient Israelitish system of demobilization be followed which was pursued when "the land rested from war" on the conclusion of the campaigns of Moses and Joshua, and, as we are told, they simply "let the people depart, every man unto his inheritance."

Already before the war had been six months in progress—in January 1915, to be exact—a scheme was prepared for the consideration of the Cabinet, containing suggestions for meeting the difficulties likely to be experienced on the conclusion of the war by the release of the large numbers of men serving in the Army and their return to civil life. It was resolved to follow generally the precedents of past wars, with, in addition, a free insurance against unemployment, and it was arranged that various existing organizations, and especially the comparatively recently created Labour Exchanges, should be made use of for fitting demobilized men into suitable employment. The proposals were generally approved, but as there seemed at that time no immediate prospect of their being put into operation they were provisionally pigeon-holed.

Later on in the war committees were appointed to deal more in detail with demobilization, *e.g.*, a Reconstruction Committee, an Army Demobilization Committee, etc., etc., and by these it was decided to grant to each soldier—

1. A furlough, with pay and separation allowances, of four weeks, from the date of demobilization.
2. A railway warrant to his home.
3. A twelve months' policy of insurance against unemployment.

>   4. A money gratuity in addition to the ordinary Service gratuity.

Various alternative methods of dispersal were considered, and the principle was at first adopted and initially followed of granting release from army service in an order of priority determined by individual industrial qualifications, with an eye at the same time to providing for a very early reconstruction of the Army after the war. It is obvious from the above that in considering and deciding upon the problems of demobilization the authorities had drawn up their scheme with a bias in favour of the national interests, and that the forces were to be dispersed in accordance with the requirements of the reconstruction of industry, and by individuals rather than by military units.

The scheme, as at the outset administered, met with much opposition both in the Press and in the Army, while a system of "Special Releases," which was no part of the original scheme, was justly open to the charge of favouritism, and Army Order No. 55 of 1919 finally abolished the principle of release on industrial grounds, and substituted that of release on grounds of age and service.

Demobilization was commenced in December, 1918, and proceeded with, under the circumstances, remarkable expedition. By February 21st, 1919, 1,848,000 men had been demobilized, and of these 85 per cent. had then already returned to industrial occupations; at one time between 5,000 and 6,000 men were being daily restored to civil life; and on July 17th, 1919, the War Minister was able to announce that nearly 3 million men had been demobilized since the Armistice, leaving 1,200,000 still in the Army, including 209,000 volunteer Regulars.

In April, 1919, what remained of the 1st Battalion Royal Dublin Fusiliers was moved from Mulheim in Germany to Le Quesnoy in France. During this month many officers and men left the Battalion, which on the 30th contained only 4 officers, 4 warrant officers, 8 sergeants, 5 corporals, 23 boys, and 45 privates.

Very early in June the cadre proceeded to Wimereux and

thence to Boulogne, where on the 16th the following embarked with it for the United Kingdom :—Captain Fisher, M.C., Second-Lieutenant Norman, Regimental Sergeant-Major Anderson, Bandmaster Caulfield, Acting Quartermaster-Sergeant Thomas, Sergeants Fraser, Ludford, Mullen, and Cameron, Sergeant-Drummer Filbey, Corporals Denning, Forrester, Hallion, and Halloran, Lance-Corporals Courtney and Darby, Privates Brien, Barrett, McDonnell, Savage, Lynch, Ruffley, Haynes, Nelson, Battersby, Clarke, Madden, Sarfield, Young, German, Whelan, and Locke; Boys Rourke, Doyle, Evans, Harris, Jones (30752), Mulcock, Powell, Saunders, Woods, Winskill, Andrews, Christian, Edwards, Griffen, Heffer, Jones (30996), Osborne, Raymond, Toner, Wood, and Woodcock.

Cadre of Battalion arrives Home. The above party landed the same day at Dover, and proceeded at once by train to Ponteland Camp, Newcastle-on-Tyne, which was reached on the 17th, and where it was attached to " X " Company, 3rd Battalion of the Regiment, being joined on June 18th by Major Heffernan, D.S.O., M.C., from leave, who assumed command of the cadre.

Here it remained until August 30th, when the Battalion was reformed, under the command of Lieut.-Colonel C. N. Perreau, C.M.G., from the 2nd Battalion.

CHAPTER VII

THE STORMY DAYS OF PEACE.
DISBANDMENT—"AVE ATQUE VALE."

WHEN at the end of August, 1919, Lieut.-Colonel C. N. Perreau, C.M.G., assumed command of the "Blue Caps," the strength of the Battalion was, in at least one respect, something quite out of the common; while the Battalion contained no more than 14 warrant officers, 31 sergeants and 537 other ranks, there were actually *ninety* officers! But on September 3rd steps were taken to bring down the number of the commissioned ranks to something like the normal, and the following were permanently posted for duty:—Lieut.-Colonel N. P. Clarke, Brevet-Major J. F. Plunkett, D.S.O., M.C., D.C.M., Captains H. A. Shadforth, O.B.E., M.C., P. J. Shears, A. S. Trigona, T. Brady, and C. G. Carruthers, M.C., Lieutenants D. R. Tittle, J. Esmonde, M.C., C. O. Matthews, C. McCann, D.C.M., A. G. L. Sidwell, A. V. Hastings, D. W. Wallis, C. A. Gamble, M. J. Price, A. W. McIntyre, A. Holman, U. 'A'. F. Williamson, J. W. G. Jones, and G. Baker, Second-Lieutenants J. McMinamin, F. Owen, H. C. Franklin, M.C., and L. R. C. Watson, with Captain and Quartermaster A. R. Williams.

The command of the companies was assigned as under:—

"A" Company—Captain H. A. Shadforth, O.B.E., M.C.
"B" Company—Captain P. J. Shears.
"C" Company—Captain T. Brady.
"D" Company—Brevet-Major J. F. Plunkett, D.S.O., M.C., D.C.M.

Brevet Lieut.-Colonel Clarke was second-in-command, Lieutenant Matthews was acting as adjutant, Lieutenant Esmonde, M.C., assistant adjutant, Lieutenant McCann, D.C.M., was

ORIGINAL EXPEDITIONARY FORCE, SERVING ON MARCH 17TH, 1920.
1ST BN. ROYAL DUBLIN FUSILIERS.

[Photo, Wm. May & Co., Ltd., Aldershot.

Top Row—Pte. Kelly L./Cpl. Bell Sergt. Berry Pte. Gash Pte. Walsh Cpl. Plunkett Pte. Stokes Pte. Doyle Pte. Canton.
Second Row—Pte. Moran Cpl. Maguire Pte. Doyle Cpl. Kerry Pte. Reilly Pte. Nulty Pte. Thompson Cpl. Connolly Pte. McBride Pte. Noone.
Third Row—C.S.M. McDermott Pte. Waters L. Sergt. Colfer Sergt. Carolan Pte. Reynolds Pte. Allen L./Cpl. Westwood L./Sergt. Fenneberg L./Sergt. Gamble
    C.Q.M.S. Fullerton C.S.M. Catley.
Front Row—Lieut. J. Esmonde, M.C. Capt. W. H. Braddell Capt. R. F. H. Massy-Westropp, M.C. Major R. M. Watson, D.S.O. Lieut.-Col. N. P. Clarke
    Major S. G. de C. Wheeler, O.B.E. Major T. J. Carroll-Leahy, D.S.O., M.C. Major J. F. Plunkett, D.S.O., M.C., D.C.M.

transport officer, Lieutenant Wallis was Lewis gun officer, while Second-Lieutenant Franklin, M.C., was in charge of the signallers.

Already in Army Order No. 266 of this year it had been announced that "His Majesty the King has been graciously pleased to signify his pleasure that a medal be granted to record the bringing of the war to a successful conclusion, and the arduous services rendered by His Majesty's forces," the riband being "centre orange, watered, with stripes of white and black on each side and with borders of royal blue"; and in the following month it was announced in Army Order 301 that the services of His Majesty's forces were to be further recognized by the grant of a second medal, to be designated "the Victory Medal," which was to be identical in design with that issued by the other Allied and Associated Powers. This medal was to be of bronze and without clasps, the riband to be "red in the centre with green and violet on each side, shaded to form the colours of two rainbows."

On October 25th the following was published in Battalion Orders:—

"With a view to encourage *esprit de corps* and perpetuate the memory of the immortal deeds of the "Blue Caps" since their inception in 1664, the Commanding Officer directs that companies and platoons will be known by the campaign and engagements in which the Battalion has taken part from time to time as under:—

"Companies and platoons in addition will still retain their alphabetical and numerical numbering.

'A' Company—'Carnatic—Mysore.'

No. 1 Platoon, 'Arcot.' No. 3 Platoon, 'Nundydroog.'
No. 2 Platoon, 'Plassey.' No. 4 Platoon, 'Pondicherry.'

'B' Company—'The Mutiny.'

No. 5 Platoon, 'Allahabad.' No. 7 Platoon, 'Cawnpore.'
No. 6 Platoon, 'Lucknow.' No. 8 Platoon, 'Oude.'

'C' Company—'South Africa.'

No. 9 Platoon, 'Colenso.'   No. 11 Platoon, 'Pieters Hill.'
No. 10 Platoon, 'Tugela.'   No. 12 Platoon, 'Laing's Nek.'

'D' Company—'Gallipoli.'

No. 13 Platoon, 'River Clyde.'   No. 15 Platoon, 'Cape Helles.'
No. 14 Platoon, 'Sedd-el-Bahr.'   No. 16 Platoon, 'Suvla Bay.'"

For some little time past the Battalion had been under orders to proceed to Bordon, and on November 7th it left Ponteland Camp by train and arrived at Witley Camp on the following day, remaining there until December 11th, when it marched to Bordon and occupied quarters in St. Lucia Barracks. It had, however, been here only exactly a week when the Battalion was placed under orders to hold itself in readiness for embarkation for the Continent for service in Silesia, but although an advance

1920 party actually proceeded to Dover on January 18th, 1920, and arrived at Cologne, the move was finally cancelled on the 24th. The Colonel-in-Chief of the Regiment, however, had been very anxious to inspect the 1st Battalion prior to embarkation, the more that the 2nd Battalion was already abroad serving in the Black Sea area, and early in January the following telegram was received by the commanding officer from Field-Marshal H.R.H. the Duke of Connaught :—

"*Please convey to all ranks my regret that on account of my illness I am unable to come down and inspect you prior to your departure for Silesia. I wish the Battalion the best of good luck for the future, and feel confident they will maintain the high standard of efficiency and discipline which has always been characteristic of the 'Blue Caps.'*"

The strength of the Battalion on January 31st stood at 54 officers, 14 warrant officers, 41 sergeants, 12 drummers, and 719 other ranks.

During the next few weeks the sportsmen of the 1st Battalion Royal Dublin Fusiliers proved their superiority over all comers in many of the events open to the whole of the Aldershot

FIELD-MARSHAL H.R.H. THE DUKE OF CONNAUGHT, K.G., COLONEL-IN-CHIEF, LEADING THE "BLUE CAPS" PAST H.M. THE KING AT ALDERSHOT, MAY 21ST, 1920.

[Photo, Gale & Polden, Ltd.

[*Photo, Gale & Polden, Ltd.*

THE OFFICERS. 1ST BN. ROYAL DUBLIN FUSILIERS, WITH MAJOR-GENERAL C. D. COOPER, C.B.
SEPTEMBER, 1920.

Back Row—2/Lieut. K. E. Hegan. Lieut. C. McCann, D.C.M. Lieut. A. V. Hastings Lieut. C. A. Gamble.
Middle Row—Lieut. J. Esmonde, M.C. 2/Lieut. R. G. Rooth Lieut. A. R. Yeates Capt. R. O. C. Bush Capt. T. Brady Capt. W. H. Braddell
 Lieut. H. C. Franklin, M.C. Lieut. J. W. G. Jones 2 Lieut. L. R. C. Watson Lieut. W. J. Shaw.
Front Row—Bt. Major T. J. Carroll-Leahy, D.S.O., M.C. Capt. A. R. Williams Major J. P. Tredennick, D.S.O., O.B.E. Bt. Lt.-Col. K. C. Weldon, D.S.O.
 Lieut.-Col. C. N. Perreau, C.M.G. Major-Gen. C. D. Cooper, C.B. Major S. G. de C. Wheeler, O.B.E. Bt. Major R. M. Watson, D.S.O.
  Capt. R. F. H. Massy-Westropp, M.C. Capt. J. A. Clarke.

THE ALDERSHOT DISTRICT

Command; thus on March 10th they won the Cross-country Running Competition with 415 points, beating the Cameron Highlanders, who were second with 412; while on the 30th the Battalion tug-of-war team won the 110st. Competition, open to all the troops of the Aldershot district.*

On May 21st His Majesty the King visited Aldershot and held a review on Farnborough Common, on which occasion the "Blue Caps" were honoured by H.R.H. the Duke of Connaught, the Colonel-in-Chief of the Regiment, marching past at the head of the Battalion. On the 25th the following divisional order was published for the information of the troops concerned:—

"*The General Officer Commanding the 1st Division wishes to express his satisfaction with the turn-out, drill, and general appearance on parade of all troops under his command on the occasion of His Majesty's Review on the 21st inst.*"

On September 24th Major-General C. D. Cooper, C.B., Colonel, Royal Dublin Fusiliers, arrived at Bordon and inspected the Battalion on parade, visited the barrack-rooms, regimental institutes, and the company gardens. The following is the text of the address made by the General to the Battalion:—

"*Colonel Perreau, officers, warrant and non-commissioned officers and men, 1st Battalion the Royal Dublin Fusiliers, the 'Blue Caps.'*

"*I can assure you it is a great pleasure to me to be with you to-day. The last time I had the honour of seeing the Battalion was when you were at Nuneaton, Warwickshire, in February, 1915; you had come home from India to take part in the Great War, and on March 17th (St. Patrick's Day) you sailed for an unknown destination. I tried my best to go and see you off and wish you 'God-speed,' but the authorities were unable to give me permission as every move of units had to be kept very secret. Well, hardly a month had passed by when you were taking part in that wonderful feat of arms, the landing at Cape Helles, April 25th, 1915. I feel sure that your splendid gallantry on that day*

* See Appendix Seventeen.

has never been excelled by any troops, if equalled; you are, I know, very proud to have belonged to the immortal 29th Division.

"*I have watched your doings in the Great War very keenly, and well know the splendid gallantry and devotion to duty of all ranks at all times; you have, indeed, kept up the traditions of our distinguished Regiment and added lustre to them; we are all very proud of our 'Blue Caps' and the services rendered by the Battalion. I sympathize very deeply with you in your heavy losses, and I know that you are all with me when I say that the memory of those gallant heroes that have fallen for our King and country will ever remain with us all.*

"*To you who have not been in the Service very long may I point out how very necessary it is for you to do your very best to get on in your profession, and to keep up the traditions of your distinguished Regiment—one second to none in the Service. Do your very best to jealously guard its reputation, think of your Regiment first and yourself afterwards, carry out all orders with alacrity, never questioning the why or wherefore; pay every attention to your instructors and help your officers and non-commissioned officers to the utmost. You may depend that they will do their best for you. Take a pride in your Regiment and yourselves.*

"*To-morrow you are celebrating Lucknow Day; how well all ranks have emulated the great example of all those who took part in the Indian Mutiny in 1857; it was in that campaign that you were called the 'Blue Caps,' a name I know you are all very proud of. I will not detain you any longer, and I beg to thank you, Colonel Perreau, for the honour you have done me in allowing me to see your Battalion on parade, and I congratulate all ranks on the excellent turn-out and steadiness under arms. You have all my very best wishes, and never fear that my interest in the Battalion will ever fail.*"

On Christmas Day the following message was received by the Commanding Officer from Lieutenant-General Sir Aylmer Hunter-

[Photo, Gale & Polden, Ltd.

RESERVISTS, 1ST BN. ROYAL DUBLIN FUSILIERS.
CALLED UP ON STRIKE DUTY, APRIL, 1921.

Weston, the former commander of the 29th Division and VIIIth Corps :—

" A line this Christmas Day to send greetings to each officer, warrant officer, non-commissioned officer and man of the Battalion that did such splendid service in the incomparable 29th Division. To that band of heroes that served with me in the 29th Division and VIIIth Army Corps I send special greetings; but all who join your Battalion inherit its traditions and become imbued with the Battalion spirit, which made the wearers of the little long red triangle distinguished throughout the war for Comradeship, Grit and Devotion to duty. Best wishes to you each and all from your old commander and comrade."

On the last day of the year 1920 the strength of the Battalion was 42 officers, 12 warrant officers, 9 staff sergeants, 34 sergeants, 8 lance-sergeants, 41 corporals, 18 drummers, and 628 privates.

1921 In the early spring of the new year there was very considerable unrest in the coal industry, leading a little later to what was known as the great coal strike. On March 1st the industry became free, after many years of control, from all restrictions on pithead prices and inland distribution. There had been an attempt in November, 1920, to put the miners' wages on a better footing, but the depression of trade had caused all the advances secured by the miners to be wiped out; and in January, 1921, it appeared that coal was being produced at an actual loss to the colliery owners. The decontrol of the mines was to have come in at the end of August, but Government sought to end it on March 31st. In the discussions between the owners and the miners, however, which now were hurried on to arrange wages and profits, no agreement seemed possible, and the miners' leaders suddenly sent notices to their districts directing the men to cease work at midnight on March 31st.

The Government replied by the issue of a Royal Proclamation declaring the existence of a state of emergency, and, in order to prevent the mines being flooded and a national industry irretrievably ruined, called for volunteers to save the mines and carry on the transport services, while inviting ex-service men and others to enlist in a Defence Force for the preservation of order. Troops also were sent up from Aldershot to London, where they were camped in the different parks so as to be at hand in the event of disturbance, and among those troops sent at short notice to the capital was a detachment of 24 officers and 445 other ranks of the "Blue Caps" from Bordon.

This party left St. Lucia Barracks on April 16th, reached London on the same day, and encamped in Victoria Park. The following are the names of the officers accompanying the detachment :—Lieut.-Colonel Perreau, Majors Higginson, Wheeler, Weldon and Tredennick, Captains Watson, Carroll-Leahy and Braddell, Lieutenants Tittle, Byrne, O'Morchoe, Gamble, Yeates, Jones, McCann, and Watson, Second-Lieutenants Harrison, Renny, Eassie, Rooth, and Hegan, Captain and Quartermaster Williams, and the Rev. Father Coghlan.

The Army Reserve having also been called up, a large number of reservists joined while the headquarters of the Battalion was camped in Victoria Park, but on April 21st, when all risk of disturbance of the peace appeared to be over and the strike showed signs of coming to an end, the detachment of the Royal Dublin Fusiliers was sent back by train to Bordon. It was not, however, until June 6th that the army reservists, to the number of 199, were finally demobilized and re-transferred to the Army Reserve. In consequence of the very considerable reduction of strength thus occasioned, the Battalion contained no more than something under 650 other ranks when it moved into Aldershot later in this month as part of the "Experimental Brigade," consisting of the 2nd Coldstream Guards, 2nd Royal Irish Fusiliers and 1st Royal Dublin Fusiliers.

The Battalion remained at Aldershot, occupying quarters in Tournay Barracks, North Camp, until August 13th, when it returned to Bordon.

In December, 1921, the following officers were borne on the strength of the Battalion :—Lieut.-Colonel C. N. Perreau,

LUCKNOW DAY, 25TH SEPTEMBER, 1921.
PAST AND PRESENT OFFICERS OF THE "BLUE CAPS" AND "OLD TOUGHS."

Back Row—2/Lieut. P. L. G. Renny   2/Lieut. W. J. F. Eassie   Lieut. R. A. Yeates   Lieut. C. A. Gamble.

Middle Row—Bt. Major T. J. Carroll-Leahy, D.S.O., M.C.   2/Lieut. R. G. Rooth   Major J. P. Tredennick, D.S.O., O.B.E.   Capt. C. H. L'E. West
Major R. G. B. Jeffreys, D.S.O.   Lieut.-Col. E. F. E. Seymour, D.S.O., O.B.E.   Major S. G. de C. Wheeler, O.B.E.   Major A. V. Hill
Bt. Major R. M. Watson, D.S.O.   Lieut. K. G. O'Morchoe   Capt. W. H. Braddell.

Front Row—Brig.-Gen. W. Bromilow, C.B.E.   Col. F. Pearse   Lieut.-Gen. Sir A. J. Godley, K.C.B., K.C.M.G.   Lieut.-Col. C. N. Perreau C.M.G.
Major-Gen. C. D. Cooper, C.B.,   Col. W. C. Riddell   Major-Gen. C. F. Romer, C.B., C.M.G.   R. A. Bacon, Esq., O.B.E.
Col.-Com. H. W. Higginson C.B., D.S.O.   Major M. P. E. Lonsdale   Major-Gen. G. N. Cory, C.B., D.S.O.

Photo, Gale & Polden, Ltd.

C.M.G., Majors R. G. B. Jeffreys, D.S.O., S. G. de C. Wheeler, O.B.E., J. P. Tredennick, D.S.O., O.B.E., and (Brevet-Lieut.-Colonel) K. C. Weldon, D.S.O., Brevet-Majors R. M. Watson, D.S.O., T. J. Carroll-Leahy, D.S.O., M.C., Captains C. H. L'E. West, W. H. Braddell, J. McM. Dickie, M.C., A. L. Elsworthy, M.B.E., and R. O. C. Bush, Lieutenants D. R. Tittle, K. G. O'Morchoe, U. A. F. Williamson, C. A. Gamble, R. 'A. Yeates, C. McCann, D.C.M., H. C. Franklin, M.C., W. J. Shaw, L. R. C. Watson, and J. H. S. Harrison, Second-Lieutenants P. L. G. Renny, W. J. F. Eassie, K. E. Hegan, and R. G. Rooth, Captain and Quartermaster A. R. Williams, and, attached, Lieutenant W. L. Clarke, education officer, and the Rev. Father J. O. Herlihy, R.C. Chaplain.

For some very considerable time past there had been a great deal of serious unrest, amounting at times to open rebellion, against the forces of government in Ireland. Martial law had for many months past been proclaimed in certain of the more disturbed areas, and had gradually been extended until the rule of the military had almost everywhere superseded that of the civil power.

On June 22nd, 1921, His Majesty the King visited Belfast and opened the Northern Parliament in state, making a special appeal to all Irishmen to join in securing peace, and as the outcome of His Majesty's speech the Prime Minister invited the heads of the Northern Government and the leaders of Sinn Fein to discuss matters with a view to a settlement at a conference in London. "Certain agreements" were provisionally arrived at, and on July 11th a truce came into force between the Crown forces and those of the Irish Republican party pending the negotiations between the British Government and the Sinn Fein leaders, and on the 18th General Macready, Commander-in-Chief in Ireland, after interviews with the chief liaison officer of the Irish Republican Army, agreed to the removal of all the restrictions on fairs and markets which had been imposed in the martial law areas.

On July 14th Messrs. Lloyd George and de Valera commenced their discussions, and some three weeks later the Government decided upon the unconditional release of all members of the Dail Eireann, interned or imprisoned, to enable them to attend the meeting of the Dail; but after sitting for some days in secret session Dail Eireann unanimously rejected the Government's peace offer. At the end of September, however, the British Premier again invited Sinn Fein to send delegates to a conference in London, and this time the invitation was accepted, and the conference opened on October 11th. The situation was more than once imperilled by certain utterances made by Mr. de Valera, such as when in a telegram to the Pope he disclaimed, on behalf of his supporters, "allegiance to the British King"; but the negotiations were continued, and finally on the morning of December 6th an agreement was reached, and the provisions thereof were at once published. The one immediately affecting the status and existence of those Irish regiments of the British Army which were recruited in that portion of Southern Ireland which was in future to be known as "the Irish Free State," was that which agreed to the establishment by the Government of the Irish Free State of a Military Defence Force, which was not, however, to exceed in size such proportion of the military establishments in Great Britain as that which the population of Ireland bore to that of Great Britain.

Another matter which seemed to have some possible bearing upon the maintenance of the Irish regiments of the British Army arose from the fact that in August, 1921, a committee of business men had been appointed by the Cabinet to advise on questions of finance and to make recommendations to the Chancellor of the Exchequer for effecting forthwith all possible reductions in national expenditure, in view of the urgent necessity for reducing expenditure in 1922 by no less a sum than *one hundred and thirty millions*. The committee was known as the "Super-Axe" Committee or, from its chairman, as the Geddes Committee, and already as early as January 28th, 1922, the leading Service paper of the day, in writing of the forthcoming publication of the report of this committee, and in anticipating the particular form which

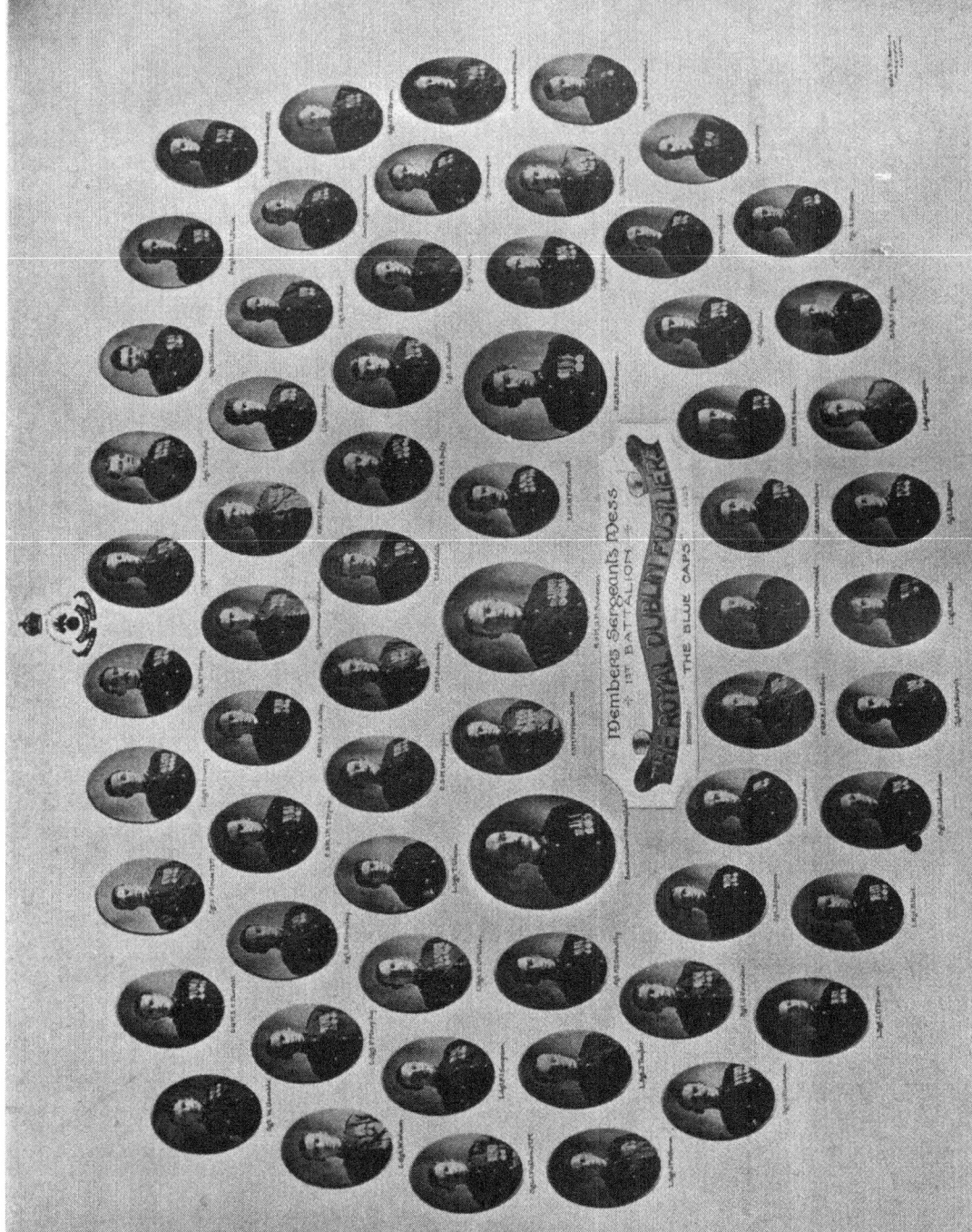

the expected proposals for economy would take, had spoken as follows :—" It seems that in any case we shall find that certain further reductions in battalions of infantry will almost certainly take place—no matter how premature and suicidal such policy may be, and we must, therefore, we fear, prepare ourselves for the worst and recognize that many historic units may be removed from the Army. At first sight, admitting that disbandment on the Geddesian scale is really to be the order of the day, it seems easy enough to decide upon the regiments and battalions from among which such disbandment can most easily occur. The recently concluded treaty with Ireland permits of the new Free State maintaining certain armed forces of its own, and doubtless the Irish regiments of the Imperial Army will cease to exist. . . . . An easy method for complying with the demands of any large-scale proposals for disbandment presents itself by virtue of the Treaty lately concluded, according to the terms of which there does not appear to be any provision whatever for maintaining as part of the British Army those Irish regiments hitherto recruited in Southern Ireland. The Irish regiments have done at least as much as have the English, the Scotch and the Welsh in the past to build up our Empire; they have gained fame in every quarter of the globe; the history of the British Army has whole volumes dedicated to the memory of Irish soldiers. But unless we can maintain depots in Ireland the Irish regiments of our Army can no longer be kept up, such Irishmen as desire to soldier in the Imperial Army must for the future serve in British regiments; and, taking everything into consideration, it seems practically inevitable that the wholesale disbandment threatened by the forecasts of the Geddes report may have to be met by the disappearance from the Army List of the greater number of our historic Irish regiments."

1922 It will be seen from the above that the year 1922 opened gloomily for the 1st Battalion Royal Dublin Fusiliers, whose existence was threatened, if, indeed, their actual dissolution was not close at hand.

The prolonged disturbances in Ireland had had the effect of interrupting the flow of recruits to the home battalion of the Royal Dublin Fusiliers, which had continued none the less to supply drafts of the usual strength to the 2nd Battalion now in India. As a result the "Blue Caps" at the beginning of 1922 were very weak, the strength on January 31st being 27 officers, 11 warrant officers, 38 sergeants, 16 drummers, and only 357 other ranks; but on February 8th, in consequence no doubt of the changes inaugurated by the formation of the Irish Free State, the Depot of the Regiment arrived at Bordon from Naas, thus securing for the Battalion a very welcome and timely reinforcement of 5 officers and 72 non-commissioned officers and men. The officers were Brevet-Lieut.-Colonel Weldon, D.S.O., Major and Quartermaster Holloway, Captain Caldbeck, and Lieutenants Moffat and Lawrence.

With the issue of the Army Estimates there was published a statement by Sir L. Worthington-Evans, the Secretary of State for War, in which it was given out that, in order to effect the necessary economy demanded by the condition of the finances of the country, it had been decided to reduce the Regular Army by 5 line cavalry regiments, or an equivalent reduction, and 24 line battalions and corresponding depots, and this decision was given effect to, so far as the infantry of the Army was concerned, in Army Order No. 78, published on March 11th, and which, in view of its historical and far-reaching importance, may here be given in full :—

Order for Disbandment. "*Reduction of Establishment.*—His Majesty the King has approved with great regret the disbandment, as soon as the exigencies of the Service permit, of the following corps and battalions of infantry of the line :—

"The Royal Irish Regiment, comprising—
    1st Battalion.
    2nd Battalion.
    3rd Battalion (Militia).

[Photo. Gale & Polden, Ltd.

REGIMENTAL COLOURS AND COLOUR BELTS
1ST BATTALION THE ROYAL DUBLIN FUSILIERS
THE "BLUE CAPS," MAY, 1922.

FATE OF THE SOUTH IRISH REGIMENTS

    4th Battalion (Militia).
    Depot.
"The Royal Irish Fusiliers (Princess Victoria's), comprising—
    1st Battalion.
    2nd Battalion.
    3rd Battalion (Militia).
    4th Battalion (Militia).
    Depot.
"The Connaught Rangers, comprising—
    1st Battalion.
    2nd Battalion.
    3rd Battalion (Militia).
    4th Battalion (Militia).
    Depot.
"The Prince of Wales's Leinster Regiment (Royal Canadians), comprising—
    1st Battalion.
    2nd Battalion.
    3rd Battalion (Militia).
    4th Battalion (Militia).
    5th Battalion (Militia).
    Depot.
"The Royal Munster Fusiliers, comprising—
    1st Battalion.
    2nd Battalion.
    3rd Battalion (Militia).
    4th Battalion (Militia).
    5th Battalion (Militia).
    Depot.
"The Royal Dublin Fusiliers, comprising—
    1st Battalion.
    2nd Battalion.
    3rd Battalion (Militia).

4th Battalion (Militia).
5th Battalion (Militia).
Depot.
" 3rd Battalion, The Royal Fusiliers (City of London Regiment).
" 4th Battalion, The Royal Fusiliers (City of London Regiment).
" 3rd Battalion, The Worcestershire Regiment.
" 4th Battalion, The Worcestershire Regiment.
" 3rd Battalion, The Middlesex Regiment (Duke of Cambridge's Own).
" 4th Battalion, The Middlesex Regiment (Duke of Cambridge's Own).
" 3rd Battalion, The King's Royal Rifle Corps.
" 4th Battalion, The King's Royal Rifle Corps.
" 3rd Battalion, The Rifle Brigade (Prince Consort's Own).
" 4th Battalion, The Rifle Brigade (Prince Consort's Own)."

On April 28th the 2nd Battalion Royal Dublin Fusiliers arrived at Bordon from India, and both battalions then seriously commenced the heart-breaking processes of disbandment.

On May 30th it was notified in orders that " His Majesty the King has honoured the Battalion by intimating his intention to receive the Colours of the Battalion and place them in safety in St. George's Chapel, Windsor Castle. The handing-over ceremony will take place at 11.30 a.m. on June 12th."

On the same day, in a special Battalion Order, the following farewell messages were conveyed to all ranks of the Royal Dublin Fusiliers :—

From Field-Marshal H.R.H. the Duke of Connaught, K.G., Colonel-in-Chief :—

"*It is with a feeling of deep sorrow that I bid farewell to the Royal Dublin Fusiliers.*

"*I have been your Colonel-in-Chief for nearly twenty years, and have seen you in many parts of the Empire. The Regiment has been in existence over 250 years, and, as the Madras and*

FAREWELL ORDERS

Bombay Fusiliers, its history is practically the history of our Indian Empire. On its Colours are names such as Plassey, Arcot, Wandiwash, Seringapatam and Lucknow, which shows where the Regiment has fought.

"It is always a sign of great achievement when a regiment receives a nickname, and the 'Blue Caps' extorted that title from the enemy in the great Indian Mutiny, and the 'Old Toughs' earned their nickname by their tenacity in the Mahratta Wars.

"'As the Royal Dublin Fusiliers the Regiment continued to play its part in the history of the British Empire. It earned the admiration of all at Talana Hill and in the battles for the Relief of Ladysmith. In the late war it is only necessary to point to the landing at Gallipoli, and to Ypres, to show that the Regiment has never ceased to keep up the standard of its former achievements in India. It was to me a source of great pride when Her Majesty Queen Victoria appointed me Colonel-in-Chief of the Regiment.

"I have presented their Colours to both Battalions, and in the late war I inspected battalions of the Regiment in France and Palestine.

"All ranks will share with me my satisfaction in knowing that His Majesty the King is going to take charge of our Colours, and it is my earnest hope that, in the future, he may be able to restore its Colours to the Regiment should the country again need its services.

"In wishing good-bye to all ranks I know that every man of the Royal Dublin Fusiliers will maintain his pride in the Regiment, and will never forget that he has worn its uniform and will ever help to maintain its glorious traditions.

(Sd.) " ARTHUR, *Field-Marshal,*

"*Colonel-in-Chief The Royal Dublin Fusiliers.*"

From Major-General C. D. Cooper, C.B., Colonel, The Royal Dublin Fusiliers :—

"*It is with feelings of deep sorrow that I write these few lines of farewell to all and sign my name for the last time as your*

Colonel, which great honour was granted me on March 13th, 1910, over twelve years ago. I have always had the greatest pride in the Battalions and in their splendid and very old traditions. I feel sure that every one of you will always have a deep affection and pride in your old Corps.

"*May every good luck attend you all.*

"*From your ever good-wisher, comrade and admirer.*

(Sd.) C. D. COOPER, *Major-General*,

"*Colonel The Royal Dublin Fusiliers.*"

On the next day, May 31st, Battalion Orders contained the following :—

"*Now that definite orders for disbandment have been received, the Commanding Officer hopes that all ranks will agree with his wish not to issue a farewell order.*

"*His feelings about disbandment and his love for the dear old Regiment are shared equally by every member of it, and cannot be expressed in words.*

"'*Spectamur Agendo.*'"

On this day the Battalion contained 25 officers, 11 warrant officers, 48 sergeants, 30 corporals, 18 drummers and 268 privates.

In Army Order No. 179, published on May 11th, instructions were issued as to the disposal of the officers and men of the battalions to be disbanded under the Army Order from which quotation has already been made. Officers were permitted to submit applications for transfer, giving five regiments in order of preference, in the case of such officers as desired to continue in the Service, while a compensation scheme was published giving the rates of retired pay and gratuities for those who elected to retire. Soldiers serving on other than normal engagements were granted 28 days' leave, with full pay and allowances, at the conclusion of which they were discharged; those serving on normal engagements were given the option of premature discharge to the Army Reserve or of transfer to another unit or corps; while men discharged compulsorily with fourteen and less than

COLOUR PARTIES OF "OLD TOUGHS" AND "BLUE CAPS" WHO PROCEEDED WITH THE COLOURS TO WINDSOR CASTLE TO HAND OVER SAME TO H.M. THE KING, 12TH JUNE, 1922.

"BLUE CAPS"

Sergt. T. Doyle   Sergt. A. D. Connolly   C.Q.M.S. G. Sexton

Major J.P Tredennick, D.S.O., O.B.E.   C.S.M. A. Cullen   Major T. J. Carroll-Leahy, D.S.O., M.C.   Capt. J. M. Mood, O.B.E. M.C.

"OLD TOUGHS"

C.Q.M.S. P. Keogh

C.Q.M.S. J. Jones   Capt. C. G. Carruthers, M.C.

[Photo, Gale & Polden, Ltd.

COLOUR PARTIES ENTERING WINDSOR CASTLE,
JUNE 12TH, 1922.

21 years' total service were considered eligible for service pensions on discharge under the general conditions of Army Order No. 325 of 1919, provided: (a) they had not less than 10 years' qualifying service, (b) they were serving on engagements to complete at least 21 years' total service, or (c) that they were serving on engagements under which they would be serving with the Colours on completing 21 years' service were they not prematurely discharged.

In consequence of the above orders officers and men were now daily being transferred to other regiments and corps from the Royal Dublin Fusiliers,* and the strength of the Battalion was constantly falling.

Ceremony at Windsor Castle. Monday, June 12th, was, as already stated, the day which had been set aside by His Majesty the King to receive from the disbanded Irish regiments the Colours which in past days they had had handed to them by Royal personages or by distinguished Generals or leaders in the field. In each case the Colour party was attended by the commanding officers of the battalions and the colonels-in-chief and colonels of the regiments, and the "Blue Caps" on this day of solemn parting were represented by the following:—

King's Colour—Major J. P. Tredennick, D.S.O., O.B.E.

Regimental Colour—Brevet-Major and Adjutant T. J. Carroll-Leahy, D.S.O., M.C.

Commander of Guard—Company Sergeant-Major A. Cullen.

Escort to Colours—Sergeants T. Doyle and A. D. Connolly.

The different Colour parties made their way from their several stations to Windsor by rail and road, and when all were assembled in the yard of the Great Western Railway Company at Windsor the order of route was formed and the last march commenced.

"The ceremony which took place this morning at Windsor," wrote one who was there, "would perhaps in pre-war days have been without any special significance to those who had not served in the Regular Army; but to-day, when practically all the

* See Appendix Eleven.

manhood of our nation has passed through the ranks of the Army in the course of a great war, the outward and visible sign of the disbanding of ten historic infantry battalions is something which few can regard unmoved.

"To-day the First and Second Battalions of the Royal Irish Regiment, the Connaught Rangers, the Leinster Regiment, the Royal Munster Fusiliers, and the Royal Dublin Fusiliers, which are being disbanded, sent their Colours, their commanding officers, and their Colour parties to Windsor, there to hand over to the safe-keeping of the Sovereign the Colours which they have cherished and which are inscribed with the names of the battles in which they have been engaged from the spacious days of Marlborough onwards. Each Colour is in itself almost an epitome of the history of the British Army.

"Forming up in the station yard at Windsor, and preceded and followed by escorts provided by the 3rd Battalion of His Majesty's Grenadier Guards, and with the band of that regiment at the head of the procession, the ten Colour parties, bearing their Colours aloft, marched up the hill to the Castle, the band playing the march past of each regiment in turn. Arrived at the entrance to St. George's Hall, the tune suddenly changed to 'Auld Lang Syne,' and so the column of Colour parties passed out of the great quadrangle.

"Within the ceremony was of a private—almost of an intimate —character. The King inspected the line of representatives of his Irish regiments, and then addressed them as follows:—

"'*We are here to-day in circumstances which cannot fail to strike a note of sadness in our hearts. No regiment parts with its Colours without feelings of sorrow. A knight in days gone by bore on his shield his coat-of-arms, token of valour and worth; only to death did he surrender them. Your Colours are the record of valorous deeds in war and of the glorious traditions thereby created. You are called upon to part with them to-day for reasons beyond your control and resistance. By you and your predecessors*

[Photo, *Daily Sketch.*

HANDING OVER THE COLOURS TO H.M. THE KING IN ST. GEORGE'S HALL,
WINDSOR CASTLE, JUNE 12TH, 1922.

THE KING'S LEAVE-TAKING

these Colours have been reverenced and guarded as a sacred trust—which trust you now confide to me.

"'*As your King I am proud to accept this trust. But I fully realize with what grief you relinquish these dearly-prized emblems; and I pledge my word that within these ancient and historic walls your Colours will be treasured, honoured and protected as hallowed memorials of the glorious deeds of brave and loyal regiments.*'

"The King and Queen shook hands cordially and in regretful farewell with each member of the Colour parties. Then followed to each commanding officer a few words expressive of very real sympathy; and then came again the personal touch when His Majesty, the head of the Army, handed to each of the several colonels a letter of good-bye addressed specially to each regiment, recalling its past history, and expressing again his grateful appreciation of services rendered."

The letter to all ranks of the "Blue Caps" ran as follows:—

"*It is with feelings of no ordinary sorrow that I address you for the last time, for I know that I am taking leave, not merely of a fine Regiment, but of great memories and great traditions which hitherto have been kept alive and embodied in you.*

"*You are the oldest of the British garrison in India. Your Second Battalion dates back to the time when Queen Catherine of Braganza brought Bombay as part of her dowry to King Charles II; your First Battalion to still remoter days. Stringer Lawrence, the teacher of Robert Clive, won many a victory with you. Clive led you to Arcot and Plassey; Eyre Coote to Wandewash; Forde to Condore.*

"*Your history is the history of early British dominance in India, and you have shown abundantly that you could fight as sternly in South Africa and in Europe as in the East Indies.*

"*To me it is a mournful task to bid you farewell. I have always taken the greatest pride in your past history, but if the glory of any fighting men be safe, then most assuredly safe is yours.*

"*You have your Colours, your trophies and your household gods which are dear to you as Honour itself. You have thought fit to entrust your Colours to me for custody, and I am very proud to take charge of them to be preserved and held in reverence at Windsor Castle as a perpetual record of your noble exploits in the field.*

"*Meanwhile be very sure that with or without external monument, the fame of your great work can never die.*

"*I thank you for your good service to this Country and the Empire and with a full heart I bid you—*

"*Farewell.*

(*Sd.*) "GEORGE R.I.

"12*th June*, 1922."

"And so," adds the writer from whom quotation has already been made, "the outstanding act of disbandment was accomplished, and soon nothing will remain of five splendid Irish regiments but a memory—and those Banners in the hall at Windsor Castle."

But very little more remains to be told. On June 23rd the cadre of the Battalion was formed of the following 5 officers:—Lieut.-Colonel Perreau, Major Jeffreys, Brevet Majors Watson and Carroll-Leahy, and Captain and Quartermaster Williams, and these with 11 warrant officers, 8 staff sergeants, 16 sergeants, 4 lance-sergeants, 17 corporals, 13 drummers and 187 fusiliers were all that was left. And so disbandment dragged on for some few weeks until, on the last day of July, 1922, there remained of the Regiment which—under the name of the Madras Europeans, Madras Fusiliers, the "Blue Caps," or the Royal Dublin Fusiliers—had endured from the days of the Stuarts and accumulated honour and Honours in all quarters of the globe, no more than the officers of the cadre.

"The 1st Battalion The Royal Dublin Fusiliers," says War Office Letter No. 20, "ceases to exist from this date."

AVE ATQUE VALE.

APPENDICES

[Appendix One.

LIST OF COMMANDING OFFICERS OF THE "BLUE CAPS."

Major Stringer Lawrence	1748
Colonel Robert Clive	1756
Major John Caillaud	1758
Colonel Joseph Smith	1766
Colonel John Wood	1768
Lieut.-Colonel Ross Lang	1769
Colonel John Brathwaite	1778
Lieut.-Colonel Eccles Nixon	1782
Lieut.-Colonel Robert Kelly	1784
Lieut.-Colonel Charles Fraser	1785
Lieut.-Colonel George Smith	1786
Colonel Matthew Horne	1788
Lieut.-Colonel George Conyngham	1795
Lieut.-Colonel John Lang	1804
Lieut.-Colonel James Junes	1806
Lieut.-Colonel Aldwell Taylor	1807
Lieut.-Colonel Sir John Malcolm, G.C.B.	1809
Major Augustus Andrews	1817
Major James A. Kelly	1819
Lieut.-Colonel Hastings M. Kelly	1823
Lieut.-Colonel Gilbert Waugh	1827
Lieut.-Colonel John Lindsay	1829
Major Hugh Kyd	1830
Lieut.-Colonel Charles A. Elderton	1832
Major James Kerr	1838
Major James A. Howden	1840
Lieut.-Colonel James Bell	1841
Lieut.-Colonel Robert H. Vivian	1843
Major Charles Butler	1844
Lieut.-Colonel Thomas A. Burke	1846
Major William Hill	1852
Lieut.-Colonel East Apthorp, K.S.F.	1854
Lieut.-Colonel Daniel H. Stevenson	1856
Lieut.-Colonel Jas. G. S. Neill, C.B., A.D.C.	1857
Major Sydenham G. C. Renaud	1857
Major John L. Stephenson, C.B.	1857
Lieut.-Colonel Michael Galwey, C.B.	1857
Lieut.-Colonel Thomas J. Fischer	1859
Lieut.-Colonel Richard Shebrick	1861
Lieut.-Colonel Thomas Raikes	1862

LIST OF COMMANDING OFFICERS

Lieut.-Colonel John Spurgin, C.S.I.	1870
Lieut.-Colonel Henry J. Jepson	1872
Lieut.-Colonel George J. Harcourt	1876
Lieut.-Colonel John Duncan	1879
Lieut.-Colonel William Cleland	1884
Lieut.-Colonel William F. Vetch	1887
Lieut.-Colonel Chas. R. Kerr	1890
Lieut.-Colonel Wm. C. Riddell	1894
Lieut.-Colonel Geo. A. Mills, C.B.	1898
Lieut.-Colonel Spencer G. Bird, D.S.O.	1902
Lieut.-Colonel & Bt. Colonel A. J. Chapman	1906
Lieut.-Colonel G. Downing	1910
Lieut.-Colonel R. A. Rooth	1914
Lieut.-Colonel & Bt. Colonel J. W. O'Dowda, C.B., C.M.G.	1915
Lieut.-Colonel C. N. Perreau, C.M.G.	1919 to July 31st, 1922 (date of Disbandment.)

[Appendix Two.

LIST OF STATIONS.

Year.		Year.	
1644	Fort St. George, Madras.	1815	Deccan.
1648	Coromandel Coast and	1817	Maheidpoor.
1748	Madras.	1818	Mallygaum.
1748	Fort St. David.	1819	Asseerghur.
1750	Pondicherry.	1824	Rangoon and Ava.
1751	Trichinopoly.	1826	Masulipatam.
1751	Madras and Arcot.	1830	Hyderabad (Deccan) and Madras.
1752	Trichinopoly.		
1755	Alighur and Calcutta; Plassey.	1840	Kamptee.
1757	Carnatic.	1842	Secunderabad.
1758	Fort St. George, Madras.	1843	Arcot and Arnee.
1759 / 1760	Wandiwash.	1845 / 1852	Bangalore, and Bellary.
1761 / 1764	Patna Mongheer.	1852	Burma and Pegu.
		1856	Madras.
1765	Carnatic.		Allahabad
1766	Bengal.	1857	Benares / Cawnpore / Lucknow. — The Mutiny.
1767	Mysore.		
1771	Tanjore.		
1772	Fort Ramnad.		Alum Bagh.
1773	Tanjore.	1858	Lucknow.
1775	Guzerat.		Fyzabad.
1778	Conjeveram.	1859	Calcutta, Madras, Bangalore.
1779	Fort Mahé.	1862	Beypore and Cannanore.
1780	Guzerat.	1868	Lucknow.
1781	Carnatic.	1870	India to Dover.
1783	Cuddalore.	1871	Aldershot.
1784	Tinnevelly.	1872	Isle of Wight.
1790	Madras.	1874	Portland.
1791	Mysore and Nundydroog.	1876	Gibraltar.
1793	Pondicherry.	1879	Ceylon.
1799	Seringapatam.	1885	Alexandria.
1800	Molucca Islands.	1886	Mullingar.
1803	Province of Cuttack.	1887	The Curragh.
1808	Masulipatam.	1890	Newry.
1809	Dutch East Indies and Madras.	1893	Sheffield.

LIST OF STATIONS

1895	Gosport.	1914	Torquay.
1897	Aldershot.	1915	Nuneaton and Kenilworth.
1899	The Curragh.	1915	Gallipoli.
1899–1902	South Africa.	1915 ⎫	
1902	Malta.	1916 ⎬	The
1905	Alexandria.	1917 ⎬	Great War.
1907	Khartoum.	1918 ⎭	
1908	Cairo.	1918	Cologne.
1909	Ahmednuggar.	1919	Ponteland.
1913	Fort St. George, Madras.	1920	Bordon.

[Appendix Three.

1st BATTALION HEADQUARTERS STRENGTH,
Previous to Proceeding to Gallipoli.

The following Officers, Warrant Officers, Non-commissioned Officers and Men form the Headquarter Section of the Battalion, and as such are not included in the Fighting Strength of Companies :—

Lieut.-Colonel R. A. Rooth. Major E. Fetherstonhaugh. Captain and Adjutant C. T. W. Grimshaw, D.S.O. Lieut. and Qr.Mr. M. J. Kennedy. Sergt.-Major W. O'Mahoney, " A " Coy. Qr.Mr. Sergt. J. Thurlow, "A" Coy. Orderly Room Clerk: 9095 Sergt. A. Gale, " D " Coy. 6662 Sergt. Dr. S. Filbey, " C " Coy. Sergt. Cook : 5702 Sergt. P. Byrne, " D " Coy. Transport Sergt. : 10388 Sergt. A. Holman, " C " Coy. 10645 A./Sergt. Mr. Shoemaker, J. Langley, " C " Coy. Orderly Room Sergt. : 6878 Qr. Mr. Sergt. J. Keogh, " D " Coy. 1154 Ar. S./Sergt. P. Bonynge, " C " Coy.

Drivers : 1st Line Transport :—

10927	Pte. Cook, " A " Coy.		6997	Pte. McKenna, " B " Coy.
9698	Pte. Byrne, " A " Coy.		7889	Pte. Lett, " C " Coy.
10588	Pte. Farrell, " B " Coy.		9466	Pte. Coffey, " C " Coy.
9536	Pte. Gallagher, " A " Coy.		6450	Pte. Darcy, " C " Coy.
6597	Pte. Harvey, " B " Coy.		10751	Pte. Hogan, " B " Coy.

Drivers : Spare Animals :—

9643 Pte. McConn, " D " Coy.   9931 Pte. Brennan, " A " Coy.

Batmen :—

9327 Pte. Jackson, " A " Coy. C.O.'s Servant.
0520 Pte. Reid, " A " Coy. C.O.'s Groom.
19993 Pte McCormack, " C " Coy. 2nd C.O.'s Servant.
0994 Pte. Exton, " C " Coy. Adjutant's Servant.
19201 Pte. Stynes, " A " Coy. Quartermaster's Servant.
5749 Pte. King, " B " Coy. Medical Officer's Servant.

Pioneers :—

6798	Sergt. Reeves, " B " Coy.		10610	Pte. Shorrocks, " C " Coy.
10494	Pte. Appleby, " A " Coy.		8878	Pte. Christie, " D " Coy.
10777	Pte. Fitzpatrick, " B " Coy.		10533	Pte. Murphy, " D " Coy.
10797	Pte. Hickey, " B " Coy.		10429	Pte. McCullagh, " D " Coy.
9800	Pte. O'Neill, " C " Coy.		11095	Pte. Doyle, " C " Coy.
10901	Pte. Booth, " A " Coy.			

Signallers :—

9015	Sergt. Laffan, ' B " Coy.		10286	Cpl. Byrne, " A " Coy.
10805	Pte. Jones, " A " Coy.		10532	Pte. Sloan, " C " Coy.
10327	Pte. Cronin, " A " Coy.		10561	Pte. McQuaile, " C " Coy.
10824	Pte. Collins, " A " Coy.		9945	Pte. Roche, " C " Coy.
10818	Pte. Kernan, " B " Coy.		8512	Pte. Johnson, " D " Coy.
9801	Pte. Mulvaney, " B " Coy.		8960	Pte. Cullen, " D " Coy.
10923	Pte. Shakespeare, " B " Coy.		10098	Pte. Cregan, " D " Coy.
11056	Pte. Kelly, " B " Coy.		10466	Pte. Burns, " D " Coy.
10852	Pte. Pielow, " D " Coy.			

Stretcher Bearers :—

10188	L./Cpl. Stevens, " C " Coy.		7217	Pte. Miller, " B " Coy.
9765	Pte. Haynes, " A " Coy.		10843	Pte. Double, " C " Coy.
9760	Pte. Coombes, " A " Coy.		10441	Pte. Nicholls, " C " Coy.

H.Q. STRENGTH PRIOR TO GALLIPOLI

9247	Pte. Fenton, " A " Coy.	10341	Pte. Herter, " C " Coy.
0972	Pte. Hodges, " A " Coy.	9759	Pte. Davies, " D " Coy.
9763	Pte. Harman, " B " Coy.	10842	Pte. Hudson, " D " Coy.
10186	Pte. Rawlinson, " B " Coy.	10975	Pte. Redding, " D " Coy.
9762	Pte. Whitham, " B " Coy.	10844	Pte. Walker, " D " Coy.

Orderlies : Medical Officer :—

10549	L./Cpl. Linton, " C " Coy.	10631	Pte. Smither, " C " Coy.

Machine Gun Sections : Lieut. G. M. Dunlop—

6461	Sergt. Emery, " D " Coy.	10275	Sergt. Harney, " B " Coy.
11047	Pte. Skingle, " A " Coy.	9591	Pte. Byrne, " C " Coy.
10962	Cpl. Price, " A " Coy.	11648	L./Cpl. Churchill, " C " Coy.
10678	Pte. Hurt, " D " Coy.	6189	Pte. O'Byrne, " D " Coy.
8831	Pte. Gough, " D " Coy.	7942	Pte. Byrne, " A " Coy.
9941	Pte. Curran, " C " Coy.	9943	Pte. Stafford, " A " Coy.
10372	Pte. Flanagan, " A " Coy.	10114	Pte. McMahon, " C " Coy.
9914	Pte. Ellis, " A " Coy.	9270	Pte. Brogan, " D " Coy.
10928	Pte. Gorey, " A " Coy.	8863	Pte. Foster, " D " Coy.
10349	Pte. Hughes, " A " Coy.	9098	Pte. Byrne, " D " Coy.
9336	Pte. Boland, " A " Coy.	10247	Pte. Connor, " D " Coy.
8476	Pte. Scanlon, " A " Coy.	7635	Pte. Hearns, " D " Coy.
5303	Pte. Eaves, " B " Coy.	9269	Pte. Byrne, " B " Coy.
9784	Pte. Cummins, " D " Coy.		

Machine Gun Drivers :—

11187	Pte. Doyle, " B " Coy.	11045	Pte. White, " C " Coy.
10446	Pte. Magee, " B " Coy.	10998	Pte. Hand, " C " Coy.
11305	Pte. McSweeney, " C " Coy.	10424	Pte. Murphy, " D " Coy.

Batman :—

9790	Pte. Cummins, " A " Coy.

The following are attached to Headquarters but still included in the Fighting Strength of Companies.

They will always parade with the Headquarter Units.

Extra Machine Gun Men :—

9651	L./Cpl. Nolan, " A " Coy.	
9666	Pte. Farrington, " A " Coy.	
9854	Pte. Yorke, " B " Coy.	To parade with Machine Gun.
11149	Pte. Butler, " C " Coy.	
11249	Pte. Redmond, " D " Coy.	
10827	Pte. Long, " D " Coy.	

Water Cart Men :—

8664	Pte Carbery, " A " Coy.	
11367	L./Cpl. Kane, " B " Coy.	
9712	Pte. Lawlor, " B " Coy.	To parade with Water Carts.
10594	Pte. Green, " B " Coy.	
10167	Pte. Kelly, " B " Coy.	

Batman :—

6249	Pte. Moyles, " B " Coy.	To parade with the Servants.

Cold Shoers :—

6540	Pte. Murphy, " B " Coy.	To parade with Transport.
11206	Pte. Harris, " B " Coy.	

Observers :—

11072 Pte. Smyth, " C " Coy.	} To parade with C.O. and Adjutant.
10906 Pte. Whelan, " D " Coy.	

The following table is attached, which shows distinctly the distribution of Companies :—

1st Battalion The Royal Dublin Fusiliers.

The following are the Details to be found by Companies under the amended figures given in "War" Establishments.

Equipment and Arms to complete to this scale are in possession of Companies.

Detail	"A"	"B"	"C"	"D"	Total
Supernumerary :—					
Brigade Servants	1	2	1	1	5
Battalion Headquarters :—					
Staff Sergeants	2	—	3	3	8
Armourer	—	—	1	—	1
Batmen	3	1	2	—	6
Pioneers	2	3	3	3	11
Signallers	4	5	3	5	17
Stretcher Bearers	4	4	4	4	16
Medical Officer's Assistant	—	—	1	—	1
Machine Gun Sections	11	3	4	10	28
Machine Gun Drivers	—	2	3	1	6
Drivers 1st Line Transport	4	4	3	1	12
Drivers Medical Cart	—	—	1	—	1
Total Headquarters	30	22	28	27	107
Company :—					
Extra Machine Gun Men	2	1	1	2	6
Batmen	—	1	—	—	1
Cold Shoers	—	2	—	—	2
Transport Men	3	3	3	3	12
Water Men (under M.O.)	1	4	—	—	5
Drummers	4	4	4	4	16
Range Takers	—	—	1	—	1
Observers	—	—	1	1	2
Other Ranks	212	207	212	212	843
Total Company :—	222	222	222	222	888
Grand Total of W.O.'s, N.C.O.'s, and Men Proceeding Overseas	253	246	251	250	1000

Nuneaton,
2/3/15.

(Sd.) C. Grimshaw, Captain,
Adjutant 1st Royal Dublin Fusiliers.

[Appendix Four

OFFICERS' ROLL OF HONOUR

Bn.
- 4 Addis, Thomas Henry Liddon, Lt., k. in a., 21/3/18.
- Agnew, Andrew Eric Hamilton, Capt., died, 3/11/18.
- 11 Allen, Arthur Haviland, 2/Lt. (Tp.), k. in a., 4/10/17.
- 10 Allgood, George, 2/Lt. (Tp.), k. in a., 15/4/17.
- 1 Anderson, Denis Vipont Friend, Capt., k. in a., 25/4/15.
- 1 Andrews, William, 2/Lt., k. in a., 25/4/15.
- 10 Armstrong, Charles Martin, 2/Lt. (Tp.), k. in a., 8/2/17.
- 8 Bagley, Arthur Bracton, M.C., Capt., d. of w., 29/10/18.
- 3 Bankes, Edward Nugent, Capt., k. in a., 26/4/15.
- 11 Barre, Gerald Benedict, 2/Lt., killed, 9/8/18 (and R.A.F.).
- 10 Barrett, Hebron, Lt. (Tp.), d. of w., 27/3/18.
- 4 Bate, Alfred Francis, Lt., k. in a., 14/3/15 (att. Leinster Regt.).
- 4 Beddoes, Henry Roscoe, Lt.-Col., drowned, 15/1/19 (att. 9th Bn.).
- 8 Belas, Reginald Charles William, 2/Lt. (Tp.), k. in a., 21/3/18.
- 5 Bell, Alfred Roy Lancaster, 2/Lt., d. of w. 17/5/15.
- 7 Bell, Lee, 2/Lt. (Tp.), k. in a., 17/10/18.
- 1 Bernard, Robert, Lt., k. in a., 25/4/15.
- 11 Blackwell, Walter, Lt. (Tp.), d. of w., 28/9/18.
- Boles, Robert Stephen, 2/Lt. (Tp.), d. of w., 6/5/18.
- 2 Boulter, Jack Edward Hewitt, M.C., 2/Lt., d. of w., 15/10/18.
- Bourke, Bertram Walter, Capt., k. in a., 9/5/15.
- 1 Boustead, Lawrence Clive, Lt., k. in a., 28/6/15.
- 5 Boyd, Frederick Ennis, 2/Lt., k. in a., 20/5/17.
- 9 Boyd, William Hatchell, 2/Lt., k. in a., 9/9/16.
- 7 Boyle, John Kennedy, M.C., Lt., died, 21/10/18 (P. of W.).
- 11 Bradley, John McDonald, Lt. (Tp.), d. of w., 30/9/18.
- 10 Brereton-Barry, William Roche, 2/Lt., k. in a., 16/8/17.
- 6 Broun, Richard Clive McBryde, Lt. (Tp.), k. in a., 6/12/15.
- 8 Burns, Robert Henry, 2/Lt. (Tp.), k. in a., 1/11/18.
- Burroughs, Bernard Prendergast, 2/Lt., d. of w., 16/3/17.
- 11 Byrne, Edward Aloysius, 2/Lt. (Tp.), k. in a., 24/4/17.
- 8 Cahill, Thomas Laurence, 2/Lt. (Tp.), k. in a., 26/3/18.
- 9 Callear, Herbert, Capt. (Tp.), k. in a., 16/8/17.
- 9 Carrette, Albert Ernest, 2/Lt. (Tp.), k. in a., 27/4/16.
- 10 Carroll, Patrick, 2/Lt. (Tp.), k. in a., 8/2/17.
- 6 Carruth, John, Lt. (Tp.), d. of w., 10/10/18 (att. R. Ir. Rif.).
- Church, Frederick James, 2/Lt., k. in a., 10/5/15.
- 8 Clarke, George Alexander, 2/Lt. (Tp.), k. in a., 21/3/18.
- 5 Clarke, Wilfred John, 2/Lt., d. of w., 9/9/16.
- 6 Clery, Daniel Richard, Lt., k. in a., 10/8/15.
- Cliff, Harold Martin, Lt.-Col., died, 1/2/17.
- 10 Close, Charles Paul, 2/Lt. (Tp.), d. of w., 14/11/16.
- Close, Henry Burke, Lt., died, 1/11/18 (att. 1/2 Bn.).
- 7 Clover, Harwood Linay, Lt. (Tp.), died, 25/12/16 (and R.F.C.).
- Colles, Arthur Grove, Capt., k. in a., 12/3/15 (att. R. Ir. Rif.).
- Conroy, Bernard, 2/Lt., k. in a., 5/7/15.
- 2 Considine, Christopher Daniel, 2/Lt., k. in a., 24/5/15.
- 7 Cooney, Charles Robert, 2/Lt. (Tp.), k. in a., 9/10/16 (att. R. Ir. Rif.).
- 9 Cooney, Edmund Luke, 2/Lt. (Tp.), k. in a., 4/6/17.
- 1 Corbet, Reginald Vincent Campbell, Lt., k. in a., 25/4/15.
- Cowley, George Evelyn, Major (Tp.), d. of w., 18/6/18 (P. of W.).
- 9 Coyne, John Joseph Aloysius, 2/Lt. (Tp.), k. in a., 10/8/17.

Bn.
1 Crawford, Sydney George, 2/Lt., drowned, 10/10/18.
7 Crichton, Aleck Godfrey, 2/Lt. (Tp.), k. in a., 16/8/15.
10 Cross, Henry Hazelock, 2/Lt. (Tp.), k. in a., 13/11/16.
   Cuffey, Maurice O'Connor, Lt., k. in a., 20/5/15.
7 Cunningham, Bernard Camelis Josh, Capt. (Tp.), k. in a., 21/3/18.
4 Cusack, Reginald Ernest, 2/Lt., died, 15/4/15.
5 Daly, Arthur Charles de Burgh, 2/Lt., k. in a., 9/9/16.
2 Damiand, Walter Henry Alexander, 2/Lt., d. of w., 2/7/16.
3 Davies, Charles Bernard, Lt., k. in a., 9/6/16.
8 Davies, Noel John, 2/Lt. (Tp.), k. in a., 27/4/16.
1 De Lusignan, Raymond, Lt., k. in a., 25/4/15.
3 Dillon, Edeveain Charles Barclay, 2/Lt., k. in a., 13/10/16.
6 Dinan, George Albert, 2/Lt. (Tp.), k. in a., 9/9/16.
8 Doherty, John, 2/Lt. (Tp.), k. in a., 16/8/17.
2 Donovan, Cyril Bernard, M.C., Lt. (Tp.), k. in a., 25/3/18.
7 Doran, Louis Godfrey, 2/Lt. (Tp.), k. in a., 23/10/16.
1 Dowling, Frederick, Lt., k. in a., 7/8/17.
2 Doyle, Christopher, 2/Lt., k. in a., 15/8/17.
6 Doyle, John Joseph, Lt. (Tp.), k. in a., 10/8/15.
8 Drury, William Symes, Lt. (Tp.), killed, 29/1/16.
1 Dunlop, George Malcolm, Capt., k. in a., 25/4/18.
2 Dunlop, John Gunning Moore, 2/Lt., k. in a., 27/8/15.
3 Dunne, John Geoffrey David Baird, Lt., died, 12/11/18.
4 Dunwoody, John Myles, 2/Lt., k. in a., 4/5/17.
4 Edwards, Brian Wallie, 2/Lt., died, 10/11/18 (and R.A.F.).
   Edwards, William Victor, Capt., k. in a., 29/12/17.
3 Ellis, Robert Percy, 2/Lt., d. of w., 6/4/18 (as P. of W.).
2 Falkiner, George Stride, 2/Lt., k. in a., 16/8/17.
4 Ferguson, James Ernest, 2/Lt., k. in a., 20/4/17.
1 Fetherstonhaugh, Edwyn, Major, d. of w., 27/4/15.
5 Finlay, Robert Alexander, Lt., k. in a., 9/5/15 (att. 1 R. Ir. Rif.).
10 Fitzgerald, Robert William, 2/Lt. (Tp.), d. of w., 4/10/18.
10 Fitzgibbon, G. J., Lt. (T./Capt.), k. in a., 20/11/17.
7 Fitzgibbon, Michael Joseph, Lt. (Tp.), k. in a., 15/8/15.
2 Floyd, Henry Murrell, Capt., k. in a., 28/6/15.
9 Forde, John Patrick, 2/Lt., d. of w., 16/8/17.
1 Frankland, Thomas Hugh Colville, Brevet-Major, k. in a., 25/4/15.
6 Freeney, Patrick Joseph, 2/Lt. (Tp.), k. in a., 8/10/18 (att. 198 L.T.M.B.).
2 French, Charles Stockley, Lt., k. in a., 25/4/15.
3 Gaffney, James, M.C., Capt. (Tp)., k. in a., 8/10/18.
   Gage, John, Capt., died, 7/11/16.
11 Gault, Arthur Alexander, 2/Lt. (Tp.), d. of w., 10/10/18.
   George, Herbert Duncan King, Lt., died, 6/4/17 (and R.F.C.) (P. of W.).
2 Gibson, Henry William, 2/Lt. (Tp.), d. of w., 27/11/16.
3 Girvin, Colin Bertram, Capt. (Tp.), died, 5/11/18.
9 Good, Thomas Henry, Capt. (Tp.), d. of w., 8/9/16.
1 Gradwell, George Francis, 2/Lt., k. in a., 28/2/17.
3 Graham, Cecil Hollingsworth, 2/Lt., k. in a., 19/9/16 (att. T.M.B.).
6 Graham, George Lyons, 2/Lt. (Tp.), k. in a., 17/8/17.
4 Gray, George, 2/Lt., killed, 28/4/16.
3 Gray, Meredith, 2/Lt., k. in a., 16/8/16 (att. 10 R. Ir. Rif.).
7 Greaves, Eric, M.C., Lt. (Tp.), d. of w., 21/11/18.
5 Green, Arthur Vivian, 2/Lt., k. in a., 17/8/17.
1 Green, Harold, 2/Lt. (Tp.), k. in a., 28/2/17.
1 Grimshaw, Cecil Thomas Wrigley, D.S.O., Major, k. in a., 26/4/15.
10 Guisani, St. John Joseph Vincent Anthony, 2/Lt. (Tp.), k. in a., 13/11/16.
11 Gyves, John James, 2/Lt. (Tp.), k. in a., 3/6/18.

OFFICERS' ROLL OF HONOUR

Bn.	
	Hackett, Henry Robert Theodore, 2/Lt., k. in a., 2/11/15.
3	Haigh, John Caleb, 2/Lt., k. in a., 2/10/18 (att. 1 R. Ir. Rif.).
	Halligan, Matthew, Lt., k. in a., 18/11/17 (and R.F.C.).
	Haines, Alec C., Lt., d. of w., 8/5/15.
	Hall, John Ramsay Fitz-Gibbon, 2/Lt., k. in a., 24/5/15.
8	Hamilton, Geoffrey Cecil Monck, 2/Lt. (Tp.), k. in a., 7/9/16.
4	Handyside, Thomas Fosbery, Lt., k. in a., 29/12/17.
6	Hare, Edward Henry, 2/Lt., k. in a., 23/9/17 (att. Yorks. Regt.).
7	Hare, George, Lt. (Tp.), k. in a., 27/12/17.
3	Harold-Barry, J., Capt., k. in a., 24/5/15.
11	Harty, Wilfrid, 2/Lt., k. in a., 8/8/17.
11	Harvey, John Alan, 2/Lt. (Tp.), k. in a., 20/11/17.
	Head, Henry d'Esterre, Lt., d. of w., 1/6/15.
4	Heenan, Thomas George Graudon, 2/Lt., k. in a., 21/3/18.
2	Helby, John Alfred Hasler, 2/Lt., d. of w., 3/8/16.
9	Hickey, Robert Francis, 2/Lt., d. of w., 16/8/17.
7	Hickman, Poole Henry, Capt. (Tp.), k. in a., 15/8/15.
1	Higginson, William Frederick, Capt., k. in a., 25/4/15.
11	Howden, Francis William, 2/Lt. (Tp.), d. of w., 30/3/18.
11	Howell, Reuben Harrison, 2/Lt. (Tp.), d. of w., 29/3/18.
8	Hughes, Bryan Desmond, M.C., Capt. (Tp.), k. in a., 6/8/18.
4	Humphrey, William, M.C., 2/Lt., d. of w., 24/10/18.
	Hunter, Ronald Gordon, 2/Lt., d. of w., 25/4/18 (P. of W.).
3	Inglis, Douglas Ian, 2/Lt., k. in a., 7/2/17.
2	Ingoldby, Roger Hugh, 2/Lt. (Tp.), k. in a., 1/7/16.
1	Jackson, William, 2/Lt. (Tp.), k. in a., 30/9/18 (att. 23 R. Fus.).
11	Jackson, Herbert, 2/Lt., k. in a., 21/3/18.
3	Johnson, Richard Digby, Major, k. in a., 24/5/15.
	Jones, Samuel Victor Charles, Lt., d. of w., 23/9/16.
3	Jones-Nowlan, Thomas Chamney, 2/Lt., d. of w., 27/5/17 (att. 1st Bn.).
	Judd, Frederick George Kerridge, 2/Lt. (Tp.), k. in a., 24/5/15.
7	Julian, Ernest Lawrence, Lt. (Tp.), d. of w., 8/8/15.
11	Karney, David Noel, T/2/Lt. (A./Capt.), k. in a., 21/3/18.
7	Kee, William, M.C., A./Capt., d. of w., 24/3/18 (as P. of W.).
11	Keenan, John, Capt. (Tp.), died, 26/3/17.
	Kempston, Robert James, Lt., k. in a., 24/5/15.
3	Kennedy, Arthur St. Clair, 2/Lt., died, 6/3/15.
9	Kettle, Thomas Michael, Lt. (Tp.), k. in a., 9/9/16.
5	Kidson, Charles Wilfrid, Lt., k. in a., 17/10/18.
2	Killingley, Hastings Grewatt, Lt., k. in a., 23/10/16.
	King, Robert Anderson Ferguson Smyly, 2/Lt., d. of w., 23/5/15.
2	Lemass, Herbert Justin, 2/Lt., k. in a., 23/10/16.
	Le Mesurier, Frederick Neil, Capt., k. in a., 25/4/15.
2	Loveband, Arthur, C.M.G., Lt.-Col., k. in a., 25/5/15.
8	Lowe, Joseph, 2/Lt. (Tp.), k. in a., 26/3/18.
9	McAllister, Charles, A./Capt., k. in a., 27/5/18.
	McBrien, Hubert John, 2/Lt. (Tp.), k. in a., 4/11/18.
9	MacCarthy, Cornelius Aloysius, 2/Lt., drowned, 19/7/17.
	McCreery, Mona J. M., Capt., died, 21/10/18.
10	McCusker, Patrick Joseph, Lt. (Tp.), k. in a., 13/11/16.
3	MacDaniel, James, 2/Lt., k. in a., 18/8/17 (and R.F.C., 57 Sqd.).
6	McGarry, William Frederick Cecil, 2/Lt. (Tp.), k. in a., 10/8/15.
11	McGuinness, John Norman, 2/Lt., k. in a., 21/3/18 (att. 2 R. Mun. Fus.).
	McGuire, Brian, 2/Lt., k. in a., 14/9/14.
7	Machutchison, William Frederick, Lt., k. in a., 26/3/18.
2	Maclear, Basil, Capt., k. in a., 24/5/15.
	Maclear, Percy, Major, k. in a., 30/8/14.

Bn.
4	McLoughlin, James Patrick, Lt., d. of w., 24/5/15 (att. R. Ir. Rif.).
4	Macnamara, George Frederick, 2/Lt., k. in a., 17/8/16 (att. 8th Bn.).
2	Macnamara, Maccon John, 2/Lt., k. in a., 26/3/18.
5	Mcnulty, Michael John, Lt., k. in a., 4/9/15 (att. 9th Bn.).
11	Mallen, William James, 2/Lt. (Tp.), k. in a., 16/8/17.
9	Malone, Joseph James, 2/Lt. (Tp.), k. in a., 16/8/17.
10	Mansfield, Harold Barton, 2/Lt. (Tp.), k. in a., 13/11/16.
5	Marchant, Charles Stewart, 2/Lt., k. in a., 4/6/17.
8	Marlow, Charles Dwyer, 2/Lt. (Tp.), k. in a., 17/8/17.
6	Martin, Charles Andrew, Capt., k. in a., 6/12/15.
3	Martin, Geoffrey Clogstoun, 2/Lt., k. in a., 2/8/16.
3	Martin, Richard Archer Walcott, 2/Lt., k. in a., 16/8/17.
1	Maunsell, Edward Richard Lloyd, Capt., k. in a., 1/7/16.
8	Maxwell, Thomas, 2/Lt. (Tp.), k. in a., 9/9/16.
10	Mehegan, Daniel Joseph, 2/Lt., k. in a., 21/3/18.
11	Millar, James Roland, Capt. (Tp.), k. in a., 16/8/17.
8	Monson, William Herbert, Capt. (Tp.), d. of w., 7/9/16.
1	Mooney, Francis, 2/Lt., k. in a., 28/2/17.
9	Mooney, David George, 2/Lt. (Tp.), k. in a., 16/8/17.
1	Moore, Athelstan, D.S.O., Major (Bt.-Lt.-Col.), d. of w., 14/10/18.
5	Moran, Gerald Charles, Lt., d. of w., 26/5/15.
2	Morgan, John Walter Rees, 2/Lt., k. in a., 1/7/16.
6	Mortimer, William Lionel Gueritz, 2/Lt. (Tp.), d. of w., 10/8/15.
8	Murphy, Edward, 2/Lt. (Tp.), k. in a., 21/3/18.
5	Murphy, James Neville Herbert, 2/Lt., k. in a., 10/5/15.
9	Murphy, William Joseph, Capt. (Tp.), k. in a., 9/9/16.
10	Neilan, Gerald Aloysius, Lt. (Tp.), killed, 24/4/16.
6	Nesbitt, William Charles, 2/Lt. (Tp.), k. in a., 15/8/15.
1	Nolan, James, M.C., D.C.M., 2/Lt., d. of w., 29/9/18.
3	Nolan-Martin, Alfred John, Capt., d. of w., 22/2/17 (att. M.G.C.).
6	O'Carroll, Francis Brendon, 2/Lt. (Tp.), k. in a., 10/8/15.
1	O'Hara, Henry Desmond, D.S.O., Lt., d. of w., 29/8/15.
9	O'Kearney-White, Ernest Francis, 2/Lt., k. in a., 9/9/16.
5	O'Neill, Frederick, 2/Lt., k. in a., 13/11/16.
3	Palmer, David Adams, M.C., A./Capt., d. of w., 25/3/18 (att. Tank Corps).
10	Palmer, Samuel William, Lt., k. in a., 27/3/18.
	Pedlow, William, M.C., A./Capt., k. in a., 12/10/18.
3	Peel, Charles William, 2/Lt., k. in a., 24/4/15.
5	Perrier, Hargrave Carroll Lumley, 2/Lt., k. in a., 8/11/18.
4	Persse, Dudley Eyre, Lt., d. of w., 1/2/15.
	Philby, Denis Duncan, Lt., k. in a., 12/11/14 (att. R. Munster Fus.).
7	Pige-Leschallas, Gilbert, Capt. (Tp.), k. in a., 15/8/15.
9	Pither, Harold Francis, 2/Lt., k. in a., 6/7/16.
9	Potter, Robert John, 2/Lt. (Tp.), k. in a., 16/8/17.
8	Poulter, Henry Chapman, Capt. (Tp.), d. of w., 29/11/17.
5	Powell, Frederick William, 2/Lt., died, 20/1/17.
6	Preston, A. J. D., Capt., k. in a., 15/8/15.
	Prince-Smith, Donald St. Patrick, Lt. (Tp.), k. in a., 24/10/17 (att. R.F.C., [16 Sqd.).
11	Quigley, Christopher, 2/Lt. (Tp.), k. in a., 21/3/18.
11	Quinn, John Patrick, Lt. (Tp.), d. of w., 20/6/17.
	Ransome, Frederick Ronald, 2/Lt., k. in a., 27/5/18.
3	Reavie, Wilfred Laurance, 2/Lt., k. in a., 16/8/17.
3	Reid, Bernard, 2/Lt. (Tp.), k. in a., 28/6/16.
9	Richards, Leslie John, 2/Lt. (Tp.), k. in a., 1/8/17.
6	Richards, William Reeves, Capt. (Tp.), k. in a., 15/8/15.
	Ridley, Herbert Leslie, M.C., Lt. (A./Capt.), k. in a., 15/7/17.

OFFICERS' ROLL OF HONOUR

Bn.	
1	Roberts, William John, 2/Lt., k. in a., 21/3/18.
	Robertson, Eric Hume, 2/Lt., k. in a., 21/3/18 (att. 48 T.M.B.).
11	Rogers, James Joseph, 2/Lt. (Tp.), k. in a., 28/3/18.
1	Rooth, Richard Alexander, Lt.-Col., k. in a., 25/4/15.
4	Rose-Cleland, Alfred Middleton Blackwood Bingham, Lt., k. in a., 1/7/16.
7	Russell, Alexander James, Lt. (Tp.), k. in a., 15/8/15.
10	Russell, Thomas Wallace, 2/Lt. (Tp.), k. in a., 13/11/16.
4	Saffery, Leslie Hall, 2/Lt., k. in a., 1/7/16.
4	Salvesen, Edward Maxwell, 2/Lt., k. in a., 25/4/15.
8	Sheridan, Leonard, Capt., k. in a., 26/3/18.
8	Sheridan, Richard Brinsley, Lt. (Tp.), killed, 7/3/16.
2	Shine, James Owen Williams, Capt., k. in a., 16/8/17.
	Sparrow, Francis, 2/Lt., k. in a., 25/4/15.
6	Stanford, Donovan Edward, 2/Lt., k. in a., 21/3/18.
6	Stanton, Robert, 2/Lt., k. in a., 7/8/15.
4	Stewart, Joseph, 2/Lt., k. in a., 16/8/17.
	Storrar, Andrew Wynne, 2/Lt., k. in a., 16/8/17 (att. 48 T.M.B.).
7	Sutherland, William, M.M., 2/Lt. (Tp.), k. in a., 7/10/18.
2	Sutton, Robert William, 2/Lt., T./Capt., k. in a., 16/10/15.
	Taylor, Adrian Aubrey Charles, Capt., k. in a., 28/6/15 (att. Egypt Police).
	Taylor, John Arthur Harold, 2/Lt., k. in a., 24/9/15.
3	Thomas, Daniel Gwyn, 2/Lt., k. in a., 25/5/15.
	Thompson, Gerald Pittis Newman, Lt., k. in a., 4/5/18 (att. 8th Bn.).
7	Tippet, Charles Henry, T./Major, k. in a., 7/8/15.
7	Tobin, Richard Patrick, Capt. (Tp.), k. in a., 15/8/15.
10	Traverse, James Hector, 2/Lt. (Tp.), k. in a., 30/11/17.
11	Tumilty, Austin, 2/Lt. (Tp.), died, 10/11/17.
3	Tweedy, Cecil Mahon, Lt., k. in a., 28/2/17.
4	Tyndall, Joseph Charles, Lt., k. in a., 2/3/15 (att. R. Ir. Rif.).
9	Tyner, Thomas Goodwin, 2/Lt. (Tp.), k. in a., 9/9/16.
8	Valentine, Robert Lepper, Lt. (Tp.), d. of w., 30/4/16.
5	Vardon, Evelyn Francis Claude, 2/Lt., k. in a., 10/5/16.
9	Verley, Albert Stuart Leonard, T./Lt., k. in a., 16/8/17.
9	Vigors, Arthur Cecil, 2/Lt. (Tp.), k. in a., 9/9/16 (att. R. Munster Fus.).
	Walkey, Francis Ashton, 2/Lt., k. in a., 17/10/18.
2	Walsh, Lionel Percy, Major (Tp.), d. of w., 4/7/16.
8	Walsh, Phillip James, T./2/Lt., k. in a., 30/11/17.
11	Ward, Bernard, 2/Lt. (Tp.), k. in a., 20/11/17.
4	Warner, Douglas Redston, 2/Lt., k. in a., 1/7/16.
7	Weatherill, Edward Theaker, 2/Lt. (Tp.), k. in a., 15/8/15.
4	White, William, 2/Lt., k. in a., 25/4/15.
3	Whitehead, Walter, 2/Lt., k. in a., 6/9/16.
11	Williams, John, 2/Lt. (Tp.), drowned, 22/10/17.
10	Wilson, Alexander Stewart, 2/Lt. (Tp.), k. in a., 20/4/17.
	Wilson, Denis Erskine, Major (Tp.), d. of w., 24/9/16.
	Wylie, J. R., 2/Lt., killed, 23/4/18 (att. R.A.F.).
	Young, Mervyn Cyril Nicholas Radford, 2/Lt., d. of w., 25/5/15.

Total number of Officers (*a*) Killed in Action, (*b*) Died of Wounds, (*c*) Killed, other than in action, (*d*) Died, from natural causes, etc. :—

269.

OTHER RANKS ROLL OF HONOUR

Total number of Warrant Officers, Non-commissioned Officers and Men (*a*) Killed in Action, (*b*) Died of Wounds, (*c*) Killed, other than in action, (*d*) Died, from natural causes, etc. :—

4508.

A complete Roll of Soldiers of The Royal Dublin Fusiliers who were killed in action or died as the result of wounds, etc., can be found in " Part 73," The Royal Dublin Fusiliers, published by H.M. Stationery Office, at Imperial House, Kingsway, London, W.C. 2, or 23, Forth Street, Edinburgh, or from Eason & Sons, Ltd., 41 & 42, Lower Sackville Street, Dublin. Price 2/6.

[Appendix Five

List of
HONOURS AND REWARDS
issued to
THE ROYAL DUBLIN FUSILIERS
for services in
THE GREAT WAR, 1914-18.

NOTE.—*This list is as accurate as possible from data available. Omissions or errors may have occurred. It is hoped that notification of same will be sent to the publishers with a view to corrections being made should a second impression become necessary.*

VICTORIA CROSS.

Curtis, Horace Augustus; sergeant (Regtl. No. 14107); 2nd Battalion. For gallantry in France. Invested 8/3/19. (*London Gazette*, 6/1/19.)

Downie, Robert; sergeant (Regtl. No. 11213); 2nd Battalion. For gallantry in France. V.C. presented by the King at Sandringham, 8/1/17. (*London Gazette*, 25/11/16.)

Ockenden, James; sergeant (Regtl. No. 10605); 1st Battalion. For gallantry east of Langemaarke, France. Invested 5/12/17. (*London Gazette*, 8/11/17.)

ORDERS OF BATH, St. MICHAEL AND St. GEORGE, DISTINGUISHED SERVICE ORDERS, MILITARY CROSSES, AND PROMOTIONS.

NAME.	RANK.	BATTALION.	HONOURS AND REWARDS.	"LONDON GAZETTE."
Alexander, Edward	2nd-Lieut.	1st	M.C.	24/9/18
Amos, Stephen Lewis	Lieut. (Temp. Capt.)	5th (attd. 152nd T.M.B.)	M.C.	4/6/17
Arnold, Norman Alfred	Temp. Lieut.	Attd. 1st	M.C.	11/1/19
Ashton, Frederic Ellis	Major (Temp. Lieut.-Col. York and Lanc. Regt.)	Attd. 7th	D.S.O.	3/6/18
Bagley, Arthur Bracton	Capt.	1st	M.C.	17/4/17
Bailey, Charles	Temp. Capt.	10th	M.C.	1/1/18
Barrett, Edward Robert	Temp. Lieut.	Attd. 2nd Bn. R. Innis. Fusiliers	M.C.	15/2/19
Beaumont, William Victor	2nd-Lieut.	Spec. Res. (attd. 2nd)	M.C.	17/9/17
Bellingham, Edward Henry Charles Patrick, Sir	Temp. Lieut.-Col. (Temp. Brig.-Gen.)	8th (R. of O., late Royal Scots)	D.S.O.	20/10/16
			C.M.G.	1/1/18
			Bt. Lieut.-Col. (A.O. 193)	30/1/20
Bergin, Charles Joseph	2nd-Lieut.	3rd (attd. 1st Bn. Royal Munster Fusiliers)	M.C.	2/12/18
Black, Walter Ian	2nd-Lieut.	Spec. Res. (att. 2nd)	M.C.	26/7/17
			Bar to M.C.	18/10/17
Boulter, Jack Edward Hewitt	2nd-Lieut.	2nd	M.C.	15/2/19
Brown, Frederic Elliott	Lieut.	3rd, and No. 84 Sqdn. R.F.C.	M.C.	22/4/18
			Bar to M.C.	22/6/18
Browne, Bernard Joseph (M.M.)	Temp. 2nd-Lieut.	11th (attd. 10th)	M.C.	18/2/18
Burke, John	Qr.Mr. and Hon. Maj.	2nd	M.C.	1/1/17
			D.S.O.	3/6/19
Burke-Savage, Ivan	Temp. Lieut.	10th (attd. 1st)	M.C.	1/1/19
Burrowes, Alfred Edward	Temp. 2nd-Lieut.	9th (attd. 2nd)	M.C.	1/1/18
Byrne, Louis Campbell	Lieut. (A./Capt.)	Attd. 2nd	M.C.	18/10/17
			Bar to M.C.	18/2/18
			D.S.O.	15/2/19
Byrne, Richard	Qr.Mr. and Hon. Lieut.	Service	M.C.	2/2/16
Calwell, William Maunsell	Temp. Capt.	10th (attd. 19th Entr. Bn.)	M.C.	16/9/18
Cameron, William Bedford St. George	Lieut.	3rd (attd. 1st)	M.C.	1/1/19
Carew, Robert John Henry	Capt.		M.C.	1/1/17
			Bt. Major	3/6/19
Carroll-Leahy, Thomas Joseph	Capt. and Bt. Major		M.C.	1/1/15
			Bt. Major	4/6/17
			D.S.O.	1/1/19

HONOURS AND REWARDS

Carruthers, Colin Gordon	Capt.	Attd. 24th	M.C.	2/5/16
Carson, William Roland	Temp. Lieut.	—	M.C.	8/3/19
Chandler, George Hamilton	Lieut. (A./Capt.)	Spec. Res. (attd. 1st)	M.C.	26/11/17
Clarke, Norman Percy	Major	—	Bt. Lieut.-Col.	1/1/19
Clarke, Thomas Scott	Temp. 2nd-Lieut., 2nd Bn. R. Irish Regt.	Attd. 1st Bn.	M.C.	8/3/19
Corballis, Edward Roux Littledale	Capt.	R.D.F. and R.F.C.	D.S.O.	1/1/18
Cory, George Norton (D.S.O.)	Major	R.D.F.	Bt. Lieut.-Col.	18/2/15
			Bt. Col.	1/1/17
			C.B.	3/6/18
			Major-Gen.	1/1/19
Cox, John Francis	Temp. 2nd-Lieut.	10th	M.C.	26/1/17
Crawford, Gilbert Malcolm	Temp. Capt.	7th (attd. 2nd)	M.C.	8/3/19
Crozier, Herbert Charles	Capt.	1st	M.C.	3/7/15
Cullen, Patrick John	2nd-Lieut. (A./Capt.)	1st (attd. 1st Bn. R. Irish Rifles)	M.C.	1/2/19
Cuninghame, Henry Maurice Benedict Gun.	Lieut. (Temp. Capt.)	Spec. Res. (attd. 1st)	M.C.	17/4/17
Dalton, James Emmet	Temp. 2nd-Lieut.	7th (attd. 9th)	M.C.	20/10/16
Darling, Sydney George	Temp. 2nd-Lieut.	9th (attd. 1st)	M.C.	16/9/18
Davies, Douglas Joseph	2nd-Lieut.	5th (attd. 10th)	M.C.	3/6/18
Devlin, David	2nd-Lieut.	3rd (attd. 2nd)	M.C.	8/3/19
Devoy, Joseph Charles Brendin	Lieut. (A./Capt.)	1st	M.C.	4/2/18
Dickie, James MacNeece	Capt.	—	M.C.	23/6/15
Dickie, T. W.	Capt.	Spec. Res.	Bt. Major	1/1/18
Dickson, Thomas Cedric Harold	Capt. (A./Major)	4th (attd. 13th Bn. R. Innis. Fus.)	M.C.	3/6/19
Dobbs, John Fritz Kivas	Capt.	Attd. 1st Bn. R. Ir. Rif.	M.C.	30/1/20
Dolan, John Joseph	2nd-Lieut.	2nd	M.C.	16/9/18
Donovan, Cyril Bernard	Temp. 2nd-Lieut (A./Capt.)	—	M.C.	1/1/18
Duff-Taylor, Squire	Capt.	4th (attd. 2nd)	M.C.	3/6/18
Egan, Nicholas Joseph	Temp. 2nd-Lieut.	9th	M.C.	27/7/16
Esmonde, James	Lieut.	Attd. 6th	M.C.	1/1/18
Fisher, Clarence George Cary	Temp. 2nd-Lieut.	8th (attd. 1st)	M.C.	16/9/18
Frankland, Thomas Hugh Colville	Capt.	—	Bt. Major	18/2/15
Franklin, Hubert Charles	Temp. 2nd-Lieut.	8/9th	M.C.	4/2/18
Gaffney, James	Lieut.	Spec. Res. (attd. 2nd)	M.C.	11/12/16
Galbraith, Hugh	Temp. 2nd-Lieut.	10th (attd. 19th Entr. Bn.)	M.C.	16/9/18

NEILL'S "BLUE CAPS"

NAME.	RANK.	BATTALION.	HONOURS AND REWARDS.	"LONDON GAZETTE."
Gehrke, Richard Arthur	Lieut.	5th Spec. Res. (attd. 30th M.G. Coy.)	D.S.O.	25/11/16
Gibbs, George Howard	Lieut. (Temp. Major)	4th (attd. Vth Corps as T.M. officer)	M.C.	3/6/19
Glegg, James Donie	Capt.	2nd	M.C.	4/6/17
Goodbody, Jerome Marcus	Temp. Lieut.	10th (attd. 4th Bn. North'd Fus.)	M.C.	24/9/18
Greaves, Eric	Temp. Lieut.	7th (attd. 2nd)	M.C.	2/4/19
Grove, James Robert Wood	Capt. (Temp. Major)	—	Bt. Major	3/6/19
Guilbride, Francis Langford	Temp. Capt.	8th	M.C.	24/6/16
Hamlet, Francis Aylmer	Lieut. (A./Capt.)	3rd (attd. 2nd Bn. Tank Corps)	M.C.	3/6/19
Hannin, William Francis	Temp. Lieut.	6th	M.C.	8/3/19
Harcourt, Harry Gladwyn	Temp. Lieut. (A./Capt.)	Attd. 51st Bn. M.G.C.	M.C.	3/6/18
			D.S.O.	26/7/18
			Bar to D.S.O.	21/1/20
Harrison, Herbert Berkeley	Lieut. (A./Capt.)	1st (attd. 1/6th Bn. Glouc. R.)	M.C.	2/4/19
Harvey, William James	Lieut.	Spec. Res. and No. 102 Sqdn. R.F.C.	M.C.	22/6/18
Haskard, John McDougall	Major (Temp. Lieut.-Col.)	—	D.S.O.	1/1/17
			Bt. Lieut.-Col.	1/1/18
			C.M.G.	1/1/17
Hatt, Frederick (Regtl. No. 5531)	Regtl. Sergt.-Major	2nd	M.C.	1/1/17
			Bar to M.C.	16/9/18
Hawtrey, Eric Edmund Harcourt	Temp. 2nd-Lieut.	Attd. 1st	M.C.	8/3/19
Hayes, Hugh Joseph	Capt.	4th (attd. 6th)	M.C.	1/1/17
Healy, Christopher Francis	Temp. 2nd-Lieut.	8th	M.C.	3/6/19
Healy, Maurice	Capt.	4th (attd. Labour Corps)	M.C.	4/6/17
Heffernan, James Gerald Patrick	Temp. Capt.	9th	D.S.O.	3/6/19
Henchy, Alphonso Watson	Temp. 2nd Lieut.	10th	M.C.	24/1/17
Henderson, E. (Regtl. No. 10819)	Company Sergt.-Major		M.C.	18/2/15
Higgins, Richard Leo	Temp. 2nd-Lieut.	10th (attd. 9th Bn. R. Innis. Fus.)	M.C.	17/4/17
Higginson, Harold Whitla	Major and Bt. Col. (Temp. Lt.-Col., Temp. Brig.-Gen., Temp. Major-Gen.)	—	Bar to M.C.	15/2/19
			D.S.O.	14/1/16
			Bt. Lt.-Col.	3/6/16
			Bt. Col.	1/1/18
			Bar to D.S.O.	16/9/18
			C.B.	1/1/19

HONOURS AND REWARDS

Hill, Charles	Temp. 2nd-Lieut.	9th	M.C.	17/9/17
Horrell, Joseph Betts	2nd-Lieut.	5th (attd. 2nd)	M.C.	8/3/19
Hughes, Bryan Desmond	Temp. 2nd-Lieut.	8th	M.C.	24/6/16
Hughes, James Allan	Lieut.	Spec. Res. (attd. 6th Bn. L. N. Lancs. R.)	M.C.	15/10/18
Humphrey, William	2nd-Lieut.	4th (attd. 2nd)	M.C.	15/2/19
Hunt, John Patrick	Temp. Capt. (now Temp. Major, A./Lieut.-Col.)	8th (now Gen. List)	D.S.O.	20/10/16
			Bar to D.S.O.	26/7/18
			C.M.G.	3/6/19
Hurst, Nicholas	Temp. 2nd-Lieut.	9th	M.C.	20/10/16
Hurst, Nicholas	Capt. 9th Gurkha Rif. (I.A.)	—	Bar to M.C.	10/6/21 to date 1/8/20
Jeffreys, Richard Griffith Bassett	Major (Temp. Lieut.-Col.)	2nd	D.S.O.	1/1/18
Jeffries, William Francis	Capt. (A./Major)	Spec. Res.	D.S.O.	26/7/18
Jowett, Harold Arthur	Temp. 2nd-Lieut.	1st (attd. 6th)	M.C.	25/11/16
Julian, Arthur Wellesley	Lieut.	Spec. Res. (attd. 10th)	M.C.	4/6/17
Kane, Michael Harry Kirkpatrick	Lieut.	Spec. Res. (attd. 10th)	M.C.	18/2/18
Kee, William	Temp. Lieut.	7th	M.C.	25/11/16
			Bar to M.C.	16/9/18
Kelly, Daniel	Temp. Capt. R.A.M.C.	Attd. 1st Bn.	M.C.	4/6/17
Kendrick, Edward Holt	Bt. Major (Temp. Lieut.-Col.)	R.D.F. (comdg. 11th Bn. Suffolk Regt.)	Bt. Major	4/6/17
			D.S.O.	1/1/18
			Bt. Lieut.-Col.	3/6/19
Kidd, William Ruddock	2nd-Lieut.	Spec. Res. (attd. 8th)	M.C.	22/9/16
Kiernan, Farrell Michael	Temp. Capt.	2nd	M.C.	2/4/19
Laffan, Paul	2nd-Lieut.	1st	M.C.	26/11/17
Lamblin, Douglas Raymond	Lieut.	5th (attd. 2nd)	M.C.	8/3/19
Law, Robert	Capt.	1st	M.C.	22/9/16
Lind, Walter Peterson	Temp. 2nd-Lieut.	8th	M.C.	24/6/16
Lindsay, Walter Charles (M.V.O.)	Lieut.-Col.	Spec. Res.	Bt. Col.	1/1/19
Little, Edward Gerald	2nd-Lieut.	Attd. 7th	M.C.	16/8/17
Lloyd, Percy Gamaliel Whitelocke	Temp. 2nd-Lieut.	11th (attd. 2nd)	M.C.	17/12/17
Loveband, Arthur	Lieut.-Col.	R.D.F.	C.M.G.	18/2/15
McElnay, George Herbert	Lieut.	3rd (attd. 2nd)	M.C.	8/3/19
McFeely, Cecil Michael	Lieut.	1st	D.S.O.	17/4/17
				26/11/17
			Bar to M.C.	8/3/19

172   NEILL'S "BLUE CAPS"

NAME.	RANK.	BATTALION.	HONOURS AND REWARDS.	"LONDON GAZETTE."
McGowan, Patrick John	Temp. 2nd-Lieut.	11th (attd. 1st)	M.C.	24/9/18
McGrath, John Augustine	Temp. 2nd-Lieut.	11th (attd. 9th)	M.C.	18/-/17
McKenna, John	2nd-Lieut.	3rd (attd. R. Ir. Rif.; attd. 107th L.T.M.B.)	M.C.	15/2/19
Mackenzie, Ian Dawson	2nd-Lieut. (Temp. Lieut.)	3rd (attd. 1st)	M.C.	1/1/18
McMahon, Vincent Matthew	Temp. 2nd-Lieut.	10th	M.C.	26/1/17
Maguire, Robert	Temp. 2nd-Lieut.	7th	M.C.	26/9/17
Massy-Westropp, Ralph Frederick Hugh	Capt.	R.D.F.	M.C.	3/6/19
Matson, Colin	Lieut.	Attd. 10th M.G.C.	M.C.	4/6/17
Matthews, Horace Lionel	Temp. Capt.	8th	M.C.	4/6/17
May, John Paul (M.M.)	2nd-Lieut.	Attd. 1st Bn. R. Muns. Fus.	M.C.	2/12/18
Miller, John Stephen	Temp. 2nd-Lieut.	Attd. 6th	D.S.O.	8/3/19
Molesworth, Edward Algernon	Major	—	D.S.O.	15/10/15
Monson, William Herbert	Temp. Capt	8th	M.C.	24/6/16
Montgomery, Malcolm Ronald	2nd-Lieut.	2nd	M.C.	18/2/18
Moore, A.	Major	—	Bt. Lieut.-Col.	1/1/18
Morris, Samuel	2nd-Lieut.	2nd	M.C.	15/2/19
			Bar to M.C.	2/4/19
Noblett, George Harris	2nd-Lieut. (A./Capt.)	3rd (attd. 1st)	M.C.	11/1/19
			Bar to M.C.	15/2/19
Nolan, James (D.C.M.)	2nd-Lieut.	1st	M.C.	16/9/18
O'Connor, Matthew John	2nd-Lieut.	R.D.F. and 50th Bn. M.G.C.	M.C.	15/2/19
O'Connor, Peter John	Temp. 2nd-Lieut.	8th	M.C.	24/6/16
O'Donnell, Michael Francis	Temp. 2nd-Lieut.	8th (attd. 1st)	M.C.	11/1/19
			Bar to M.C.	8/3/19
			2nd Bar to M.C.	8/3/19
O'Dowda, James Wilton	Lieut.-Col. (Temp. Brig.-Gen.)	R.D.F. and Staff	Bt.-Col.	3/6/16
			C.M.G.	22/12/16
			C.B.	7/2/18
			D.S.O.	3/7/15
O'Hara, Henry Desmond	Lieut.	10th (attd. Bn. R. Muns. Fus.)	M.C.	18/6/17
O'Malley, Victor David	Capt. (Temp.)	3rd (attd. 2nd)	Bar to M.C.	15/2/19
O'Sullivan, Gerald Patrick	Lieut.	Spec. Res. (attd. 1st)	M.C.	8/3/19
Oulton, William Plato	Capt.		M.C.	7/12/15
			Bar to M.C.	18/2/18

HONOURS AND REWARDS

Name	Rank	Unit	Honour	Date
Palmer, David Adams	2nd-Lieut.	Spec. Res. (attd. 8th)	M.C.	20/12/16
Parker, Harry (Regtl. No. 27362)	Coy. Sergt.-Major	8th	M.C.	14/11/16
Perreau, Charles Noël	Major (Temp. Col. 5/2/15, Temp. Brig.-Gen. Canadian Militia 10/12/18)	2nd (employed Colonial Office as Comdt. R.M.C. of Canada)	C.M.G. (for services in connection with the War)	4/6/18
Patterson, Ronald More	Lieut. (A./Capt.)	Spec. Res. (attd. 2nd)	M.C.	19/8/17
Pedlow, William	Lieut. (A./Capt.)	2nd	M.C.	18/2/18
Petit, Gorth	2nd-Lieut.	2nd	M.C.	18/2/18
Philippe, Douglas George	2nd-Lieut.	4th	M.C.	17/9/17
Popham, F. S.	Capt.	Spec. Res.	Bt. Major	1/1/18
Power, Frederick Thomas Alfred	Lieut.	2nd	M.C.	17/9/17
Quigley, Eugene Patrick	Temp. Lieut.	9th	M.C.	20/10/16
Renny, Lewis Frederick	Major	Staff, R.D.F.	D.S.O.	23/6/15
			Bt. Lieut.-Col.	1/1/17
			C.M.G.	1/1/18
			Bt.-Col.	3/6/19
Ridley, Herbert Leslie	Lieut. (Temp. Capt.)	1st	M.C.	1/1/17
Robinson, John Poole Bowring	Major	—	D.S.O.	4/6/17
			C.M.G.	1/1/19
Romer, Cecil Francis	Major and Bt. Lieut.-Col. (Temp. Col. on the Staff)	—	C.B.	18/2/15
			Bt. Col. and A.D.C. (extra) to the King	14/1/16
			C.M.G.	1/1/17
			Major-Gen.	11/1/19
Ross, Frederick George	2nd-Lieut.	5th (attd. 1st)	M.C.	1/1/19
Seymour, Evelyn Francis Edward	Major (A./Lieut.-Col.)	Attd. 10th	D.S.O.	1/1/18
Shadforth, Harold Anthony	Capt.	Attd. 6th	M.C.	8/3/19
Staples, John Vincent	Temp. 2nd-Lieut.	Attd. 2nd	M.C.	8/3/19
Stirke, Henry Richard	Temp. Major	9th (attd. 2nd)	D.S.O.	18/2/18
Stirling, Walter Francis	Major	R. of O. (late R.D.F.)	M.C.	1/1/18
			Bar to D.S.O.	8/3/19
Synnott, Frederick William	Capt.	Spec. Res. (attd. 10th and 19th Entr. Bn.)	M.C.	16/9/18
Thompson, Albert Charles	Temp. Lieut.-Col.	8th	D.S.O.	1/1/18
Thompson, Frank Septimus	Temp. Lieut.	8th	M.C.	24/6/16
Tippet, Herbert Charles Coningsby	Capt.	4th	M.C.	1/1/19
Treacher, Frederick	Lieut.	—	M.C.	14/1/16
			Bt. Major	3/6/19

NAME.	RANK.	BATTALION.	HONOURS AND REWARDS.	"LONDON GAZETTE."
Tredennick, James Paumier	Major (Temp. Lieut.-Col.)		D.S.O.	14/1/16
Watson, Ronald Macgregor	Capt.		D.S.O.	18/2/15
			Bt. Major	1/1/17
Weir, Andrew Herbert	Temp. Lieut.	Attd. 1st	M.C.	8/3/19
Weldon, Kenneth Charles	Major		D.S.O.	1/1/17
			Bt. Lieut.-Col.	3/6/19
White, Herbert	Temp. Lieut. (A./Capt.)	9th	M.C.	26/7/18
Whyte, William Henry	Lieut. (Temp. Major A./Lieut.-Col.)	R. of O., R.D.F. (attd. 6th Bn.)	D.S.O.	3/6/19
			D.S.O.	1/1/18
Wolfe, William Cooper	2nd-Lieut.	Spec. Res. (attd. 2nd)	M.C.	16/9/18

THE ORDERS OF THE BRITISH EMPIRE, MILITARY DIVISION, 1914–20.

NAME.	RANK.	BATTALION.	HONOURS AND REWARDS.	"LONDON GAZETTE."
Bell, Lee	2nd-Lieut.	11th	M.B.E.	7/6/18
			Transferred to Mil. Div.	15/4/19
Bromilow, Walter	Col.	R.D.F.	C.B.E., Grade III	3/6/19
Byrne, Richard, M.C.	Capt. and Qr.Mr.	R.D.F.	O.B.E., Grade IV	3/6/19
De Courcey Wheeler, Samuel Gerald	Temp. Lieut.-Col.	R.D.F.	O.B.E., Grade IV, with effect from 3/6/19	12/12/19
Elsworthy, Alexander Lockhart	Capt.	2nd	M.B.E., Grade V	3/6/19
Halligan, Joseph Thomas	Capt.	R.D.F.	O.B.E., Grade IV	1/1/19
Henry, Hugh	Major (Spec. Res.)	Late 3rd	O.B.E., Grade IV, with effect from 3/6/19	12/12/19
Keegan, Michael, M.M.	Capt. (A./Major)		O.B.E., Grade IV	3/6/19
Lanigan-O'Keefe, François Stephen			M.B.E., Grade V	3/6/19
Meldon, James Austen	Lieut.-Col.	4th	C.B.E., Grade III	3/6/19
Mood, John Muspratt, M.C.	Capt. (Temp. Major)	R.D.F., seconded M.G.C.	O.B.E., Grade IV	3/6/19
Moore, James Stuart Hamilton	T./Capt. (Gen. List, Intelligence H.Q., Eastern Command)	G.S.O.3, R.D.F.	O.B.E., Grade IV	3/6/19

HONOURS AND REWARDS

NAME.	RANK.	BATTALION.	HONOURS AND REWARDS.	"LONDON GAZETTE."
Robinson, Robert Hervey StClair	Lieut.-Col.	5th	M.B.E., Grade V (transferred to Mil. Div., *Lond. Gaz.*, 23/1/20)	8/1/19
Seymour, Evelyn Francis Edward D.S.O.	Major	R.D.F.	O.B.E., Grade IV	3/6/19
Shadforth, Harold Anthony	Capt.	R.D.F. (attd. 6th)	O.B.E., Grade IV	20/3/19
Shore, Alfred George	Lieut. (Temp. Capt.)	3rd	M.B.E., Grade V	3/6/19
Smithwick, Standish George	Major	R.D.F.	O.B.E., Grade IV	3/6/19
Tredennick, James Paumier, D.S.O.	Major	R.D.F.; D.A.A.G. 63rd (R.N.) Div.	O.B.E., Grade IV	3/6/19
Ward, John	Major	R.D.F.	O.B.E., Grade IV	1/1/19

NEILL'S "BLUE CAPS"
DISTINGUISHED CONDUCT MEDAL.

NAME.	REGTL. NO.	RANK.	BATTALION.	"LONDON GAZETTE."
Ainger, A. G.	28934	Private	6th	12/3/19
Alexander, E.	9529	Sergeant	8th	20/12/16
Benson, R. H., M.M.	27691	Sergeant	1st	12/3/19
Brophy, P.	4907	Sergeant	5th	24/1/17
Byrne, L.	8901	C.Q.M.S.	1st	22/10/17
Byrne, M.	16105	Private	9th	20/10/16
Byrne, S.	10774	A./Sergeant	1st	22/1/16
Callaghan, E.	17988	Private	2nd	15/3/16
Carrick, J.	16980	C.S.M.	9th	20/10/16
Chittenden, B.	7574	Bandsman	2nd	17/12/14
Conneys, P.	22813	L./Corporal	2nd	18/2/18
Cooke, W.	8672	A./Sergeant	2nd	30/6/15
Cooney, C.	10256	Sergeant	1st	6/9/15
Cowell, J.	14627	Sergeant	9th	20/10/16
Cullen, L.	6847	Sergeant	9th	19/11/17
Cullen, T.	10159	Sergeant	1st	1/1/19
Cullen, T.	10113	Private	1st	5/8/15
Cummins, W.	6603	C.S.M.	2nd	16/5/16
Bar to D.C.M.	—	—	—	12/3/19
Curley, W. P.	9508	Corporal	2nd	14/1/16
Delaney, P.	9364	Sergeant	1st	26/11/17
Dennis, J. M.	28923	Sergeant	6th	12/3/19
Devoy, J.	10335	Sergeant	1st	2/2/16
Doherty, J.	14507	C.S.M.	8th	24/6/16
Donfield, J.	10414	A./Corporal	9th	25/8/17
Dunne, D.	24580	Private	5th	24/1/17
Dyke, C. P.	9761	Private	1st	16/5/16
Ferguson, S.	6128	Sergeant	1st	3/7/15
Ford, J.	17811	Private	1st	16/11/15
Fox, H.	4823	C.S.M.	12th	30/1/20
Furphy, A.	18364	C.S.M. 2nd Bn. R. Mun. Fus.	Late 10th	3/10/18
Gaynor, F. J.	10090	Sergeant	2nd	18/2/19
Gibson, G.	16531	Corporal	1st	12/3/19
Gormley, T.	21233	Corporal	1st	5/12/18
Green, W. C. C.	27780	Sergeant	2nd	18/2/19
Bar to D.C.M.	—	—	—	18/2/19
Greenwood, L. B.	10544	C.S.M.	1st	12/3/19
Guest, A.	14153	A./Sgt.-Major	7th	2/2/16
Hall, R. S.	5039	C.S.M.	2nd	1/4/15
Halloran, M.	18341	Corporal	1st	3/6/19
Healy, R.	14705	Sergeant	8th	24/6/16
Hurley, J. F.	10374	Private	1st	1/1/17
Jennings, T.	10641	Private	1st	16/5/16
Kane, Patrick	10592	Corporal	1st	4/3/18
Kavanagh, R.	8087	Private	2nd	3/6/15
Kelly, C.	11330	Private	2nd	14/1/16
Kelly, E.	28182	Private	8th	1/1/18
Knight, H.	10515	Sgt. (A./R.S.M.)	2nd	1/1/19
Knightley, A. G.	24078	Sergeant	2nd	12/3/19
Lamb, P.	25439	Private	1st	5/12/18
Lennon, M.	15729	Sergeant	8th	24/6/16
Lowe, W.	29318	Private	10th	3/6/18
McManus, J., M.M.	40313	Sergeant	1st	12/3/19
McNamara, F.	10132	Corporal	1st	6/9/15
McPartlin, M., M.M.	21379	Sergeant	1st	30/10/18
Maloney, J.	7100	C.S.M.	2nd	14/1/16
Mangan, P. J.	16540	Sgt. (A./C.S.M.)	—	20/10/16
Moran, P.	7094	Private	2nd	3/6/18
Mulligan, F.	5834	Private	1st	26/11/17

HONOURS AND REWARDS

NAME.	REGTL. NO.	RANK.	BATTALION.	"LONDON GAZETTE."
Murphy, H.	13190	A./R.S.M.	1st	22/10/17
Murray, F.	11371	Private	2nd	3/9/18
O'Brien, D.	20155	Sergeant	6th	12/3/19
O'Brien, J.	9581	L./Corporal	1st	26/11/17
O'Brien, J. F.	13886	C.S.M.	9th	19/11/17
O'Connor, J.	8746	Sergeant	6th	3/6/16
O'Keefe, J.	18763	Sergeant	8th	24/6/16
O'Leary, J.	10310	Sergeant	1st	3/6/19
Perrott, H.	9266	Sergeant	1st	12/3/19
Perry, F.	15834	Sergeant	2nd	18/2/19
Bar to D.C.M.	—	—	—	18/2/19
Roache, J.	9559	L./Sergeant	8th	20/10/16
Robinson, H.	14275	C.S.M.	7th	25/11/16
Ryan, E.	8669	Sergeant	2nd	14/1/16
Shanahan, M.	43052	A./Corporal	2nd	1/5/18
Smith, A.	8222	Sergeant	9th	20/10/16
Stafford, J.	27322	Private	Formerly 10th	3/10/18
Starkie, J.	15828	Private	20th	18/2/19
Stead, T. R.	17748	Private	1st	2/2/16
Stokes, J.	9150	A./Corporal	2nd	19/11/17
Tait, T.	14613	C.S.M.	8th	25/8/17
Waine, P.	11167	Sergeant	1st	22/10/17
Bar to D.C.M.	—	—	—	26/11/17
Wall, C. J.	24478	Corporal	1st	26/11/17
Watts, M.	9121	Private	1st	3/6/19

MILITARY MEDAL.

NAME.	REGTL. NO.	RANK.	BATTALION.	"LONDON GAZETTE."
Acheson, J.	7/13817	Sergeant	7th	22/1/17
Archbold, M.	27247	Private	9th	16/11/16
Aylward, J. J.	26464	L./Corporal	10th	19/2/17
Banbury, D.	27463	Private	1st	14/5/19
Barry, J.	12007	Private	6th	17/6/19
Bass, C. A.	24093	Sergeant	2nd	17/6/19
Bastin, W. G.	15244	Sergeant	9th	19/11/17
Batchelor, S.	22172	Pte. (A./Cpl.)	1st	21/10/18
Bates, H.	22204	L./Corporal	1st	11/11/16
Batley, B.	266607	L./Corporal	1/6th	18/6/17
Behan, T.	16451	Pte. (Cpl.)	6th	23/7/19
Benson, R. H.	27691	Corporal	1st	17/6/19
Billman, G.	27820	Private	6th	20/8/19
Bingham, J.	21139	Private	8th	10/8/16
Blades, J.	29697	Sergeant	2nd	17/6/19
Blake, W.	5837	Private	1st	17/4/17
Blayney, G.	16907	Private	2nd	19/11/17
Blostein, P.	43172	Private	2nd	17/9/17
Blyth, R. J.	13857	Sergeant	1st	11/2/19
Boland, F. C.	14920	L./Corporal	2nd	17/6/19
Boon, W.	10464	C.Q.M.S.	2nd	11/11/16
Bowen, C.	7/24250	Sergeant	7th	22/1/17
Boyce, P.	24274	Private	2nd	17/6/19
Bramble, D.	10882	A./Corporal	1st	17/4/17
Brannan, P.	22434	Private	6th	23/7/19
Brazington, J.	28936	Corporal	6th	17/6/19
Brennan, T.	5610	Private	2nd	11/11/16
Brierley, E.	20041	Private	8th	19/11/17
Brooks, J.	5008	Sergeant	1st	14/1/18
Brophy, P.	4907	Sergeant	1st	18/10/17
Brown, D.	21193	L./Corporal	8th	16/11/16

NAME.	REGTL. NO.	RANK.	BATTALION.	"LONDON GAZETTE."
Brown, G.	8471	Corporal	1st	17/6/19
Brown, T.	30741	Private	1st	11/2/19
Browne, B. J.	25579	Private	10th	19/2/17
Browne, T.	11515	Private	2nd	13/3/18
Brunton, G.	27907	Private	1st	21/10/18
Bryan, E.	13197	Sergt.-Dmr.	6th	9/7/17
Bryan, S.	43610	Private	6th	20/8/19
Buggy, M.	16108	Private	2nd	23/7/19
Burke, J.	10809	C.Q.M.S.	2nd	6/8/18
Burke, J.	8/17090	Sergeant	8th	14/9/16
Butler, C.	5696	Private	8/9th	23/2/18
Butler, T.	18631	Private	1st	14/1/18
Byrd, B.	16517	Sergeant	8th	16/11/16
Byrne, A.	14874	Sergeant	2nd	19/11/17
Byrne, J.	8868	Private	2nd	13/3/18
Byrne, J.	9590	Private	2nd	22/1/17
Byrne, J.	24807	Private	1st	11/2/19
Byrne, L.	8901	Sergeant	1st	11/11/16
Byrne, P.	1823	Private	1st	11/2/19
Byrne, T.	5460	Private	2nd	6/8/18
Cahill, J.	9829	Sergeant	2nd	29/8/18
Callaghan, J.	12699	Private	6th	17/6/19
Campbell, J.	8/15473	Sergeant	8th	14/9/16
Cantillon, R.	18613	Private	2nd	11/11/16
Carr, J.	1/17528	Private	7th	25/4/16
Carroll, J.	8249	Sergeant	2nd	6/1/17
Carroll, M.	9808	Private	1st	21/9/16
Carroll, P.	19392	Pte. (Cpl.)	9th	19/11/17
Carter, J.	8337	Private	2nd	4/2/18
Cashel, J.	43539	Private	2nd	14/5/19
Cassidy, F.	25659	Private	8th	16/11/16
Chambers, A. S.	24110	Private	2nd	23/7/19
Chisolm, A.	30570	Private	2nd	23/7/19
Christian, T.	20014	Pte. (L./Cpl.)	1st	29/8/18
Clark, J.	18369	Private	2nd	11/11/16
Cleary, W. P.	20103	Private	6th	9/12/16
Clifton, R.	14444	Private	8th	16/11/16
Clifton, W.	28444	Pte. (A./L./Cpl.)	2nd	23/7/19
Coen, T.	27995	Private	6th	17/6/19
Collier, R.	5452	Private	2nd	11/11/16
Connell, L.	29912	A./Sergeant	1st	11/2/19
Connolly, E. P.	30170	Private	1st	17/6/19
Connolly, P.	10237	Private	2nd	20/8/19
Conroy, P.	30520	Private	1st	17/6/19
Cooney, M.	26734	Private	9th	18/10/17
Crawford, T.	15544	L./Corporal	9th	17/9/17
Crealy, C.	6889	Sergeant	1st	14/1/18
Crosby, T.	15590	Private	9th	18/10/17
Crowley, W.	15794	Private	8th	10/8/16
Crudden, P.	10834	Corporal	2nd	19/11/17
Bar to M.M.	—	—	—	13/3/18
Cullen, M.	43524	Private	1st	17/6/19
Cummins, P.	25455	Private	1st	11/2/19
Cummins, W.	20881	Private	1st	11/2/19
Curran, P.	40549	L./Corporal	9th	17/9/17
Currie, A.	13039	Sergeant	1st	17/4/17
Dagg, P.	18621	Corporal	8th	17/9/17
Daintree, T.	43182	Private	2nd	13/3/18
Daly, P.	11669	Private	2nd	18/7/17
Bar to M.M.	—	—	—	13/3/18
2nd Bar to M.M.	—	—	—	14/5/19

HONOURS AND REWARDS

NAME.	REGTL. NO.	RANK.	BATTALION.	"LONDON GAZETTE."
Davies, W.	265370	Private	6th	18/7/17
Davis, A. W.	43232	Private	2nd	19/11/17
Davis, F.	27357	Private	2nd	13/3/18
Delaney, J.	1/7874	Corporal	6th	14/1/18
Delaney, P.	9364	C.S.M.	1st	11/2/19
Devine, P.	12687	Corporal	6th	30/1/20
Devitt, W. H.	25570	Private	1st	17/6/19
Devlin, T.	22358	Pte. (L./Cpl.)	1st	14/5/19
Doherty, J.	18370	A./Corporal	2nd	11/11/16
Doherty, T.	27069	Private	9th	17/9/17
Donfield, J.	1/10414	Corporal	9th	22/1/17
Donohoe, T.	19582	Private	1st	14/1/18
Downie, R.	11213	Sergeant	2nd	11/11/16
Doyle, C.	19412	Cpl. (A./Sergt.)	10th	13/3/18
Doyle, J.	30818	Private	2nd	23/7/19
Doyle, P.	4998	Private	1st	14/1/18
Doyle, T.	31346	Corporal	1st	11/2/19
Drake, T.	10314	L./Corporal	2nd	14/5/19
Dunn, H.	28132	Private	2nd	13/3/18
Dunne, J.	21859	Private	2nd	13/3/18
Durr, T. F.	26956	A./Sergeant	2nd	18/7/17
Ebbitt, J.	15797	Sergeant	8th	17/9/17
Egan, F.	9771	Corporal	2nd	11/11/16
Bar to M.M.	—	Sergeant	—	17/6/19
Eglington, J. J.	10640	Sergeant	1st	17/6/19
Bar to M.M.	—	—	—	17/6/19
Ellis, J.	23063	Pte. (L./Cpl.)	8th	11/5/17
Elsey, F.	29011	Private	2nd	17/6/19
Fallon, J.	20102	Sergeant	1st	17/6/19
Felton, W.	16888	L./Corporal	8th	10/8/16
Finerty, J.	18472	L./Corporal	1st	18/10/17
Finlay, A.	10099	Corporal	1st	21/10/18
Finnie, J. R.	29250	Corporal	1st	14/5/19
Flynn, W.	20825	L./Corporal	1st	18/10/17
Foley, J.	40297	Private	1st (attd. 86th T.M. Bty.)	14/1/18
Ford, H. J.	15841	Corporal	2nd	17/6/19
Foster, R.	16223	Private	8th	17/9/17
Bar to M.M.	—	—	—	21/10/18
Foster, W.	40819	Private	1st	11/2/19
Fox, C.	9851	Private	1st (attd. 86th T.M. Bty.)	14/1/18
Fox, E. J. W.	15712	L./Sergeant	1st	6/8/18
Fox, J.	26503	Private	1st	11/2/19
Fray, W. A.	29150	Corporal	2nd	17/6/19
Freeman, P.	9223	Private	2nd	14/5/19
Fullerton, J.	9504	L./Corporal	2nd	11/11/16
Gable, E.	14757	Private	7th	6/1/17
Gaffney, M.	26965	Sergeant	2nd	21/12/16
Gallagher, J.	9536	Private	1st	9/7/17
Galvin, P.	19730	Private	6th	17/6/19
Gannon, P.	6/11864	Private	6th	22/1/17
Gasteen, F. E.	27317	Sergeant	1st	17/6/19
Geddes, R.	17577	Pte. (L./Cpl.)	1st	25/4/18
Gee, J.	40208	Private	1st	14/5/19
Gibson, G.	16531	Corporal	1st	11/2/19
Gill, A.	28816	Private	2nd	14/5/19
Gill, H. P.	40890	Pte. (L./Cpl.)	8th	19/11/17
Gleeson, R.	11481	Corporal	9th (attd. 48th T.M. Bty.)	17/9/17
Glynn, C.	8259	Pte. (L./Cpl.)	2nd	13/3/18

NAME.	REGTL. NO.	RANK.	BATTALION.	"LONDON GAZETTE."
Glynn, T. P.	23253	Corporal	1st	17/6/19
Bar to M.M.	—	—	—	17/6/19
Godden, C.	14315	Private	1st	29/8/18
Goldsborough, J.	30339	Pte. (L./Cpl.)	1st	11/2/19
Goode, A. E.	40535	Corporal	1st	11/2/19
Gorman, P.	11642	Private	2nd	19/11/17
Gorry, J.	24825	Cpl. (L./Sgt.)	1st	29/8/18
Goulding, M.	18944	L./Corporal	9th	21/8/17
Grace, L.	9692	Private	1st	14/1/18
Gray, R.	14245	Private	2nd	23/7/19
Green, M.	28739	Private	1st	18/10/17
Green, P.	23438	Private	2nd	13/3/18
Griffen, J.	8639	L./Corporal	9th	17/9/17
Guinane, T.	19342	Sergeant	1st	11/2/18
Halleron, J.	7075570	L./Corporal	2nd	14/1/21
Hamill, J.	20020	Corporal	1st	21/10/19
Hamilton, P.	11291	Corporal	1st	14/5/19
Hanley, P.	12968	L./Corporal	2nd	17/6/19
Bar to M.M.	—	—	—	20/8/19
Hanlon, P.	27757	Private	1st	21/10/18
Hardy, F.	5698	Private	2nd	23/7/19
Harrington, M.	19062	Private	1st	17/4/17
Hart, W. T.	3/12005	Private	9th	21/9/16
Hayes, R.	5780	Private	1st	11/11/16
Heeney, N.	23928	Pte. (A./L./Cpl.)	1st	14/5/19
Herbert, J. J.	19005	Sergeant	1st	11/2/19
Hession, A.	9344	Private	2nd	13/3/18
Hickey, J.	5573	Private	1st	11/2/19
Hoey, J.	19593	L./Corporal	8th	10/8/16
Hogan, J.	16811	Sergeant	6th	9/12/16
Holmes, W.	5433	Sergeant	2nd	11/11/16
Hooper, E.	24294	Private	1st	11/2/19
Hooten, J.	28493	Corporal	2nd	17/6/19
Horton, H.	14870	Corporal	8th	26/3/17
Bar to M.M.	—	—	—	21/8/17
Hosie, W.	28161	Private	1st	17/6/19
Hubbard, J. T.	40247	Private	1st	11/2/19
Humphreys, H. W.	14372	Private	6th	17/6/19
Humphries, G. E.	41390	Private	1st	11/2/19
Inglesant, J.	29637	Private	6th	17/6/19
Irwin, T. F. A.	29522	Pte. (A./L./Cpl.)	2nd	23/7/19
Jeeves, V.	14391	L./Corporal	7th	6/1/17
Joceylinn, P.	11156	Private	2nd	19/11/17
Jones, W.	22916	Corporal	8th	26/3/17
Joyce, H.	27192	Private	10th	19/2/17
Kearns, P.	23678	Private	2nd	13/3/18
Keegan, T.	10880	A./Sergt.	8th	16/11/16
Keeping, B. R.	10946	Sergeant	2nd	13/3/18
Keeping, F. A.	9497	A./Corporal	8th	6/1/17
Kelly, J.	15533	Private	9th	14/9/16
Kelly, J. P.	14653	Sergeant	9th	16/11/16
Kelly, P.	8790	Private	1st	14/1/18
Kenna, E.	21076	Private	2nd	17/6/19
Kenna, G.	23219	Private	2nd	23/7/19
Kennedy, D.	18324	A./Sergeant	2nd	18/7/17
Kenny, W.	7359	Sergeant	2nd	18/7/17
Killeen, J.	19879	Private	2nd	23/7/19
Killeen, P.	11570	Private	2nd	11/11/16
King, C. J.	20079	L./Corporal	8th	11/5/17
King, H.	30183	Corporal	1st	17/6/19
Kinsella, J.	9891	Cpl. (Sergt.)	9th	19/11/17
Leonard, J.	25241	Private	10th	22/11/19

HONOURS AND REWARDS 181

NAME.	REGTL. NO.	RANK.	BATTALION.	"LONDON GAZETTE."
McCann, P.	7909	Private	8th	19/11/17
McCarten, J.	21563	Pte. (L./Cpl.)	1st	11/2/19
McCarthy, J.	43067	Corporal	1st	9/7/17
McCarthy, J.	16762	Sergeant	1st	14/1/18
McCauley, W.	18856	Sergeant	8th	10/8/16
McCormack, J. J.	27020	Sergeant	10th	19/2/17
McCormick, C.	20910	Private	1st	11/2/19
McCudden, F.	14863	L./Corporal	9th	17/9/17
McCue, E.	18645	L./Corporal	9th	14/9/16
McCullagh, G.	26447	Corporal	10th	13/3/18
McCullagh, M.	9314	Sergeant	1st	11/2/19
McDonnell, J.	19164	Corporal	1st	17/6/19
Bar to M.M.	—	—	—	20/8/19
McFarlane, J.	10814	Corporal	Late 1st	21/9/16
McGahey, G.	7069	Sergeant	2nd	14/12/16
McGann, T.	22117	Private	1st	11/11/16
McGeeney, M.	18624	Pte. (L./Cpl.)	1st	25/4/18
McGlynn, J.	20009	Private	2nd	11/11/16
McGrane, M.	8456	Private	2nd	13/3/18
McGrogan, P.	22141	Private	2nd	13/3/18
McGuirk, D.	21338	Pte. (L./Cpl.)	2nd	13/3/18
McInespie, P.	18241	Private	2nd	19/11/17
Mackew, A.	14090	Sergeant	2nd	14/5/19
McKinley, J. E.	13943	Sergeant	8th	10/8/16
McLoughlin, M.	25245	Cpl. (Sergt.)	10th	13/3/18
McLoughlin, P.	25899	Private	8th	11/5/17
McManus, J.	19870	Private	2nd	29/8/18
McManus, J.	40313	Sergeant	1st	11/2/19
McNeely, J.	23998	Sergeant	1st	17/6/19
McNicol, R.	21890	A./Corporal	1st	11/11/16
McPartlin, M.	21379	Sergeant	2nd	6/8/18
Bar to M.M.	—	—	—	21/10/18
McQueen, J.	21378	Private	1st	17/4/17
Madden, A.	25710	Private	9th	17/9/17
Bar to M.M.	—	—	—	19/10/17
Maguire, P.	8751	Private	Late 1st	11/11/16
Maher, M.	17191	Private	1st	14/1/18
Maher, M.	8/23023	Corporal	8th	14/9/16
Maher, P.	17298	L./Corporal	2nd	17/6/19
Mallon, L.	22461	Pte. (L./Cpl.)	2nd	19/11/17
Bar to M.M.	—	—	—	14/5/19
Malone, P.	22354	Private	1st	28/7/17
Mangan, P. J.	8/16540	Sergeant	8th	14/9/16
Manning, R.	9020	Private	1st	11/2/19
Marchant, W. G.	7/28515	Sergeant	7th	24/1/19
Bar to M.M.	—	—	—	20/8/19
Marks, T.	14116	L./Corporal	2nd	14/5/19
Marshall, A. W.	43546	Corporal	2nd	17/6/19
Martin, J.	15543	Private	8th	9/12/16
May, J. P.	18196	Private	7th	6/1/17
Mealey, L. P.	21136	Private	2nd	23/7/19
Meehan, J.	9138	Private	2nd	19/11/17
Merrins, J.	6568	Sergeant	2nd	4/2/18
Bar to M.M.	—	—	—	2/4/18
Miller, J.	23815	Private	2nd	19/11/17
Minogue, J. P.	19274	Private	2nd	23/7/19
Mitchell, A. J.	24717	Private	10th (attd. 54th L.R.O. Coy. R.E.)	19/11/17
Money, J. W.	43216	Pte. (A./Sgt.)	2nd (attd. 48th T.M. Bty.)	19/11/17

NAME.	REGTL. NO.	RANK.	BATTALION.	"LONDON GAZETTE."
Mooney, M.	6978	Sergeant	9th	19/11/17
Moore, P.	8272	Private	1st	11/11/16
Moran, J.	13008	Corporal	1st (attd. 48th Inf. Bde. Sig. Sec. R.E.)	29/8/18
Moran, T.	26925	Private	10th	26/5/17
Morrisey, T.	23002	Corporal	1st	28/9/17
Bar to M.M.	—	—	—	14/1/18
Mortimer, F. J.	30108	Private	2nd	23/7/19
Mulhall, P.	27634	Pte. (L./Cpl.)	1st	30/1/20
Mulhall, T.	6/12082	L./Corporal	Late 6th	26/4/17
Mullen, A.	15074	Sergeant	2nd	20/8/19
Mullen, M.	40055	Private	2nd	13/3/18
Mulligan, E.	7163	Private	1st	14/1/18
Mulligan, F., D.C.M.	5834	Private	1st	14/5/19
Bar to M.M.	—	—	—	23/7/19
Mulrenan, T.	25970	Private	10th	26/4/17
Murphy, J.	21612	Cpl. (A./Sgt.)	8th	19/11/17
Murphy, J.	26136	Private	1st	11/2/19
Murphy, J.	15061	Private	1st	11/2/19
Murray, F., D.C.M.	11371	Private	2nd	14/5/19
Murray, J.	27979	Pte. (A./L./Cpl.)	1st	14/5/19
Murray, J.	17074	Private	1st	17/6/19
Murray, J.	26629	Private	8th	19/11/17
Murray, M.	10300	Private	2nd	29/8/18
Bar to M.M.	—	—	—	17/6/19
Navin, T.	24605	Private	1st	9/7/17
Neville, J.	25857	Private	1st	9/7/17
Newell, A.	24219	Private	2nd	17/6/19
Newman, W.	13693	Corporal	9th	14/9/16
Newton, F. P.	9211	C.S.M.	1st	11/2/19
Bar to M.M.	—	—	—	17/6/19
Norfolk, W. V.	28774	L./Corporal	2nd	14/5/19
Norman, R.	28018	Pte. (A./L./Cpl.)	1st	11/2/19
Normoyle, M.	17239	Corporal	9th	19/11/17
O'Brien, J.	10055	L./Corporal	1st	3/6/16
O'Brien, J.	13886	Sergeant	9th	16/11/16
O'Brien, J., D.C.M.	9581	Corporal	1st	11/2/19
Bar to M.M.	—	—	—	17/6/19
O'Brien, P.	10924	L./Corporal	1st	3/6/16
O'Brien, R.	23727	Private	1st	20/10/19
O'Byrne, L.	6189	A./Sergeant	1st	11/11/16
O'Connell, M.	26174	L./Corporal	10th	19/2/17
O'Connor, H.	12015	Cpl. (A./L./Sgt.)	2nd	19/11/17
O'Donnell, C.	7124	L./Corporal	1st	11/11/16
O'Haire, P.	8598	Private	1st	25/4/18
O'Neill, T.	21339	L./Corporal	9th	10/8/16
O'Toole, D.	25501	Private	10th	19/2/17
Ockenden, J.	10605	Sergeant	1st	28/9/17
Owen, A.	28776	Private	2nd	23/7/19
Parsons, G.	8056	Private	5th	24/1/17
Patterson, W. P.	30501	Private	1st	11/2/19
Peters, A. E.	6/14311	Corporal	6th	2/11/17
Petty, H. E.	28221	Private	8th	19/11/17
Pim, J.	10410	Pte. (A./L.Cpl.)	1st	11/2/19
Powell, T.	18277	Private	2nd	17/6/19
Preece, G. R.	25437	Sergeant	10th	24/1/17
Prestage, R.	10347	Sergeant	1st	18/10/17
Price, H.	26059	Private	9th	19/11/17
Price, J.	10616	Private	2nd	19/11/17
Priest, T.	25462	Sergeant	10th	19/2/17

HONOURS AND REWARDS

NAME.	REGTL. NO.	RANK.	BATTALION.	"LONDON GAZETTE."
Pudney, E. J.	31272	Private	6th	20/10/19
Quinn, J.	8/15102	Private	8th	14/9/16
Quinn, J.	12894	Private	9th	19/11/17
Redmond, W.	10722	Private	10th	26/4/17
Regan, C. C.	21097	Private	1st	11/2/19
Regan, J.	24016	Private	2nd	17/6/19
Reid, G.	21584	Private	2nd	17/6/19
Reilly, P.	9042	Cpl. (L./Sgt.)	9th	19/11/17
Reilly, T.	27045	Private	1st	17/6/19
Rex, P. C.	9025	Private	1st	3/6/16
Roache, A.	5068	Private	2nd	11/11/16
Roberts, J. F.	16878	Corporal	2nd	18/7/17
Bar to M.M.	—	—	—	13/3/18
Robinson, J.	18870	Private	9th	19/11/17
Roe, P.	11416	Private	2nd	3/6/16
Roebuck, J.	28547	Pte. (L./Cpl.)	2nd	17/6/19
Rogers, J.	40312	Corporal	1st	14/1/18
Ryan, P.	43135	Private	6th	20/8/19
Ryder, J.	25794	Private	1st	11/2/19
Sandar, W.	24040	Private	2nd	13/3/18
Sargeant, T.	18773	Private	1st	6/8/18
Saunders, J.	7842	Private	1st	14/1/18
Scallon, W.	19191	Private	9th	16/11/16
Scott, J.	14095	Private	8th	17/9/17
Scully, J.	12209	Private	1st	14/5/19
Bar to M.M.	—	—	—	23/7/19
Seddon, G.	22177	Private	1st	14/1/18
Shinkwin, T.	8775	Corporal	2nd	18/7/17
Short, E. J.	25975	Private	10th	26/5/17
Singleton, J.	26941	Pte. (L./Cpl.)	2nd	23/7/19
Skegg, C.	14306	L./Sergeant	6th	17/6/19
Skinner, F. C.	28560	L./Corporal	2nd	17/6/19
Smith, J.	9834	Private	2nd	19/11/17
Smith, M.	8145	Private	2nd	13/3/18
Smith, R.	14548	Private	8th	10/8/16
Sneddon, R.	7165	Private	2nd	17/6/19
Spratt, E. A.	26721	Private	10th	19/2/17
Bar to M.M.	—	—	—	13/3/18
Stowe, T.	27686	Private	2nd	17/6/19
Street, L.	14384	L./Corporal	8th	10/8/16
Tait, T.	14613	Sergeant	8th	10/8/16
Taylor, G.	43203	Private	1st	14/5/19
Territt, J.	10026	Private	1st	18/10/17
Bar to M.M.	—	—	—	14/1/18
Thomas, A.	11542	Sergeant	1st	11/2/19
Thurlow, W.	21731	Sergeant	6th	17/6/19
Tierney, J.	21170	Private	1st	11/11/16
Townsend, F.	25184	Private	1st	18/10/17
Tracey, T.	18929	Private	1st	21/9/16
Tracy, J.	9622	Private	2nd	11/11/16
Turton, W.	3/19688	Corporal	7th	25/4/18
Valentine, P.	11163	Sergeant	1st	11/11/16
Wade, J.	9240	Sergeant	1st	17/6/19
Walker, H.	40726	Private	1st	11/2/19
Bar to M.M.	—	—	—	17/6/19
Wallace, C. N.	6642	Sergeant	2nd	6/1/17
Walls, J.	12137	A./Sergeant	1st	11/2/19
Bar to M.M.	—	—	—	23/7/19
Walsh, J.	13269	Private	2nd	12/12/17
Walsh, M.	6745	Sergeant	2nd	11/11/16
Watson, J.	41004	Private	1st	18/10/17

NAME.	REGTL. NO.	RANK.	BATTALION.	"LONDON GAZETTE."
Webb, J.	9072	Private	2nd	18/7/17
Wharf, E.	40388	Private	1st	11/2/19
Whelan, P.	10776	A./Corporal	1st	11/11/16
White, H.	9980	Pte. (L./Cpl.)	2nd	13/3/18
Whittaker, L.	9709	Sergeant	8th	11/5/17
Wilkinson, T.	19115	Private	1st	17/6/19
Wilson, J. H.	15901	Sergeant	9th	14/9/16
Wood, A.	10652	C.Q.M.S.	2nd	3/6/19
Worrell, W.	13119	Private	8th	21/9/16

MERITORIOUS SERVICE MEDAL.

NAME.	REGTL. NO.	RANK.	BATTALION.	"LONDON GAZETTE."
Berry, W. P.	8898	Sergeant	2nd	17/6/18
Boon, W.	10464	C.Q.M.S.	2nd	30/1/20
Burke, J.	10809	C.Q.M.S.	2nd	3/6/19
Cahill, J.	9829	Sgt. (A./C.Q.M.S.)	2nd	3/6/19
Cameron, J.	15955	Sergeant	1st	3/6/19
Clements, W. H.	7/14401	Private	7th	26/4/17
Connolly, R. W.	15825	C.S.M.	10th	17/6/18
Cops, F. O.	12123	R.Q.M.S.	1st	17/6/18
Cornish, J.	12170	Sergeant	6th	3/6/19
Coyne, J.	7/13760	C.S.M.	7th	13/2/17
Daly, J.	4956	R.S.M.	—	22/2/19
Darling, S. G.	7/15273	Sergeant	7th	26/4/17
Fitzpatrick, F. H.	29404	Q.M.S. (A./S.M.)	—	12/12/19
Frost, G. F.	6/12325	R.S.M.	6th	18/6/17
Galloway, E. H.	25356	Sgt. (A./C.S.M.)	—	18/1/19
Geraghty, H.	8658	Sergeant	1st	17/6/18
McKeown, D.	15117	R.Q.M.S.	8/9th	17/6/18
Mangan, W.	6/13553	C.Q.M.S.	6th	17/12/17
Marrett, E. A. R.	43537	Pte. (A./Q.M.S.)	2nd	3/6/19
Money, J. W.	43216	Sergeant	2nd (attd. 48th T.M. Bty.)	17/6/18
O'Connor, J. J.	8859	R.Q.M.S.	2nd	17/6/18
Purcell, P.	15120	Q.M.S.	Depot	12/12/19
Shoetensack, W. G.	28557	Private	7th	3/6/19

HONOURS AND REWARDS

MENTIONED IN DESPATCHES, 1914–20.

NAME.	RANK.	BATTALION.	THEATRE OF WAR.	"LONDON GAZETTE."
Atherley, C. E.	Temp. Lieut. (Service Bn. Yorkshire L.I.)	Attd. 1st	Dardanelles	5/11/15, p. 10999
Allan, J. H.	Capt. (Temp. Major)	1st attd. 1/7th Manch.	Egypt	6/7/17, p. 6769
Addis, G. T.	Capt. (Spec. Res.)	4th (attd. 2nd)	France	21/12/17, p. 13373
Adcock, H.	Pte. (Regtl. No. 27802)	6th	France	24/5/18, p. 6101
Bousted, L. C.	Lieut.	1st	France	9/7/19, p. 8710
Brennan, T.	L./Cpl. (Regtl. No. 5610)	2nd	Dardanelles	5/11/15, p. 10999
Bryan, E.	Cpl. (Regtl. No. 13197)	Service	France	1/1/16, p. 56
Burrowes, A. E.	Sergt. (Regtl. No. 14150)	Service	Dardanelles	28/1/16, p. 1204
Bellingham, E. H. C. P., D.S.O.	Temp. Lieut.-Col. (Lieut. R. of O., Temp. Brig.-Gen.)	8th	France	28/1/16, p. 1204
Byrd, B.	Sergt. (A./C.S.M.) (Regtl. No. 16517)	8th	France	4/1/17, p. 240
Burke, F. W. R.	L./Sergt. (Regtl. No. 25692)	10th	France	25/1/17, p. 946
Brown, F. E.	Lieut.	3rd (attd. R.F.C.)		15/5/17, p. 4754
Burke, J., M.C., D.C.M.	Qr.Mr. and Hon. Major	2nd	France	17/2/15, p. 1668
			France	21/12/17, p. 13373
			France	9/7/19, p. 8710
Burke, J.	Sergt. (Regtl. No. 6/14885)	6th	Egypt	14/6/18, p. 7054
Byrne, R. C., M.C.	Qr.Mr. and Hon. Capt.	6th	Dardanelles	28/1/16, p. 1204
			Egypt	14/6/18, p. 7054
Beveridge, E. W.	Lieut. (attd. 34th D.S. Coy. R.E.)	4th	France	9/7/19, p. 8710
Byrne, L. C., D.S.O., M.C.	Lieut. (A./Major)	2nd	France	9/7/19, p. 8710
Bailey, H. T.	Cpl. (A./L./Sergt.) (Regtl. No. 15372)	2nd	France	9/7/19, p. 8710
Brown, C. H.	Sergt. (Regtl. No. 43472)	1st	France	9/7/19, p. 8710
Boon, W., M.M.	C.Q.M.S. (Regtl. No. 10464)	2nd (Wrexham)		30/1/20, p. 1227
Campbell, F. C. G.	Lieut. (40th Pathans)	Attd. 2nd	France	17/2/15, p. 1668
Cooke, —	Cpl. (Regtl. No. 8672)	2nd	France	17/2/15, p. 1668
Curley, W. P.	Cpl. (Regtl. No. 9508)	2nd	France	22/6/15, p. 6003
Crozier, H. C.	Capt.	1st	Dardanelles	5/8/15, p. 7666
Cooney, C.	Sergt. (Regtl. No. 10256)	1st	Dardanelles	5/8/15, p. 7666
Cummins, W.	Sergt. (Regtl. No. 6603)	1st	Dardanelles	5/8/15, p. 7666
Carew, R. J. H.	Capt. (Temp. Major, 83rd Bde. Machine Gun Officer)	2nd	France	5/5/16, p. 4519
			Salonika	1/1/16, p. 56
			Salonika	11/6/18, p. 6918
				5/6/19

NAME.	RANK.	BATTALION.	THEATRE OF WAR.	"LONDON GAZETTE."
Campbell, J.	Temp. Sergt.-Major (Regtl. No. 13507), also Qr.Mr. and Hon. Lieut.	8th	Dardanelles	28/1/16, p. 1204
			France	25/5/17, p. 5166
Carruthers, C. G.	Capt.	1st	France	21/12/17
			Dardanelles	5/11/15, p. 10999
			Dardanelles	5/5/16, p. 4519
Clarke, N. P.	Major	2nd	Dardanelles	13/7/16, p. 6956
			France	17/2/15, p. 1668
Cory, G. N.	Major and Bt. Col. (Temp. Major-Gen.)	R.D.F., Staff	Egypt	21/6/16, p. 6182
			France	9/12/14, p. 10535
			France	17/2/15, p. 1648
			France	1/1/16, p. 3
			Salonika	25/9/16, p. 9342
			Salonika	6/12/16
			Salonika	21/7/17, p. 7448
			Salonika	11/6/18, p. 6918
			Salonika	31/1/19, p. 1474
			Mesopotamia	9/9/21
Cox, P. G. A.	Bt. Major (Temp. Lieut.-Col.), Ret. Pay, R. of O.	6th	Dardanelles	28/1/16, p. 1204
			Salonika	13/7/16, p. 6942
			Salonika	6/12/16
Corcoran, J.	Pte. (Regtl. No. 15632)	8th	France	4/1/17, p. 240
Corballis, E. R. L.	Capt.	2nd (attd. R.F.C. Staff)	France	17/2/15
			France	15/5/17, p. 4754
Culbert, W.	Sergt. (A./Q.M.S.) (Regtl. No. 10365)	1st	France	11/12/17, p. 12911
Cahill, W.	Sergt. (A./Q.M.S.) (Regtl. No. 18859)	8th	France	25/5/17, p. 5166
Cullen, A. A.	Temp. 2nd-Lieut.	6th	France	25/5/17, p. 5166
Curtis, H. A.	Cpl. (A./Sergt.) (Regtl. No. 7/14107)	7th	Salonika	21/7/17, p. 7453
Curran, P.	R.Q.M.S. (Regtl. No. 1/9593)	7th	Salonika	21/7/17, p. 7454
Conarchy, W. C.	Temp. 2nd-Lieut.	8th	France	28/11/17, p. 12485
Cowley, G. E.	Capt. (Temp. Major)	Attd. 8th	France	21/12/17, p. 13373
Cameron, J.	Sergt. (Regtl. No. 15955)	1st	France	21/12/17, p. 13373
Cops, F. O.	R.Q.M.S. (Regtl. No. 12123)	1st	France	21/12/17, p. 13373
Considine, T. J.	Capt.	5th (attd. 1st)	France	9/7/19, p. 8710
Coombs, J. H.	Sergt.-Dmr. (Regtl. No. 28826)	2nd	France	28/12/18, p. 15162
			France	9/7/19, p. 8710
Dickie, J. MacN.	Lieut.	2nd	France	22/6/15, p. 6003

HONOURS AND REWARDS

Devoy, J.	Sergt. (Regtl. No. 10335)	...	7th	Dardanelles	28/1/16, p. 1204
Downing, G.	Lieut.-Col. (R. of O.)	...	7th	Dardanelles	28/1/16, p. 1204
Dyke, C. P.	Pte. (Regtl. No. 9761)	...	—	Dardanelles	5/5/16, p. 4519
Daly, U. de B.	Capt.	...	4th	Home "A" List	25/1/17, p. 944
Doran, W. A.	Temp. Capt.	...	9th	France	25/5/17, p. 5166
Dee, G. S.	Temp. 2nd-Lieut.	...	7th	Salonika	28/11/17, p. 12485
Douglas, R. G.	Lieut. (Temp. Capt.)	...	2nd	Egypt	16/1/18, p. 934
Delaney, A. S.	Staff (Temp. Major)	...	—	Egypt	5/6/19, p. 7172
Eales, R. W.	Lieut. (Temp. Capt.)	...	5th (attd. 2nd)	France	24/5/18, p. 6101
Esmonde, L. G.	Pte. (Regtl. No. 7/15351)	...	7th	Salonika	6/12/16, p. 11936
Esmonde, James, M.C.	Lieut.-Col.	...	—	(List "A," Ireland)	25/1/17, p. 944
	Lieut. (A./Capt.)	...	Attd. 6th	Salonika	28/11/17, p. 12485
Ekins, E. W.	Pte. (Regtl. No. 28873)	...	2nd	France	9/7/19, p. 8710
Frankland, T. H. C.	Capt.	...	2nd	France	17/2/15, p. 1668
Ferguson, S.	Sergt. (Regtl. No. 6128)	...	1st	Dardanelles	5/8/15, p. 7666
Fletcher, D. A.	Lieut. (Temp. Capt.) 2nd Cameron Highrs.		Attd. R.D.F.	Salonika	6/12/16, p. 11939
Finnigan, J.	Pte. (Regtl. No. 43128)	...	—	Home "A" List	25/1/17, p. 946
Forbes, A.	Sergt. (Regtl. No. 7/14774)	...	7th	Salonika	28/11/17, p. 12485
Fitzgerald, P.	C.Q.M.S. (A./C.S.M.) (Regtl. No. 9952)		1st	France	9/7/19, p. 8710
Graham, A.	C.S.M. (Regtl. No. 6203)	...	2nd	France	22/6/15, p. 6003
Guest, A.	R.S.M. (Regtl. No. 14153)	...	7th	Dardanelles	28/1/16, p. 1204
Gibbs, G. H.	Temp. 2nd-Lieut.	...	—	Salonika	28/11/17, p. 12485
Grove, J. R. W.	2nd-Lieut. (A./Capt.)	...	4th	France	25/5/17, p. 5166
Glegg, J. D., M.C.	Capt. (Temp. Major)	...	1st (attd. R.F.C.)	North Russia	16/1/19, p. 823
Gibbs, J. L. A.	Capt.	...	2nd, Staff	France	5/7/19, p. 8492
	Lieut. (A./Capt.)	...	4th (attd. 5th Field Surv. Bn., R.E.)	France	9/7/19, p. 8710
Gilder, A. W.	Sergt. (Regtl. No. 40518)	...	2nd (attd. H.Q. 48th Inf. Bde.)	France	9/7/19, p. 8710
Hall, R. S.	C.S.M. (Regtl. No. 5039)	...	2nd	France	19/10/14, p. 8356
Hatt, F. W.	Sergt.-Major (Regtl. No. 5531)	...	2nd	France	17/2/15, p. 1668
	R.S.M.	...	2nd	France	24/5/18, p. 6101
Henderson, E.	C.S.M. (Regtl. No. 10819)	...	1st	France	17/2/15, p. 1668
Hayes, R.	Pte. (Regtl. No. 5780)	...	2nd	France	5/11/15, p. 10999
Hayden, P.	Pte. (Regtl. No. 9470)	...	Attd. 7th	France	1/1/16, p. 56
Harrison, R.S.M.	Major 51st Sikhs	...	1st (attd. 7th)	Dardanelles	28/1/16, p. 1204
Hoey, C. B. R.	Capt. (Temp. Major)	...		Dardanelles	28/1/16, p. 1204

(See also page 194.)

NAME.	RANK.	BATTALION.	THEATRE OF WAR.	"LONDON GAZETTE."
Haig, T.	C.S.M. (Regtl. No. 14972)	7th	Dardanelles	28/1/16, p. 1204
Higginson, H. W., C.B., D.S.O.	Major and Bt. Col. (Temp. Major-Gen.)	Staff	France	1/1/16, p. 6
			France	15/6/16, p. 5951
			France	4/1/17
			France	15/5/17, p. 4748
			France	11/12/17, p. 12914
			France	20/5/18, p. 5947
			France	20/12/18, p. 14928
Harvey, C. D.	Temp. Lieut.	7th	France	5/7/19, p. 8493
Haskard, J. McD., C.M.G., D.S.O.	Major (Temp. Brig.-Gen.)	Staff	Salonika	6/12/16, p. 11939
			France	4/1/17
			France	15/5/17, p. 4748
			France	11/12/17, p. 12914
			France	20/5/18, p. 5947
			France	20/12/18, p. 14928
Heffernan, J. G. P.	Temp. Capt.	8/9th (attd. 1st)	France	4/1/17, p. 240
	Temp. Major		France	24/5/18, p. 6101
Hunt, J. P., C.M.G., D.S.O., D.C.M.	Temp. Major (A./Lieut.-Col.)	Attd. 8th	France	15/7/19, p. 8710
			France	4/1/17, p. 240
	Gen. List		France	21/12/17, p. 13373
	Gen. List, Comdg. 1st Bn. R. Irish Rifles		France	28/12/18, p. 15162
Holmes, W.	Sergeant (Regtl. No. 5433)		France	10/7/19, p. 17
Henderson, J. S.	C.S.M. (Regtl. No. 14779)	2nd	France	4/1/17, p. 240
	A./R.S.M.	10th	Home "A" List	25/1/17, p. 946
Holloway, L.	Gen. List		France	25/5/17, p. 5166
Harney, J.	Hon. Capt. and Qr.Mr.	7th	Salonika	21/7/17, p. 7454
Hamlet, G. T.	Pte. (Regtl. No. 27952)	10th	France	21/12/17, p. 13373
Harrison, E. N.	Temp. Capt.	10th	France	24/5/18, p. 6101
Halligan, J. T.	C.Q.M.S. (Regtl. No. 7/28,484)	7th	Egypt	14/6/18, p. 7054
	Capt. (2nd-Lieut. late Leinster Regt.; Adjt. and Qr.Mr. Cadet School)		France	28/12/18, p. 15162
Harcourt, H. G., D.S.O., M.C.	Lieut. (A./Major)	Attd. 51st Bn. M.G. Corps	France	28/12/18, p. 15162
Hawes, C. E.	Temp. Lieut. (Temp. Major)	Staff	Archangel	11/6/20, p. 6456
			France	15/5/17
Ingoldby, R. H.	Temp. 2nd-Lieut.	2nd	France	5/7/19, p. 8493
Johnson, R. D.	Major	3rd (attd. 2nd)	France	1/1/16, p. 56
			France	22/6/15, p. 6003

HONOURS AND REWARDS

Jennings, T.	Pte. (Regtl. No. 10641)	1st (attd. 2nd)	Dardanelles	5/5/16, p. 4519
Jeffreys, R. G. B.	Major (A./Lieut.-Col.)	—	France	4/1/17, p. 240
			France	25/5/17, p. 5166
Jeffries, W. F., D.S.O.	Capt. (A./Major)	3rd	France	21/12/17, p. 13373
			France	4/1/17
Jones, H.	Pte. (Regtl. No. 10944)	6th	France	28/12/18, p. 15162
Keegan, M.	2nd-Lieut.	R.D.F. (attd. R.F.C.)	France	9/7/19, p. 8710
Kendrick, E. H., D.S.O.	Capt., Bt. Major (Temp. Lieut.-Col.)	Attd. 11th Bn. Suff. Regt. and 34th Bn. M.G. Corps	France	4/1/17, p. 204
			France	25/5/17, p. 5166
			France	21/12/17, p. 13373
			France	28/12/18, p. 15162
			France	9/7/19, p. 8710
Kee, W., M.C.	C.S.M. (Regtl. No. 14132)	7th (attd. 1st)	Dardanelles	28/1/16, p. 1204
	Temp. Lieut.	7th (attd. 1st)	France	24/5/18, p. 6101
Lonsdale, M. P. E.	Major (R. of O.)	7th	Dardanelles	28/1/16, p. 1204
Lynch, C.	C.S.M. (Regtl. No. 25573)	10th	Dardanelles	28/1/16, p. 1204
			Home	25/1/17, p. 946
Leahy, T. J., D.S.O., M.C.	Capt., Bt. Major	2nd	France	19/10/14, p. 8356
			France	9/12/14, p. 10546
			France	15/6/15
			France	1/1/16, p. 56
			France	4/1/17, p. 198
			France	15/5/17, p. 4749
			France	11/12/17, p. 12916
			France	20/5/18, p. 5948
			France	28/11/17, p. 14929
Losty, P. P.	C.Q.M.S. (Regtl. No. 2/10034)	6th	Salonika	28/11/17, p. 12485
Lawrence, L. A.	Lieut. (A./Capt.)	4th (attd. 9th)	France	21/12/17, p. 13373
Lunn, J. S.	Capt.	4th	Egypt	14/6/18, p. 7054
			Egypt	12/1/20, p. 504
Langley, B.	Sergt. (Regtl. No. 10645)	1st	France	28/12/18, p. 15162
Loveband, A., C.M.G.	Lieut.-Col.	2nd	France	17/2/15, p. 1668
Loveband, G. Y.	Temp. Capt.	6th	Egypt	22/1/19, p. 1156
Lloyd-Blood, L. I. N., M.C.	Lieut.	5th (attd. 2nd)	France	9/7/19, p. 8710
Loydall, J.	Sergeant (No. 16646)	2nd	France	25/5/17
Massy-Westropp, R. F. H.	Lieut.	2nd	France	4/12/14, p. 10296
Murphy, P.	Cpl. (Regtl. No. 7755)	2nd	France	22/6/15, p. 6003
Molesworth, E. A.	Major	1st	Dardanelles	5/8/15, p. 7666
Maclear, B.	Capt.	2nd	France	1/1/16, p. 56

NAME.	RANK.	BATTALION.	THEATRE OF WAR.	"LONDON GAZETTE."
Mulhall, P.	Pte. (Regtl. No. 10714)	1st	Dardanelles	5/5/16, p. 4519
Murphy, W. H.	2nd-Lieut.	4th	France	4/1/17, p. 240
Murphy, W. J.	Temp. Capt.	9th	France	4/1/17, p. 240
Meldon, J. A.	Lieut.-Col.	4th	Home "A" List	25/1/17, p. 945
MacDaniel, J. R.	2nd-Lieut.	3rd	France	25/5/17, p. 5166
Merry, J.	Qr.Mr. and Hon. Lieut.	9th	France	25/5/17, p. 5166
Macdermott, A. W.	Temp. Capt.	7th	Salonika	21/7/17, p. 7453
Marchant, W. G.	Cpl. (Regtl. No. 7/28515)	7th (now E. Yorks Regt.)	Salonika	21/7/17, p. 7454
McAuley, H. T. B.	L./Sergt. (A./Sergt.) (Regtl. No. 40300)		Salonika	28/11/17, p. 12485
McFeely, C. M., D.S.O., M.C.	Capt.	1st	France	21/12/17, p. 13373
Maguire, R., M.C.	Temp. 2nd-Lieut.	1st	France	21/12/17, p. 13373
Moore, A., D.S.O.	Major	1st		
	Lieut.-Col. New Zealand Infantry	Otago Bn.	Dardanelles	5/11/15, p. 11003
	Major	R.D.F.	France	21/12/17, p. 13373
Murray, A. H.	Temp. 2nd-Lieut. (A./Capt.)	9th	France	25/5/17, p. 5166
Moore, C.	Cpl. (L./Sergt.) (Regtl. No. 8840)	8th	France	21/12/17, p. 13373
Matson, C., M.C.	Lieut. (A./Major)	Secd. 47th Bn. M.G. Corps	France	24/5/18, p. 6101
McCann, C.	Lieut.	3rd (attd. 6th)	France	9/7/19, p. 8710
Maffett, C. W.	Capt.	1st	France	9/7/19, p. 8710
Nolan, E.	Regtl. No. 24910	5th	Home "A" List	25/1/17, p. 946
Neill, C.	Temp. Lieut.	10th (attd. 11th Hants.)	France	24/5/18, p. 6101
O'Hagan, C. E.	Sergt. (Regtl. No. 5753)	2nd Bn.	France	17/2/15, p. 1668
O'Hara, H. D.	Lieut.	1st	Dardanelles	5/8/15, p. 7666
O'Brien, J.	Pte. (Regtl. No. 10055)	1st	Dardanelles	5/11/15, p. 10999
O'Brien, P.	L./Cpl. (Regtl. No. 10924)		Dardanelles	5/5/16, p. 4519
			Dardanelles	5/11/15, p. 10999
			Dardanelles	5/5/16, p. 4519
O'Dowda, J. W., C.B., C.M.G.	Lieut.-Col. and Bt. Col. (Temp. Brig.-Gen.)	1st	Dardanelles	13/7/16, p. 6943
			Mesopotamia	19/10/16, p. 10048
			Mesopotamia	15/8/17, p. 8329
			Mesopotamia	12/3/18, p. 3112
			Mesopotamia	27/8/18, p. 9985
			Mesopotamia	21/2/19, p. 2588
			Mesopotamia	5/6/19, p. 7234

HONOURS AND REWARDS

Name	Rank	Bn.	Theatre	Gazette
O'Donnell, M. F.	Sergt. (Regtl. No. 17393)	7th	Salonika	6/12/16, p. 11939
Oulton, W. P., M.C.	Capt.	1st	France	4/1/17, p. 240
O'Neill, F.	2nd-Lieut. (killed)	5th	Home "A" List	25/1/17, p. 945
O'Connor, J. J.	Q.M.S. (Regtl. No. 8859)	2nd	France	22/6/15, p. 6003
O'Malley, V. D., M.C.	R.Q.M.S.		France	25/5/17, p. 5166
	Temp. Capt.	10th	France	25/5/17, p. 5166
			France	24/5/18, p. 6101
O'Malley, P.	Pte. (Regtl. No. 6/12871)	6th	Salonika	21/7/17, p. 7454
O'Neill, J.	Temp. Lieut.	8/9th	France	24/5/18, p. 6101
Preston, A. J. D.	Capt.	7th	Dardanelles	28/1/16, p. 1204
Palmer, L. S. N.	Temp. Capt.	7th	Dardanelles	28/1/16, p. 1204
Popham, F. S.	Capt.	5th	Home "A" List	25/1/17, p. 945
Pedlow, W.	2nd-Lieut. (A./Capt.)	2nd	France	21/12/17, p. 13373
Plunkett, J. F., D.S.O., M.C., D.C.M.	Capt. (Temp. Lieut.-Col.)	1st (attd. 13th Bn. R. Innis. Fus.) Attd. 15th Bn. R. Innis. Fus.	France	28/12/18, p. 15162
Padley, A. C.	Lieut.	9th	France	9/7/19, p. 8710
			Siberia	14/1/20, p. 665
Ray, A. W.	Sergt. (Regtl. No. 6704)	2nd	France	19/10/14, p. 8356
Richards, W. R.	Capt.	6th	Dardanelles	28/1/16, p. 1204
Robinson, H.	C.S.M. (Regtl. No. 14275)	7th	Dardanelles	28/1/16, p. 1204
Rex, P. C.	Pte. (Regtl. No. 9025)		Dardanelles	5/5/16, p. 4519
Romer, C. F. C.B., A.D.C.	Lieut.-Col. and Bt.-Col. (Temp. Brig.-Gen.; Major-Gen.)	Staff	France	9/12/14, p. 10535
			France	17/2/15, p. 1650
			France	22/6/15, p. 6010
			France	1/1/16, p. 9
			France	15/6/16, p. 5923
			France	4/1/17, p. 201
			France	15/5/17, p. 4751
			France	11/12/17, p. 12919
Renny, L. F.	Major (Temp. Brig.-Gen.)	Staff	France	17/2/15, p. 1650
			France	22/6/15, p. 5979
			France	1/1/16, p. 9
			France	15/6/16, p. 5923
			France	4/1/17, p. 201
			Home	12/2/18, p. 1934
			France	5/7/19, p. 8498

NAME.	RANK.	BATTALION.	THEATRE OF WAR.	"LONDON GAZETTE."
Robinson, J. P. B., C.M.G., D.S.O.	Major (A./Lieut.-Col.)	Staff	France	4/1/17, p. 201
			France	15/5/17, p. 4751
			France	11/12/17, p. 12919
			France	20/5/18, p. 5950
Rickerby, S.	Cpl. (Regtl. No. 11695)	2nd	France	20/12/18, p. 14933
Rawlings, H. W.	L./Cpl. (Regtl. No. 6/14305)	6th	Salonika	4/1/17, p. 240
Robertson, G. McM., D.S.O, M.C.	Capt. (A./Lieut.-Col.)	10th N. Staffs Regt. (attd. 10th Bn. R.D.F.) 2nd Bn. N. Staffs Regt. (attd. 2nd Bn. Manch. Regt.)	France France	21/7/17, p. 7454 24/5/18, p. 6101 21/12/17
Shanks, W. J.	2nd-Lieut.		France	28/12/18
Stead, T.	Pte. (Regtl. No. 17748)	2nd	France	9/7/19, p. 56
Stephens, P.	2nd-Lieut. (Temp. Capt.)	—	Dardanelles	1/1/16, p. 1204
Stirke, H. R., D.S.O.	Temp. Major	4th	France	28/1/16, p. 240
		9th (attd. 2nd)	France	4/1/17, p. 6101
Synnott, F.	Sergt. (Regtl. No. 16177)	9th	France	4/1/17
Silcox, B.	Temp. 2nd-Lieut.	Gen. List (attd. 7th)	France	24/5/18, p. 6101
Seymour, E. F. E.	Major (A./Lieut.-Col.)	10th	Salonika	25/5/17, p. 5166
Shine, J. O. W.	Capt.	Attd. 9th	France	25/11/17, p. 12485
Shadforth, H. A.	Capt.	6th	France	21/12/17, p. 13373
Shirren, A. G.	C.S.M. (Regtl. No. 15150)	1st	Egypt	21/12/17, p. 13373
Stirling, W. F., D.S.O. M.C.	Major (R. of O.)	1st and Staff	France Egypt	30/4/19, p. 5445 24/5/18, p. 6101 11/6/20, p. 6452
Shears, P. J.	Capt. (A./Major)	1st (attd. 11th Bn. Hampshire Regt.)	France	28/12/18, p. 15162
Scott, W. G.	Temp. Lieut. (A./Capt.)	4th (attd. Labour Corps)	France	9/7/19, p. 8710
Sheehy, E.	Lieut. (A./Capt.)	4th	France	9/7/19, p. 8710
Swetman, F.	Pte. (Regtl. No. 28641)	6th	France	9/7/19, p. 8710
Tredennick, J. P., D.S.O.	Major (Temp. Lieut.-Col.)	2nd (attd. 18th London Regt.)	France	1/1/16, p. 56 5/7/19, p. 8500
Tarleton, G. W. B.	Lieut.	2nd	France	1/1/16, p. 56
	Capt.	—	France	21/12/17, p. 13373

HONOURS AND REWARDS

Treacher, F., M.C.	Lieut.	2nd	France	1/1/16, p. 56
	Capt.		France	5/7/19, p. 8500
Thompson, P. T. L.	Temp. Capt. (killed)	6th	Dardanelles	28/1/16, p. 1204
Tobin, R. P.	Capt.	7th	Dardanelles	28/1/16, p. 1204
Thompson, A. C.	Temp. Major (Temp. Lieut.-Col.)	8th	France	4/1/17, p. 240
			France	25/5/17, p. 5166
			France	21/12/17, p. 13373
Tippet, H. C. C.	Capt.	4th and Staff	France	11/12/17, p. 12921
Tittle, D. R.	Lieut. (A./Capt.)	2nd (attd. 1st Bn. Conn. Rangers)	Egypt	5/6/19, p. 7181
Taylor, C.	Cpl. (Regtl. No. 7/24256)	6th (attd. H.Q. 10th Div.)	Egypt	12/1/20, p. 504
Wheeler, S. G. de C.	Capt.	2nd	France	17/2/15, p. 1668
	Major		France	28/12/18, p. 15162
Whelan, J.	Pte. (Regtl. No. 10974)	1st	Dardanelles	5/8/15, p. 7666
West, J.	Sergt. (Regtl. No. 17141)	7th	Dardanelles	28/1/16, p. 1204
Wilkinson, G. N.	Temp. Capt.	7th	Dardanelles	28/1/16, p. 1204
Williams, A. E.	Pte. (Regtl. No. 17750)		Dardanelles	5/5/16, p. 4519
Watson, R. M., D.S.O.	Capt.	2nd	France	17/2/15, p. 1668
			France	15/6/15, p. 5924
			France	15/6/16, p. 5923
			France	4/1/17
			France	20/12/18, p. 14935
Whyte, W. H.	Temp. Major (A./Lieut.-Col.) (Lt. R. of O.)	6th	Dardanelles	5/7/19, p. 8501
			Salonika	6/12/16, p. 11939
			Salonika	28/11/17, p. 12485
Whittaker, L.	Sergt. (Regtl. No. 9709)	8th	France	4/1/17, p. 240
Watson, F. H.	Pte. (Regtl. No. 19200)	Late 4th	Home "A" List	25/1/17, p. 946
Wilson, F. A.	Temp. Lieut. (A./Capt.)	1st	France	25/5/17, p. 5166
Wallis, D.	C.S.M. (Regtl. No. 11435)	1st	France	25/5/17, p. 5166
West, M.	Pte. (Regtl. No. 8207)	1st	France	25/5/17, p. 5166
Whelan, J.	Sergt. (Regtl. No. 9210)	10th	France	21/12/17, p. 13373
Whitton, W. J.	C.S.M. (Regtl. No. 10636)		France	21/12/17, p. 13373
Weldon, K. C., D.S.O.	Major (Temp. Lieut.-Col.)	2nd Bn.		
Watson, J. W.	Sergt. (Regtl. No. 15703)	2nd	France	9/7/19, p. 8710
White, M.	Cpl. (Regtl. No. 9878)	1st	France	9/7/19, p. 8710
Wilkins, A.	Pte. (Regtl. No. 14091)	6th	France	9/7/19, p. 8710
White, H., M.C.	Sergt.-Major (Regtl. No. 9/15206)	9th	France	4/1/17, p. 240
	Temp. Lieut. (A./Capt.)		France	28/12/18, p. 15162
			France	9/7/19, p. 8710

HOME SERVICES AWARDS.

The names of the undermentioned have been brought to the notice of the Secretary of State for War for valuable services rendered in connection with the war:—

NAME.	REGTL. NO.	RANK.	BATTALION.	"LONDON GAZETTE."
Agnew, A. E. H.	—	Capt.	—	13/8/18, p. 180
Annetts, A. E.	111126	Col.-Sergt.	3rd	28/8/19, p. 400
Boyle, H.	29405	W.O. Cl. II. (S.Q.M.S.)	—	4/11/18, p. 225
Briggs, G. E.	—	Bt. Col. (R.P.)	R.D.F.	13/8/18, p. 180
Brennan, T.	25521	Pte. (A./Sergt.-Dmr.)	3rd	28/8/19, p. 401
Browne, J.	29406	Col.-Sergt. (A./W.O. Cl. II., S.Q.M.S.)	—	4/11/18, p. 225
Browne, J.	29406	S.Q.M.S.	—	15/3/19, p. 273
Byrne, J.	9608	R.Q.M.S.	—	28/8/19, p. 441
Byrne, J.	9607 (now 12292 7th Bn. R. Ir. Regt.)	Sgt. (A./R.Q.M.S.)	1st	27/3/19, p. 304
Byrne, L., D.C.M., M.M.	13/561	C.Q.M.S.	3rd	28/8/19, p. 401
Caulfield, C. E.	10726	Bandmaster	1st	27/3/19, p. 304
Collins, F. R.	—	Capt.	—	25/3/19, p. 278
Daly, J.	4956	R.S.M.	3rd	28/8/19, p. 402
Darby, W. G.	29437	Col.-Sergt. (A./W.O., Cl. II., S.Q.M.S.)	—	4/11/18, p. 225
Dawson, F.	10530	Sergt. (A./Col.-Sergt.)	—	25/3/19, p. 279
Dickie, T. W.	—	Capt.	—	24/2/17, p. 9
Doyle, O.	9897	C.S.M.	3rd	28/8/19, p. 403
Drewett, J.	13518	Q.M.S.	—	27/3/19, p. 305
Farrell, M.	13561	Col.-Sergt.	3rd	28/8/19, p. 403
Fitzpatrick, F. H.	29404	S.Q.M.S.	—	27/3/19, p. 305
French, D.	—	Major	—	13/8/18, p. 182
Gillespie, W.	16388	R.S.M.	—	24/2/17, p. 37
Grattan-Esmonde, L.	—	Major (Temp. Lieut.-Col.)	—	24/2/17, p. 13
Greenland, H.	12169	C.S.M. (A./R.S.M.)	3rd	28/8/19, p. 404
Hoey, C. B. R.	—	Major	—	27/3/19, p. 298
Howis, J. E.	29440	Pte. (A./Sergt.)	—	27/3/19, p. 307
Jackson, W.	20147	W.O., Cl. II. (S.Q.M.S.)	Depot	4/11/18, p. 226
Johnson, A. M.	—	Major	—	13/8/18, p. 183
Keogh, E. J. L.	—	Major	3rd	28/8/19, p. 398
Lindsay, W., M.V.O.	—	Lieut.-Col.	—	24/2/17, p. 19
Loughran, W.	15805	Sergt.	3rd	28/8/19, p. 405
McGrath, J.	5137	Cpl. (A./Sergt.)	3rd	28/8/19, p. 406
Murphy, H. P.	—	Temp. Lieut. (Temp. Capt.)	—	28/8/19, p. 441
Murphy, W.	22197	C.S.M. (A./R.S.M.)	—	13/3/18, p. 150
Parry, T.	10634	Cpl.	3rd	28/8/19, p. 406
Partridge, H.	5903	C.S.M.	3rd	28/8/19, p. 406
Perreau, C. N.	—	Col., Canadian Forces	—	24/2/17, p. 49; 5/7/18
Popham, F. S.	—	Capt. and Bt. Maj.	—	28/8/19, p. 441

HONOURS AND REWARDS

NAME.	REGTL. NO.	RANK.	BATTALION.	"LONDON GAZETTE."
Reddy, T. F.	19183	Pte. (A./Sergt.)	7th	27/3/19, p. 309
Reid, A. A.	29426	Pte. (A./Sergt.)	—	4/11/18, p. 226
Reid, A. A.	29426	Pte. (A./Sergt.)	—	27/3/19
Shanley, P.	11308	Sergt.	3rd	28/8/19, p. 407
Smith, J.	29398	S.M.	—	25/3/19, p. 282
Smithwick, S. G.	—	Major	—	28/8/19, p. 399
Tighe, M. H.	—	Lieut.	3rd	15/3/19, p. 273
Townsend, A.	5736	C.Q.M.S.	3rd	28/8/19, p. 408

FOREIGN AWARDS, 1914-18.

NAME.	RANK.	BATTALION.	REWARDS.	"LONDON GAZETTE."
Boylan, Frank	Pte. (Regtl. No. 15155)	8/9th	Belgian Decoration Militaire	15/4/18
Brady, Thomas	Capt.	—	French Croix de Guerre avec Palme	15/12/19
Brophy, Peter	L./Cpl. (Regtl. No. 32603)	—	Russian Medal on St. Stanislas Riband	16/7/21
Brown, Frederick Elliott	Lieut.	—	French Croix de Guerre	14/7/17
Bryan, Edward	Sergt. (Regtl. No. 13197)	6th	Serbian Cross of Karageorge, 1st Class, Gold Star (with Swords)	21/4/17
Burke, John Patrick	Sergt. (Regtl. No. 12970)	9th (attd. 48th T.M. Bty.)	French Croix de Guerre	1/5/17
Byrne, John	Pte. (Regtl. No. 9590)	2nd	Montenegrin Medal for Merit (silver)	9/3/17
Byrne, Lawrence	C.Q.M.S. (Regtl. No. 8901)	1st	French Croix de Guerre	17/12/17
Campbell, Charles Wilson	C.Q.M.S. (Regtl. No. 24700)	10th	Belgian Croix de Guerre	12/7/18
Connolly, Joseph	L./Sergt. (Regtl. No. 9392)	2nd	French Croix de Guerre	14/7/17
Cooke, William	Sergt. (Regtl. No. 8672)	2nd	Russian Medal of St. George, 2nd Class	25/8/15
Corballis, Edward Roux Littledale	Capt.	R.D.F and R.F.C.	French Legion d'Honneur (Chevalier)	14/7/17
Cory, George Norton	Major and Bt. Lieut.-Col.	R.D.F.	Russian Order of St. Anne, 3rd Class (with Sword)	15/2/17
	Major-Gen.	R.D.F.	Greek Order of the Redeemer (Grand Commander)	10/10/18
	Bt. Col. (Temp. Major-Gen.)	General Staff	Serbian White Eagle, Class III (with Swords)	7/6/19
	Major-Gen.	M.G.G.S., G.H.Q.	Greek M.C., 2nd Class	21/7/19
	Major-Gen	General Staff	French Croix de Guerre avec Palme	21/7/19
	Major-Gen.	General Staff	French Legion of Honour (Commandeur)	21/8/19
Courtney, John	Cpl. (L./Sergt.) (Regtl. No. 22493)	9th	Russian Cross of St. George, 4th Class	15/2/17
Cox, Patrick Godfred Ashley	Capt. and Bt. Major (Temp. Lieut.-Col.)	6th	French Croix d'Officier, Légion d'Honneur	21/4/17
Cummins, William	Sergt. (Regtl. No. 6603)	1st	Serbian Cross of Karageorge (with Swords), 4th Class	15/2/17
Darling, Sydney George, M.C.	2nd-Lieut. (A./Capt.)	1st (S.B.) attd. 1st	French Croix de Guerre avec Etoile en argent	19/6/19
Devoy, Joseph	Sergt. (Regtl. No. 10335)	1st	French Medaille Militaire	24/2/1
Dillon, John	Pte. (Regtl. No. 40436)	1st	Belgian Croix de Guerre	12/7/168

HONOURS AND REWARDS

Name	Rank	Bn.	Decoration	Date
Doogan, Michael Joseph	A./C.S.M. (Regtl. No. 10902)	R.D.F., attd. Army Gym. Staff	Belgian Croix de Guerre	4/9/19
Elston, William Thomas	Cpl. (A./L./Sergt.) (Regtl. No. 15346)	2nd	Belgian Croix de Guerre	12/7/18
Falkiner, Frederick	L./Sergt. (Regtl. No. 7/14166); 2nd-Lieut. R. Ir. Rifles	7th	Italian Bronze Medal for Military Valour	31/8/17
Gavin, Peter	Pte. (A./L./Cpl.) (Regtl. No. 6/11937)	6th	Serbian Silver Medal	15/2/17
Gibson, George, M.M.	Cpl. (Regtl. No. 16531)	1st	French Croix de Guerre avec Etoile en bronze	19/6/19
Glegg, James Dowie, M.C.	Capt.		Belgian Croix de Guerre	4/9/19
Gorry, Joseph	Cpl. (A./L./Sergt.) (Regtl. No. 24825)	8/9th	Belgian Croix de Guerre	12/7/18
Grove, James Robert Wood	Bt. Major		Russian Order of St. Anne, 3rd Class, with Swords and Bow	16/7/21
Hall, R. S.	C.S.M. (Regtl. No. 5039)	2nd	French Medaille Militaire	5/11/14
Halligan, Joseph Thomas, O.B.E.	Capt. (Temp. Major)		French Croix de Guerre avec Palme	8/3/20
Harcourt, Harry Gladwyn, D.S.O., M.C.	Lieut.	R.D.F. (attd. M.G.C.)	Russian Order of St. Stanislas, 2nd Class (with Swords)	16/7/21
Harvey, Charles Dacre	Temp. Capt.	7th	Egyptian Order of the Nile, 4th Class	9/11/18
Hawes, Cecil Ernest	Temp. Lieut. (Temp. Capt.)		Serbian White Eagle, 5th Class	15/2/17
Hayes, Robert	Pte. (Regtl. No. 5780)	1st	French Croix de Guerre	24/2/16
Healy, Patrick	Pte. (Regtl. No. 21450)	8/9th	Belgian Decoration Militaire	15/4/18
Hoey, Charles Bayly Robert	Major		Order of the Star of Roumania (Officer)	20/9/19
Holmes, Geoffrey Gordon	Temp. Lieut.	1st	French Croix de Guerre avec Etoile en bronze	19/6/19
Higginson, H. W., C.B., D.S.O.	Major and Bt. Col. (Temp. Major-Gen.)	Staff	Order of the Star of Roumania (Commandeur)	—/—/19
			French Légion d'Honneur (Officier)	—/—/19
Irwin, Thomas	L./Cpl. (Regtl. No. 5728)	Spec. Res. (attd. 1st)	French Croix de Guerre	24/2/16
Jenkins, Cuthbert Esmond	Temp. Lieut. (A./Capt.)		French Croix de Guerre avec Palme	17/8/18
Kavanagh, Martin	Sergt. (Regtl. No. 13431)	9th	French Croix de Guerre	14/7/17
Kendrick, Edward Holt, D.S.O.	Bt. Major (Temp. Lieut.-Col.)	R.D.F. & M.G.C.	French Légion d'Honneur (Chevalier)	22/11/18
			French Légion d'Honneur (Officier)	21/8/19

NAME.	RANK.	BATTALION.	REWARDS.	"LONDON GAZETTE."
Leahy, Thomas Joseph	Lieut.	2nd	French Croix de Chevalier, Légion d'Honneur	3/11/14
Lynch, Christopher	L./Cpl. (Regtl. No. 8542)	1st	French Croix de Guerre avec Etoile en Vermeil	14/7/17
McLoughlin, Michael J.	Sergt. (Regtl. No. 25245)	10th	Belgian Croix de Guerre	12/7/18
McNeely, Joseph	Sergt. (Regtl. No. 23998)	1st	Belgian Croix de Guerre	4/9/19
Martin, Charles Andrew	Temp. Lieut.	Service	Serbian Order of the White Eagle, 5th Class	9/3/17
Metcalfe, Maurice Owen	Cpl. (A./Sergt.) (Regtl. No. 14289)	10th	French Croix de Guerre	10/10/18
Moore, Patrick	Pte. (Regtl. No. 8272)	1st	Serbian Silver Medal	15/2/17
Neill, Charles	Temp. Lieut.	1st	Belgian Croix de Guerre	4/9/19
O'Carrol, Frederick W. J.	Capt.	5th	French Croix de Guerre	21/7/19
Ockenden, James, V.C.	Sergt. (Regtl. No. 10605)	1st	Belgian Croix de Guerre	12/7/18
O'Dowda, James Wilton	Lieut.-Col. and Bt. Col. (Temp. Brig.-Gen.)	—	Serbian White Eagle, 3rd Class	15/2/17
O'Leary, James	Sergt. (Regtl. No. 10310)	1st	Belgian Decoration Militaire avec Croix de Guerre	26/11/19
Plunkett, Joseph Frederick, D.S.O., M.C., D.C.M.	Capt. (Temp. Lieut.-Col.)	R.D.F. (attd. 13th Bn. R. Innis. Fus.)	French Croix de Guerre avec Etoile en Vermeil	19/6/19
Ray, A. W.	(Regtl. No. 6704)	2nd	French Medaille Militaire	5/11/14
Roche, Michael	Cpl. (A./Sergt.) (Regtl. No. 10570)	2nd	Roumanian Medaille Barbatie si Credenta (3rd Class)	20/9/19
Romer, Cecil Francis, C.B., C.M.G., A.D.C.	Lieut.-Col. and Bt. Col., Major-Gen.	General Staff	Russian Order of St. Anne, 2nd Class	15/2/17
			French Légion d'Honneur, Croix d'Officier	2/6/17
Sinnott, Lawrence	C.S.M. (Regtl. No. 6/10485)	6th	Russian Cross of St. George, 3rd Class	15/2/17
Stirke, Henry Richard, D.S.O.	Temp. Major		Belgian Croix de Guerre	12/7/18
Stirling, Walter Francis, D.S.O., M.C.	Major (Temp. Lieut.-Col.)		Hedjaz, The Nahda Order, 2nd Class	8/3/20
Stokes, James	Pte. (Regtl. No. 9150)	2nd	French Medaille Militaire	14/7/17
Swifte, Latham Coddington	Major	5th	Italian Croce di Guerra	21/8/19
Tansey, Patrick	L./Cpl. (Regtl. No. 6/13135)	6th	Serbian Gold Medal	15/2/17
Tarleton, Gerald Waldon Browne, M.C.	Lieut.	R.D.F. (attd. Service Bn.)	Serbian Order of the White Eagle, 5th Class	21/4/17
Waine, Patrick, D.C.M.	C.S.M. (Regtl. No. 11167)	1st	Belgian Croix de Guerre	12/7/18
Weldon, Kenneth Charles	Major (Temp. Lieut.-Col.)	Attd. 7/8th R. Ir. Fus.)	French Légion d'Honneur (Officier)	14/7/17
Whyte, William Henry	Lieut. (Temp. Major)	R. of O., R.D.F. (attd. R. Ir. Fus.)	Serbian Order of the White Eagle, 4th Class	21/4/17

APPENDICES

[*Appendix Six*

HONOURS SELECTED FOR REGIMENTAL COLOURS AND ARMY LIST.

The following is a list of Honours in connection with the Great War to be placed on the Regimental Colours, together with additional Honours for insertion in the Army List, as selected by the Regimental Committee composed as under, and in accordance with instructions contained in War Office letter No. 20/Gen., No. 5000 (Q.M.G. 7) of February 15th, 1923, Army Order 338, dated September 4th, 1922, and Army Council Instruction No. 458 of September 8th, 1922 :—

The Committee met in London on January 16th and March 12th, 1923, and Battalions were represented as follows :—

Chairman—Major-General C. D. Cooper, C.B., Colonel Royal Dublin Fusiliers.

Secretary—Lieut.-Colonel C. N. Perreau, C.M.G., late Commanding 1st Bn. Royal Dublin Fusiliers.

Representing :—

1st Battalion—Bt. Major T. J. Carroll-Leahy, D.S.O., M.C.

2nd Battalion—Col.-Comdt. H. W. Higginson, C.B., D.S.O., A.D.C.
 Bt. Lieut.-Colonel K. C. Weldon, D.S.O.
 Major J. Burke, D.S.O., M.C., D.C.M.

5th Battalion—Lieut.-Colonel F. H. Macnamara.

6th Battalion—Capt. J. Esmonde, M.C.

8th Battalion—Lieut.-Colonel Sir E. H. C. P. Bellingham, Bt., C.M.G., D.S.O.

9th Battalion—Lieut.-Col. J. P. Hunt, C.M.G., D.S.O., D.C.M.

10th Battalion—Lieut.-Col. E. F. Seymour, D.S.O., O.B.E.

NOTE.—Representatives of the 3rd, 4th, and 7th Battalions were unavoidably absent, but sent letters in connection with the war services of their Battalions.

LIST OF HONOURS FOR THE COLOURS.

MONS.
MARNE.
YPRES, 1915, 1917.
GALLIPOLI, 1915, 1916.
MACEDONIA, 1915, 1916, 1917.

SOMME, 1916, 1918.
CAMBRAI, 1917, 1918.
PALESTINE, 1917, 1918.
HINDENBURG LINE.
SELLE.

ADDITIONAL HONOURS FOR INSERTION IN ARMY LIST.

Operations.	Battles. (For Honours in Army List.)	Battalion of Regiment on behalf of whom Honour was claimed.	Brigade, Division, or Formation serving with.
Retreat from Mons: Aug. 23rd–Sept. 5th, 1914	1. Le Cateau	2nd Battalion	10th Bde., 4th Div.
Advance to the Aisne: Sept. 6th–Oct. 1st, 1914	2. Retreat from Mons	,, ,,	,, ,, ,, ,,
	3. Aisne, 1914	,, ,,	,, ,, ,, ,,
Operations in Flanders, 1914: Oct. 10th–Nov. 22nd	4. Armentières	,, ,,	,, ,, ,, ,,
Summer Operations, 1915: Mar.–Oct.	5. St. Julien	,, ,,	Attached 84th Brigade.
	6. Frezenberg	,, ,,	10th Bde., 4th Div.
Operations on the Somme: July 1st–Nov. 18th, 1916	7. Bellewaerde	,, ,,	,, ,, ,, ,,
	8. Albert	1st Battalion	86th Bde., 29th Div.
	9. Delville Wood	2nd Battalion	10th Bde., 4th Div.
	10. Guillemont	8th Battalion	48th Bde., 16th Div.
		9th Battalion	,, ,, ,, ,,
	11. Ginchy	8th Battalion	,, ,, ,, ,,
		9th Battalion	,, ,, ,, ,,
	12. Morval	2nd Battalion	10th Bde., 4th Div.
	13. Transloy	,, ,,	,, ,, ,, ,,
	14. Ancre Heights	10th Battalion	189th Bde., 63rd Naval Division.
	15. Ancre, 1916	,, ,,	189th Bde., 63rd Naval Division.
The Arras Offensive: April 9th–May 15th, 1917	16. Arras, 1917 (Scarpe battles)	1st Battalion	86th Bde., 29th Div.
	17. Scarpe, 1917	10th Battalion	189th Bde., 63rd Naval Division.
Flanking operations round Bullecourt: April 11th–June 16th	18. Bullecourt	2nd Battalion	48th Bde., 16th Div.
		8th Battalion	,, ,, ,, ,,
		9th Battalion	,, ,, ,, ,,
Flanders Offensive: June 7th–Nov. 10th, 1917	19. Messines, 1917	2nd Battalion	,, ,, ,, ,,
		8th Battalion	,, ,, ,, ,,
		9th Battalion	,, ,, ,, ,,

HONOURS FOR ARMY LIST

Flanders Offensive: June 7th–Nov. 10th, 1917 (*contd.*)	20. Langemarck, 1917	2nd Battalion	48th Bde., 16th Div.
		8th Battalion	" " "
		9th Battalion	" " "
The Offensive in Picardy: Mar. 21st–April 5th, 1918	21. St. Quentin	1st Battalion	" " "
	22. Bapaume, 1918	2nd Battalion	" " "
		8th Battalion	" " "
		9th Battalion	" " "
The Breaking of the Hindenburg Line: Aug. 26th–Oct. 12th, 1918	23. St. Quentin Canal	2nd Battalion	148th Bde., 50th Div.
	24. Beaurevoir	" "	198th Bde., 66th Div.
Final advance	25. Cambrai, 1918	6th Battalion	" " "
	26. Sambre	2nd Battalion	148th Bde., 50th Div.
		6th Battalion	" " "

MACEDONIA.

Retreat from Serbia on Salonika: Dec., 1915	27. Kosturino	6th Battalion	30th Bde., 10th Div.
Operations in Struma Valley: 1916–1918	28. Struma	7th Battalion	" " "
		" "	" " "

DARDANELLES.

Helles Operations: April 25th, 1915–Jan. 8th, 1916	29. Landing at Helles	1st Battalion	86th Bde., 29th Div.
Anzac and Suvla Operations: April 25th–Dec. 20th, 1915	30. Krithia	" "	" " "
	31. Suvla	1st Battalion	86th Bde., 29th Div.
	32. Sari Bair	6th Battalion	30th Bde., 10th Div.
	33. Landing at Suvla	7th Battalion	" " "

EGYPT AND PALESTINE.

Second Offensive: Oct. 27th–Nov. 16th, 1917	34. Gaza	6th Battalion	30th Bde., 10th Div.
		7th Battalion	" " "
Jerusalem Operations: Nov. 17th–Dec. 30th, 1917	35. El Mughar	" "	" " "
	36. Nebi Samwil	" "	" " "
	37. Capture of Jerusalem	" "	" " "

[*Appendix Seven*

DESCRIPTION OF MEMORIALS erected to the Memory of Officers, W.Os., N.C.Os. and Men of The Royal Dublin Fusiliers who laid down their lives for King and Country in the Great War, 1914–1918.

IN WESTMINSTER CATHEDRAL.

With the approval and co-operation of the surviving Officers and Men of the Irish Regiments a committee was formed shortly after the cessation of hostilities of the Great War (1914–1918), for the purpose of establishing a permanent Memorial to the Officers, Non-commissioned Officers, and Men of Irish Regiments killed in that war, and it was proposed that this Memorial should take the form of a Chapel dedicated in Westminster Cathedral, with books containing the names of those who lost their lives.

Cardinal Bourne offered St. Patrick's Chapel in the Cathedral for this purpose, and, although the original idea was to decorate and complete the entire Chapel, owing to lack of funds, modifications had to be made. Each Regiment which has subscribed is to be represented by a panel in the Chapel, and the books of names are to be kept in a suitable receptacle.

There can be no more fitting place for such a record than a Cathedral in the heart of the British Empire. The Chapel will be a lasting Memorial to those who so gallantly and grandly upheld the honour of the Irish Regiments, and it is hoped to make it a shrine worthy of the supreme sacrifice.

IN THE CHAPEL OF THE ROYAL MILITARY COLLEGE, SANDHURST.

A Memorial to Officers of the Royal Dublin Fusiliers, who were Cadets at the Royal Military College.

The Memorial will consist of a White Marble Slab with the names of the Officers as under, surrounded by a frame of carved oak, and with the crest of the Regiment coloured and carved in the oak at the top.

DESCRIPTION OF MEMORIALS

Inscription on R.M.C. Memorial.

Roll of Officers,
Cadets at the R.M.C.,
who served in
THE ROYAL DUBLIN FUSILIERS
and who
Died for King and Country
in
THE GREAT WAR OF 1914–1918.

1914

Lieut.-Colonel P. Maclear	Captain H. O. Davis

1915

Capt. D. V. F. Anderson	2/Lieut. R. A. F. S. King
Lieut. R. V. C. Corbet	2/Lieut. M. C. N. R. Young
Lieut. R. de Lusignan	Capt. B. Maclear
Capt. G. M. Dunlop	2/Lieut. H. D'E. Head
Bt. Major T. H. C. Frankland	Capt. A. A. C. Taylor
Capt. F. N. Le Mesurier	Lieut. L. C. Boustead
2/Lieut. B. McGuire	Capt. H. M. Floyd
Lieut. R. Bernard	Lieut. H. D. O'Hara, D.S.O.
Major E. Fetherstonhaugh	2/Lieut. J. A. H. Taylor
2/Lieut. M. O'C. Cuffey	2/Lieut. H. R. T. Hackett.

1916

Capt. E. R. L. Maunsell	Major D. E. Wilson
2/Lieut. W. H. A. Damiano	2/Lieut. H. J. Lemass
2/Lieut. J. A. H. Helby	Lieut. H. G. Killingley
Lieut. S. V. C. Jones	

1917

2/Lieut. G. F. Gradwell	Lieut. F. Dowling
Lieut. H. D. K. George	Capt. J. O. W. Shine
Capt. H. L. Ridley, M.C.	2/Lieut. G. S. Falkiner

1918

2/Lieut. E. H. Robertson	Lieut. G. P. N. Thompson
2/Lieut. M. J. Macnamara	Lieut. W. Pedlow, M.C.
2/Lieut. R. G. Hunter	Bt. Lieut.-Col. A. W. Gordon

1919

Lieut.-Col. H. R. Beddoes

This Memorial is erected by their Comrades in proud recognition of their gallantry and supreme sacrifice, and of all other Officers, Warrant Officers, Non-commissioned Officers and Men of The Royal Dublin Fusiliers who gave their lives in the Great War, 1914–1919.

"*Spectamur Agendo.*"

MEMORIAL IN R.C. CHAPEL, BORDON CAMP.

A Stained Glass Window.

Erected by the
OFFICERS 1ST BN. THE ROYAL DUBLIN FUSILIERS
(Neill's "Blue Caps")
To the glorious and imperishable Memory of their Comrades
who fell at
GALLIPOLI
1915.

Also five other windows erected in the same chapel by A, B, C and D Companies and Sergeants' Mess in memory of the landing at Gallipoli.

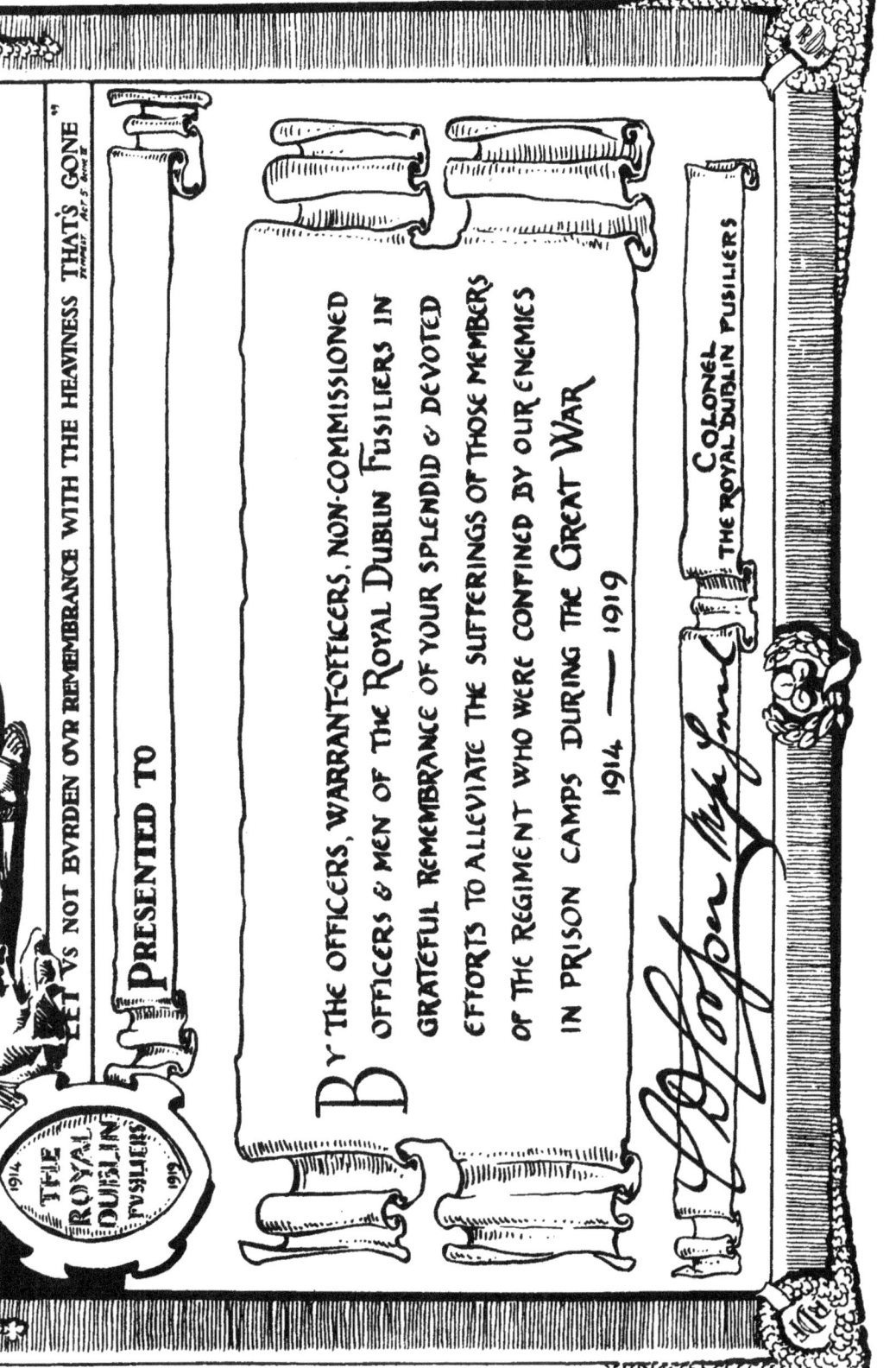

[*Appendix Eight*

WHAT OUR WOMEN DID FOR THE REGIMENT
During the Great War.

The work for the men of the Royal Dublin Fusiliers was inaugurated by the Committee of the Dublin Women's Unionist Club at a meeting held in August, 1914, at the offices of the Club at No. 10, Leinster Street, Dublin, and commenced with the collection and dispatch of a large quantity of newspapers, magazines and books to the battalions of the Regiment serving with the Expeditionary Force in France and Flanders, until the Camp Libraries made unnecessary any individual provision of literature for the troops.

The very urgent appeal made by an Irish woman to the Committee of the Club early in 1915 for food to be sent to those of the Royal Dublin Fusiliers who were prisoners of war at Limburg in Germany, caused the Committee to concentrate their energies on this work, until ever-increasing numbers and the regulations published by Government necessitated larger measures of relief. One of the workers then proposed the co-ordination of work of all kinds for the Regiment under a Central Advisory Committee for the Regimental Area of the City and County of Dublin and the Counties of Wicklow, Carlow and Kildare, and this Advisory Committee then became "The Dublin County Association for the Administration of Voluntary Work," and "The Regimental Care Committee for Prisoners of War" as approved by the War Office.

The following were some of the Branches of the Central Advisory Committee :—

Women's Branch, Royal Dublin Fusiliers Clothing Committee, 102, Grafton Street, Dublin. (Clothing for men at the Front and some branches of the Prisoners of War Committee.) Chairman : Lady Moore. Hon. Secretary : Miss Dickson.

The Dublin Committee, Prisoners of War, 65, Merrion Square. (Food and Clothing.) President : Lady Arnott. Secretary : Miss Rosalie Hamilton. Hon. Treasurer : Miss Croker.

The County Kildare Committee, Courthouse, Naas. (Food for Prisoners of War.) President : The Countess of Mayo.

Dundrum, County Dublin, Prisoners of War Committee. (Food.) President : Mrs. Arthur Goff.

Bray, County Wicklow, Prisoners of War Committee. (Food.) President : Miss Jameson.

The Bonded Store, under the direct control of the Customs and Excise officials, for all branches, was in charge of the Dublin Committee, 65, Merrion Square, and from this branch alone over 50,000 parcels were packed by a small band of no more than 10 helpers.

The final effort of the four Counties was a Mammoth Auction of valuable gifts, held in Dublin in October, 1918, just before the Armistice, and which realised £15,000. The balance of this sum after paying off all debts amounted to £11,000 and this was handed over by the Master of the Rolls to the Trustees for the benefit of those men of the Royal Dublin Fusilier battalions who had been prisoners of war, or their dependents, and afterwards for the benefit and advancement of those of the Regiment who had served outside the United Kingdom during the war and who had not been prisoners of war.

The following were appointed trustees: Lady Arnott, D.B.E., Right Hon. L. Jonathan Hogg, and Mr. Andrew Jameson, D.L.

Perhaps the words spoken by a Woman to the first batch of repatriated Prisoners of War on arrival in Ireland from Germany, voice all that was felt and done for our soldiers during the tragic years of the Great War: "Soldiers, Welcome Home! All have thought of you, prayed for you, and now we bid you the warmest and heartiest of welcomes. We are thankful to see you back in Ireland; we rejoice that your sufferings are over and that you are coming back to those who love and care for you. We trust you will have many and happy years among those who love you, and among your fellow-countrymen who are proud of you."

The Regimental History Committee have thought that the War Record would be incomplete did it not contain this very brief account of all that Irish women did for the Regiment.

APPENDICES

[Appendix Nine

SPECIAL ORDERS ON DISBANDMENT.

SPECIAL ORDERS BY LIEUT.-COLONEL C. N. PERREAU, C.M.G.,
COMMANDING 1ST BATTALION THE ROYAL DUBLIN FUSILIERS.

No. 125. ST. LUCIA BARRACKS,
BORDON,
May 30th, 1922.

FAREWELL ORDERS.

The Commanding Officer has received the following farewell orders from the Colonel-in-Chief and the Colonel of the Royal Dublin Fusiliers:

From : Field-Marshal H.R.H. The Duke of Connaught, K.G., etc., Colonel-in-Chief, The Royal Dublin Fusiliers.

It is with a feeling of great sorrow that I bid farewell to The Royal Dublin Fusiliers.

I have been your Colonel-in-Chief for nearly 20 years and have seen you in many parts of the Empire. The Regiment has been in existence over 250 years, and as the Madras and Bombay Fusiliers its history is practically the history of our Indian Empire. On its Colours are names such as Plassey, Arcot, Wandiwash, Seringapatam and Lucknow, which show where the Regiment has fought.

It is always a sign of great achievements when a regiment receives a nickname and the "Blue Caps" extorted that title from the enemy in the great Indian Mutiny, and the "Old Toughs" earned their nickname by their tenacity in the Mahratta Wars.

As The Royal Dublin Fusiliers, the regiment continued to play its part in the history of the British Empire. It earned the admiration of all at Talana Hill and in the battles for the Relief of Ladysmith. In the late war it is only necessary to point to the Landing at Gallipoli, and to Ypres, to show that the regiment has never ceased to keep up the standard of its former achievements in India. It was to me a source of great pride when Her Majesty Queen Victoria appointed me Colonel-in-Chief of the Regiment.

I have presented their Colours to both Battalions, and in the late war I inspected Battalions of the Regiment in France and in Palestine.

All ranks will share with me my satisfaction in knowing that His Majesty The King is going to take charge of our Colours and it is my earnest hope that, in the future, he may be able to restore its Colours to the Regiment, should the country again need its services.

In wishing Good-bye to all ranks, I know that every man of the Royal Dublin Fusiliers will maintain his pride in the Regiment and will never forget that he has worn its uniform and will ever help to maintain its glorious traditions.

(Sd.) ARTHUR, Field-Marshal,
Colonel-in-Chief, The Royal Dublin Fusiliers.

From : Major-General C. D. Cooper, C.B.
Colonel, The Royal Dublin Fusiliers.

It is with feelings of deep sorrow that I write these few lines of farewell to all, and sign my name for the last time as your Colonel, which great honour was granted me on March 13th, 1910, over 12 years ago. I have always had the greatest pride in the Battalions, and of their splendid and very old traditions. I feel sure every one of you will always have a deep affection and pride in your old corps.

May every good luck attend you all from your ever good wisher, comrade and admirer.

(Sd.) C. D. COOPER, Major-General,
Colonel, The Royal Dublin Fusiliers.

BATTALION ORDERS BY LIEUT.-COLONEL C. N. PERREAU, C.M.G., COMMANDING 1ST BATTALION THE ROYAL DUBLIN FUSILIERS.

No. 126.　　　　　　　　　　　　　ST. LUCIA BARRACKS,
Sheet 1　　　　　　　　　　　　　　　　BORDON,
　　　　　　　　　　　　　　　　　　May 31st, 1922.

737. DISBANDMENT.
1644—1922.

Now that definite orders for disbandment have been received, the Commanding Officer hopes that all ranks will agree with his wish not to issue a farewell order.

His feelings about disbandment and his Love for the dear old Regiment are shared equally by every member of it and cannot be expressed in words.

"*Spectamur Agendo*"

(Sd.) T. J. CARROLL-LEAHY, Major,
Adjutant 1st Bn. The Royal Dublin Fusiliers.

SPECIAL ORDERS ON DISBANDMENT

St. Lucia Barracks,
Bordon.
May 27th, 1922.

From: The Officer Commanding,
The "Blue Caps."

To: Major-General C. D. Cooper, C.B.,
Colonel, The Royal Dublin Fusiliers.

Sir,

I have to acknowledge receipt of your letter of the 25th instant, enclosing the farewell order of Field-Marshal His Royal Highness The Duke of Connaught, Colonel-in-Chief, The Royal Dublin Fusiliers, to the Battalion under my command.

Will you please convey to His Royal Highness the grateful thanks of all ranks of the "Blue Caps" for his sympathy in the sad hour of their disbandment.

The story of our traditions will never fade and we are proud to think that the services of the Regiment in South Africa gained for us the signal honour of a deeply sympathetic Royal Colonel-in-Chief.

The "Blue Caps" would much appreciate it if His Royal Highness would convey on their behalf to His Majesty The King the grateful thanks of the Battalion for the high honour he has conferred on it by accepting their Colours for safe custody.

I have the honour to be,
Sir,
Your obedient Servant,
(Sd.) C. N. Perreau, Lieut.-Colonel,
Commanding 1st Bn. The Royal Dublin Fusiliers.

St. Lucia Barracks,
Bordon.
May 27th, 1922.

Dear General,

All ranks of the "Blue Caps" are intensely moved by your farewell order to them.

Coming as it does from one who has had 54 years' direct connection with the old Regiment it is doubly valued.

We realise that no one could have had the interests of the Regiment more at heart through all those years and we trust it will be a source of consolation in your hour of great sorrow, that you and your dear wife always held the affection and esteem of every Royal Dublin Fusilier—that your sorrow is our sorrow.

We shall greatly miss you at the Regimental Dinner and on the occasion of handing over our Colours to H.M. The King.

Yours very sincerely,
(Sd.) C. N. PERREAU.

Major-General C. D. COOPER, C.B.
   Colonel, The Royal Dublin Fusiliers.

[Appendix Ten

OFFICERS ON THE STRENGTH OF THE "BLUE CAPS," JULY 31st, 1922 (date of Disbandment), at Bordon.

Lieut.-Colonel C. N. Perreau, C.M.G. (*Commanding*).
Major R. G. B. Jeffreys, D.S.O.
Major S. G. de C. Wheeler, O.B.E.
Major & Brevet Lieut.-Colonel K. C. Weldon, D.S.O. (*Depot*).
Major J. P. Tredennick, D.S.O., O.B.E.
Captain & Brevet Major R. M. Watson, D.S.O.
Captain & Brevet Major T. J. Carroll-Leahy, D.S.O., M.C. (*Adjutant*).
Captain W. H. Braddell.
Captain A. L. Elsworthy, M.B.E.
Captain W. E. Caldbeck (*Depot*).
Lieutenant D. R. Tittle.
Lieutenant J. B. Moffat (*Depot*).
Lieutenant C. A. Gamble.
Lieutenant L. R. C. Watson (*Assistant Adjutant*).
Lieutenant J. H. S. Harrison.
Lieutenant P. L. G. Renny.
Lieutenant W. J. F. Eassie.
2/Lieutenant K. E. Hegan.
2/Lieutenant R. G. Rooth.
2/Lieutenant B. Tarleton.
2/Lieutenant H. W. H. Houghton.
Major & Quartermaster L. Holloway (*Depot*).
Captain & Quartermaster A. R. Williams.
Rev. J. O'Herlihy, C.F. (*attached*).
Lieutenant W. L. Clarke, A.E.C. (*attached*).

[*Appendix Eleven*

A LIST OF OFFICERS OF THE 1st AND 2nd BATTALIONS THE ROYAL DUBLIN FUSILIERS SERVING ON DISBANDMENT, showing Units to which they were transferred, etc.

LIEUT.-COLONELS.

Perreau, C. N. ... ...
Higginson, G. S. ... ... Retires. 1/8/22.

MAJORS.

Haskard, J. McD. (Bt. Lt.-Col.) East Yorkshire Regt. 5/8/22.
Jeffreys, R. G. B. ... ... North Staffordshire Regt. 5/8/22.
Wheeler, S. G. de C. ... ... Welch Regt. 9/9/22.
Smithwick, S. G. ... ... Duke of Cornwall's Light Infantry. 19/8/22.
Weldon, K. C. (Bt. Lt.-Col.)... Sherwood Foresters. 2/8/22.
Tredennick, J. P. ... ... Bedfordshire and Hertfordshire Regt. 29/7/22.
Knox, R. F. B. ... ... King's Regt. 19/8/22.
Robinson, J. P. B. ... ... Royal Berkshire Regt. 12/8/22.
Hoey, C. B. R. ... ... Retires on Retired Pay. 15/7/22.
Crozier, H. C. ... ... King's Regt. (Liverpool)
French, D. ... ... Retires on Retired Pay. 27/8/22.

CAPTAINS.

Mood, J. M. ... ... East Yorkshire Regt. 26/8/22.
Watson, R. M. ... ... Lancashire Fusiliers. 29/7/22.
Grove, J. R. W. ... ... Bedfordshire and Hertfordshire Regt. 6/9/22.
Dobbs, J. F. K. ... ... King's Regt. 6/6/22.
Carroll-Leahy, T. ... ... Northumberland Fusiliers. 29/7/22.
Lanigan-O'Keeffe, F. S. ... Royal Welch Fusiliers. 7/10/22.
Braddell, W. H. ... ... Northumberland Fusiliers. 29/7/22.
Shadforth, H. A. ... ... Royal Scots Fusiliers. 2/9/22.
Massy-Westropp, R. F. H. Lancashire Fusiliers. 2/9/22.
Carruthers, C. G. ... ... Border Regt. 12/8/22.
Shears, P. J. ... ... Border Regt. 12/8/22.
Kendrick, E. H. ... ... Tank Corps.

OFFICERS SERVING ON DISBANDMENT

Tarleton, G. W. B. ... Border Regt. (India). 2/8/22.
Glegg, J. D. ... East Yorkshire Regt. 26/8/22.
Elsworthy, A. L. ... Royal Scots Fusiliers. 16/9/22.
Maffett, C. W. ... Black Watch. 12/8/22.
Treacher, F. ... South Staffordshire Regt. 16/9/22.
Gillett, N. C. ... Tank Corps.
Walters, J. P. ... Duke of Cornwall's Light Infantry. 7/10/22.
Caldbeck, W. E. ... Bedfordshire and Hertfordshire Regt. 2/9/22.
Brady, T. ... Retires, Receiving a Gratuity. 23/7/22.

Lieutenants.

Tittle, D. R. ... King's Own Regt. 30/8/22.
Byrne, L. C. ... Royal Scots Fusiliers. 2/9/22.
O'Morchoe, K. G. ... Gordon Highlanders. 16/9/22.
Moffat, J. B. ... East Yorkshire Regt. 9/9/22.
Arnold, W. J. ... East Lancashire Regt. 20/9/22.
Matson, C. ... Gloucestershire Regt. 4/10/22.
Douglas, R. G. ... Gloucestershire Regt. 4/10/22.
Stitt, W. H. ... Welch Regt. 9/9/22.
Craig-McFeely, C. M. ... Border Regt. 26/7/22.
Power, F. T. A. ... Royal Corps of Signals, Welch Regt.
Williamson, U. A. F. ... Tank Corps.
Gamble, C. A. ... Royal Army Service Corps (Sherwood Foresters). 20/9/22.
Aylmer, H. G. ... Essex Regt. 20/9/22.
Hynes, W. H. ... Gloucestershire Regt. 14/10/22.
Carroll, S. J. M. ... Cameronians (Scottish Rifles). 9/9/22.
Harcourt, H. G. ... South Wales Borderers. 9/9/22.
Mulholland, G. F. ... Royal Warwickshire Regt. 20/9/22.
Harrison, H. B. ... Royal Welch Fusiliers. 26/8/22.
Lawrence, L. A. ... West Yorkshire Regt. 12/8/22.
Shepard, D. C. A. ... Border Regt.
Dolan, J. J. ... Manchester Regt.
Flewett, T. E. ... Border Regt.
Chadwick, T. A. H. ... Norfolk Regt. 5/8/22.
Norman, D. S. ... East Yorkshire Regt. 26/8/22.
Condron, M. A. ... Retires, Receiving a Gratuity. 20/7/22.
Watson, L. R. C. ... Royal Corps of Signals, Northumberland Fusiliers. Seconded. 4/8/22.
FitzGerald, M. H. ... East Yorkshire Regt. 26/8/22. Seconded for Service Royal Air Force. 16/8/22.

Russell, G. D. R. ... ... Prince of Wales's Volunteers. 29/7/22.
Harrison, J. H. S. ... ... West Yorkshire Regt. 29/7/22. King's African Rifles. 1/9/22.
Renny, P. L. G. ... ... South Staffordshire Regt. 2/8/22.
Eassie, W. J. F. ... ... Loyal North Lancashire Regt. 29/7/22.

Second-Lieutenants.

Hegan, K. E. ... ... Loyal North Lancashire Regt. 29/7/22.
Rooth, R. G. ... ... West Yorkshire Regt. 12/8/22.
Tarleton, B. ... ... Northumberland Fusiliers. 5/8/22.
Houghton, H. W. H. ... Sherwood Foresters. 26/8/22.

Quartermasters.

Major Holloway, L. ... ...
Capt. Williams, A. R. ... Tank Corps. 2/10/22.
Capt. Dowling, J. E. ... Black Watch. 25/9/22.

[Appendix Twelve

COPY OF ARMY LIST FOR JULY, 1922
(THE LAST BEFORE DISBANDMENT)
SHOWING ROLL OF OFFICERS OF THE ROYAL DUBLIN FUSILIERS 1ST AND 2ND BATTALIONS.

1545	1546	1547	1548

THE ROYAL DUBLIN FUSILIERS.
[To be Disbanded.]

[102]

No. 11 District.

The Royal Tiger, superscribed "Plassey," "Buxar," and with motto, '*Spectamur Agendo*' underneath.
The Elephant, superscribed, "Carnatic," "Mysore."
"Arcot," "Condore," "Wandiwash," "Pondicherry," "Guzerat," "Sholinghur," "Nundy Droog,"
"Amboyna," "Ternate," "Bauda," "Seringapatam," "Kirkee," "Maheidpoor,"
"Beni Boo Alli," "Ava," "Aden," "Mooltan," "Goojerat," "Punjaub,"
"Pegu," "Lucknow," "Relief of Ladysmith," "South Africa, 1899-1902."

Agents—Mr C. R. McGrigor, Bt. & Co.

Regular and Militia Battalions.
Uniform—Scarlet. *Facings*—Blue.

1st Bn. (102nd Foot)	.. Bordon.	3rd Bn. (Kildare Mil.)	Naas.
2nd ,, (103rd ,,)	.. Bordon.	4th ,, (R. Dublin City Mil.)	Dublin.
		5th ,, (Dublin County Mil.)	Dublin.
Depôt ..	.. Bordon.	Record Office .. Hamilton.	

Colonel-in-Chief — Field-Marshal H.R.H. The Duke of Connaught and Strathearn, K.G., K.T., K.P., G.C.B., G.C.S.I., G.C.M.G., G.C.I.E., G.C.V.O., G.B.E., Col. Gren Gds. and R.A.S.C., and Col. in Chief The Inniskillings, H.L.I., Rifle Bde. and R.A.M.C., *Personal A.D.C. to the King* — 7Nov03

Colonel .. .. .. Cooper, Hon. Maj.-Gen. C. D., C.B., *ret. pay* 13Mar.19

Officer Commanding Depôt — Weldon, Maj. (bt. lt.-col.) K. C., D.S.O., R. D. Fus. .. 28Dec.21

1st and 2nd Battalions. (Regular.)

Lt.-Colonel.
1 Perreau, C. N., *C.M.G.* 26May19
2 Higginson, G. S. 26Sept.21

Majors.
2 Haskard, J. McD., *C.M.G., D.S.O.*, p.s.c. [t] 26Apr.15
 bt. lt.-col. 1Jan.18
Jeffreys, E. G. B., *D.S.O.* 1Sept.15
1 Wheeler, S.G. de C., *O.B.E.* 1Sept.15
2 Smithwick, S. G., *O.B.E.* 1Sept.15
d. 1 Weldon, K. C., *D.S.O.* 1Sept.15
 bt. lt.-col. 3June19
1 Tredennick, J.P., *D.S.O., O.B.E.*, (s.c.) 1Sept.15
e.a. Knox, R. F. B. 1Sept.15
s. Robinson, J. P. B., *C.M.G., D.S.O.*, p.s.c. 1Sept.15
 bt. lt.-col. 26June22
(1) Hoey, C. B. R. 18Jan.17
Crozier, H. C., *M.C.* (*Supt. Phys. Trng.*) 18Jan.17
2 French, D. 18Jan.17

Captains.
2 Mood, J. M., *O.B.E., M.C.* 7Aug.13
1 Watson, R. M., *D S O.* 5Aug.16
 bt. maj. 1Jan.17
t. Grove, J. R. W. 2Sept.14
 bt. maj. 1June19
e.e. Dobbs, J. F. K., *M.C.* 14Dec.14
1 Carroll-Leahy, T. J., *D.S.O., M.C.*, (S.C.), Adjt. 26Apr.15
 bt. maj. 3June17
Lanigan-O'Keeffe, F. S., *M.B.E.* (*Spec. Empld.*) 23Apr.15
1 Braddell, W. H. 10ct.15
e.a. Shadforth, H. A., *O.B.E., M.C.* 10ct.15
s. Massy-Westropp, R. F. H., *M.C.* 10ct.15
2 Carruthers, C. G., *M.C.* 26Jan.16
(1) Shears, P. J. 15Aug16
t.c. Kendrick, E. H., *D.S.O.* 15Oct.16
 bt. maj. 3June17
2 Turidon, G. W. B., *M.C.* 1Jan.17
2 Glegg, J. D., *M.C.* 1Jan.17
Elsworthy, A. L., *M.B.E.* (i) 1Jan.17

Captains—contd.
2 Maffett, C. W. 1Jan.17
s. Treacher, F., *M.C.* 1Jan.17
 bt. maj. 3June19
t.c. Gillett, N. C. 20Apr.17
t.e. Walters, J. P. 14Sept.17
m. Caldbeck, W. E. 9Sept.20
 22June19
(1) 2Brady, T. 22June19

Lieutenants
1 Tittle, D. R. 30Aug.15
c.o. Byrne, L. C., *D.S.O., M.C.* 26Jan.16
c.o. O'Morchoe, K. G. 6June16
d. 1 Moffat, J. B. 6June16
e.o. Arnold, W. J. 20June16
2 Matson, C., *M.C.* 24June16
e.a. Douglas, R. G. 21July16
2 Stitt, W. H., *D.S.O., M.C. Adjt.* 24July16
2 Craig-McFeely, C.M., *D.S.O., M.C.* 24July16
c.s. Power, F.T.A., *M.C.* 20Dec.16
t.c. Williamson, U A. F. 1Jan.17
1 Gamble, C. A. 1Jan.17
3 Aylmer, H. G. 1Jan.17
2 Hynes, W. H. 1Jan.17
t.c. Carroll, S. J. M. 14Nov.17
t.v. Harcourt, H. G., *D.S.O., M.C.* (*Adjt. Aux. Force. India*) 26Nov.17
c.o. Mulholland, G. F. 23Dec.17

Lieutenants—contd.
2 Harrison, H. B., *M.C.* 16Jan.18
d. 2 Lawrence, L. A. 21Apr.18
2 Shepard, D C A. 27Apr.18
2 Dolan, J. J., *M. C.* 28May19
2 Flewett, T. E. 21June19
2 Chadwick, T. A. H. 21June19
2 Norman, D. S. 21June19
2 Condron, M. A. 6July19
1 Watson, L. R. C. 20Dec.20
2 FitzGerald, M. H. 20Dec.20
2 Russell, G. D. B. 20Dec.20
1 Harrison, J. H. S. 16July21
1 Renny, P. L. G. 17Dec.21
1 Eassie, W.J. F. 17Dec.21

2nd Lieutenants.
1 Began, K. E 16July20
1 Rooth, R. G. 15July20
1 Tarleton, B. 23Dec.21
1 Houghton, H. W H. 23Dec.21

Adjutants.
1 Carroll-Leahy, T. J., *D.S.O., M.C.*, *capt.* 16 Oct. 19
2 Stitt, W. H., *D.S.O., M.C., U.* 1Nov.19

Quarter-Masters.
m. Holloway, L. 28Nov.08
 maj. 1July17
1 Williams, A. R. 8Mar.13
 capt. 1July17
Dowling, J. E. 25Aug.14
 capt. 25Aug.17
 15Oct.21

[Appendix Thirteen

DISTRIBUTION OF OFFICERS' AND SERGEANTS' MESS PROPERTY.

COMMITTEE OF ADJUSTMENT, ROYAL DUBLIN FUSILIERS.

Meeting held at the Army and Navy Club, on Friday, June 9th, 1922.
The following were present :—
    Colonel Elford Pearse.
    Colonel Commandant H. W. Higginson, C.B., D.S.O.
    Lieut.-Colonel C. N. Perreau, C.M.G.
    Lieut.-Colonel G. S. Higginson.
    Major D. French.
    Major R. M. Watson, D.S.O.
Major-General C. F. Romer, C.B., C.M.G., was unable to attend.

IT WAS DECIDED :—

1. That certain articles as shown in the Inventory, should be sent to the Royal United Service Institution.

2. That articles as shown on the Inventories presented by past and present officers and other persons should be returned to the donors, or their heirs and successors for safe custody.

2A. In the case of articles presented by more than one person, such articles will be disposed of by drawing lots amongst those persons who are living at the time.

In the event of there being no survivors amongst the donors the Commanding Officers and sub-committees of Battalions shall have discretionary powers of disposal.

3. That the articles as shown in the Inventories (*i.e.* those won by the Battalions and those not presented by individuals) should be distributed among those officers of the 1st and 2nd Battalions who were members of the Royal Dublin Fusiliers Dinner Club in 1922, and who are willing to undertake the safe custody of these.

4. That miscellaneous articles, viz., furniture, books, pictures, etc., should be disposed of under instructions to be issued by the Commanding Officers and their sub-committees of the 1st and 2nd Battalions respectively.

5. That the silver forks and spoons should be stored for three years, and in the event of the Regiment not being reconstituted as laid down in para. 6, these should be distributed amongst those officers, or their heirs and successors, serving on the strength of the Regiment on the date of disbandment.

6. That the articles dealt with under paras. 2 and 3, should be distributed on the understanding that they shall be returned to the Regiment in the event of its being reconstituted as a Regiment of the Imperial British Army; *i.e.* that it must form part of the British Army *as it now does*, and is not part of any Army of the Irish Free State.

7. That if the Regiment is not reconstituted as laid down in para. 6, within three years of the date of disbandment, the articles enumerated in paras. 2 and 3, should become the property of the persons in whose custody they were placed.

8. That all articles not claimed within one month of the date of the posting of the notification relating thereto, will be redistributed by the Committee.

9. That power be given to Commanding Officers and sub-committees of the 1st and 2nd Battalions to make presentations of plate to :—

(1) H.M. The King.

(2) Field-Marshal H.R.H. The Duke of Connaught, K.G., Colonel-in-Chief, The Royal Dublin Fusiliers.

(3) R. A. Bacon, Esq., O.B.E.

(4) The Committee, Royal Dublin Fusiliers Prisoners of War Fund, viz., Lady Arnott, Sir G. Cochrane and J. Whiteside Dane, Esq.

[*Appendix Fourteen*

DISPOSAL OF THE SILVER AND MESS PROPERTY
1st Bn. The Royal Dublin Fusiliers.

The Madras Cup (Item No. 10) has been sent to H.M. The King.

The two seven-light Candelabra (Items Nos. 13 and 14) have been sent to Field-Marshal H.R.H. The Duke of Connaught, K.G., etc.

The following articles have been sent to the Royal United Service Institution:—

    Item No. 1.   ⎫
    Item No. 2.   ⎬ Neill Centrepiece and Stand.
    Item No. 4.   South African War Cup.
    Item No. 5.   Rifle Challenge Cup.
    Item No. 23. Silver Aghdan.
    Item No. 33. Cannon Cigar Lighter.
    Item No. 48. One Wine Cooler.
    Item No. 50. Maheidpoor Snuff Mull.
    Item No. 74. One Complete Dish.
    Item No. 80. One Complete Dish.

All the medals.
Busby Badge, 1862–1881.
Busby Badge, 1881–1914.
Regimental Crest.
Sergeant Drummer's Sash.
Relics of "River Clyde."
Drum carried at Relief of Lucknow.
Pictures of:—
    Lord Clive,
    General Stringer-Lawrence.
    Sir John Malcolm.
    Sir Eyre Coote.
One Plate and one Coffee Cup of dinner service.
One Spoon and one Fork.

The remainder of the silver if presented has been returned to the donor, and if not presented distributed amongst the members of the Royal Dublin Fusiliers Dinner Club.

OFFICERS' MESS SILVER
1ST BATTALION THE ROYAL DUBLIN FUSILIERS.
THE "BLUE CAPS," MAY, 1922.

[Photo, Gale & Polden, Ltd.

SERGEANTS' MESS SILVER OF THE "BLUE CAPS."

[Photo, Gale & Polden, Ltd.

MESS PROPERTY

COPIES OF LETTERS IN REGARD TO DISTRIBUTION OF SPECIAL ITEMS OF SILVER.

St. Lucia Barracks,
Bordon.
23rd June, 1922.

Sir,

It is the unanimous wish of all the Officers of the Battalion under my command, that His Majesty should be asked to honour us by accepting as a memento, a silver two handled cup, presented by the Citizens of Madras, in 1913, on the occasion of the return of the Battalion to the city of its origin, and its home for over two hundred years.

As I am unaware of the necessary procedure in this case, I should be most grateful for your advice.

I have the honour to be,
Sir,
Your Obedient Servant,
C. N. Perreau, Lieut.-Colonel,
Commanding 1st Bn. The Royal Dublin Fusiliers
(late Royal Madras Fusiliers).

The Lord Chamberlain,
Buckingham Palace.

Buckingham Palace,
26th June, 1922.

Dear Sir,

Your letter of the 23rd instant, to the Lord Chamberlain, has been laid before the King.

I am commanded to say with what appreciation His Majesty has received the expressed wish of the Officers under your Command that he should accept as a memento a silver two handled cup, presented by the Citizens of Madras in 1913, on the occasion of the return of the Battalion to the city of its origin, and its home for over two hundred years.

The King will gladly accept this interesting gift and treasure it in remembrance of your distinguished Regiment.

Yours very truly,
Stamfordham.

Lieutenant-Colonel C. N. Perreau, C.M.G.,
Commanding 1st Bn. The Royal Dublin Fusiliers
(late Royal Madras Fusiliers),
St. Lucia Barracks,
Bordon.

BUCKINGHAM PALACE,

DEAR SIR,

The Silver Two-Handled Cup, which you were so kind as to bring here, has been handed to the King, and I am commanded to express to you and the Officers of the 1st Battalion, The Royal Dublin Fusiliers, His Majesty's sincere thanks for this gift, which will be treasured among the Royal Plate as a memento of a Regiment whose great and distinguished career has been terminated through circumstances beyond its control.

Yours very truly,
STAMFORDHAM.

Lieutenant-Colonel C. N. PERREAU, C.M.G.,
  Commanding 1st Bn. The Royal Dublin Fusiliers,
    St. Lucia Barracks,
      Bordon.

ST. LUCIA BARRACKS,
BORDON.
27th June, 1922.

DEAR SIR MALCOLM,

It is the wish of all the Officers of the "Blue Caps" that His Royal Highness should accept from them some mark of their great admiration and appreciation of all he has done for them during the period he has been their Colonel-in-Chief.

The Officers would like His Royal Highness to accept two seven branch candelabra—one silver, one Sheffield plate—and which have been in possession of the Mess for over 150 years.

The Sergeants' Mess are most anxious His Royal Highness should accept a Silver Soup Tureen on stand, presented to their Mess by the Citizens of Madras in 1858, in commemoration of the fine achievements of the Battalion as Madras Fusiliers, during the Mutiny.

If His Royal Highness will honour us by accepting these pieces of silver, I would take steps to send them up by motor car later on, when we deposit other pieces of silver in the Royal United Service Institution.

Yours sincerely,
C. N. PERREAU,
Lieut.-Colonel,
Commanding 1st Bn. The Royal Dublin Fusiliers.
(Neill's "Blue Caps.")

SIR MALCOLM MURRAY,
  Clarence House,
    St. James's.

SILVER CUP

PRESENTED BY THE CITIZENS OF MADRAS TO THE
1ST BN. THE ROYAL DUBLIN FUSILIERS
(FORMERLY THE 1st MADRAS FUSILIERS)

On the Return of the Regiment in February, 1913, to Madras, the City of its Birth and its Home for over 200 years.

Presented by the Officers' Mess of the "Blue Caps" to H.M. the King, August, 1922.

TRAY   [*Photos, Gale & Polden, Ltd.*

PRESENTED TO THE
1ST BN. THE ROYAL DUBLIN FUSILIERS
BY THE OFFICERS' MESS

To Commemorate the Officers who served with the Battalion during the Great War.

MESS PROPERTY

> CLARENCE HOUSE,
> ST. JAMES'S, S.W.,
> *24th July*, 1922.

DEAR COLONEL PERREAU,

    I am desired by H.R.H. The Duke of Connaught to ask you to express to the Officers of the Battalion under your Command his most grateful thanks for the splendid pair of silver Candelabra, which they have so kindly sent for his acceptance. His Royal Highness very much appreciates this mark of their regard for their former Colonel-in-Chief, and he wishes to assure them how much he will value their present.

    Should the Battalion be at any time re-formed as a part of the Imperial Army, His Royal Highness would, of course, be prepared to return the Candelabra to the Officers' Mess.

> Believe me,
> Yours sincerely,
> MALCOLM MURRAY, *Lieut.-Colonel*,
> *Comptroller to H.R.H. The Duke of Connaught.*

Lieutenant-Colonel C. N. PERREAU, C.M.G.,
   Commanding 1st Bn. Royal Dublin Fusiliers,
      St. Lucia Barracks,
         Bordon.

[Appendix Fifteen

CEREMONIAL OF THE RECEPTION OF THE COLOURS OF THE DISBANDED SOUTHERN IRISH REGIMENTS BY THE KING at Windsor Castle on Monday, the 12th June, 1922, at 11.30 a.m.

On Monday, the 12th June, 1922, at 11.30 a.m., in St. George's Hall, Windsor Castle, the King will take over the Colours of the following Regiments :—

    The Royal Irish Regiment,
    The Connaught Rangers,
    The Prince of Wales's Leinster Regiment (Royal Canadians),
    The Royal Munster Fusiliers, and
    The Royal Dublin Fusiliers.

His Majesty will also receive a Regimental Engraving offered by the South Irish Horse.

The detachments from the six Regiments will travel by the 9.55 a.m. train from Paddington Railway Station, arriving at Windsor G.W. Railway Station at 10.42 a.m.

On arrival at Windsor Railway Station the Colour Parties will proceed to the Royal Waiting Room, where the Colours will be unfurled.

The detachments will be met at Windsor Railway Station by an Escorting Party of 100 all ranks of the Third Battalion, Grenadier Guards, accompanied by the Band of the Regiment.

The Escorting Party will Present Arms as the five Colour Parties march out of the Royal Waiting Room with the Colours.

The six detachments of the Irish Regiments will be formed up in the following order, *i.e.*:—

    The Royal Irish Regiment,
    The Connaught Rangers,
    The South Irish Horse,
    The Prince of Wales's Leinster Regiment (Royal Canadians),
    The Royal Munster Fusiliers,
    The Royal Dublin Fusiliers.

The detachments, headed by the Band and one-half the Escorting Party, the other half bringing up the rear of the Column, will march to the Quadrangle of the Castle.

At the gateway of the Castle, the Troops will be met by Lieutenant-Colonel The Marquis of Cambridge, Governor and Constable of Windsor Castle.

On arrival in the Quadrangle of Windsor Castle, the six detachments of the Irish Regiments will enter by the Grand Entrance and proceed to St. George's Hall, the Escorting Party, with Band, remaining in the Quadrangle.

To the Officers, Warrant Officers, Non-Commissioned Officers and Men of the Royal Dublin Fusiliers.

It is with feelings of no ordinary sorrow that I address you for the last time; for I know that I am taking leave not merely of a fine regiment, but of great memories and great traditions which hitherto have been kept alive and embodied in you.

You are the oldest of the British garrison in India. Your second battalion dates back to the time when Queen Catherine of Braganza brought Bombay as part of her dowry to King Charles II; your first battalion to still remoter days. Stringer Lawrence, the teacher of Robert Clive, won many a victory with you. Clive led you to Arcot and Plassey; Eyre Coote to Wandewash; Forde to Condore. Your history is the history of early British dominance in India, and you have shown abundantly that you could fight as sternly in South Africa and in Europe as in the East Indies.

To me it is a very mournful task to bid you farewell—I have always taken the greatest pride in your past history, but if the glory of any fighting men be safe, then most assuredly safe is yours.

You have your Colours, your trophies and your household gods, which are dear to you as honour itself. You have thought fit to entrust your Colours to me for custody, and I am very proud to take charge of them, to be preserved and held in reverence at Windsor Castle as a perpetual record of your noble exploits in the field.

Meanwhile, be very sure that, with or without external monument, the fame of your great work can never die.

I thank you for your good service to this Country and the Empire, and with a full heart I bid you—Farewell.

George R.I.

12th June, 1922.

RECEPTION OF COLOURS BY THE KING

The six detachments of the Irish Regiments will form up in St. George's Hall facing the windows, in the following order, numbering from the right :—
1. The Royal Irish Regiment,
2. The Connaught Rangers,
3. The South Irish Horse,
4. The Prince of Wales's Leinster Regiment (Royal Canadians),
5. The Royal Munster Fusiliers,
6. The Royal Dublin Fusiliers.

The King, accompanied by Field-Marshal His Royal Highness The Duke of Connaught (Honorary Colonel of the South Irish Horse and Colonel-in-Chief of the Royal Dublin Fusiliers), will enter St. George's Hall at 11.30 a.m. Upon His Majesty taking up his position facing the centre of the line, a Royal Salute will be given, the Colours will be lowered, and the Band in the Quadrangle will play the National Anthem.

The King will then inspect the six detachments and resume his place facing the centre of the line.

His Majesty will address the detachments; after which the Ceremony of Presentation of the Colours will take place, concluding with the offering by the South Irish Horse of the Engraving.

On the conclusion of the Ceremony a Royal Salute will be given, the Band in the Quadrangle playing the National Anthem.

His Majesty leaves St. George's Hall.

Dress.   Service Dress.
   Grenadier Guards. Full Dress.
   Detachments from Irish Regiments wear Medals and Breast Decorations.

COMPOSITION OF THE SIX DETACHMENTS FROM IRISH REGIMENTS :—

THE SOUTH IRISH HORSE.

Honorary Colonel	F.M. H.R.H. The Duke of Connaught.
Colonel	Lieutenant-Colonel I. W. Burns-Lindow, D.S.O.
Second in Command	Major R. Smyth.
Adjutant	Captain R. Dease.
	Sergeant Goodchild.

THE ROYAL IRISH REGIMENT.

Colonel	Major-General J. Burton Forster, C.B.
O.C. 1st Battn.	Major F. Call, D.S.O.
King's Colour	Lieutenant J. J. Burke-Gaffney, M.C.

Regimental Colour ...	Lieutenant W. C. V. Galwey, M.C. R.S.M. C. Field. C.S.M. J. Bridger, M.S.M. Sergeant H. Taylor, M.M. Sergeant W. Dunne, D.C.M.
O.C. 2nd Battn. ...	Lieutenant-Colonel G. A. Elliot, M.C.
King's Colour	Lieutenant W. C. L. Shee.
Regimental Colour ...	Lieutenant E. C. Beard, M.C. R.S.M. R. Burns. C.S.M. J. Cussens, D.C.M. C.S.M. J. Bergin. C.S.M. B. Harris.

The Connaught Rangers.

O.C. 1st Battn. ...	Lieutenant-Colonel W. N. S. Alexander, D.S.O. Captain F. D. Foott. Captain W. O'Brien. M.C. Sergeant Wallace. Sergeant Malone. Sergeant Scott.
O.C. 2nd Battn. ...	Lieutenant-Colonel H. F. N. Jourdain, C.M.G. Lieutenant G. B. Champion. Lieutenant C. G. Gaden, M.C. R.S.M. M. J. Monaghan, M.C. Bandmaster G. Landrock. Acting R.S.M. P. J. Finucane, D.C.M.

The Prince of Wales's Leinster Regiment (Royal Canadians).

Colonel	Major-General G. F. Boyd, C.B., C.M.G., D.S.O.
O.C. 1st Battn. ...	Colonel E. T. Humphreys, C.M.G., D.S.O. Captain T. B. Deane. Lieutenant F. A. Levis. C.S.M. A. Bradley, M.M. C.S.M. J. Newton. C.Q.M.S. A. Madden.
O.C. 2nd Battn. ...	Lieutenant-Colonel R. A. H. Orpen-Palmer, D.S.O. Captain W. S. Caulfeild, M.C. Captain T. E. M. Battersby. R.S.M. C. H. Smith, M.C., D.C.M. C.S.M. J. Finn. Colour-Sergeant J. Cannon.

The Royal Munster Fusiliers.

Colonel	...	Lieutenant-General Sir H. S. G. Miles, G.C.B., G.C.M.G., G.B.E., C.V.O.
O.C. 1st Battn.	...	Lieutenant-Colonel J. A. F. Cuffe, C.M.G., D.S.O.
		Major G. W. Geddes, D.S.O.
		Captain G. R. Prendergast.
		C.Q.M.S. Fitzmaurice.
		Private McNamara.
		Private Wynne.
O.C. 2nd Battn.	...	Lieutenant-Colonel H. S. Jervis, M.C.
King's Colour	...	Major C. R. Rawlinson.
Regimental Colour	...	Lieutenant and Adjutant C. B. Callander, M.C.
		R.S.M. J. Ring, M.C., D.C.M.
		Lance-Corporal J. Foley.
		Private J. Merner, M.M.

The Royal Dublin Fusiliers.

Colonel-in-Chief	...	F.M. H.R.H. The Duke of Connaught.
O.C. 1st Battn.	...	Lieutenant-Colonel C. N. Perreau, C.M.G.
King's Colour	...	Major J. P. Tredennick, D.S.O., O.B.E.
Regimental Colour	...	Major T. J. Carroll-Leahy, D.S.O., M.C.
		C.S.M. A. Cullen.
		Sergeant T. Doyle.
		Sergeant A. D. Connolly.
O.C. 2nd Battn.	...	Lieutenant-Colonel G. S. Higginson.
King's Colour	...	Captain J. M. Mood, O.B.E., M.C.
Regimental Colour	...	Captain C. G. Carruthers, M.C.
		Colour-Sergeant J. A. Jones.
		Colour-Sergeant P. Kehoe.
		Colour-Sergeant G. Sexton.

[*Note.*—Major-General C. D. Cooper, C.B., Colonel of The Royal Dublin Fusiliers, was unavoidably prevented from being present.]

[Appendix Sixteen

ARMY RIFLE ASSOCIATION. 1921 MEETING.
Successes of the "Blue Caps."

Queen Victoria Cup.—The 1st Royal Dublin Fusiliers were placed 6th, with a score of 1,405, in Series (A).

King George Cup was won by the 1st Royal Dublin Fusiliers who were awarded Challenge Cup and eight A.R.A. silver medals.

SERIES (A).
RESULT OF THE COMPETITION, 1921.
Number of entries, At Home, 17.

Winners:
1ST BATTALION THE ROYAL DUBLIN FUSILIERS.

Officer Commanding Battalion—Lieut.-Colonel C. N. Perreau, C.M.G.
Fired at Longmoor, 21st September, 1921.
Captain of the Team—Lieutenant L. R. C. Watson.

	Barrel Number of Rifle.	H.P.S.	Practices 1 (20)	Practices 2 (20)	Practices 3 (30)	Total (70)
2/Lieutenant P. L. G. Renny	61361		15	17	21	53
Lieutenant L. R. C. Watson	7181		20	11	21	52
Lieutenant K. G. O'Morchoe	1653		14	12	18	44
Captain C. H. L'E. West	36886		11	14	18	43
Major S. G. de C. Wheeler, O.B.E.	8964		13	11	18	42
Major R. M. Watson, D.S.O.	10256		15	10	15	40
Lieutenant C. McCann, D.C.M.	3334		14	13	12	39
2/Lieutenant R. G. Rooth	2305		13	13	12	38
Totals			115	101	135	351
Averages			14.37	12.62	16.87	43.87

Average of team 43.87.

Officers Superintending:
- At the Butt: Lieut. F. A. L. Cooper, R.G.A.; Lieut. H. B. Truscott, R.G.A.
- At the Firing Point: Lieut. A. E. Smith, M.C., M.M., R.G.A.; Lieut. A. P. Lambooy, R.G.A.

Young Soldiers Cup.—The 1st Royal Dublin Fusiliers were placed 5th, with only 3 points below 3rd.

Henry Whitehead Cup was won by the 1st Royal Dublin Fusiliers, who were awarded the Challenge Cup and 50 A.R.A. bronze medals.

SERIES (D).
RESULT OF THE COMPETITION, 1921.
Number of Entries, 7.

Winners:
1ST BATTALION THE ROYAL DUBLIN FUSILIERS.

Officer Commanding Battalion—Lieut.-Colonel C. N. Perreau, C.M.G.
Fired at Longmoor.

[*Photo, Gale & Polden, Ltd.*

WINNERS OF THE HENRY WHITEHEAD CUP, 1921.
1ST BN. THE ROYAL DUBLIN FUSILIERS.

Top Row—Bdmn. G. Wood   Bdmn. W. Toner   L. Cpl. J. Harris   Bdmn. T. Andrews   Bdmn. W. Raymond   Bdmn. J. Fitzgerald
Second Row—Fus. J. Costigan   Fus. J. Corcoran   Fus. J. Doran   Bdmn. H. Nelson   L. Cpl. C. Keegan   Fus. J. Bell   Fus. R. Rawlinson
Third Row—Sergt. F. Manktelow   Sergt. E. Godfrey   Fus. W. Nash   Sergt. A. Childerhouse   Sergt. A. Wood   Sergt. M. Ludford   Sergt. G. Blackman   L. Sergt. J. W. Deegan   Sergt. T. English   Sergt. J. Dolan
Front Row—R.S.M. G. H. Anderson   Lieut. C. A. Gamble   Lieut. K. G. O'Morchoe   Capt. W. H. Braddell   Major S. G. de C. Wheeler, O.B.E.   Lieut. D. R. Tittle   Lieut. J. H. S. Harrison   C.S.M. (1. of M.) T. Byrne   C.Q.M.S. J. Byrne.

THE HENRY WHITEHEAD CUP.

THE KING GEORGE CUP.

SHOOTING SUCCESSES

Rank, Name and Company.	Aggregate Scores. H.P.S. 265	Rank, Name and Company.	Aggregate Scores. H.P.S. 265
R.S.M. G. H. Anderson (D)	228	Major S. G. de C. Wheeler, O.B.E. (D)	201
Sergt. E. Godfrey (D)	227	C.Q.M.S. J. Byrne (B)	201
C.S.M.I.M. T. Byrne (D)	225	Sergt. T. English (C)	201
Sergt. M. Ludford (C)	225	Bdm. H. Nelson (A)	201
Sergt. A. Childerhouse (B)	220	Capt. W. H. Braddell (D)	199
Lieut. K. G. O'Morchoe (A)	219	Pte. W. Nash (D)	199
Cpl. J. Mogan (B)	219	Sergt. J. Bradley (D)	198
Pte. P. Pepper (C)	217	Cpl. W. Raymond (B)	198
Sergt. R. Wood (A)	215	Bdm. G. Wood (A)	195
Sergt. F. Manktelow (C)	214	Capt. J. Esmonde, M.C. (A)	194
Lieut. C. McCann, D.C.M. (D)	212	Sergt. B. Kinsella (D)	194
Sergt. J. Deegan (C)	212	Bdm. J. Harris (A)	194
Pte. R. Rawlinson (C)	211	Cpl. E. D'Oney (C)	193
Pte. J. Bell (C)	210	Pte. H. Osborne (D)	193
Pte. C. Keen (C)	209	Pte. J. Doran (A)	192
Lieut. D. R. Tittle (C)	208	Pte. T. Fitzgerald (A)	192
Sergt. A. D. Connolly (D)	208	Lieut. C. A. Gamble (B)	191
Lieut. L. R. C. Watson (D)	207	2/Lieut. R. G. Rooth (B)	191
Bdm. W. Toner (A)	207	Pte. E. Hanton (B)	191
Bt. Lt.-Col. K. C. Weldon, D.S.O. (A)	205	Pte. T. Byrne (C)	191
Capt. J. MacN. Dickie, M.C. (A)	205	Pte. J. Corcoran (A)	191
Sergt. G. Blackman (A)	205	Cpl. C. Keegan (D)	190
Sergt. J. Dolan (B)	205	Lieut. J. H. S. Harrison (A)	189
Pte. R. Evans (C)	205	Sergt. A. Murphy (D)	189
Pte. T. Costigan (C)	205		
Pte. T. Andrews (D)	204	Total	10,195
		Average	203.90

SERIES (D).

H.P.S. 13,250

1	1st Royal Dublin Fusiliers	Longmoor	10,195*	
2	3rd Coldstream Guards	Pirbright	9,935	
3	2nd Leinster Regiment	Colchester	9,824	TOTAL—
4	2nd Connaught Rangers	Dover	9,082	50 Bronze
5	1st Coldstream Guards	Pirbright	9,042	Medals.

Two other teams competed.

*The Challenge Cup and 50 A.R.A. Bronze Medals.

In the Company Match, "D" Company, Major S. G. de C. Wheeler, O.B.E., were placed 4th, with a score of 472.

In the Hopton Cup (Platoon Competition), No. 15 Platoon of "D" Company were placed 3rd, equal with the 2nd Rifle Brigade, with a score of 162.

In the Duke of Connaught Cup (Officers' Revolver Shoots), the 1st Royal Dublin Fusiliers were placed 20th, equal, of 61 teams, with a score of 582.

[*Appendix Seventeen*

SPORTING SUCCESSES of the "Blue Caps" from the Period of Reorganization, August, 1919, to Disbandment, July, 1922, in the Aldershot Command.

BOXING.
(Officer in Charge : Lieut. C. McCann, D.C.M.)

No. 6 Group, A.C.A.A. Championships, February 1st, 1920.

Won Officers' Heavy-Weight (Lieut. Rice, silver medal).
Won Officers' Middle-Weight (Lieut. Franklin, M.C., silver medal).
Won Officers' Welter-Weight (Lieut. McCann, D.C.M., silver medal).
Second in Other Ranks' Middle-Weight (Cpl. Gray, silver medal).
Won Other Ranks' Light-Weight (Pte. Anderson, silver medal).
Won Other Ranks' Bantam-Weight (Pte. O'Brien, silver medal).
Second in Other Ranks' Fly-Weight (Pte. McDonald, bronze medal).
Won Boys' Fly-Weight (Boy Murphy, silver medal).

Battalion won Officers' and Boys' Team Competitions in above Competition.

No. 6 Group, A.C.A.A. Individual Championships, March 20th, 1920.

Won Officers' Welter-Weight (Lieut. McCann, D.C.M., silver medal).
Won Other Ranks' Catch-Weight (Sergt. Doyle, silver medal).
Won Other Ranks' Fly-Weight (Pte. Morgan, silver medal).
Won Boys' Bantam-Weight (Boy Vary, silver medal).
Second in Boys' Fly-Weight (Boy Stanway, bronze medal).

Aldershot Command Unit Team Competition, March 28th, 1920.

Won Boys' Bantam-Weight (Boy Vary, silver medal).
Won Boys' Feather-Weight (Boy Murphy, silver medal).
Won Boys' Fly-Weight (Boy Cauldfield, silver medal).
Second in Boys' Light-Weight (Boy Baird, bronze medal).

Above Team won Boys' Shield.

Won Other Ranks' Catch-Weight (Sergt. Doyle, silver medal).

Aldershot Command Individual Championships, April 8th–9th, 1920.

Won Boys' Feather-Weight (Boy Vary, silver medal).
Won Boys' Fly-Weight (Boy Murphy, silver medal).
Won Other Ranks' Fly-Weight (Pte. Morgan, silver medal).

Novices' Boxing Competition, Aldershot Command, November 15th–16th, 1920.

Light-Weight Winner, Fusilier Betts.
Bantam-Weight Winner, Fusilier Murphy.

Class " A " Officers.

Walk-over for Challenge Cup : Lieut. Tittle, Lieut. Franklin, Lieut. McCann.

Class " C " Boys.

Feather-Weight Winner : Boy Carroll.
Fly-Weight Runner-up : Boy James.

The Battalion tied with 4th Hussars for 1st place and Challenge Shield.

BATTALION FOOTBALL TEAM, THE "BLUE CAPS."

Winners Aldershot Command Senior League, Season 1921-22; Army Football Association Cup,
Fifth Round, 1920-21; Fourth Round, 1921-22.

L. Cpl. W. Brindle   L./Cpl. R. Bovenizer   L. Sergt. B. Hurt
Sergt. W. Berry   L./Cpl. F. Packer   Fus. T. Sandford   Fus. W. Jarmain   C.Q.M.S. J. Fullerton
Cpl. G. Kershaw   Cpl. H. Dreher   Lieut. K. E. Hegan   Sergt. W. Gamble   Sergt. Ludford

[*Photo, Gale & Polden, Ltd.*

HOCKEY TEAM, THE "BLUE CAPS."

Season 1920-21—Played 14; won 8, lost 4, drawn 2 games. Total Goals—For 36, Against 27.
Winners, Garrison Knock-out Competition; and Runners-Up Aldershot Command A.A. Shield.
Season 1921-22—Played 17; won 14, lost 2, drawn 1. Total Goals—For 79, Against 18.

Cpl. J. D'Orey   Fus. C. Hewitt   Fus. W. Gilley   C.S.M. W. Murphy   Cpl. W. Carter   Lieut. D. R. Tittle   Sergt. T. English
Sergt. W. Hannigan   Lieut. W. J. F. Eassie   Lieut. C. A. Gamble (*captain*)   Cpl. A. Courtney   C.Q.M.S. L. Sully

TUG-OF-WAR TEAM, THE "BLUE CAPS."

1919-20—Winners, Aldershot Command Bronze Medal Tournament; No. 6 Group A.C.A.A. 110 stone and Catchweights; 110 stone A.C. Championship, June, 1920; Runners-Up Catchweights.

1920-21—Winners, Aldershot Command Bronze Medal Tournament; No. 6 Group A.C.A.A. 110 stone and Catchweights; A.C. Championship, 110 stone; Challenge Cup, presented by Aldershot Gymkhana Committee, open to H.M. Forces.

1922—Runners-Up Aldershot Command Bronze Medal Tournament.

Fus. Kavanagh   Fus. Murphy   Fus. O'Hara   Fus. Costigan   Fus. Mannion   Fus. Boddy   Cpl. J. Finnegan
Fus. P. McKeown   Sergt. L. P. Grace, M.M. (coach)   Lieut. L. R. C. Watson   Sergt. T. Doyle   L./Cpl. P. Kelly

BOXING TEAM, THE "BLUE CAPS." 1919–21.

Second in Team Competition, Bordon Garrison, 1919 (Nov.).   Won Team Competition, Bordon Garrison, 1919 (Dec.).
Won Team Competition, Bordon Garrison, 1920 (Nov.).   Won Team Competition, Bordon Garrison, 1921 (Feb.).
Won Men's Shield, Aldershot Command, 1921 (Nov.).   Tied with 4th Hussars for 1st Place and Boys' Challenge Shield, Aldershot Command, 1920 (Nov.).   Won Boys' Team Competition, Bordon Garrison, 1920 (Nov.).
Tied with 3rd Royal Fusiliers for Boys' Competition, Bordon, 1921 (Feb.).   Won Boys' Shield, Aldershot Command, 1921 (Mar.).   ARMY CHAMPIONSHIP—Individual, Welter-Weight. Lieut. C. McCann, D.C.M., winner, May, 1921.

Boy Myers   Boy C. Hewitt   Boy Ward   Sergt. T. Doyle   Fus. Brown   Boy Raithes   Fus. Collins
Boy Wilkes   Fus. Murphy   Lieut. C. McCann, D.C.M.   Sergt. B. Duggan   Sergt. J. Fallon   Cpl. J. Doherty
Fus. Edwards

SPORTING SUCCESSES

Bordon Garrison Boxing Competition, November, 1920.

Class "B."

Heavy-Weight Winner: Fusilier Connolly.
Middle-Weight Winner: Fusilier Grey.
Welter-Weight Runner-up: Fusilier Edwards.
Light-Weight Winner: Fusilier Betts.
Feather-Weight Winner: Sergeant Duggan.
Bantam-Weight Runner-up: Fusilier Murphy.
Fly-Weight Runner-up: L./Corporal O'Brien (24).

Battalion won Team Competition with 33 points.

Class "B," Boys.

Light-Weight Winner: Boy Mulraney.
Feather-Weight Runner-up: Boy Carroll.
Bantam-Weight Winner: Boy Doherty.
Fly-Weight Winner: Boy James.

Battalion won Boys' Competition with 11 points.

Bordon Boxing Competition, February 3rd–4th, 1921.

Light Heavy-Weight Winner: Sergeant Doyle.
Middle Heavy-Weight Winner: Fusilier Grey.
Welter-Weight Runner-up: Fusilier Edwards.
Light-Weight Winner: Fusilier Betts.
Feather-Weight Winner: Sergeant Duggan.
Bantam-Weight Winner: Fusilier Murphy.

Battalion won Team Competition with 17 points.

Class "C," Boys.

Light-Weight Runner-up: Boy Doyle.
Feather-Weight Runner-up: Boy Ward.
Bantam-Weight Winner: Boy Smith.

Battalion tied with 3rd Royal Fusiliers for 1st place, 4 points each.

Aldershot Command Boxing Competition, March, 1921.

Fly-Weight Runner-up: Fusilier McDonnell.

Class "C," Boys.

Fly-Weight Winner: Boy Smith.
Bantam-Weight Winner: Boy Collins.
Light-Weight Runner-up: Boy Doyle.

Battalion won Unit Team Challenge Shield for Class "C" Boys.

Result of Army Boxing Championship held at Aldershot, May 3rd–4th, 1921.

Individual Entries.

Officers' Welter-Weight Winner: Lieut. C. McCann, D.C.M., 1st Royal Dublin Fusiliers.

Imperial Service Boxing Championship.

Light Weight Runner-up: Lieut. C. McCann, D.C.M., 1st Royal Dublin Fusiliers.

NOVICES' BOXING, ALDERSHOT COMMAND TEAM COMPETITION, 1921.
Winner Other Ranks: 1st Royal Dublin Fusiliers with 36 points.
Enlisted Boys: 1st Royal Dublin Fusiliers placed 2nd with 16 points.

TUG-OF-WAR.
(Officer in Charge: Lieut. J. Esmonde, M.C.)

March 30th, 1920: Won 110 Stone Aldershot Command Championship. Bronze medals to team.

OLYMPIA, JUNE, 1920.

Beaten in Semi-Final of 105 Stone Competition. The Battalion Team was the last Army Team in to be beaten.

PENTATHLON.
Lieut. H. C. Franklin, M.C., was in charge of teams.

February 24th, 1920: Won No. 6 Group, A.C.A.A. Championship. Bronze medals for team.
March 9th, 1920: Won Aldershot Command Unit Championship. Silver medals for team.

FOOTBALL XI.
(Captain: Lieut. K. E. Hegan.)

Winner of Aldershot Command Senior League for Season, 1921–1922; Army Football Association Challenge Cup, 5th Round, 1920–21; Army Football Association Challenge Cup, 4th Round, 1921–22.

HOCKEY XI.
(Captain: Lieut. Gamble.)

Season, 1920–21:—Won 8, Lost 4, Drawn 2. Won Bordon Garrison Knockout Competition. Runner-up Aldershot Command A.A. Shield, losing to R.A.S.C. by 1 goal to 2.
Season, 1921–22:—Played 17: Won 14, Lost 2, Drawn 1.

CROSS COUNTRY RUNNING.
(Team Captain: Lieut. D. R. Tittle).

January 21st, 1920: Won Squadron, Battery and Company, No. 6 Group, A.C.A.A. Competition. ("C" Company), medals for team.
January 28th, 1920: "C" Company finished fifth in A.C.A.A. 4-mile run.
March 1st, 1920: Won Regimental, No. 6 Group, A.C.A.A. Bronze medals Silver medals to Pte. Dermody (1st), Pte. Trigg (4th).
March 10th, 1920: Won Aldershot Command Unit Championship. Awarded Shield and Bronze Medals to team. Silver medal to Pte. Dermody (2nd).
March 16th, 1920: Sixth in Army Championship.
March 31st, 1920: Won Regimental No. 6 Group, A.C.A.A. bronze medals. Silver medal to Pte. Dermody (1st).
April 19th, 1920: Won Regimental No. 6 Group, A.C.A.A. Championship. Shield and bronze medals to team.
December 1st, 1920: Third in Comrades Relay Race at Aldershot.
January 26th, 1921: "D" Company, "Blue Caps" 4th place in Inter-Company 4-Mile Cross Country Run. Fusilier Trigg finished 5th of all.

CROSS-COUNTRY RUNNING TEAM, THE "BLUE CAPS."

1919-20—Winners Silver Cup, Silver and Bronze Medals, No. 6 Group A.C.A.A. Aldershot Command Challenge Shield and Medals.
1920-21—Runners-Up Aldershot Command Challenge Shield.
1921-22—Runners-Up Aldershot Command Challenge Shield. Winners A.C.A.A. Pair Race.

Fus. W. Nash Fus. J. Corcoran Fus. Hanrahan Cpl. W. Carter Fus. Wade Fus. Humphrey Fus. Gallagher
Fus. C. Lebane L. Sergt. F. Simpson Fus. J. Trigg Lieut. D. R. Tittle Fus. C. Grogan Sergt. A. Childerhouse Fus. Murray
Fus. Wolohan Fus. Gaughan

[Photo, Gale & Polden, Ltd.

REGIMENTAL DESIGN, SHOOTING AND SPORTS PRIZES FOR "BLUE CAPS."

Regimental Medal for Sporting Competitions.
1st—Silver Gilt.   2nd—Silver.   3rd—Copper.

Regimental Spoon for Rifle Competitions.

[Appendix Eighteen

BATTALION MAGAZINE.

Early in 1922, the desirability of issuing a Battalion Magazine was brought forward and the Commanding Officer asked Capt. A. L. Elsworthy, M.B.E., to assume the duties of Editor.

The Magazine was first issued in the month of February, 1922, and was called "The Blue Cap."

It was decided to make an issue monthly and to distribute it among past and present "Blue Caps," thereby maintaining the traditional *esprit de corps* of the "Blue Caps."

Unfortunately after the issue of three numbers, the order for disbandment came along and terminated what was already proving to be a valuable asset to the Battalion.

[*Appendix Nineteen*

PARTICULARS OF BEQUESTS MADE TO THE "BLUE CAPS."

It is hoped that the Trustees of the Neill Fund will permit the revenue from the capital sum to continue for a period of five years from the date of disbandment to enable the money to be distributed amongst deserving cases of N.C.O.'s transferred to other units or discharged.

Lieut.-Colonel J. W. Royce Tomkin, T.D. (late 1st Royal Dublin Fusiliers) most generously assented to the balance credit of his fund, on the disbandment of the Battalion, being paid into the Regimental History Fund of the Battalion.

To his generosity is largely due the fact that the "Blue Caps" have been able to prepare for the press a History of Neill's Blue Caps from 1664 to disbandment.

This work will be published by Messrs. Gale & Polden, of Aldershot, whose Manager, Mr. C. S. Seager, an old friend of our Battalions, has taken the greatest interest and pains to make the work a complete success.

RULES OF THE "NEILL FUND."

1. That the sum of (four thousand six hundred) Rupees 4,600 be invested in Government Securities in the names of Lieut.-Colonel R. HAMILTON and Mr. H. NELSON.

2. That these gentlemen be the first Trustees, and that in case of either of them leaving the Presidency for more than six months, he endorse over the Securities to his successor in, or the then incumbent of, the office of Deputy Secretary to Government in the Military Department, or Chairman of the Chamber of Commerce, as the case may be.

3. That in the event of the decease of a Trustee, the survivor endorse over the paper to himself and the successor of the Trustee deceased, jointly.

4. That the Trustees have the management of the Fund, and that they sign an engagement to administer it strictly according to these rules.

5. That the interest of the Fund be transmitted yearly to the OFFICER IN COMMAND OF THE REGIMENT for distribution as follows :—

(1) One gratuity of (one hundred) Rupees 100 to be given annually to the most deserving Serjeant, who may take his pension; or who, being enlisted under the limited Service Act, may quit the Regiment at the expiration of his time.

BADGES AND BUTTONS

FULL DRESS— (1) Busby Grenade   (2) Tunic Grenades   (3) Tunic Buttons
SERVICE DRESS— (4) Cap Badge   (5) Collar Grenades   (6) Buttons
BLUE UNDRESS— (7) Collar Grenades
MESS DRESS— (8) Lapel Grenades   (9) Buttons for Jacket and Waistcoat
(10) SHOULDER BADGE FOR RANK AND FILE

BEQUESTS

(2) One gratuity of (seventy) Rupees 70 to the most deserving Corporal under similar conditions.

(3) One gratuity of (fifty) Rupees 50 and of (thirty) Rupees 30 to the most deserving Privates under similar conditions.

(4) No gratuity to be given in any case where the discharge has been by purchase.

(5) These rules to apply also to Staff Serjeants of the Corps, and to men removed to Staff employ, who may have served with the Regiment ten years, or were on service in the mutinies of 1857, 1858 and 1859 without limit as to time with the Corps.

(6) Any gratuities not distributed in one year may be added as separate gratuities to the list for the year following.

(7) The selections for gratuities to be made by the Commanding Officer of the Regiment.

R. HAMILTON, LIEUT.-COL. } Trustees.
H. NELSON,

MADRAS,
8th September, 1860.

RULES OF ROYCE TOMKIN FUND.

(Commenced 25th January, 1907.)

The income from the investments and securities shall be paid to the Commanding Officer, the Second in Command and the Senior Captain for the time being of the 1st Bn. The Royal Dublin Fusiliers (hereinafter called " The Officers ").

The Officers shall distribute such income quarterly or half-yearly amongst such of the N.C.O.'s and men of the said Battalion, and the wives of such N.C.O.'s and men as are of good character and have become incapacitated through wounds or ill-health or impoverished through no fault of their own and are selected by the Officers as being in their opinion deserving of pecuniary assistance.

[Appendix Twenty

THE ROYAL DUBLIN FUSILIERS ASSOCIATION.
(Formed in 1910.)

Patron: Field-Marshal H.R.H. THE DUKE OF CONNAUGHT, K.G., K.T., K.P., G.C.B., G.C.S.I., G.C.M.G., G.C.I.E., G.C.V.O., G.B.E., Colonel-in-Chief The Royal Dublin Fusiliers.

President: Major-General C. D. COOPER, C.B., Colonel of the Regiment.

Vice-President: Brigadier-General G. DOWNING.

Hon. Treasurer: Lieut.-Colonel E. ST. G. SMITH.

Secretary: Major R. BAKER, D.S.O.

Hon. Medical Adviser: Colonel Sir W. T. de C. WHEELER, F.R.C.S., 23, Fitzwilliam Square, Dublin.

Temporary Office: 77, Grosvenor Square, Rathmines, Dublin.

The Objects of the Association are—

1. To maintain connection between the men serving in The Royal Dublin Fusiliers and old comrades, and to promote friendship and association amongst those now in civilian life interested in their old Regiment.

2. To promote the welfare of discharged soldiers of the Royal Dublin Fusiliers who are members of this Association, by assisting them to obtain situations, and generally to aid members in establishing themselves respectably in civilian life.

3. To assist financially any member who, through no fault of his own, has fallen into bad health, and is unable to earn his own livelihood or who is out of employment and in distressed circumstances, if the Committee to whom application is made deem the applicant worthy; and also to assist financially widows or children of members who are in distressed circumstances.

4. In case of death to provide for the burial of any member, if aid is required.

5. To foster *esprit de corps* and promote recruiting for the Regiment, and to make widely known the advantages of service in the Regiment, and to create a brotherhood between the non-commissioned officers and men after discharge from either Battalion.

6. To make application to the authorities on behalf of veterans for pensions where none have already been granted, or for increased allowance where only small sums are received.

Keeping the above objects in view, any member of the Association should inform the Committee of any suitable situation which he may know to be vacant.

Members who are desirous of employment should make their wants known to the Secretary.

At the Meeting of the Past and Present Officers of the Regiment, held in London on the 9th March, 1922, it was decided to continue the Regimental Association after the disbandment of the Regiment.

It is expected that in the near future applications for assistance will be much increased owing to so many men, now in military employment in Ireland, losing their employment as a result of the withdrawal of troops from the country.

There are many men, most of them still serving, who, having paid for from four to ten years membership after discharge, will have a claim on the Association until the expiration of these periods.

In these circumstances it is hoped that all Officers will continue their subscriptions. The rate of Annual Subscription is 10/6 for Subalterns and 21/- for higher ranks. Subscriptions may be paid through Messrs. Cox & Co., or sent direct to the Secretary, Major Baker, D.S.O., 77, Grosvenor Square, Rathmines, Co. Dublin.

[*Appendix Twenty-one*

REGIMENTAL ARMY AGENTS.

The suspension of business by Messrs. Sir C. R. McGrigor, Bart., & Co., on October 18th, 1922, came as a great shock to the Regiment, who have banked with the firm since July 30th, 1862. The losses sustained by the Regiment as a whole and individual members are heavy. So far a dividend of 5s. in the £ has been paid.

The sympathy of the entire Regiment goes out to Mr. R. A. Bacon, O.B.E. Mr. Bacon has been identified with the Regiment since June, 1880, and during this long period by his never failing help, and intense interest in the officers and their families has endeared himself to everyone. The continued success of the Regimental Annual Dinner is due to his able management and unceasing efforts to make it a real re-union of past and present officers.

[*Note.*—Since the above was written the War Office have very generously come to the help of the sufferers with a dividend of 10/- in the £.]

[*Appendix Twenty-two*

REGIMENTAL SONG

(Common to both Battalions).

I

COME, boys, we'll sing of gallant lads,
  "Old Toughs" of bygone days;
A roll of names we claim our own,
  And wreathe with choicest bays;
Of days ere Britain's name was great
  In India's burning zone,
Yet shone with brightness guarded there
  By our "Old Toughs" alone.

CHORUS.

"Old Toughs" were they, "Old Toughs" are we!
  And through the coming years
We'll keep that name without a stain
  As "Dublin Fusiliers."

II

Two hundred years and more, my boys,
  Since first was marched away
From Britain's shore our fine old corps,
  To keep for her—Bombay;
And there, when Englishmen were few
  And foes were strong around,
Their only safeguard many a year
  In our "Old Toughs" was found.

Chorus—"Old Toughs" were they, etc.

III

As time sped on and gave command
  For Britain's sway to spread,
Bombay sent forth her pioneers,
  Who in the vanguard led;
They led a hundred fights, my lad!

They stormed the strongest wall !
And Irishmen were there, who shed
　　Their heart's best blood through all.
Chorus—" Old Toughs " were they, etc.

IV

No tale of ancient chivalry,
　　No mediæval lays,
Can tell of deeds more wonderful
　　Than since those early days,
When, first as " Bombay Regiment,"
　　Then " Bombay Fusiliers,"
They wrapt with glory Britain's name
　　Through twice a hundred years.
Chorus.—" Old Toughs " were they, etc.

V

Our Colours, boys, but little tell
　　The fame of our old corps ;
A dozen flags we well could fill,
　　And maybe even more ;
Through length and breadth of Hindostan,
　　Bombay, Madras, Bengal,
From Plassy, east, to Aden, west,
　　" Old Toughs " is stamped on all.
Chorus.—" Old Toughs " were they, etc.

VI

Some names we never should forget,
　　Of men, in days gone by,
Who went, with " hope forlorn," through death,
　　To plant our standard high ;
At Ahmedabad, like Hieme and Fridge,
　　Who led a dauntless few ;
At S'ringapatam, where Graham died ;
　　At Mooltan, Bennett too.
Chorus—" Old Toughs " were they, etc.

VII

The hearts at home throbbed warm, my lads,
    When those brave deeds were told,
Of heroes we may call our comrades ;
    Should our hearts grow cold ?
From Arcot down to Mut'ny days,
    From Havelock back to Clive,
The " Toughs " have won a glorious name,
    'Tis ours to keep alive.

Chorus—" Old Toughs " were they, etc.

VIII

Should we be ever called to share
    In scenes like those of yore,
We know the stuff that's in us, lads,
    Will bring us to the fore.
But times of peace must try our pluck
    With test both close and keen ;
For honour, boys, then keep our name,
    Like shamrocks, fair and green.

Chorus—" Old Toughs " were they, etc.

MELODY OF REGIMENTAL SONG.

INDEX

ACHEUX, 64
Achi Baba, 19, 21
Addis, 2/Lieut., 72, 76
Albert, 64
Aldershot, Bn. moves to, 140
Allen, 2/Lieut., killed, 91
Allenby, Gen., 77
Alexander, 2/Lieut., 113
Alexandria, Bn. arrives at, 16; sails from, 17; arrives at, 61; embarks for France, 62
Amalgamation Munsters and Dublins, 39; of both Battalions, 109
Amiens, 74, 106
Ancre, The, 65, 77
Anafarta Ridge, 52
Anderson, Lieut. D. V. P., 5; Capt., 10, 15, 24, 29, 40
Anderson, R.S.M., 129, 133
Andrews, 2/Lieut. W., 16, 25, 36, 40
Anzac, 52, 57, 59
Armentières, 77
Armies, First, 64, 67; Second, 64, 76; Third, 64, 77, 82, 105; Fourth, 64, 76, 77, 82; Fifth, 72, 77, 105
Armstrong, Lieut. & Q.Mr. C. W., 62
Army Corps, VIIIth
Army, re-organization of, 99
Arnold, Lieut. N. A., 124, 129
Arras, 77, 82; battle of, 83, et seq., 84, 99
Aubigny, 107
Auchonvillers, 65
Aywaille, 125

BAGLEY, Lieut. A. B., 5; Capt., 76, 79, 80
Bailey, Capt. C., 124
Baker, C.Q.M.S., 25, 36
Baker, 2/Lieut., 83; Lieut., 134
Bapaume, 75
Barre, 2/Lieut. G. B., 94
Barisis, 99
Barrett, Pte., 133
Barry, Lieut., 74, 84
Battersby, Pte., 133

Beach, "S," 19, 25; "V" 21, 25, 34, 37, 61; "W," 19, 21, 25, 34, 37, 61; "X," 19, 21, 25, 34, 37, 60, 61; "Y," 19, 25, 34, 52, 61
Beaumetze, 91
Beaumont Hamel, 65-67, 70-72, 77
Beauval, 64, 72
Bedding, C.Q.M.S. G., 25, 36
Bedell-Sivright, 2/Lieut. T., 93, 94; Lieut., 96
Belas, 2/Lieut. R. C. W., killed, 108
Bellary, 4
Bensberg, 126
Berg Gladbach, 127, 129
Bernafay Camp, 76
Bernard, Lieut. R., 5, 10, 15, 25, 36, 40
Blackwell, Lieut., killed, 120
Blair-White, 2/Lieut. J. H., 76
Blake, 2/Lieut. G. M., 85, 121; Lieut., 124, 129
Birdwood, Gen., 56, 60, 61
Boles, 2/Lieut. R. S., 93, 94; died of wounds, 111
Bolster, Lieut. G. W., 108
Bonnar, Capt. J. C., 93, 94, 124
Bondues, 122
Bonyage, O.R.S. P., 24
Bordon, Bn. arrives at, 136; returns to, 140
Bourke, 2/Lieut. E. C., 124, 129
Boulogne, cadre embarks from, 133
Boustead, 2/Lieut. L. C., 5, 8, 10, 15, 24, 26, 36, 40; killed, 47
Boys, Andrews, Christian, Doyle, Edwards, Evans, Griffen. Harris, Heffer, Jones (30752), Jones (30996), Mulcock, Osborne, Powell, Rourke, Saunders, Toner, Winskill, Wood, Woodcock, Woods, 133
Braddell, Capt., 140, 141
Brady, Capt. T., 134
Breakell, 2/Lieut., 121
Brennan, C.Q.M.S., 25
Brien, Pte., 133
Brigades—32nd, 54; 33rd, 54; 38th, 57; 48th, Bn. joins, 92, 93; 86th, 11, 23, 49, 54, 57, 86, Bn. leaves, 91, 126; 87th, 47, 49, 54, 57, 86; 88th, 67, 86; 156th, 46.

INDEX

Briscoe, 2/Lieut. W. R. W., 108
Brodhurst-Hill, Capt. A., 5, 10
Broembeck River, 90
Brown, 2/Lieut. C. J., 124, 129
Browne, Lieut. G. C. T., 93, 94
Bruce, Capt. G. E. (3rd Bn.), 45, 46
Buckley, 2/Lieut., 128, 129
Burke-Savage, 2/Lieut., 120
Burns, 2/Lieut. H., 94
Burns, 2/Lieut. R. H., 94
Burroughs, Lieut., 81
Bush, Capt. R. O. C., 141
Byng, Gen., 59, 93, 105
Byrne, Corpl., 55
Byrne, 2/Lieut. E. A., killed, 84
Byrne, Lieut., 140

CALDBECK, Lieut. W. E., 93, 94
Camber Beach, 34
Cambrai, Battle of, 96
Cameron, Lieut. W. B. St. G., 76, 93, 94
Cameron, Sergt., 133
Campbell, Pte., 81
Cape Helles, 18, 19, 25
Cape Suvla, 19
Cape Tekke, 18, 37
Cappy, 105
Carew, Lieut. R. J. H., 5
Carnoy, 76, 77
Carroll-Leahy, Capt., 140, 141; Brevet Major, 149, 152
Carruthers, 2/Lieut. C. G., 5, 10, 15; Lieut., 25, 40; Capt., 51, 61, 62, 74, 134
Cassidy, Lieut. J., 124
Casson, Col., relieves Col. Cayley, 45
Caulfield, Bdmr., 133
Cavan, Gen. Lord, 91
Cayley, Lieut.-Col., 44; Major-Gen., 110, 127, 130
Chadwick, 2/Lieut., 121
Chandler, Capt. G. H., 93, 94, 108
Cheape, Brig.-Gen., 88, 91, 110, 127
Chocolate Hill, 53
Chudleigh, 2/Lieut., 111, 124, 129
Clarke, Lieut. and Q.Mr., 76, 94
Clarke, Capt. N. P., 52; Major, 76, 78, 88; Lieut.-Col., 134
Clarke, Pte., 133
Clarke, 2/Lieut. G. A., killed, 108
Clarke, 2/Lieut. T. S., 124
Cleland, 2/Lieut., 62
Cléty, 109
Coakley, 2/Lieut., 128, 129
Coal Strike, 139, 140
Coffee, Pte., 117

Coghlan, Rev. Father, 140
Coldwell, 2/Lieut., 121
Cologne, entry into, 126, 129
Colours, handed over on leaving Torquay, 11; orders re safe-keeping of, 146
Combles, 75
Condé, 76
Condron, 2/Lieut. M. A., 111, 124, 129
Conerney, 2/Lieut. C. J. G., 120, 124, 129
Congratulatory Orders, 42
Congreve, Gen., 97, 105; Corps losses in, 108
Connaught, Duke of, message from, 55, 136, 137; farewell order, 146
Connolly, Sergt. A. D., 149
Conran, 2/Lieut., 128, 129
Considine, Lieut. T. J., 94; Capt., 124, 129
Cooke, 2/Lieut., 128, 129
Cooper, Major-Gen., 12, 137; farewell order, 147
Cooney, 2/Lieut., 111, 118
Copland, 2/Lieut. C. A., 52, 62
Corbet, 2/Lieut. R. V. C., 5, 8, 10, 15, 40
Corbie, 76, 77, 82
Corps, IInd, 119; IIIrd, 65; IVth, 93; Vth, 93; VIth, 93; VIIth, 97; VIIIth, 65, 72; Xth, 65, 72; XIIIth, 65; XVth, 65, 119; XVIIIth, 93, 107; XIXth, 106
Courtney, L./Cpl., 133
Court St. Etienne, 125
Courtrai, 122, 126
Coventry, 15
Cowley, Capt. G. E., 93, 94, 108
Cox, 2/Lieut., 98
Crawford, 2/Lieut. S. G., 93, 94
Crawford, 2/Lieut. G. P. G., 94, 108
Cripps, Lieut. A. S. (Som. L.I.), 45
Croisilles, 94
Crozier, Capt. H. C., 4, 10, 15, 24, 26, 33, 40
Cullen, Sergt. G., 125
Cullen, C.S.M. A., 149
Cummins, Corpl., 36
Curran, C.Q.M.S. P., 24

DARB-EL-HAJ, 62
Darby, L./Cpl., 133
Dardanelles, 29th Div., ordered to, 13; Force, composition of, 14
Darley, 2/Lieut. 118

INDEX

Darling, Capt., 117, 121, 124
de Boer, Lieut., R.A.M.C., 16, 24, 40
Delany, Capt. A. S., 124
Delville Wood, 76
De Lisle, Gen., 46, 53, 89, 90, 91, 110
De Lusignan, 2/Lieut. R., 5, 10, 15; Lieut., 25, 34, 40
Demobilization begins, 128
Denning, Corpl., 133
Dernancourt, 74
Designations of companies and platoons, 135
De Tott's Battery, 37
Devoy, 2/Lieut., 41, 66, 83, 91–94
De Wolf, Capt., 54, 57, 60
Dickenson, Capt. E. (Yorks. Regt.), killed, 47
Dickie, Major, 129, 141
Dickson, 2/Lieut., R.F.A., 108
Disbandment Orders, 144
Disbandment, regiments for, 144–146
Disposal of officers and men of disbanded regiments, 148
Distribution of forces on 6/8/15, 50
Divisions—4th, 64, 66; 10th, 50, 52; 11th, 52, 53, 54, 60; 13th, 50, 57, 60, 61; 16th, Bn. transferred to, 88; 29th, Bn. joins, 11, 12, 23, 35, casualties at landing, 45; "Incomparable," 48, 50, 52–54, 60, 61, 66; transferred to XVIIIth Corps, 82, Bn. leaves, 81, returns to, 109, 110, broken up, 129; 31st, 64, 66; 42nd, 14, 45, 46, 50, 61; 48th, 64, 66; 52nd, 46, 50, 61; 53rd, 50, 52, 53, 60; 54th, 52, 53; Royal Naval, 50
Dobbs, Lieut. J. F. K., 5
Domqueur, 64
Doughty-Wylie, Lieut.-Col., 35, 36
Douglas, Maj.-Gen., 48
Doullens, 72
Dover, Bn. Cadre lands at, 133
Doyle, Corpl., 54
Doyle, Sergt., 36, 149
"Dubsters," 45
Dundon, 2/Lieut., 129
Dunlop, Lieut. G. M., 5, 10, 15; Capt., 24, 29, 40
Dunne, Lieut., 81, 124
Durward, 2/Lieut. R. G. S., 59, 62, 69

Eassie, Lieut., 140, 141
Eaucourt l'Abbaye, 75
Eclusier, 105

Egypt, Bn. sails to, 61
El Kubri, 62
Elliott, Lieut. L. R., 124, 129
Ellis, A./Brig.-Gen., 130
Elphick, Lieut. R., 69
Elsworthy, Capt. A. L., 141
Elverdinghe, 87
Emden, 6 et seq.
Epéhy, 97, 101
Ervine, 2/Lieut., J. St. J. E., 93, 94, 111
Eski Hissarlik, 20, 21
Esmonde, Lieut. J., 134
Evacuation of Gallipoli decided on, 56, 57

Farmar, Maj., 36, 41
Fenning, Lieut. G. S., 53
Fenton, Sergt., 94
Fergusson, C.S.M., 36, 38, 41
Fetherstonhaugh, Maj. E., 5, 10, 15, 24, 29, 40
Filbey, Sergt.-Dmr., 133
Finn, Rev. Father, 16, 40
Fisher, 2/Lieut. and Adjt. C. G. C., 125; Capt., 129, 133
Floyd, Lieut. H. M., 4, 10, 25, 45; Capt., killed, 47
Foch, Marshal, 65; assumes supreme command, 108
Forrester, Corpl., 133
Fort St. George, 4, 10
Fox, C.S.M., 25
Franklin, 2/Lieut. H. C., 134, 135, 141
Fraser, Sergt., 133
French, Capt. D., 5, 10, 15, 25, 29, 31, 40
Froissy, 105

Gabe Tepe, 20
Gallipoli, 18 et seq.; plan of attack, 20; Bn. leaves, 61
Gamble, Lieut. C. A., 134, 140, 141
German, Pte., 133
Germany, advance into, 125
Geoghan's Bluff, 47
George, Capt. L. E. (Som. L.I.), 45; killed, 47
Gibbons, 2/Lieut. 128, 129
Gibbs, 2/Lieut. J. L. A., 76
Gibraltar, 16
Ginchy, 75
Gough, Gen., 72, 77, 97, 105
Gourlay, 2/Lieut. W. W., 108

INDEX

Gouy, 84
Gradwell, 2/Lieut. G. F., 76 ; killed, 81
Grandcourt, 77
Greaney, 2/Lieut. J. A., 108
Green, 2/Lieut., killed, 81
Greenlees, 2/Lieut. C. F. (Queen's), 59, 62, ; killed, 69
Grimshaw, Capt. C. T. W., 5, 10, 15, 25, 33, 36, 40
Grove, Lieut. J. R. W., 5, 10 ; Capt., 15, 24, 39.
Guillemont, 75, 77
Gully Beach, 45, 49, 61
Gully Ravine, 47
Gun-Cuninghame, Lieut. H. M. B., 66, 76, 79, 80, 84
Guret, 2/Lieut., 111
Gyves, 2/Lieut. J. J., 93, 94 ; killed, 113

HAIG, Gen. Sir D., 71 ; F.M., 126
Haldane, Gen., 93
Halloran, Corpl., 133
Halloy, 82
Halsted, Lieut. A. L. (Rifle Bde.), killed, 47
Hamel, 108, 109
Hamilton, Gen. Sir I., 12, 20, 50, 55, 56, 63
Hamilton, 2/Lieut. A. H., 125
Hannen, Lieut. W. F., 51, 52
Hardecourt, 77
Hardeghem, 110
Hare, Brig.-Gen., 11, 23, 28 ; wounded, 44
Harris, 2/Lieut. D. W., 93, 94
Harrison, 2/Lieut., 140 ; Lieut., 141
Hastings, 2/Lieut., 91, 134
Hawes, Lieut., 54 ; Capt., 62
Hawtrey, Lieut., 87, 122
Haynes, Pte., 133
Hazebrouck, 114, 118, 119
Healy, 2/Lieut. M. F., 76
Hébuterne, 65
Heffernan, Lieut.-Col., 129, 133
Hegan, Lieut., 140, 141
Hegarty, 2/Lieut., 84
Herlihy, Rev. Father, 141
Hernon, 2/Lieut. A. F., 76, 84
Helles, 51, 57, 60, 61, 70
Hickey, 2/Lieut., 129
Higginson, Capt. W. F., 5, 6, 10, 15, 24, 34, 40
Higginson, Major G. S., 140
Hill 53, 53 ; Hill 112, 53

Hinkson, 2/Lieut. C. A., 125
Hoey, Capt. C. B. R., 5
Hollom, 2/Lieut. G. B. (Middlesex Regt.), 59, 62
Holman, 2/Lieut. A. R., 76, 124 ; Capt., 129
Holmes, 2/Lieut. G. G., 124, 129
Horne, Gen., 77
Horrell, 2/Lieut. 128, 129
Hosford, 2/Lieut. J., 15, 25, 40
Hostilities cease, 123
Howell, 2/Lieut. R. H., 93, 94 ; killed, 108
Howden, 2/Lieut. F. H., killed, 108
Hughes, Capt., killed, 114
Hunt, Major J. P., 98
Hunter, 2/Lieut. R. G., 108
Hunter-Weston, Gen., 12, 21, 22, 44, 46, 69, 110, 138

INDIA, British Battalions in, 4
Ireland, unrest in, 141 *et seq.*
Irwin, Pte., 55
Ismail Oglu Tepe, 52, 53

JACKSON, 2/Lieut. E. W., 94
Jacob, Lieut.-Gen. Sir C., 119
Jacobs, Lieut. G. C., 62
Jeffreys, Major R. G. B., 141, 152
Jones, Lieut. J. W. G., 134, 140
Jones-Nowlan, 2/Lieut., 84
Johnson, Capt. A. M., 4, 5, 10, 15, 26, 29, 40
Johnston, 2/Lieut. J. E., 91, 93, 94

KAIAJIK Aghala, 53
Kavanagh, C.S.M., 114
Kavanagh, Pte., buried at sea, 16
Kee, Lieut. W., 93, 94 ; A./Capt., 108
Kelly, Major, R.A.M.C., 76, 81
Kelly, Rev. Father, 128, 129
Kemmel Hill, 118
Kennedy, Lieut. & Q.Mr., 5, 10, 16, 24, 45
Kent, 2/Lieut., 81
Kephalos, 55
Kereves Dere, 37
Khoja Chemen Tepe, 50
Kidson, 2/Lieut., 83
Kiernan, Lieut. F. M., 108
Kilid Bahr, 20

INDEX

Killingley, 2/Lieut. A. V. G., 76
Kinneen, 2/Lieut. W. P., 76
King, Lieut. L. A., 93, 94
Kingcombe, Lieut. A. K. (Yorks Regt.), died of wounds, 47
King's speech and farewell order, 150, 151
Kiretch Tepe Sirt, 53, 58
Kirwan, 2/Lieut. C., 111
Kitchener, Lord, 55–57
Kneafsey, 2/Lieut. A. M., 76; Lieut., 93, 94
Knight, Lieut. A. E. (Rifle Bde.), died of wounds, 47
Krithia, 20, 37
Kum Kale, 19, 35

La Fère, 99
Laffan, 2/Lieut. P. 93, 94
Langemaarke, 90
Lanigan-O'Keeffe, Lieut. F. S., 5, 10, 15, 16, 25, 40; Capt., 83
Layton, 2/Lieut. M., 93, 94, 120
Ledeghem, 120, 121
Lempire, 101
Lemnos, island of, 17, 21, 49
Lendrum, Capt. A. C., 93, 94, 95, 96
Lennon, 2/Lieut., 111
Le Quesnoy, 132
Le Sars, 75
Letchworth, A./Capt. H. M., 103, 108
Locke, Pte., 133
London, Bn. moves to, 140
Loos, 65
Lord, Lieut. G., 124, 129
Loupart, 77
Louvencourt, 65
Lowe, 2/Lieut. S., killed, 108
Ludford, Sergt., 133
Lynch, Pte., 133
Lys, battle of the, 115 *et seq.*; crossing of the, 122

McAllen, 2/Lieut. H., 111, 124
McCann, 2/Lieut. A. J., killed, 91
McCann, Lieut. C., 33, 134, 140, 141
McCarthy, 2/Lieut. P., 94, 108
McCormack, Lieut. F. H., 62, 72
McDonnell, Pte., 133
McFeely, Lieut. C. M., 78, 79, 80; Capt., 121, 124
McGowan, 2/Lieut., 111, 113, 129
McGuire, Pte., 55
MacHutchinson, Lieut. W. F., 108
Macintosh, Pte., 81

McIntyre, A./Capt. A. W., 91, 134
McKenzie, 2/Lieut. I. D., 76, 80
Mackillop, 2/Lieut. D., 93, 94, 108
McMinamin, 2/Lieut. J., 134
McNulty, Lieut., 117; killed, 118
McWilliam, 2/Lieut. W. A., 94, 96
Madden, Pte., 133
Madras, bombardment of, by *Emden*, 7
Maffett, 2/Lieut. C., 24, 30, 40; Capt., 62
Maguire, A./Capt. R., 94, 108
Mailley-Maillet, 65
Malassise Farm, 100, 101
Malta, 16
Mametz Wood, 74
Mansfield, Lieut. T. M. L. M., 5
Markomania, 6, 7
Marshall, Maj.-Gen., 38
Marseilles, Bn. arrives at, 64
Martin, 2/Lieut. W., 111, 124, 129
Mason, 2/Lieut. T. W. H., 76
Matthews, Capt. C. O., 76, 134
Maunsell, Capt. E. R. L., killed, 69
Maunsell, 2/Lieut. J. E. B., 69
Meaulte, 76, 77
Medals granted for the war, 135
Meldon, Lieut.-Col., assumes command of Bn., 122, 124
Mericourt, 82, 106
Merry, Lieut. & Q.Mr. J., 125
Mex, camp at, 16; Bn. leaves, 17
Milburn, Lieut. R.A.M.C., 108
Minesweepers, *Clacton*, 26; *Newmarket*, 26; *Whitby Abbey*, 27
Miraumont, 77
Moffatt, Capt. G. M., 62
Molesworth, Capt. E. A., 4, 10, 15; Major, 24, 36, 37, 40
Molony, Capt. A. W., 5, 10, 15, 24, 26, 29, 34, 40
Monchy, 83
Monro, Gen. Sir C., 56, 57
Montgomery, 2/Lieut., 113
Mood, Capt. J. M., 5, 10, 15, 25, 34, 40
Mooney, 2/Lieut. F., 76,; killed, 81
Moore, Maj. A., 88; Col., 93, 98, 109; killed, 121, 122
Morris, Capt., R.A.M.C., 125
Morris, 2/Lieut., 128, 129
Morval, 77
Mudros, 59; Bay, 21, 24, Harbour, 17, 49, 50, 60, 61
Mulheim, 129, 132
Mullen, Sergt., 133
Muller, Capt. von, 6
Murphy, 2/Lieut. B. B., 76
Murphy, 2/Lieut. E., killed, 108

INDEX

Neill, 2/Lieut. T. W. R., 62, 69
Neill, Lieut. C., 124, 129
Nelson, Lieut.-Col. H., assumes command of Bn., 60, 62, 76, 78, 88
Nelson, Pte., 133
Nibrunesi Point, 20
Nieppe, forest of, 110
Nolan, 2/Lieut. J., 108; killed, 120
Norman, 2/Lieut. D. S., 124, 129, 133
Noblett, 2/Lieut. G. H., 93, 94; Capt., 117, 118, 120
Nuneaton, Bn. moves to, 11

O'Carroll, 2/Lieut. W. T., 76, 81, 91
O'Carroll, Lieut. C. J., 124
Ockenden, Sergt., wins V.C., 89, 90
O'Connor, Sergt., 54
O'Donnell, Lieut., 110, 117, 121, 122
O'Dowda, Lieut.-Col., 54, 57
O'Hara, Lieut. H. D., 5, 10, 15, 24, 26, 32, 40, 45, 63
O'Keefe, C.S.M., 25
Oliver, Pte., 36
O'Mahoney, R.S.M., 24
O'Morchoe, Lieut., 140, 141
Osborne, Lieut. E., 53
O'Reilly, 2/Lieut. J. P., 124
O'Toole, Pte., 36
Oulton, Capt. W. P., 76, 93, 94–96, 124
Owen, 2/Lieut. F., 118, 134
Oxley, 2/Lieut. F. R., 62

Papote, 111
Passerelle Farm, 86
Peacey, Lieut. R. S., 108
Pearson, 2/Lieut. A. J. W., 62, 69; killed, 69
Pentland, Lord, 9
Peronne, 104, 106
Perreau, Lieut.-Col., assumes command, 133, 134, 137, 140, 152
Pernois, 84
Philby, Lieut. D. D., 5
Ploegsteert, 115 *et seq.*
Plumer, Gen., 76, 114, 126
Plunkett, Bt.-Maj. J. F., 134
Plymouth, Bn. arrives at, 11
Ponteland Camp, 133
Pont Rémy, 64
Poperinghe, 73, 74, 119
Power, Rev. Father, 62, 76, 125, 128
Price, Lieut. M. J., 134
Proyart, 106, 107

Rawlinson, Gen., 65, 72, 76, 77
Redmond, Pte., 32
Regiments, British—Cold. Gds., 140; Con. Rang., 150; Essex, 51; Gren. Gds., 85, 150; Hampshire, 26, 32, 36, 104; K.O.S.B., 21, 55; Lanc. Fus., 11, 21, 38, 39, 45, 62, 67, 78, 79, 110, 116–119; Leicester, 103, 104; Leinster, 150; Mdlx., 88, 89, 115; R. Munster Fus., 11, 26, 32–38, 45, 103, 150; R. Fus., 11, 21, 38, 39, 45, 60, 67, 68, 78, 92, 110, 116, 119; R. Irish, 94, 129, 150; R.I. Fus., 140; Warwick, 129; S.W. Bor., 21, 73
Reilly, 2/Lieut., 84, 114
Reinforcements reach Gallipoli, 48
Renny, 2/Lieut., 140, 141
Riccard, Capt. C. B. J., 45
Ridley, Lieut. H. L., 60; Capt., 62, Adjt., 76; killed, 85
Rigg, Maj. W. T., 93, 98, 122
Riordan, Lieut. W. J., 124
Roberts, 2/Lieut. W. S., killed, 108
Robertson, 2/Lieut. W. J., 62, 69
Robertson, 2/Lieut. E. H., 76
Rogers, 2/Lieut. H. G. (Som. L.I.), 45; killed, 47
Rogers, Capt. R. J. (Rifle Bde.), killed, 47
Rogers, 2/Lieut., 84
Ronayne, Maj., R.A.M.C., 12
Ronssoy, 103
Rooth, Lieut. R. G., 140
Rooth, Lieut.-Col. R. A., 5, 9–11, 15, 24, 33, 40
Rose-Cleland, 2/Lieut. A. M. B. B., 62; killed, 69
Ross, 2/Lieut. F. G., 111, 113, 124, 129
Roye, 76
Rucker, Lieut. C. E. E., 47
Ruddervoorde, 123
Ruffley, Pte., 133
Ryan, Capt., 120

Sailly-Saillisel, 77
St. Eloi, 65
St. Emilie, 97, 104
St. Jean, 73
St. Lucia Barracks, 136 *et seq.*
Saisseval, 76, 77
Sarfield, Pte., 133
Sari Bair, 19, 51, 52
Saules Farm, 85
Savage, Lieut., 129
Savage, Pte., 133
Scimitar Hill, 53, 54

INDEX

Scott, 2/Lieut. D. F., 62
Scott, 2/Lieut. A., 129
Scale, 2/Lieut. E. A., 91
Sedd-el-Bahr, 27, 28, 31-36
Sellars, Lieut. (K.O.S.B.), 46
Semmence, 2/Lieut., 120
Serre, 65, 66, 70, 72, 77
Seymour, Maj. E. F. E., 66
Shadforth, Capt. H. A., 134
Shaw, Lieut. W. J., 141
Shaw, Maj.-Gen., 11, 12, 62
Shears, Capt. P. J., 93, 94, 134
Sheehan, 2/Lieut. M. J., 124, 129
Shine, Lieut. J. O. W., 4, 10
Ships—R.N., *Euryalus*, 26; *Queen Elizabeth*, 28; French, *Dupleix*, 10
Sidwell, Lieut. A. G. L., 134
Silesia, Bn. ordered to, 136
Smith, C.S.M., 24, 33
Smith, 2/Lieut., 91
Smithwick, Capt. S. G., 5
Spa, 125
Spankie, 2/Lieut. H. V., 62, 69
Spiess, 2/Lieut. W. F., 93, 94, 120
Steenbeck River, 86
Ster, 125
Stewart, 2/Lieut., 120, 122
Stopford, Lieut.-Gen., 48, 52
Stirling, Capt. W. F., 45
Somme, The, 64; battle of, 66 *et seq.*; battle of, 1918, 101 *et seq.*
Suez, 62
Sulajik, 53
Sulz, 126
Susuk Kuju, 53
Suvla, attack opens, 50, 54, 55-60
Suvla Bay, 52, 53

Taylor, Capt. A. A. C., 45, 47
Taylor, 2/Lieut. J. A. H., killed, 55
Tenedos, 15, 21, 24, 25
Thomas, A./Q.M.S., 133
Thompson, Lieut., killed, 111
Thurlow, R.Q.M.S., 24
Tighe, 2/Lieut. M. H., 69
Tighe, Lieut. R. E., 124
Tincourt, 104
Tittle, Lieut. D. R., 134, 140, 141
Tooth, Lieut. A. G., 54, 62, 76, 84
Torquay, Bn. arrives at, 11
Transports—*Alaunia*, 15, 21; *Assaye*, 10; *Ausonia*, 15-17, 21, 61; *Caledonia*, 21, 61; *Haverford*, 15; *Hazel*, 60; *Malda*, 10; *Minominee*, 62; *Prince Abbas*, 53; *River Clyde*, 25-28, 31-35, 38, 61, 63; *Serangbee*, 61

Tredennick, Maj., 140, 141, 149
Trigona, Capt., 62, 66, 134
Trotter, 2/Lieut. J., 62, 74
Tully, 2/Lieut., 128, 129
Tumility, 2/Lieut. A., 93, 94; killed, 95
Turkish trench, 66
Turk's tribute to British, 43
Tweedy, Lieut. C. M., 76, 78; killed, 81

Unwin, Capt., 28

Verdun, 65
Villers Bretonneux, 106
Villers Faucon, 97
Vlamertinghe, 73

Wagner, 2/Lieut. D.P., 93, 94, 120, 124
Wall, Corpl., 96
Wallis, 2/Lieut. D. W., 91-94, 129, 134, 135
Walters, 2/Lieut. J. P., 15, 24, 40
Ward, Lieut.-Col. T., commands Bn., 51, 54
Ward, 2/Lieut. B., 93, 94; killed, 96
Warner, 2/Lieut. D. R., 62, 69
Watson, Bt.-Maj. R. M., 140, 141, 152
Watson, 2/Lieut. L. R. C., 134, 140, 141
Watts, Gen., 105
Weldon, Lieut.-Col. K., 109, 140, 141
West, Capt., C. H. L'E., 141
Weywertz, 125
Whelan, Pte., 133
Wheeler, Maj., 140, 141
Wieltje Salient, 73
Williams, Capt. & Q.Mr., 129, 134, 141, 152
Williamson, 2/Lieut. J. F., 93, 94, 108, 124, 129
Williamson, Lieut. U. A. F., 134, 141
Willis, Sergt., 30
Wilson, 2/Lieut. F. A., 62; Capt., 76
Windsor Castle, ceremony at, 148 *et seq.*
Wolley-Dod, Col. O.C., commands 86th Bde., 46
Wood, 2/Lieut., 128, 129
Wormhoudt, 72, 74

Yeates, Lieut. R. A., 140, 141
Young, 2/Lieut. F. G. (Som. L.I.), 45
Young, Pte., 133
Ypres, 64, 65, 73-76, 84 *et seq.*, 120

Zighin Dere, 37

www.ingramcontent.com/pod-product-compliance
Lightning Source LLC
Chambersburg PA
CBHW080541230426
43663CB00015B/2672